THE HAMLYN ENCYCLOPEDIA OF
FREEZING

AUDREY ELLIS

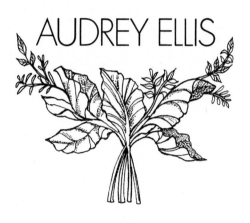

HAMLYN
London · New York · Sydney · Toronto

Acknowledgements

Published by
The Hamlyn Publishing Group Limited
London · New York · Sydney · Toronto
Astronaut House, Feltham, Middlesex,
England
© Copyright The Hamlyn Publishing
Group Limited 1977

ISBN 0 600 33146 6

Printed in Italy by New Interlitho, Milan

The author and publishers would like to thank the following for their help in sponsoring the colour photographs for this book:

British Poultry Meat Association: pages 65, 66, 67, 68 · British Sausage Bureau: page 215 · British Sugar Bureau: pages 55, 56, 95, 96 · British Turkey Federation: pages 106, 107, 108 · Brook Bond Oxo Limited: page 238 · Cadbury Typhoo Food Advisory Service: pages 118, 186, 256 · Carnation Milk Bureau: page 187 · Danish Food Centre: page 148 · Del Monte Foods Limited: page 226 · DRG Bettapak: pages 117 (co-sponsored), 158 · Electrolux Limited: pages 135, 157, 175, 185 · H.P. Bulmer Limited: page 198 · James Robertson and Sons Limited: page 225 · John West Foods Limited: pages 105, 227 · Lyons Tetley Limited: pages 35, 36, 37, 38 · McDougalls Home Baking Bureau: page 18 · New Zealand Lamb Information Bureau: pages 136, 176 · Philips Electrical Limited: page 255 · Pointerware (U.K.) Limited: page 17 · Quaker Oats Limited: page 237 · RHM Foods Limited: page 216 · Sharwoods Limited: page 228 · Taunton Cider Company: page 188 · Terinex Limited, manufacturers of Look roasting film: pages 77, 78 · The Tupperware Company: page 145 · Thompson and Morgan Limited: page 117 (co-sponsored) · Westphalia Pumpernickel Company: pages 146, 147

Black and white photographs kindly supplied by:
Bejam Group Limited: page 75 · Black and Decker: page 10 · Braby Group Limited: page 111 · Buitoni: page 93 · Danish Food Centre: page 9 · DRG Bettapak: page 91 · Hamster Baskets: page 58 · Lakeland Plastics Limited: pages 59, 84 · Li-Lo: page 121 · The Prestige Group Limited: page 11 · The Tupperware Company: pages 47, 123 · Thorpac Limited: pages 7, 122 · Wall's Ice Cream: page 73 · Young's Seafoods Limited: page 82

Equipment and additional information kindly supplied by: Addis Limited, Alcan Polyfoil Limited, B.G.M. Limited, Electrolux Limited, Lakeland Plastics Limited, Thorpac Limited, The Tupperware Company.

Colour photographs by **John Lee** and **Roy Rich**, Angel Studios

Illustrated by **Judy Millman**

Contents

Introduction

This encyclopedia has been written for readers who want to know more about the science of freezing, and its practical applications to the art of using a home freezer well. Few owners fully exploit the capacity of their freezers to make day-to-day catering easier, and life generally more pleasant.

Saving money is in modern economic conditions important to all of us. Calculated savings could now include the cost of travel and the value of our wasted time in going too often to the shops. When we come to weigh the advantages of enjoying a more varied choice of food throughout the year against the cost of running a home freezer, it is satisfying to find that the economies achieved eventually balance out the initial investment. Right from the start, it should be possible to equate savings in bulk buying with spending extra money on a wider and perhaps more luxurious selection of food.

In Part I, there is a truly comprehensive dictionary of freezing terms you may have found puzzling in the past. There are, at a glance, all the charts you need to consult on processing food for excellent and consistent results.

In Part II, suggestions are made for widely differing uses of a freezer, to suit many lifestyles. Yours may not exactly match any of these, but they should act as a valuable guide to create a pattern to suit your particular lifestyle.

In Part III, there are recipes most families need at various times, on which you can model your own solutions to individual problems in catering.

These sections have been studied, subjected to criticism and suggestions from a number of families who have put them to the test. Therefore this book has not been created as a dry, scientific treatise, but as a realistic and sensible aid to real people. I hope it will be of help and interest to you.

Audrey Ellis

My gratitude is especially due to
Jill Spencer, Chief Home Economist of the Hamlyn Test Kitchen
Christine Curphey, Co-ordinator of equipment testing

Organisations offering useful services to the public on domestic freezing.
University of Bristol, Research Station, Long Ashton, BRISTOL, BS18 9AF. *Head of Home Food Preservation* Mr. D. J. Cook, MSc, FIFST, MIBiol, MAHE.
The Electrical Association for Women, 25 Fouberts Place, LONDON, W1V 2AL. *Director* Mrs. Ann McMullan. Contact for news of home freezing courses.
The Food Freezer and Refrigerator Council, 25 North Row, LONDON, W1R 2BY. Contact for general advice on freezing and freezers.
Freezer Family The magazine for keeping up-to-date with new developments in the field of freezing.

Part I

A Glossary
of Freezing Terms

A

ACCELERATED FREEZE DRYING
This method of preserving food should not be confused with food *preservation* by freezing. It is a sophisticated method of drying a variety of foods, a typical example widely available being coffee. The food is first frozen and then put under vacuum before being gently heated. The water in the food, present in the form of ice, passes from solid ice to water vapour without becoming liquid and is removed from the food in that form. When reconstituted the food re-absorbs water more quickly and successfully than conventionally dried foods.

ACIDIC FOODS
Fruit is the prime example of an acidic food, which makes it excellent for freezing. After picking, fruit tends to continue ripening until it eventually becomes over-ripe and spoils. Vegetables, however, are non-acidic and begin to decay as soon as they are picked due to a special enzyme action. Most vegetables require blanching to inactivate the enzymes, or they decay to a minor extent even in the frozen state. Some vegetables are not affected during a comparatively short period of storage. See *BLANCHING.

ADHESIVE FREEZER TAPE
An adhesive tape which does not peel off at low temperatures. It is available in a clear form, and also an opaque form on which the contents of the pack can be written without fading.

AIR EXCLUSION
There are three ways to exclude unwanted air from freezer bags.
1. By moulding the bag closely round the food with one's hands to force out surplus air before sealing.
2. By drawing the air out with a straw or with a freezer vacuum pump. If using a straw, fix a twist tie loosely round the neck of the bag, insert the straw, suck out the air until the bag collapses round the food, withdraw the straw and tighten up the tie quickly. If using a pump, gather the bag round the pump with one hand, extract the air, remove the pump, tightening your grip round the bag at the same time, and seal at once.
NOTE: Never breathe out through a straw into a bag, as this may introduce germs into the pack.
3. By immersing the lower part of the bag into a bowl of cold water, thus forcing out the surplus air. Hold the neck of the bag above the water and loosely fix a twist tie. When displacement of the air is complete, tighten the tie and lift the bag out of the water.
NOTE: The outside of the bag must be dried before freezing or it will form an overcoat of ice.

The best way to exclude unwanted air from a rigid-based container is to fill air spaces with crumpled foil. When packing food in a parcel, fold in the wrapping tightly for the same purpose.

AIR PURIFIERS
The Thorpac air purifier consists of a carbon pad encased in a streamlined white plastic shell. The unit simply clips on to a shelf or basket in your freezer or fridge and absorbs stale odours. It is active for up to two years.

'Fridge Fresh' is an air purifier in the form of a polystyrene 'egg' with ventilation holes at either end, containing a sachet of activated charcoal granules. It is effective for up to three months in a domestic freezer.

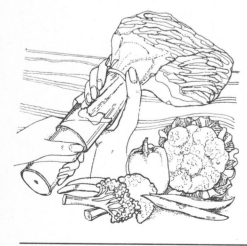

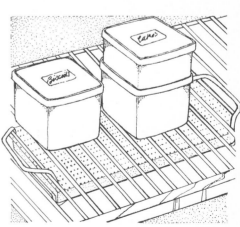

AIR SPACES There are two kinds of air spaces in freezer packs.
1. Unwanted spaces caused by the shape of the food inside the pack. These will cause dehydration of the food and loss of flavour, and should be eliminated as far as possible.
2. Necessary spaces for the expansion of the water content of the food on freezing. Foods with a low water content require very little (*e.g. joints of meat*). Foods with a high water content (*e.g. soups*) may require up to one-tenth of their total volume for expansion.
See *HEADSPACE.

AIRTIGHT SEAL A closure which totally prevents the passage of air.

ALARM SYSTEM This shows a break in the electrical circuit resulting in an undesirable rise in the temperature inside the freezer. Most freezers are fitted with a light panel and if there is a power failure or the freezer has been accidentally disconnected no light will show on the panel. If the red light shows continuously, this indicates that there is a mechanical fault or failure to close the door or lid.

   There are two other systems indicating an extreme temperature rise.
1. A winking light inside the cabinet which is clearly visible through a small porthole in the door.
2. A battery-operated alarm system with a sensor head which triggers off an audible alarm if the temperature rises 0·5°C/33°F above the pre-set temperature on the sensor head. With the B.G.M. alarm, a 10-metre/32·5-feet length of lead is provided to connect the freezer to the kitchen, or any other convenient place where the alarm would be heard.

ALLOCATION OF FREEZER SPACE
This is governed by such factors as the size of your family, their daily eating pattern, the home produce available and the amount you entertain. Space is usually divided among:

1. Commercial food products.
2. Bulk purchased meat and poultry.
3. Home-packed vegetables and fruit.
4. Home-packed made-up dishes.
5. Bread, cakes, sandwich packs and sundries (*e.g. sauces*).

ALMONDS See *NUTS.

ALTITUDE At an altitude of over 750 metres/2,500 feet, water boils at a slightly lower temperature, and longer time must be allowed for blanching. Between 750 and 1,500 metres/2,500 and 5,000 feet, it is recommended to allow half as long again, and above 1,500 metres/5,000 feet, twice as long.

ALUMINIUM FOIL This moisture-vapour-proof material is particularly useful in sheet form as it can be moulded exactly to the shape of the food and crimped together to make it seal without taping. It is available in two thicknesses (domestic and heavy duty, sometimes simply described as 'freezer foil'). It is also used for freezer packaging in the form of shaped containers with or without lids, and shaped gussetted bags. Foil pudding basins lined with vinyl are ideal for foods with an acid content which might damage the foil during long storage.
See *PACKAGING.

AMBIENT ATMOSPHERE The air immediately surrounding the freezer. In a confined space with inadequate ventilation, the heat generated by the freezer cannot easily be dissipated; therefore the ambient atmosphere is consistently too hot, so the freezer must work harder to maintain the necessary low temperature inside the cabinet. If the ambient atmosphere is humid, condensation may form on the cabinet and cause rust.

ANTI-OXIDANT A chemical agent used to prevent discoloration of food. The chemical uses up its available oxygen and thus reduces the activity of natural oxydising enzymes in the food; an effect of which is to induce discoloration of many foods.
See *DISCOLORATION.

APPLE Hard fruit available in many cooking and dessert varieties, all suitable for freezing in some form. Storage time in sugar or syrup pack 9–12 months, dry without sugar and as purée 6–8 months.
See *FRUIT PREPARATION AND PACKING, *DISCOLORATION, *DEFROSTING.
HELPFUL HINT: Raw apple slices can be packed with blackberries or any other juicy red berry fruits which stain the apple pink and disguise discoloration. Apple peel can be blanched and frozen for use later in jellies, especially those using fruits low in pectin. Windfalls are apples which fall early from the tree due to high winds; although frequently blemished the

good parts of the fruit can be frozen.

APRICOT Stone fruit suitable for freezing. The stone should always be removed, but a few kernels added to the packed fruit improve the flavour. Storage time in sugar or sugar syrup pack 9–12 months, dry without sugar and as purée 6–8 months.
See *FRUIT PREPARATION AND PACKING, *DISCOLORATION, *DEFROSTING.

ARTICHOKE, GLOBE Fleshy-leafed vegetable of which only the bases of the leaves and the artichoke 'heart' are edible; the inner hairy 'choke' must always be discarded. Discard any coarse outer leaves before blanching as they impart a bitter taste. It is possible to freeze whole artichokes but only the 'hearts' freeze really successfully. Storage time 10–12 months. See *VEGETABLE PREPARATION AND PACKING, *DISCOLORATION, *DEFROSTING.

ARTICHOKE, JERUSALEM A root vegetable only suitable for freezing as a cooked purée. Storage time 10–12 months. See *VEGETABLE PREPARATION AND PACKING, *DISCOLORATION, *DEFROSTING.

ASCORBIC ACID This is a synthetic Vitamin C product available from chemists in crystal or tablet form. Crystals are preferable because they are cheaper and more easily soluble. A weak solution of ascorbic acid may be added to some foods when preparing them for freezing, to replace lost Vitamin C and prevent discoloration.
See *DISCOLORATION, *ENZYMES.

ASPARAGUS Vegetable (of which the stalk and undeveloped flower head are eaten) which freezes well. Storage time 10–12 months.
See *VEGETABLE PREPARATION AND PACKING, *DEFROSTING.
HELPFUL HINT: To save space in packing the stalks are usually trimmed to an even length. The stalk trimmings can be used for soup.

AUBERGINE (US EGGPLANT) An imported vegetable with dark purple or black glossy skin and a firm flesh, only suitable for freezing cooked or in made-up dishes. Best used when young otherwise the high proportion of seeds makes the texture gritty. Storage time 10–12 months.
See *VEGETABLE PREPARATION AND PACKING, *DEFROSTING.
HELPFUL HINT: To retain the delicate flavour, slice aubergines, sprinkle with salt and allow to stand for 30 minutes before rinsing off and blanching.

AVOCADO A stone fruit usually treated as a vegetable although the flesh can be used to make sweets such as ice cream. It does not freeze well whole, but is quite successful in the form of a purée with lemon juice, combined with cream cheese to make a dip, or in soups. Storage time 4–6 months. See *DISCOLORATION, *VEGETABLE PREPARATION AND PACKING, *DEFROSTING.

BABY FOODS Lightly seasoned foods with a smooth texture, which can easily be digested by infants as an introduction to solids. When preparing fruit, vegetables, fish, meat and poultry dishes for the family, seasoning and flavouring may be deferred until the cooking process is completed, and part of the food reserved to be sieved or liquidised and packed in small portions. Extra care should be taken to ensure that all the cooking utensils used are perfectly clean. Freeze in small containers suitable for one meal. Great attention must be paid to hygiene in defrosting and reheating frozen baby foods. Storage time 3–4 months.
See *DEFROSTING.

BACON Cured pork which reacts differently to freezing than does fresh meat. This is due to salt and other ingredients in the curing brine.
Preparing bacon for freezing. Mould joints of bacon in foil to exclude air. Place wrapped joint in a polythene bag, withdraw air and seal. For rashers, chops and steaks use dividers between layers and pack as for joints. If you freeze down bacon at home, remember that it must be completely fresh for the best result. Smoked bacon can be stored for longer than unsmoked bacon.

Any commercially vacuum-packed bacon can be stored up to 20 weeks in the frozen state; home-wrapped joints of smoked bacon up to 8 weeks; unsmoked bacon joints up to 5 weeks; home-wrapped smoked rashers, chops and steaks up to 8 weeks; unsmoked up to 4 weeks. A special ready-frozen pack of either smoked or unsmoked rashers by Danepak Ltd. is available at many freezer centres. It contains five 225 g/8 oz vacuum packs, all of which keep in the freezer for 25 weeks.
See *DEFROSTING.

NOTE: Some other types of wrapping resemble the vacuum pack, so when buying to freeze at home inspect carefully and make sure you buy genuine vacuum packs and that the vacuum has not been accidentally punctured, in which case the pack goes slack and loses rigidity. Over-wrap with another polythene bag for protection.

HELPFUL HINT: Sealed packets of bacon rashers, steaks and chops can be thawed in hot water if required immediately. Remove from the hot water as soon as the bag becomes flexible, and dry outside of bag before snipping it open with scissors.

BAG SEALER A non-electric sealer which requires no heat, takes up little storage space or could be wall mounted. A substantial one made of polystyrene stands on a firm base with rubber treads, but there are cheaper, lighter models available. The twisted end of the bag to be sealed is fitted into the top of the sealer, leaving just sufficient headspace above the food. The sealer forces a length of self-adhesive tape round the neck of the bag at this point, joins tightly into a ring and cuts free all in the same action. Replacement reels of tape are available to fit the sealers. This method of sealing bags has long been available to butchers. It is quicker than sealing with a twist tie although it means you cannot open and reclose bags.
See *PACKAGING.

BANANA Tropical fruit which can be frozen as a purée with sugar and lemon juice, and in cooked dishes. When defrosted the colour is always darker, and both flavour and texture resemble that of slightly over-ripe fruit. To serve straight from the freezer, cut bananas in half, peel them, insert wooden sticks in the cut end and dip in melted chocolate. Open freeze on non-stick vegetable parchment and wrap individually in cling film or foil. They can also be frozen sliced and combined with sweetened whipped cream to serve as a frosted dessert. Exposure to the air causes some discoloration of the peeled fruit, very rapid once it is cut (except in canned fruit salad). Storage time 6 months.
See *FRUIT PREPARATION AND PACKING, *DISCOLORATION, *DEFROSTING.

HELPFUL HINT: If combined with other cooked fruits the banana flavour predominates and any discoloration is disguised. Loose bananas, which are frequently cheaper, are excellent for this purpose.

BASIC RULES Memorise the following six rules:
1. Choose only the freshest and best foods for freezing.
2. Keep food, hands, utensils, packing materials scrupulously clean.
3. Cook, cool, pack and freeze fast. Do not overcook made-up dishes which may receive further cooking before serving.
4. Use moisture-vapour-proof materials, ensuring both the exclusion of unnecessary air and a completely airtight seal.
5. Label packs clearly, record them if you keep a freezer log and use within the period of maximum quality.
6. When trying a new recipe or commercial pack, make sure the family approves before investing too heavily.
7. Do not overstock on any particular food. You may pay out more than it is worth to you in keeping the freezer running and be short of space for other essential items.

BASKETS Made of plastic-coated steel wire which are useful accessories and almost indispensable in a chest freezer. Those with reversible handles which hang from the rim of the chest to slide along it are the best buy, as the handles can also be turned inwards for stacking inside the cabinet. (Hamster Baskets will supply complete sets tailor-made to order to fit your freezer.) Do not overload baskets making them too heavy to lift without difficulty. See *BLANCHING BASKETS, *FREE-FLOW TRAYS.

BATCH BAKING By combining a number of recipes with suitable ingredients and making a work plan so that the oven is in constant use, you can prepare a selection of baked goods for the freezer in a two-hour session (or in a whole afternoon if you have time to spare). A typical example would be the use of a basic sponge mixture flavoured and coloured in several ways, pastry tartlets with various fillings using egg yolks in the pastry and the fillings, and meringues or macaroons to use up the egg whites. Or, the egg whites could be used for an angel cake and the yolks for almond paste. To make the most economical use of your time, oven heat and ingredients, follow the work plan carefully.
HELPFUL HINT: Team up with another freezer owner. It is a great advantage to arrange with a friend who also owns one to have a big baking session together so that you can exchange part of your baking and have a wider selection for your freezer.

BATTERS Can be frozen uncooked, prepared ready for use. Food coated in batter should be cooked until pale golden brown before freezing and refried to a rich golden brown for serving. Batter puddings (*e.g. Yorkshire pudding*) should be baked in individual portions for freezing, then defrosted and reheated in the same baking tins in a hot oven to restore their crispness. Storage time uncooked batter 3–4 months, cooked batter puddings 3 months.

BEANS Broad, French and runner beans are all suitable for freezing. As the season for these popular vegetables is an extended one it is more important than with other vegetables to date packs of home-grown crops and use them up in rotation. Storage time 10–12 months.
See *VEGETABLE PREPARATION AND PACKING, *DEFROSTING, *GROWING GUIDE for varieties recommended for freezing.

BEEF As it comes from such a large animal the capital outlay for a bulk purchase is one of the largest you are likely to make. It is the hardest of all meats to judge for quality, which in any case depends on being hung properly (from 10–14 days before freezing).

Cuts of beef. A side of beef includes both forequarter and hindquarter. The forequarter is the smaller of the two and contains most of the cheaper, coarser cuts. The hindquarter is larger and includes most of the roasting and other choice cuts. A whole forequarter or hindquarter is usually too large a purchase for one family but may be split between two freezer owners.

Large packs of the cuts you particularly want are more economical than buying day to day requirements. If you do buy in bulk at a flat rate per kg/lb, take into account the waste in the form of bones and excess fat which you may not be able to use. Without committing yourself to such a large investment you can still benefit by buying beef 'packs' of the cuts you prefer. As the cuts are known by different names in various parts of the country, the following guide to bulk buying beef is given with some alternative names, although these will not cover all local variations.

Other bulk purchases of beef are available and here is a general guide as to what cuts are included. When buying beef in this manner it is essential to check with the butcher exactly what cuts you are going to get.

PONY – chuck and blade, plus back and short ribs.
Approximate weight:
30–40 kg/65–90 lb.
Bone and fat: 20–25%.

CROP – pony plus neck and fore ribs.
Approximate weight:
45–60 kg/100–130 lb.
Bone and fat: about 25%.

TOP BIT – topside, silverside, top rump and leg.
Approximate weight:
45–57 kg/100–125 lb.
Bone and fat: 20–25%.

TOP BIT AND RUMP – topside, silverside, top rump, leg and rump (possibly including fillet and skirt).
Approximate weight:
55–64 kg/120–140 lb.
Bone and fat: 20–23%.

RUMP OF BEEF (Scottish) – silverside, top rump, steak mince.
Approximate weight:
23–32 kg/50–70 lb.
Bone and fat: Minimal.

RUMP OF BEEF WITH POPE'S EYE (Scottish) – fillet, pope's eye, steak mince, silverside, rump steak.
Approximate weight:
32–45 kg/70–100 lb.
Bone and fat: Minimal.

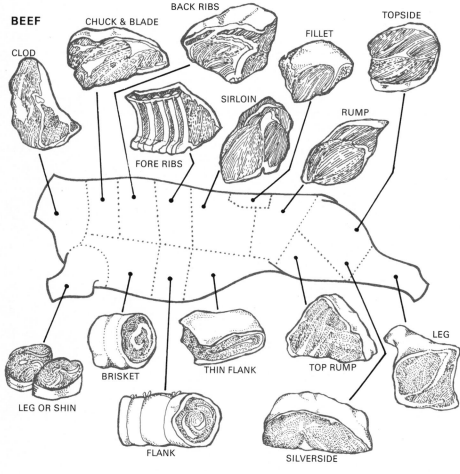

BEEF

CLOD
CHUCK & BLADE
BACK RIBS
FILLET
TOPSIDE
SIRLOIN
FORE RIBS
RUMP
LEG OR SHIN
BRISKET
THIN FLANK
TOP RUMP
LEG
FLANK
SILVERSIDE

Cuts included	Possible alternative names	Preparation	Suitable cooking method
Flank	Boiling beef	Joints boned and rolled	Braising, pot roasting
Thin flank	Nine hole	Joints boned and rolled	Stewing, boiling
Leg	Shin Hough	Cubes, mince	Stewing, boiling, minced beef dishes
Brisket		Joints boned and rolled	Pot roast – can be salted for boiling
Clod	Sticking Neck	Cubes, mince	Stewing, minced beef dishes
Chuck and blade	Shoulder	Small joints boned and rolled, slices, cubes	Braising, stewing, in puddings
Fore ribs	Long ribs Banjo Standing ribs	Joints on bone or boned and rolled, steaks	Roasting, grilling
Back ribs	Middle rib	Joints on bone or boned and rolled	Slow roasting, pot roasting
Feather steak	Feather blade	Steaks	Frying, grilling
Top ribs	Oven buster	Joints on bone, mince	Slow roasting, pot roasting, braising, minced beef dishes
Flat ribs	Leg of mutton cut Chuck tops	Joints on bone, mince	Slow roasting, pot roasting, braising, minced beef dishes

Cuts included	Possible alternative names	Preparation	Suitable cooking method
Sirloin (including wing rib)		Joints on bone or boned and rolled, steaks	Roasting, grilling, frying
Fillet	Undercut	Joint, steaks	Roasting, grilling, frying
Rump	Pope's eye	Joints, steaks	Roasting, grilling, frying
Topside	Buttock Round steak (topside and silverside together)	Joints	Slow roasting (if not top quality), braising, pot roasting
Silverside		Joints	Pot roasting, can be salted for boiling
Top rump	Rump steak Thick flank Bed of beef First cutting	Joints, sliced	Slow roasting (if top quality), braising, pot roasting
Leg	Hough	Slices, cubes	Stewing
Hindquarter flank		Cubes, mince	Stewing, minced beef dishes
Goose skirt		Cubes	Stewing, in puddings and pies

FOREQUARTER OF BEEF
Approximate weight: 55–68 kg/120–150 lb
Percentage of bone and fat to be expected: 30–35%

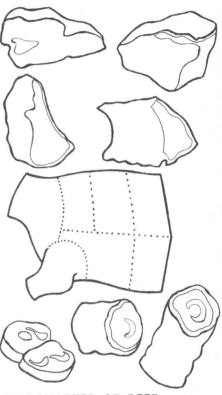

HINDQUARTER OF BEEF
Approximate weight: 68–82 kg/150–180 lb
Percentage of bone and fat to be expected: 28–35%

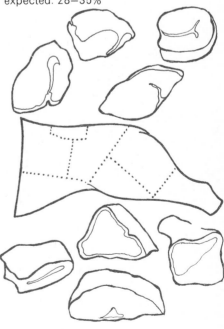

BEETROOT Root vegetable which requires to be fully cooked before freezing. Small ones freeze best. To prevent 'bleeding' of the juices and loss of colour and flavour, beetroot should be cooked whole. The skin should be rubbed off and the root removed after cooking. If the texture is not sufficiently good for use in salads, frozen beetroot may be reheated and served as a hot vegetable. Storage time 10–12 months.
See *VEGETABLE PREPARATION AND PACKING, *DEFROSTING.

BILBERRY Berry fruit sometimes described as blueberry or 'blaeberry'; suitable for freezing raw, cooked, in the form of purée, syrup or jam. Storage time in sugar, or sugar syrup pack, or as a syrup 9–12 months, dry without sugar 6–8 months.
See *FRUIT PREPARATION AND PACK-ING, *UNCOOKED FREEZER JAMS, *DEFROSTING.

BISCUITS These can be frozen baked, unbaked or as a ready-mixed dough in the form of a roll wrapped in foil. Thin slices can be cut from the partially-defrosted roll and baked off. Storage time baked 3 months, un-baked 4–6 months.

BLACKBERRY Soft berry fruit suit-able for freezing raw, cooked, in the form of purée, syrup or jam. Storage time in sugar, or sugar syrup pack, or as a syrup 9–12 months, dry without sugar 6–8 months.
See *FRUIT PREPARATION AND PACK-ING, *UNCOOKED FREEZER JAMS, *DEFROSTING.

BLACKCURRANT See *CURRANTS.

BLANCHING A method of scalding food, mainly vegetables, before freez-ing to prevent changes in colour, flavour, texture and nutritional value (caused by enzyme activity). In the case of green vegetables the natural colour is intensified by blanching. The process is as follows:
1. Use a large saucepan which easily accommodates 4 litres/7 pints water, a blanching basket and approximately 450 g/1 lb prepared vegetables. Heat the water to boiling point.
2. Place the prepared vegetables in a blanching basket and immerse in the water. Bring back to the boil as quickly as possible.
3. Begin timing from this moment, according to the blanching instruc-tions (see *VEGETABLE PREPARATION AND PACKING). Timing must be exact as under-blanching will not entirely halt enzyme activity and over-blanching may spoil the texture and colour of the food.
4. Remove the basket immediately time is up and hold under running water to cool the vegetables quickly. If this is impossible, dip the basket sev-eral times in and out of a bowl of iced water.
5. Drain blanched vegetables on absorbent kitchen paper or a clean folded tea towel. Pack when com-pletely cold. Make up packs of the weight you most frequently require. If larger packs are needed and part of the contents must be removed while still in the frozen state, open freeze to ensure a free flow.
6. Remember that vegetables must

move freely in the boiling water and that this water should be renewed after four uses.

See *PRESSURE BLANCHING, *BLANCHING BASKETS, *ENZYMES, *FREE-FLOW FREEZING, *VEGETABLE PREPARATION AND PACKING.

HELPFUL HINT: If you have no blanching basket the vegetables can be boiled freely, scooped out into a colander with a slotted draining spoon and cooled in the colander, but the timing by this method is often inaccurate.

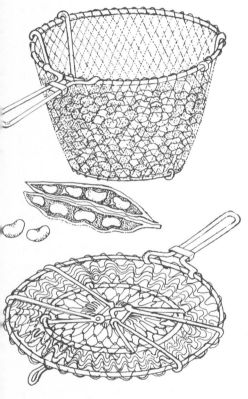

BLANCHING BASKETS Collapsible or rigid-based metal baskets with a finer mesh than that of a frying basket, really an essential accessory to blanching. The light collapsible type of basket is best as it does not slow down the return of the blanching water to boiling point to the same extent as a heavy rigid basket. It is also easier to store when not in use. If you possess two baskets, blanching is a quicker process as one batch of vegetables can be cooled down and put to drain while another batch is being blanched. The two-basket method really requires the use of a timer.

BLAST FREEZING A commercial method of quick freezing where the product is passed through a tunnel inside which there is a violent circulation of refrigerated air. The product is carried along the tunnel on a mesh belt through which the cold air can pass, or it is prepackaged, laid on shelves on a trolley and moved slowly through the tunnel.

BOILABLE BAGS Some bags suitable for freezing can be placed in boiling water to defrost and reheat the contents. None is suitable for blanching as it is too difficult to judge the timing. There are three types available.
1. Light gauge and high density polythene bags.
2. Polyester film bags also suitable for exposure to dry heat in the oven.
3. Gussetted laminated foil bags. The first two types require care in sealing as surplus air needs to be smoothed out between the surface of the food and the seal. This is necessary as air trapped inside the bag expands when heated and if excessive might cause the bag to burst. The closure can be a plastic-coated metal twist tie, or a special twine which shrinks when it becomes wet during reheating and makes an even more effective seal. The best way to use the twine is to make a goose-neck tie, twisting the

Blanched peas cooled in a colander under the cold tap and packed in rigid-based containers or gussetted bags lined with foil to make firm base.

Boilable bags. Right: filled with vegetables and fastened with a twist tie. Below: fastened with twine and the corner snipped off for easy pouring of a sauce.

bag neck firmly and folding it over, then tying firmly round the loop. The advantage of bags made from polyester material is that it is equally possible to place the bags on a baking tray in oven heat to defrost and reheat if this is more convenient. The third type of boilable bag is sealed by placing a twist tie across the mouth of the bag and folding the top over several times, turning the ends of the twist tie back to keep it in place. Some are printed with a panel and stripes in contrasting colour for easy identification with space to note the contents, quantity and date of freezing.

HELPFUL HINT: Polythene boilable bags can sometimes be re-used if very carefully washed and smoothed out while warm. If not intended for re-use it is often easier to cut off one lower corner of the bag diagonally and squeeze out the contents, particularly if it is a soup or sauce.

BONUS COOKING A method of cooking in large quantities which provides one portion of the food for immediate eating and two or more other portions to freeze down. There is a saving in preparation time and it enables you to take advantage of a bargain purchase.

BRAINS Offal which require to be blanched. They are best frozen in a sauce to disguise discoloration. Storage time 3 months.
See *OFFAL, *DISCOLORATION.

BREAD Both yeast and baking powder breads freeze well whether cooked or in the form of dough.
Cooked loaves and rolls with a soft crust store longer than those with a crisp crust as this tends to dehydrate and 'shell off' within a week; slices can be quickly separated and toasted from the frozen state. Sandwiches made with partially defrosted bread keep fresh for a long time. Mould cooked loaves in foil or cling film for freezing. Specially shaped long polythene bags are available for French loaves. Pack rolls in convenient quantities in polythene bags. Loaves wrapped in foil can be placed frozen in a moderately hot oven (200°C, 400°F, Gas Mark 6) for 35–40 minutes, according to size, to defrost. Allow 15 minutes for rolls (unwrapped loaves 20–25 minutes, but the crusts will tend to burn). To defrost rolls under the grill, brush with cold water and place under a hot grill for 5 minutes, turning once.
Commercially part-baked bread and rolls are best defrosted before baking.

Smoked cod in orange sauce (page 152)

Bread mix chains: Miniature cottage loaves, poppy seed plait, slashed herby loaf; Flat cottage loaf, cobblestone loaf (pages 214, 217)

Bread doughs can be frozen either before or after proving. The former should be stored in oiled polythene bags which require to be loosened to allow the dough to rise as it defrosts.

Baked goods made from enriched doughs (with a high fat content) have less tendency to dehydrate than ordinary breads. Frozen croissants and brioches can be packed like rolls and reheated without covering or damping. Storage time white and brown baked bread 4 weeks; crusty bread 1 week only; commercially part-baked bread 4 months; unrisen dough – plain white and brown bread 8 weeks, enriched bread 5 weeks; risen dough 3 weeks; enriched baked bread 6 weeks. See *DEFROSTING, *SANDWICHES.
NOTE: Savoury loaves to be served hot can be prepared in advance and then frozen. Make cuts 2–4 cm/1–1½ inches apart along a French or Vienna loaf almost through to the base. Spread the cut surfaces with softened butter flavoured with crushed garlic or garlic salt, or a mixture of grated cheese and chopped fresh herbs. Press the loaf back into shape and mould closely in foil. When required, place the wrapped loaf, still frozen, in a moderately hot oven (200°C, 400°F, Gas Mark 6) for 30–40 minutes, according to size. Storage time 1 week.

BREAD CROÛTONS See *CROÛTES/ CROÛTONS.

BREADCRUMBS Any leftover bread, providing it is fresh, can be frozen in the form of breadcrumbs which need not be defrosted for use. It is best to pack them in small polythene bags so that you can break up the contents with your fingers through the bag. Storage time 3 months.
HELPFUL HINT: Breadcrumbs fried in butter until crisp and golden brown can be packed when cool for freezing, also in polythene bags. Use them to top savoury gratin dishes or, if mixed with sugar, to top puddings. Storage time 3 months.

BRINE PACK Over-mature vegetables, particularly green beans, can be frozen but may be tough in texture when defrosted. Packing in brine tends to soften them. Make a brine solution by dissolving 2 tablespoons salt in 1 litre/1¾ pints boiling water. Cool and chill before pouring over the blanched vegetables, allowing 1–2 cm/½–1 inch headspace in the container. Storage time 12 months.
HELPFUL HINT: Defrost and drain before cooking as the vegetables may taste too salty. If necessary they can be cooked in unsalted boiling water.

BROCCOLI Green vegetable with thick stems and tight undeveloped flowering heads which freezes well. Choose tender sprigs and cut out thicker stems. Calabrese, often sold as broccoli, has good compact green heads. Storage time 10–12 months.
See *VEGETABLE PREPARATION AND PACKING, *DEFROSTING.

BRUSSELS SPROUT Green vegetable bearing sprouts on the main stem which freezes well. Special care must be taken to cool and chill blanched sprouts before packing as their strong odour has a tendency to permeate the container or bag. For this reason, open freezing on trays is inadvisable. Storage time 10–12 months.
See *VEGETABLE PREPARATION AND PACKING, *DEFROSTING.

BULK BUYING A means of saving money by buying a sufficiently large quantity to obtain a low price. It also saves time as you do not need to shop so frequently, but care must be taken to ensure that all the food will be used within a reasonable period and that the cost and inconvenience of storage is not excessive. It is unwise to buy any commodity in large quantities if you are likely to have insufficient freezer space to accommodate it, or have a repetitive diet as a result. Decide what items will justify the outlay of capital, then shop around to discover the best value and quality. Make a realistic calculation on the true saving effected. Remember that you may have to pay something for delivery so try to arrange to collect purchases yourself. Some foods such as frozen vegetables are free-flowing or easily divided. But make sure that fish fillets, for example, are individually frozen or packed with dividers so that you never need to defrost a whole pack to remove one portion.

At certain times it may be possible to buy fruit, vegetables, fish and poultry cheaply from local suppliers, but always take care to ensure the food is fresh and that you have the time available for the preparation involved. Dressing and drawing poultry is time-consuming and not to everyone's taste.

When buying meat in bulk, allow for the percentage of fat and bone included in the purchase price calculated per kg/lb. Insist on having the meat hung, butchered and packed in portions in convenient quantities, properly marked. Do not omit to collect the bones for stock, the fat for dripping and, if applicable, head and trotters for brawn.
See *MEAT BUYING.

BUTCHER'S WRAP A method of wrapping meat or any other food of a regular shape which has a low water content and would not easily be damaged. Use a square sheet of polythene or foil. Place diagonally across one corner. Bring corner over and tuck under the meat, then roll forward bringing the corners on either side into the centre. Continue rolling and ensure that the folded wrapping narrows towards the opposite corner. Seal the point with freezer tape.

BUTTER All butter for freezing should be made from pasteurised cream. When the price is lower than usual and you decide to stock up on butter, be careful that it is quite fresh. Over-wrap the paper cover with cling film in convenient-sized packs. Storage time unsalted 6 months, salted 4 months.
See *DEFROSTING.
Butter pats or curls should be open frozen before packing in rigid containers, interleaving the layers.
Flavoured butters, such as *maître d'hôtel* butter, should be chilled until firm enough to mould. Turn out on to wet cling film or polythene and make into a long roll about 4–4·5 cm/ 1½–1¾ inches in diameter. Roll and shape through the wrap. To serve, unwrap the portion required and cut into slices on a board while still in the frozen state. Storage time 3 months. If garlic is contained in the flavouring, only 1 month.

BUYING A FREEZER Make sure that you are buying one of the three following four-star types; a chest, refrigerator/freezer, or upright freezer, and not a conservator. To justify the description of 'freezer' the appliance must be capable of storing ready-frozen food and of freezing the manufacturer's recommended weight of fresh food (usually 10% of the freezer's total capacity) within any 24-hour period. This must be done without reducing the quality or storage life of frozen food already being stored. An appliance capable of both functions will be marked with the following four-star symbol on the rating plate and the BEAB Mark.

BS 3456 is a stringent and comprehensive specification, published by The British Standards Institution, which covers the standards of safety for household electrical appliances. It is to this specification that the BEAB carries out tests.

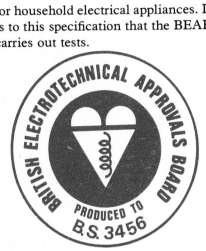

Freezers are not identical in their performances although the same four-star rating applies to both the British Standard and the European Standard. Tests carried out by European manufacturers are often less stringent than ours. The British Standard freezer tests are based on the *highest* temperature of the *warmest* pack put into the freezer. The German DIN standard is calculated on the *average* temperature of the food to be frozen. It is best to follow the manufacturer's instructions exactly when loading your freezer.

When comparing prices, look for extras which may make the more expensive of two models the better bargain. These include condensation control, sorting shelves, interior light, door locks, drainage outlets, front flaps on shelves, automatic defrost, work top, castors, adjustable feet, adjustable thermostat, counterbalanced lid, fast freeze switch, warning light. However, expensive models, very slightly shop-soiled, are sometimes offered at a reduced price.
See ★SECONDHAND FREEZERS.

CABBAGE Leafy vegetable available in white, green and red varieties. Only suitable for freezing in the cooked form. All frozen cabbage tastes better when combined with other spicy flavours in made-up dishes. (Chinese cabbage requires the minimum blanching and therefore has a short storage life because it is served almost crisp with oriental dishes.) Storage time 3–4 months.
See ★VEGETABLE PREPARATION AND PACKING, ★DEFROSTING.

CAKES All cooked undecorated cakes freeze well, also layer cakes with fillings. Baked commercial cake mixes are particularly successful. Some icings (*e.g. glacé icing*) tend to crack or sweat when defrosted. A Victoria sandwich batter can be frozen uncooked. A 50 g/2 oz Victoria sandwich mixture is the right amount to make a 18 cm/7 inch cake layer, and will fill a Tupperware cereal bowl comfortably for freezing.

Basic sponge layers of various flavours can be packed in pairs in polythene bags with dividers. You may wish to remove single layers from packs of different flavours or colours to make up fancy gâteaux (*e.g. Battenberg cake*).

Large decorated cakes are best open frozen until the decorations are hard, then packed in a rigid-based container with a seal, thus preventing damage by accidentally placing a heavy pack on top of the cake in the frozen state. Or, put the frozen cake in a large polythene bag. Draw out surplus air and seal, then place the pack inside a cardboard carton with a lid for extra protection.

Small decorated cakes are easily damaged even in the frozen state. Open freeze on baking trays. Arrange in layers with foil or non-stick vegetable parchment dividers in a shallow large-based container. It is difficult to arrange small cakes to fit a deep container. Storage time unbaked or baked 3 months.

HELPFUL HINT: To make it easy to remove large cakes from their containers, take a long narrow piece of foil or greaseproof paper and fold it several times to make a wide ruler shape, which must be long enough to press down the side of the container, across the bottom and up the other side, leaving two protruding ends large enough to grasp. When the cake is packed you can tuck the ends in under the seal. They can then be used to lift the cake out of the container easily. Storage time 3 months.
See *DEFROSTING, FILLINGS.

CANDIED FRUIT Either whole fruit or peel keeps much better in the freezer than in a container exposed to a warm atmosphere. Pack in small quantities in polythene containers for fast thawing. Storage time 12 months.

CANNED FOODS These can be frozen successfully but since they are fully cooked tend to become mushy if exposed to too much heat or rough treatment when defrosted (*e.g. stirring*). Catering cans can be opened, part of the contents used at once and the remainder divided between small containers for freezing.

CAPACITY The usable inside volume of the freezer cabinet, measured in litres or cubic feet. When buying a freezer always check whether the capacity mentioned is net or gross. For instance an upright freezer might have 295 litres/10·4 cubic feet gross capacity, 270 litres/9·5 cubic feet net. The difference in gross and net capacities in chest freezers is usually less (*e.g. 305 litres/10·5 cubic feet gross, 297 litres/10·5 cubic feet net*). The manufacturer sometimes suggests the weight of food the freezer can be expected to store, but this depends on the type of food, its weight for volume and the shape of the packs. As a general rule you can reasonably expect to store about 10 kg/22 lb of food in 30 litres/1 cubic foot of freezer space.

CARAMEL A simple toffee made of sugar and water and poured out to set on an oiled baking tray, or used to line moulds for *crème caramel*. It can be crushed when hard and frozen for decorating. Storage time 12 months. See *CUSTARDS.

CARBON DIOXIDE In its solid form it is referred to as 'dry ice' and often used as a coolant for refrigerated transport. It evaporates at a steady rate and it is possible to calculate the quantity required to keep a specific weight of food frozen for a specific length of time. It should never be handled without gloves, allowed to come in contact with the food itself or be placed inside a freezer cabinet.

CARROT Root vegetable which freezes well blanched or in made-up dishes. Young carrots can be frozen whole, unblanched, for short-term storage. Storage time blanched 10–12 months, unblanched 3 months.
See *VEGETABLE PREPARATION AND PACKING, *DEFROSTING.
HELPFUL HINT: It is useful to have small packs of neatly sliced or diced carrots in store to add to stews or other cooked vegetables for salads (*e.g. Russian salad*).

CASH AND CARRY A store where customers who have a permit to shop may buy dry goods as well as frozen food in bulk and can frequently effect extra savings by shopping under one roof. Prices are often lower than at freezer centres as these stores are suppliers to small retail traders virtually at wholesale prices.

CASSEROLES Dishes which need long slow cooking for which a number of ingredients have to be prepared. They are particularly suitable for chain cooking and bonus cooking because much time can be saved in preparing a large quantity, using one portion and freezing the remainder for future use. Oven heat which might otherwise be wasted can often be utilised for casseroles. Ingredients which tend to go mushy (*e.g. potato topping*) are best added when the dish is defrosted and reheated. Storage time 4–6 months.

See *PACKAGING.

HELPFUL HINT: Made-up casserole dishes packed in shaped foil containers defrost and reheat quickly as aluminium is a good heat conductor. The dishes can be re-used if carefully treated and can be moulded to alter the shape slightly to fit an awkward space in the oven.

CATERING PACKS Larger packs than would normally be practical for family use at an economical price. The food is much easier to handle if the packs are immediately divided and repacked into convenient meal-size portions.

CAULIFLOWER A green vegetable with creamy white compact head (the 'curd') which freezes well blanched. Cauliflower florets can be frozen unblanched for short-term storage. Storage time blanched 10–12 months, unblanched 3 months.

See *VEGETABLE PREPARATION AND PACKING, *DEFROSTING.

CAVITY ICE A layer of frost deposited on the inner surface of a pack caused by food dehydrating into air pockets inside the pack. Leaving too much headspace inside the pack or making an imperfect seal will produce this damaging result.

CELERIAC Vegetable with a bulbous root similar to celery which freezes fairly well blanched. Storage time 10–12 months.

See *VEGETABLE PREPARATION AND PACKING, *DEFROSTING.

HELPFUL HINT: Cut into matchsticks and steam blanch for 1 minute only if for use in salads such as *Céleri rémoulade*. The dressing disguises the slightly flabby texture of the defrosted vegetable.

CELERY Vegetable with a long stem and bulbous root which freezes well blanched for use in cooked dishes. Storage time 10–12 months.

See *VEGETABLE PREPARATION AND PACKING, *DEFROSTING.

HELPFUL HINT: Coarse outer stems may be stringy and unsuitable for serving as a vegetable. These can be packed separately for use in soups and stews which will be strained or liquidised before freezing.

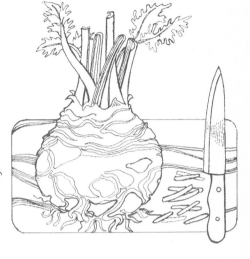

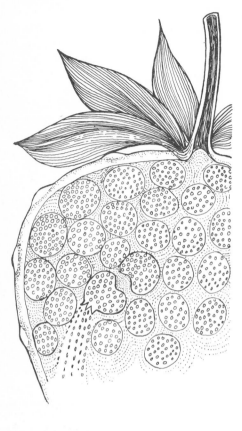

CELL DAMAGE This is most often caused by ice crystal formation, or the disturbance of the balance of osmotic pressure, or by both.

Ice crystal formation. All food consists of cells containing and surrounded by solutions mainly formed of water. The expansion of this water as it freezes ruptures the cell walls and causes small ice crystals to form which, if the process is slow, congregate and form larger ice crystals. This effect is not noticeable in the frozen state, but on thawing the collapse of cell structure is quite apparent, and is most damaging in foods with a high water content and delicate cell structure. This damage, unlike that caused by osmotic pressure, is irreversible and can only be disguised by presenting the whole food to be eaten while still semi-frozen, forming into a purée or serving cooked.

Zone of cell damage. The various constituents of food freeze at different temperatures and as food approaches the point at which every element is frozen the temperature descent curve flattens out, lengthening the period of time food takes to pass through this vital zone when large ice crystals tend to form. The more quickly food is frozen, the more quickly it passes through this zone with less cell damage caused by the formation of large ice crystals.

Balance of osmotic pressure. All food contains a solution of nutrients, minerals and vitamins in water both inside the cells (intercellular) and in the spaces between the cells (intracellular). When food is frozen ice crystals are formed which puncture the cell walls and, on defrosting, allow some of the intercellular liquid to escape, resulting in changes in the texture of the food. Generally the faster the food is frozen the smaller the ice crystals and the consequent damage. The change is also more marked in food with delicate cell walls (*e.g. strawberries*) than in food where they are tougher (*e.g. meat*). There is also a crit-

ical balance between the comparative strengths of the intercellular and intracellular solutions which are only separated by a thin, semi-permeable membrane, the cell wall. The fact that the intercellular liquid usually freezes first disturbs this balance and causes some of the liquid from inside the cells to seep out through the porous wall, thus collapsing the cell.

How to minimise the damage. Cook whole vegetables, all of which have a relatively high water content, from the frozen state. Eat raw whole fruits before they are fully defrosted. This is best achieved by thawing them in the refrigerator, covered to protect them from cross-contamination of the delicate flavour by other foods, and to keep the outer surfaces of the fruit chilled while the centres defrost sufficiently to be eatable. The fruit will be more evenly thawed and retain a better texture because it loses less moisture than if thawed at room temperature.

In other foods with a high water content such as eggs, milk and cream, there is no such 'structural' problem. An egg is one single cell; milk and cream have no cell structure, but are emulsions mainly of fat globules and water. In vegetables and fruit purées, such as mashed potato and apple sauce, the cell structure has been deliberately destroyed before freezing.

CHAIN COOKING A way of saving time and money by buying a basic ingredient in bulk (*e.g. minced beef*) and producing from it a wide variety of dishes (*e.g. meat balls, meat loaf, bolognese sauce*). A basic bread dough could be used to provide a chain, making pizzas, loaves and rolls. A basic white sauce prepared in bulk could provide a sauce chain by converting it into cheese sauce, caper sauce and onion sauce.

CHAIN FREEZING If presented with the problem of having more fresh food to freeze down than can be accommodated in the freezer, certain rules should be followed.

1. Items which deteriorate quickly (*e.g. offal*) should be frozen first.

2. Secondly, freeze vulnerable items (*e.g. minced and sliced meat*) with many cut surfaces likely to oxidise. Store these meanwhile in the refrigerator.

3. Leave the least vulnerable items until last (*e.g. joints*) but keep in as cold a place as possible. Avoid handling and exposure to temperature changes. Items which have not been frozen as quickly as you would wish should be specially labelled to remind you to use these first.

HELPFUL HINT: If you have made a bulk purchase of beef, the joints may improve by being matured for the extra time. Butchers frequently hang beef for 8–10 days whereas it could be hung up to 14 days to mature fully. This does not apply to other meats.

CHEESE All varieties of cheese freeze well providing they are very closely wrapped.

Cream, curd and cottage cheeses freeze well wrapped in foil or in their own plastic containers, but sometimes require beating or sieving to improve the texture after defrosting. They are particularly suitable for dips and dressings. Typical examples are Demi-Sel and Kraft Philadelphia.

Soft cheeses with a natural crust are better removed from the box and closely moulded with cling film or foil unless they are already wrapped in foil portions. Typical examples are Camembert, Brie and Pont l'Evêque.

Semi-hard cheeses with a rind have a smooth close texture and are little affected by freezing. They should be moulded in cling film or foil. Typical examples are Gouda and Edam.

Hard cheeses, especially those with a crumbly texture, tend to become more crumbly on defrosting. Wrap as for semi-hard cheeses. Typical examples are Cheddar and Caerphilly.

Blue cheeses all tend to crumble when thawed and are therefore best used for salads, dips and dressings. A typical example is Danish Blue.

Cheeses made from goats' milk tend to develop a slight 'off' flavour when frozen. All cheeses should be fully mature. Left-over pieces of cheese, or those which crumble when defrosted can be grated and frozen in small quantities in bags to use for cooking. Processed cheeses in small portions are best frozen in their foil wrappings inside the box provided, or with an overwrap, as the foil is not freezer-proof. Open sandwiches or bun halves with a savoury topping intended for toasting under the grill are particularly successful if processed cheese is used as the final layer. When the bread is fully defrosted, the cheese melts just sufficiently under exposure to heat to turn brown at the moment the remaining ingredients are warmed through. Storage time cream and soft cheeses 3 months, semi-hard and hard cheeses 6 months.

See *DEFROSTING.

CHEESECAKES Both the baked and unbaked varieties freeze well, but the methods of preparation are somewhat different.

Baked cheesecakes. Follow the recipe until the cake is baked. Cool, remove from tin on to a cake plate or foil plate. Open freeze until firm then wrap in polythene, cling film or foil.

Unbaked cheesecakes. Make up the topping, pour it into the cake tin and freeze. Place the prepared crumb base on this and press down with a metal spoon. Return to the freezer for a further 10 minutes, remove from the cake tin by inverting on to a cake plate or foil plate. While still chilled, wrap as for baked cheesecakes.

Cheesecakes in pastry cases. Cases may be prepared in advance, frozen empty and defrosted before filling with an uncooked mixture.

All cheesecakes are best decorated at serving time but before the surface has thawed.

See *DEFROSTING.

CHERRY White, red and black cherries all freeze well raw, with or without sugar or in sugar syrup. Stoned cherries can be more closely packed but the stones are easier to remove after freezing. Storage time in sugar or sugar syrup pack 9–12 months, dry without sugar 6–8 months.
See *FRUIT PREPARATION AND PACKING, *DEFROSTING.

CHEST FREEZER Shaped like a box with a hinged lid, controls on the front panel and ventilation grid on one panel. Available in sizes from 100–900 litres/3·5–32 cubic feet. A chest freezer requires more wall and floor space than an upright freezer, is particularly suitable for a kitchen site and requires defrosting only once a year. It is easier to store large uneven shaped packs such as meat in bulk, and to pack tidily with the use of removable baskets, but it sometimes poses a problem to those below average height who have difficulty in reaching the bottom. The fast freeze compartment is usually situated above the motor and sometimes the evaporator coils are arranged more closely together within the shell of the cabinet to give greater freezing capacity in that area. The evaporator system is enclosed within this shell and is not visible.
See *LAYERED STORAGE.

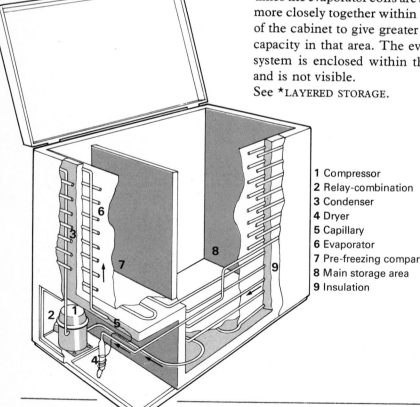

1 Compressor
2 Relay-combination
3 Condenser
4 Dryer
5 Capillary
6 Evaporator
7 Pre-freezing compartment
8 Main storage area
9 Insulation

CHESTNUT Can only be frozen whole for a short time even when blanched as chestnuts develop a musty 'off' flavour. Since they are always used cooked they are better frozen in the cooked form, if possible as a purée. Storage time whole 3 weeks, purée 3 months.
See *NUTS, *DEFROSTING.
HELPFUL HINT: Whole blanched chestnuts freeze well in the form of *marrons glacés*.

CHICKEN One of the most versatile freezer foods, which freezes well whole or jointed, raw or cooked, and in made-up dishes. *Poussins* are baby chickens 4–6 weeks old usually roasted whole. Spring chickens are 6–10 weeks old, either roasted whole or split and grilled or fried. Frying chickens (US Broilers) are 3–4 months old and suitable for roasting whole or jointing and grilling or frying. Roasters are 6–12 months old and suitable for roasting whole or jointing and sautéeing. Capons are 6–12 months old and suitable for roasting whole. Hens are boiling fowls over 1 year old which require long slow cooking and are not suitable for roasting.

Frozen chickens have been killed, plucked, drawn and frozen without allowing quite sufficient time to hang and therefore are improved in flavour by being thawed out slowly at least overnight and preferably for 24 hours before cooking. Chickens sold straight from the farm by the case may not be the bargain you expect if they are not oven ready. They may require to be plucked and drawn! Storage time 12 months, giblets 3 months.
See *POULTRY, *DEFROSTING.
NOTE: Freezing a stuffed chicken reduces its storage time to 3 months and extra defrosting and cooking time must be allowed. Bread stuffings do not have such a long storage life as the poultry itself, and take a long time to thaw. It is unwise to freeze chickens with the giblets inside because this also reduces the storage time.

CHICORY (US BELGIAN ENDIVE)
Vegetable of which the white shoots are suitable for freezing blanched or in made-up dishes. Unblanched chicory is not suitable to freeze for use in salads, and the slightly bitter flavour is intensified by freezing. Storage time 10–12 months. See ★VEGETABLE PREPARATION AND PACKING, ★DEFROSTING, ★DISCOLORATION.

CHILLING The reduction of the temperature of food to approximately 4·4°C/40°F, which is that inside the average refrigerator cabinet. The temperature of food has a direct bearing on the loss of nutrients and spoilage through bacterial activity. It is necessary for both raw and cooked foods, if not to be eaten at once, to be chilled.
1. Raw food left in a warm atmosphere is also exposed to the risk of increased bacterial contamination through multiplication of existing bacteria.
2. Cooked food (*e.g. meat stew*) which passes down slowly through the temperature range at which bacteria multiply quickly (25–7°C/77–45°F) and until cold enough to put in the freezer, could be a health hazard when defrosted. Since the temperature inside the average refrigerator cabinet is approximately 4°C/39°F, the more quickly food can be cooled and reduced to this temperature, the less opportunity there is for deterioration. Always keep chilled food covered. See ★FAST FREEZING.

CHINAGRAPH PENCILS Where it is difficult to affix a label these pencils will write on any surface, even glass, and do not fade during long-term freezer storage. They write more easily on a slightly warm surface. If the pack is already chilled or frozen, hold the tip of the pencil near a source of heat.

CHINESE CABBAGE See ★CABBAGE.

Wrapping and packing whole chickens and chicken portions.

CHOCOLATE A popular flavouring, chocolate is excellent for freezing in cakes, sweetmeats, sauces, desserts, biscuits, puddings, ice creams and fillings. Cocoa gives the strongest flavouring, and although melted chocolate can be combined with other ingredients to make butter cream or fudge icing, melted chocolate alone is not suitable as an icing. The surface tends to go grey and to sweat when defrosted. Chocolate shapes and caraque (scrolls or flakes) to be used as decorations are better frozen separately. Melted chocolate poured out to form a thin layer on non-stick vegetable parchment and allowed to set can be cut out in squares, diamonds or triangles, or even shaved off in curls with the blade of a knife. A few of these carefully arranged in a small rigid-based polythene container are useful for special occasions. Storage time 2 months.
See *DEFROSTING.
HELPFUL HINT: Small rose leaves with stems can be used to prepare chocolate leaves by spreading melted chocolate on the underside of each leaf. When set pull the leaves away, starting from the stem end. Store as above.

CHOUX PASTRY This can be frozen in the form of uncooked paste, in bulk or piped out in shapes, or baked. Raw choux paste in bulk must be fully defrosted and slightly warmed before piping, but piped shapes can be baked from the frozen state. Use a large piping bag with plain nozzle and pipe out small walnut-size pieces for puffs or 5-cm/2-inch lengths for éclairs, on to non-stick vegetable parchment. Open freeze, then pack in layers in rigid-based containers. If frozen baked, it is better slightly to underbake choux pastry puffs and defrost by placing in a moderately hot oven (190°C, 375°F, Gas Mark 5) while still in the frozen state. They defrost, become crisp and slightly browner in 15–20 minutes. If not rebaked the defrosted puffs are somewhat limp and flabby, and for this reason it is better to freeze them unfilled. Storage time baked or unbaked 4–6 months.

CHUTNEY Uncooked chutney can be made by mixing all the ingredients together with a spiced vinegar syrup, and can be frozen without the trouble of cooking, provided it is appreciated that the chutney will not keep long after defrosting. It should therefore be frozen in small polythene or glass containers which can be used up within a week and kept in the refrigerator once it is thawed. Let the mixture stand overnight, to combine the flavours thoroughly, before packing; avoid using foil containers. Storage time 6–8 months.

CITRUS FRUIT Genus including oranges, lemons, limes, grapefruit, and such fruits as satsumas, mandarins, clementines, tangerines, ugli fruit and ortaniques. They all freeze well sliced or segmented, and the juicier ones in the form of juice. Seville oranges, only suitable for making marmalade, can be frozen whole during their short season and defrosted later when you have time to make preserves. The zest can be grated or thinly peeled from all these fruits and mixed with sugar to freeze for use in cooking. Storage time in sugar or sugar syrup pack 9–12 months, juices 4–6 months, whole Seville oranges 6 months.
See *FRUIT PREPARATION AND PACKING, *DEFROSTING.

COCONUT Moist fresh white flesh of the coconut freezes well, grated or shredded, with either sugar or coconut milk. Storage time 10–12 months.
See *DEFROSTING.

COD Lean fish which freezes well. Storage time 6 months, coated in breadcrumbs or batter 3 months.
See *FISH PREPARATION AND PACKING, *DEFROSTING.

COFFEE As a flavouring coffee is excellent for freezing in cakes, sweet-meats, sauces, desserts, biscuits, puddings, ice creams, fillings. Ground coffee can be used in some cases instead of ground nuts, or added as an extender to ground nuts. Coffee made from granules or instant powder can be made up extra strong for use in cooking or coffee essence can be used. Very strong coffee-flavoured ice cubes are useful to add to cold milk to make instant iced coffee. Strong coffee, well sweetened can be poured over crushed ice, to be served as *Caffé Granita*. Storage time as freshly roasted coffee beans 10–12 months, repacked instant coffee 3 months, as cubes 2 months.
HELPFUL HINT: The addition of a small proportion of strong coffee to chocolate flavouring intensifies the taste of the chocolate, especially after freezing.

COLD AIR LOSS In theory, chest freezers are more efficient than the upright freezers. Cold air is heavy. Warm air is lighter, moister and more turbulent. When you raise the lid of a chest freezer, cold air has no tendency to rise and be displaced by warm air. When you open the door of an upright freezer, the cold air inside tends to slip out at the bottom causing warm moist air to rush in at the top. In effect, if the freezer is fully packed at the bottom there is little displacement of cold air. In practice, though (providing the door is not frequently opened or left open for long) there is not much difference in freezing efficiency between the two types. However, the moisture in any warm air which does invade the freezer inevitably condenses and forms frost inside the freezer cabinet, and all packs exposed to temperature changes defrost and refreeze to some slight degree which may prove to be harmful.

COLD CHAIN A trade term referring to the passage of frozen foods from factory to home freezer.

COMMERCIALLY FROZEN FOOD
Many foods which are not possible to freeze successfully at home may be available commercially frozen because of the techniques used by manufacturers. The quick reduction to an extremely low temperature is the secret of their success. Always remember that commercially frozen food has been in storage for some time before you buy it and this reduces the length of time for which you can expect to store it in your own freezer.

COMPRESSOR A pump of either the piston or rotary type, operated by a motor to compress the refrigerant vapour, which then passes into the condenser and becomes a liquid.

CONDENSATION GUARD An anti-condensation device to be used when the freezer is sited in a moist ambient atmosphere.

CONDENSER A system of long pipes with a large surface area which transfers heat to the outside air.
There are two main types used in chest freezers.
1. The skin condenser consists of a series of metal tubes welded under the outer walls of the cabinet. Heat produced by the refrigerant gas condensing within them is given out through the walls of the cabinet to the outer air. Freezers with this type of condenser dissipate the heat through the walls of

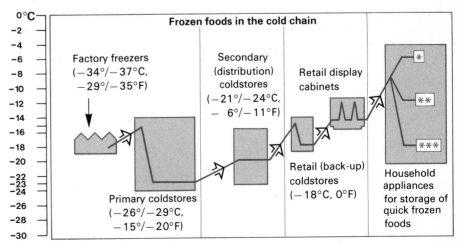

Frozen foods in the cold chain

Factory freezers (−34°/−37°C, −29°/−35°F)

Secondary (distribution) coldstores (−21°/−24°C, −6°/−11°F)

Retail display cabinets

Primary coldstores (−26°/−29°C, −15°/−20°F)

Retail (back-up) coldstores (−18°C, 0°F)

Household appliances for storage of quick frozen foods

the cabinet; therefore the outside of the cabinet may feel warm when the compressor is running. This type requires plenty of space for air to circulate freely all round the freezer.

2. The fan-cooled condenser. A fan forces air over the tubes in which the refrigerant gas is circulating. As the gas condenses to a liquid, the air becomes hot and is passed through a grill into the air outside the cabinet.

Upright freezers are usually described as static plate machines as the condenser pipes are painted black and are placed externally at the back of the cabinet.

CONSERVATOR An appliance for storing food which is already frozen at a temperature, usually 0°C/32°F, which cannot be reduced in order to freeze down fresh food. It frequently has a removable instead of a hinged lid and does not qualify for the four-star rating. If an opportunity arises to buy one in good working order cheaply, and you have the space to accommodate it, it is useful to provide extra storage space for food that has already been frozen down quickly in your own freezer, or for frozen food bought from a shop.
See *BUYING A FREEZER.

CONTAMINATION Food to be frozen must be prepared with great attention to hygiene since the process of freezing does not kill bacteria as cooking does, nor does it entirely halt the process of decay due to enzyme action. When defrosted these processes of spoilage continue often at a greater rate than before, and if the food is not to be thoroughly cooked at this stage, there may be a harmful proportion of food poisoning organisms in it. Contamination can be guarded against in three ways:
1. Food itself, hands, utensils and wrapping or packing materials must be clean.
2. Food awaiting packing for the freezer must not be exposed to the air,

where, for example, spores of moulds might settle on it, or it might be touched by dirty hands, or be contaminated by domestic animals or insects.
3. All utensils such as knives, mincers and blenders must be constantly kept clean, using plenty of hot water, frequently changed. Bacteria reproduce rapidly in warm water containing any food scraps. (This applies even more stringently to packs, containers or materials which have been used before.)
Resumption of bacterial growth takes place after thawing, which not only returns food to a temperature suitable for its consumption, but to one which again encourages bacterial growth. When removed from its pack the food is once more vulnerable to further contamination, and it is therefore safest to avoid handling, and to defrost food while still wrapped and sealed in the refrigerator where it never reaches the temperature of great bacterial activity. This applies especially to foods which will not be reheated or recooked, and reheating should be taken to a temperature of at least 88°C/190°F, not merely warmed to blood heat.
See *ENZYMES, *REFREEZING.

COOKED FOODS Hot food should be cooled as rapidly as possible before packing for freezing, or if frozen in the container in which it was cooked, before sealing. This minimises the risk of bacterial contamination by multiplication, which is bound to take place while food lingers around the temperature level (about 25°C/77°F) when bacterial growth is most active. The food should not be sealed while it is still warm because condensation will form inside the pack as it becomes colder. Nor should the surface be left exposed to the air for longer than is absolutely necessary because, besides the activity of food poisoning micro-organisms and enzymes affecting food taste and texture, it may be exposed to

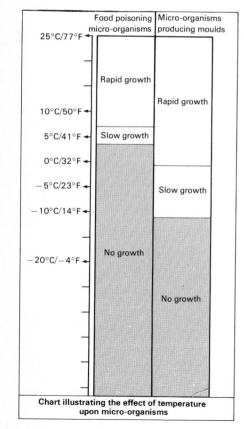

Chart illustrating the effect of temperature upon micro-organisms

airborne organisms producing mould. The best procedure is as follows:

1. Cool cooked foods quickly until low enough in temperature to be packed ready for freezing and placed in the refrigerator to chill.

2. Cover and seal as soon as food is completely cold, to prevent it taking up cross flavours in the refrigerator.

3. Place the chilled packs in the coldest possible place in the freezer. This may be against the walls of the fast freeze compartment in a chest, or on any shelf formed by evaporator coils in the upright.

COOLING PREPARED FOODS It is difficult to cool large quantities of cooked foods such as stews. The best method of dealing with such a large quantity is to divide it between a number of deep dishes and place them in a large bowl of cold water, preferably containing ice cubes. Or transfer portions direct to suitable shaped foil containers or boilable bags ready for freezer storage before cooling in the bowl of water, taking care that the level of the water will not rise too much if a number of open containers are placed in it.

CORN (US MAIZE) An edible grain. The ear can be frozen whole (*i.e. corn-on-the-cob*) or the kernels stripped from the ear and frozen (*i.e. sweet corn*). The fibrous 'silk' is discarded.
Whole cobs must be young and juicy to be worth freezing. Test by piercing with a skewer; unless plenty of juice spurts out the corn will be dry and floury when cooked. The blanched

cobs should be separately wrapped in cling film and then packed together in moisture-vapour-proof containers as they have a tendency to dehydrate.
NOTE: Although treated as a vegetable, corn cobs require to be fully defrosted before cooking.
Sweet corn kernels are grains, not vegetables, but they are treated for freezing by blanching in the same way. Storage time 10–12 months.
See *VEGETABLE PREPARATION AND PACKING, *DEFROSTING.

CORNFLOUR Sauces thickened with cornflour are less likely to separate when in the frozen state than those thickened with flour. However, all sauces suitable for freezing can be restored in texture if whisked briskly for about 1 minute when completely defrosted.

COURGETTE (US ZUCCHINI) A small variety of vegetable marrow which freezes well blanched, sliced and sautéed in butter, or in made-up dishes. It has a slight tendency to become bitter when cooked so take this into account when adding seasoning. Storage time 10–12 months.
See *VEGETABLE PREPARATION AND PACKING, *DEFROSTING.

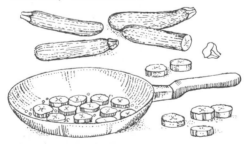

COURT BOUILLON A liquid prepared by simmering vegetables, herbs and seasonings in water, sometimes with the addition of wine or vinegar, then used for cooking fish. It is useful to strain any that is left over, cook it further to reduce and concentrate, then freeze in an ice tray to make cubes for storage in the freezer. The addition of fish bones produces a stronger stock known as *Fumet*. If there is vinegar in

the stock the frozen cubes should be stored in polythene containers or bags, not in aluminium foil containers. Storage time 3 months.

CRAB A shellfish which freezes fairly well when cooked and the meat removed from the shell for packing. The delicate flavour tends to diminish during storage. Storage time 3 months.
See *FISH PREPARATION AND PACKING.

CRANBERRY Berry fruit suitable for freezing in the form of purées and sauces. Storage time in sugar 9–12 months, purée 6–8 months.
See *FRUIT PREPARATION AND PACKING, *DEFROSTING.

CREAM Whipping cream, especially if lightly whipped with a pinch of sugar to act as a stabiliser, freezes extremely well, as does clotted cream. Single cream and soured cream, which both have a butterfat content below 40%, frequently separate because of their high water content and cannot be reconstituted, although the texture can be somewhat improved by warming the cream slightly and then beating it. Double cream, treated in the same way as whipping cream, also freezes well but tends to become grainy in texture when defrosted. The addition of single cream in the proportion of three parts double to one part

single produces a better result.
Piped cream rosettes can be open frozen on non-stick vegetable parchment and then packed in layers in a shallow rigid-based container. The rosettes can easily be transferred in the frozen state to decorate cakes and sweets, especially if a warm palette knife is used to remove them from the parchment. Storage time 6 months, clotted cream 12 months.

CROSS-CONTAMINATION The transfer of flavour and aroma from one food pack to another inside the freezer cabinet. As frozen food is stored for much longer periods than refrigerated foods, but also in a closed cabinet, the danger of cross-contamination is much greater unless packs are fully sealed inside moisture-vapour-proof wrappings or containers. Strongly flavoured foods (*e.g. cooked curries, chopped raw onion*) are frequent culprits and packs containing such foods are better over-wrapped.

CROÛTES/CROÛTONS Shapes cut from slightly stale white bread and fried in a mixture of oil and butter until crisp and golden brown. The most usual shapes for croûtes are circles, triangles and rectangles. Croûtons, which are smaller, are usually cut in the shape of small cubes or crescents. Both types should be well drained and completely cooled before packing. Storage time 6 weeks.
See *DEFROSTING.

CRUMBLES Toppings for sweet or savoury dishes made from fat rubbed into flour with or without the addition of sugar. The complete dish may be frozen unbaked or the crumble mixture may be made up and frozen separately in polythene bags ready to be firmly packed over raw fruit and sugar or a cooked savoury mixture. Crumbles should be baked from frozen in a moderately hot oven (200°C, 400°F, Gas Mark 6) for 45 minutes. Storage time 4–6 months.

CRYOVAC SHRINK-WRAPPING A commercial process by which individual cuts of meat are enclosed in high-clarity, shrinkable polythene bags. Air is extracted from the bags which are treated in a heat tunnel to conform closely to the shape of the meat and then sealed. Several of these packs may then be placed together and 'shrink-packed' into a single larger bag. The meat remains completely visible even in the frozen state.

CUCUMBER The long fleshy fruit of a creeping and climbing plant, usually eaten raw as a salad vegetable but not suitable to freeze in this form as the high water content causes a distinct alteration in the texture on freezing. Cucumber can be frozen raw, without blanching, grated or liquidised for soups or mousses, and also mixed with cream cheese and seasonings to make a dip. Diced cucumber, lightly sautéed in butter, can be frozen to serve as a hot vegetable or as part of a made-up dish. Storage time 6 months.
See *VEGETABLE PREPARATION AND PACKING, *DEFROSTING.

CURED MEATS Apart from bacon, other cured meats can be frozen raw (e.g. *pickled silverside of beef*) or cooked (e.g. *ham*), but the fat is quickly inclined to become rancid in storage. Although salt petre is added to brine or dry salt for curing, this is usually to improve the colour. The salt itself, having impregnated the meat, causes dehydration by drawing the moisture out to the surface before the centre (especially near the bone) has time to putrify. Over-wrap to avoid risk of cross-contamination. Cooked cured meat stores well sliced, without dividers. There is less likelihood of the thawed meat being dry than with uncured meats as the texture is moister but the storage time is considerably less (especially if the meat is heavily salted). Storage time raw 6 weeks, cooked 3 months.
See *BACON, *DEFROSTING.

CURRANTS White, red and black currants are all suitable for freezing raw, cooked and in the form of purée, syrup and jam. Storage time in sugar or sugar syrup pack 10–12 months, dry without sugar and as purée, syrup or jam 6–8 months.
See *FRUIT PREPARATION AND PACKING, *DEFROSTING.

CURRIES The mixture of spices in curries tends to mellow and improve the flavour in the frozen state. Small containers of both mild and hot curry sauces are extremely useful as they can be quickly thawed and reheated to mix with cooked meat, chicken, eggs or vegetables to provide a meal at short notice. Storage time meat or vegetable curries 4–6 months, curry sauce 8 months.
See *DEFROSTING.
HELPFUL HINTS: Curry sauce in a boilable bag can be defrosted and reheated in a saucepan of boiling water while eggs are being hard-boiled – a meal in 20 minutes from scratch.

If possible, store curries and curry sauces in disposable containers as the smell is almost impossible to remove.

CUSTARDS A mixture of whisked eggs, warm milk and sugar in the proportion of 7 eggs, 65 g/2½ oz sugar to 1 litre/1¾ pints milk. Freeze in shaped foil containers which can be lined previously with caramel. The custards should be open frozen until solid then sealed. Cook from frozen in a *bain marie* in a moderate oven (190°C, 375°F, Gas Mark 5) for 45 minutes (small), 1 hour (large). Storage time 4–6 months.
See *CARAMEL.

Cornflour custards tend to weep when frozen as part of a trifle. Canned custard, being completely homogenised, gives the best result but does not completely set. Make trifles slightly less moist than usual, and the separation of home-made custard will be less noticeable.

DAILY FREEZING CAPACITY The quantity of fresh food which can be added to the freezer as a single load to be frozen down in 24 hours. This should be stamped on the rating plate.
See *BUYING A FREEZER.

DAIRY PRODUCE All dairy produce freezes well in some form.
See *BUTTER, *CREAM, *CHEESE, *MILK.

DAMSON Stone fruit which can be frozen raw, cooked and in the form of a purée. Storage time in sugar or sugar syrup pack 9–12 months, dry without sugar and as purée or jam 6–8 months.
See *FRUIT PREPARATION AND PACKING, *DISCOLORATION, *DEFROSTING.

DEEP FREEZING A term often used as being synonymous with quick freezing. Commercially frozen food is often stored well below −18°C/0°F, which lengthens the storage life at peak quality. The term 'deep freeze' is sometimes used as a trade mark.

DEFROSTING There are three methods suitable for various foods, as follows:
Defrosting under running water. This is possible with packs that are watertight, placing the food preferably under cold running water but warm if haste is essential. To judge when food will slip out easily, turn the pack over. Allow 20–35 minutes, according to the size of the pack and the temperature of the water, for crisp foods (*e.g. fresh fruits*). Allow 15–20 minutes in very warm water for foods that will not lose texture (*e.g. stews*). Food at the centre of the pack which still remains frozen can be carefully broken up with a fork.
Defrosting at room temperature. This is suitable for foods in packs small enough to enable the contents to defrost in less than 3 hours. Large packs require many hours, even in an ambient temperature of 21°C/70°F, which means the outer layer of food will reach the temperature at which bacteria again become active, long before the centre is defrosted.

If berry fruits have been packed in layers with dividers, each divider can be removed and placed on a baking tray to thaw at room temperature, leaving the bottom layer in the container. When the fruit can be gently removed with a warm spatula it can be used immediately, which speeds up defrosting considerably.
Defrosting in a refrigerator. This is suitable for all foods (except vegetables and commercial packs with instructions to cook from the frozen state). It takes longer than defrosting at room temperature and the food must be covered as cross flavours are easily absorbed inside a closed refrigerator.

Coffee float (page 253); Holiday biscuits (page 209)

Marshmallow coffee mousse; Marshmallow chocolate mousse (page 153)

Marble mocha cake (page 252)

Meatballs with Swedish meatball sauce (page 205)

Defrosting Timetable

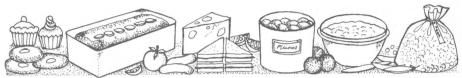

Food	Approximate time in refrigerator	Approximate time at room temperature'	Notes
BISCUITS		15–30 minutes	Spread out.
BREAD Large loaf		3–6 hours	Or, wrap whole loaf in foil. Place in a moderately hot oven (200°C, 400°F, Gas Mark 6) for 35–45 minutes, depending on size. Toast slices from frozen.
Pumpernickel		2–3 hours	
Sandwiches	3 hours	2–4 hours	Thaw wrapped or spread out for 1 hour.
BUTTER	4 hours	2 hours	
CAKES — cooked			Unwrap iced cakes before thawing, leave plain cakes wrapped.
large (plain)		2–4 hours	
frosted layer		up to 4 hours	
rich fruit		12 hours	
small		1–2 hours	
uncooked mixtures		2–3 hours	Thaw wrapped then fill tins and bake.
icings/fillings			Stand wrapped in warm water for about 2 hours.
CHEESE	12 hours per 450 g/1 lb	4 hours per 450 g/1 lb	Thaw wrapped. Grated cheese can be used from frozen.
CHEESECAKES	Overnight		
CHESTNUTS		4 hours	
CHOCOLATE			Use the decorative shapes from frozen.
CREAM (over 40% butterfat)	12 hours per 600 ml/1 pint	1–2 hours per 600 ml/1 pint	Use rosettes from frozen.
CROÛTES/CROÛTONS			Reheat from frozen.
CRUMBLES			Reheat from frozen in a moderately hot oven (200°C, 400°F, Gas Mark 6) for 30 minutes; reduce heat to 180°C (350°F, Gas Mark 4) and cook for a further 20 minutes.
DIPS	Overnight		Or, hold container under warm water until dip can be broken with a fork.
DUMPLINGS		1 hour, depending on size	Or, bake fruit dumplings from frozen in a moderately hot oven (190°C, 375°F, Gas Mark 5) for 20 minutes.
FISH			
oily, whole — herring, mackerel, salmon, salmon trout, sprats, trout, whitebait	6–10 hours per 450 g/1 lb	3–5 hours per 450 g/1 lb	Can be cooked, wrapped in foil, from frozen.
oily, steaks and fillets — herring, mackerel, salmon, salmon trout, trout	4–8 hours per 450 g/1 lb	3–4 hours per 450 g/1 lb	Interleave and spread out to defrost. Can be cooked from frozen.
shellfish	10–12 hours per 450 g/1 lb	3 hours per 450 g/1 lb	
smoked — cod, haddock, herring (kipper), mackerel, salmon, salmon trout, trout	5 hours per 450 g/1 lb	2–2½ hours per 450 g/1 lb	

Food	Approximate time in refrigerator	Approximate time at room temperature	Notes

white, whole —
    cod, haddock, hake,
    halibut, plaice, sole
	6–8 hours per
	450 g/1 lb
		3–4 hours per
		450 g/1 lb
			Can be cooked, wrapped in foil, from frozen.

white, steaks and fillets —
    cod, haddock, hake,
    halibut, plaice, skate, sole,
    turbot
	4–6 hours per
	450 g/1 lb
		2–3 hours per
		450 g/1 lb
			Interleave and spread out to defrost. Can be cooked from frozen.

FLANS, sweet and savoury
    cases
    filled
		1 hour
		4 hours	

FRUIT
soft fruits, skinless —
    bilberry, blackberry, logan-
    berry, raspberry, strawberry
	6–7 hours	2–3 hours	

soft fruits, with tough skins —
    apricot, banana, cherry,
    cranberry, currants, damson,
    elderberry, gooseberry, grape,
    greengage, melon, nectarine,
    peach, pineapple, plum
    fig
	7–8 hours	3–4 hours
		
		1½ hours	

hard fruits — apple, pear, rhubarb		3 hours	
coconut		2 hours	

citrus fruits —
    grapefruit, lemon, lime,
    orange
		1–3 hours	

fruit purées and syrup packs	6–8 hours	2–4 hours	
HORSERADISH		2–3 hours	
MEAT bacon — joints	6 hours per 450 g/1 lb	2 hours per 450 g/1 lb	
— rashers		1 hour	
chops, steaks, sausages	6 hours	2 hours	Interleave and spread out to defrost. Or, cook from frozen allowing twice as long.
joints	5 hours per 450 g/1 lb	2 hours per 450 g/1 lb	Slow roast, covered, from frozen, allowing 1 hour per 450 g/1 lb.
cured/ham	6 hours per 450 g/1 lb	2 hours per 450 g/1 lb	
minced meat and offal	10–12 hours per 450 g/1 lb	1–1½ hours per 450 g/1 lb	
cooked dishes — casseroles			Reheat from frozen in a moderately hot oven (200°C, 400°F, Gas Mark 6) for 1 hour; reduce the heat to 180°C (350°F, Gas Mark 4) and cook for a further 40 minutes. Or, reheat in a saucepan.
curries			Reheat in saucepan or double boiler.
pâtés — whole	Overnight	6–8 hours	
— sliced		1 hour	
terrines	Overnight	6–8 hours	
MERINGUES individual		2 hours	
layers		2–3 hours	
MILK		2 hours	Can be reheated from frozen.
MOUSSES, sweet and savoury	Overnight		

Food	Approximate time in refrigerator	Approximate time at room temperature	Notes
PANCAKES			
unfilled	Overnight	about 1 hour	
filled			Reheat in a moderately hot oven (200°C, 400°F, Gas Mark 6) for about 30 minutes.
PASTA – cooked			Defrost by turning into boiling water, leave until the water comes to the boil again, drain and serve.
PASTRY			
uncooked dough		3–4 hours	Defrost only sufficiently to make it easier for rolling.
uncooked pies		2–4 hours	Place frozen in a hot oven (220°C, 425°F, Gas Mark 7) for about 1 hour, depending on size.
cooked pies		2–4 hours	Place in preheated oven and bake as usual.
uncooked choux dough		3–4 hours	
cooked choux dough		1 hour	Then crisp in a moderate oven (180°C, 350°F, Gas Mark 4). Or, cook from frozen in a moderate oven for 10 minutes.
PLATE MEALS			Reheat in a moderately hot oven (200°C, 400°F, Gas Mark 6) for 30 minutes.
PIZZA – unbaked			Cook in a hot oven (220°C, 425°F, Gas Mark 7) for 30–35 minutes.
POULTRY AND GAME			
chicken–			Make sure pack of giblets has been removed and that no ice crystals linger in the cavity, since quick roasting may not raise the temperature of the bony structure of the bird to a high enough temperature to destroy all harmful micro-organisms.
(over 2 kg/4½ lb)	1–1½ days		
(under 2 kg/4½ lb)	12–16 hours	1–1½ days, covered, in a cool place.	
chicken portions	5–6 hours per 450 g/1 lb	1 hour per 450 g/1 lb	Can be poached in boiling stock from frozen.
duck (1·5–2·5 kg/3–5½ lb)	1–1½ days		
game birds –	12–16 hours		
grouse, partridge, pheasant...			
goose (2–6·25 kg/4½–14 lb)	1–2 days		
pigeon	12–16 hours	1–1½ days, covered, in a cool place	
rabbit and hare –			
(over 2 kg/4½ lb)	1–1½ days		
(under 2 kg/4½ lb)	12–16 hours		
turkey–			
(over 7·25 kg/16 lb)	2–3 days		
(under 7·25 kg/16 lb)	1–2 days		
venison	5 hours per 450 g/1 lb		After fully defrosting, wash in 1 part vinegar to 2 parts water before cooking.
PUDDINGS			
cooked sponge			Steam from frozen, allowing 45 minutes for a 900-ml/1½-pint pudding. Or, remove packaging and cook wrapped in foil.
uncooked sponge			Allow 2½ hours cooking time for a 900-ml/1½-pint pudding.
suet, sweet and savoury –			
uncooked			Steam from frozen for 5 hours.
cooked			Steam from frozen for 2½–3 hours.
RICE – cooked		1 hour	Heat defrosted rice with a little water for about 5 minutes. Or, heat from frozen in boiling, salted water until water reboils.
SOUFFLÉS – cold		3–4 hours	

Food	Approximate time in refrigerator	Approximate time at room temperature	Notes
SOUPS AND STOCKS			Reheat from frozen.
STUFFINGS		2–3 hours	
SWEETS		1–2 hours	
VEGETABLES			Cook from frozen.
Exceptions:			
artichoke, Jerusalem		1–2 hours	
aubergine, slices		1–2 hours	Should be dried thoroughly before using.
beetroot	9–10 hours	2–3 hours	
mung beans (bean sprouts)		1–2 hours	
mushrooms	2 hours	1 hour	Or, can be cooked from frozen in casseroles, etc.
olives	2 hours	1 hour	
vegetable purées – avocado, celeriac, pumpkin...		2–4 hours, depending on size of pack	Or, heat from frozen, stirring from time to time.
YEAST – fresh		30 minutes	Or, may be grated coarsely from frozen.
YOGURT	3 hours	1–2 hours	

DEFROSTING A FREEZER The frequency with which defrosting is necessary and the method adopted depends on your type of freezer. The only guide to the frequency of the defrosting cycle is the build-up of frost.

Chest freezers should only need to be defrosted once a year providing you do not have any accidental spills inside the cabinet. Watch out for a layer of frost accumulating round the top inner rim of the cabinet or the lid sealing gasket which may prevent total closure of the lid. Defrosting should be planned to take place in winter, on a cold day and when your stocks are low. Defrost as follows:

1. A clean blanket can be placed in the cabinet for a couple of hours to become completely chilled.

2. Switch off the electric current and, if convenient, pull out the plug.

3. Remove the baskets and transfer all loose packs to cardboard cartons placed close together and cover with the blanket. Use insulated portable containers if you have any.

4. If there is no drain plug, place a piece of thick absorbent material in the bottom of the freezer.

5. Place a plastic bowl or bucket of hot water inside the empty cabinet. Loosen any thick frost on the walls gently with a plastic spatula.

6. When the cabinet is completely defrosted (about 1–2 hours) remove the bucket and material and wipe the inside surfaces with hot water adding 1 tablespoon bicarbonate of soda to each generous litre/2 pints of water. Dry carefully with a clean cloth.

7. Replace the drain plug if any, switch on, close the lid and turn on the fast freeze switch. Take the opportunity to sort out your stores and within 1 hour repack the freezer.

Upright freezers require to be defrosted about twice a year because there is likely to be more build-up of frost on the shelves which are formed from refrigerant coils. Watch out for a layer of frost accumulating on these shelves, particularly the front edge where it may eventually prevent total closure of the door. Avoid defrosting in midsummer. It is better to choose a relatively cold day in spring and another in autumn. Follow the same method as for the chest freezer to defrost, making use of the drain spout if there is one. It is important to loosen thick frost on the shelves to hasten the defrosting process.

See *FREEZER CARE.

DEHYDRATION The loss of moisture from food by absorption into the cold dry air of the freezer. It occurs when the food has not been correctly wrapped in moisture-vapour-proof covering or in a moisture-vapour-proof container with an airtight seal. See *FREEZER BURN.

DELIVERY SERVICE Some firms, particularly department stores, operate a van service which delivers frozen food (packed with dry ice) within a certain radius of the town in which they are situated. In some cases stock is delivered by refrigerated transport. Food supplied in this way is usually in medium-sized packs at no great financial saving but the convenience of having your frozen food delivered to your door may make this relatively unimportant.

Dual self collection service. In rural areas where customers come from a wide radius, some freezer centres offer the choice of delivery or self collection. You can buy a freezer, the usual accessories and frozen food from their premises or order by post or telephone to have these goods delivered. Such firms usually keep in regular postal contact with their customers, supplying current stock lists, order forms and details of seasonal offers.

DENATURATION OF PROTEINS The structure of food cells is a complicated one in which protein molecules exist as gelatinous suspensions in water. One of the main damaging effects of slow freezing is that it encourages the formation of ice crystals within the tissues, some of the water being absorbed from the proteins and resulting in their dehydration and denaturation. On thawing, the protein cells are unable to reabsorb all the water and this causes 'drip loss' (*e.g. in meat*). See *DRIP LOSS.

DESSERTS See *CAKES, *FLANS, *CREAMS, *MOUSSES, *SOUFFLÉS, *ICE CREAMS.

DIAL SETTING The use of a numbered control dial enables you to set

the thermostat to keep your freezer at the temperature you choose within the range provided. This may be quite separate from the fast freeze switch.

DIPS Savoury mixtures served with potato crisps or small biscuits to be used as 'dippers'. Those based on cream cheese freeze well but any which contain a high proportion of mayonnaise are not suitable for freezing. Storage time 4 months. See *DEFROSTING.
HELPFUL HINT: Dips can often be frozen in advance for parties, in the containers from which they will be served.

DISCOLORATION This may occur in fresh foods during preparation for freezing and also by exposure to adverse conditions while in the frozen state.

During preparation discoloration takes place in many fruits and vegetables due to oxidation when the peel or skin is removed and cut surfaces are exposed to the air; these include apples, bananas, greengages, peaches, pears, plums, aubergines, avocados, cauliflower, chicory, Jerusalem artichokes, parsnips, potatoes. Other naturally white foods such as fish and cooked rice also tend to discolour slightly.

There are three ways to prevent this:
1. Cover all cut surfaces as quickly as possible by sprinkling with lemon juice, immersing in sugar syrup (*e.g. pears*) or brine in the case of vegetables (*e.g. cauliflower florets*) or temporarily in lightly salted water. This is drained off when a batch of packs is ready to be sealed.
2. Add a solution of ascorbic acid to the pack.
3. Add lemon juice or white vinegar to the water in which fruit is cooked or vegetables are blanched.
During frozen storage discoloration may occur when food has been unsuitably packed or sealed before being exposed to the effects of temperature

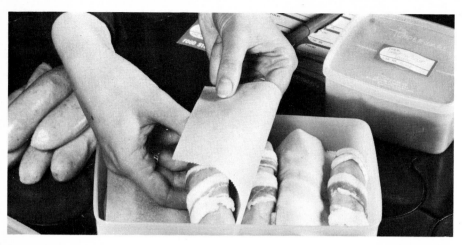

Concertina divider, using a long narrow strip of non-stick parchment.

heavy sugar syrup. A piece of crumpled foil laid over the surface of the food keeps it under the syrup and does not affect the seal.

DIVIDERS Small pieces of foil, cling film, greaseproof paper or freezer tissue (sometimes called peach-bloom paper) used to interleave layers of food and make it easy to remove individual items from a pack. Freezer tissue is available in large sheets which must be cut up or in a perforated roll. Non-stick vegetable parchment is particularly effective used in this way but may be costly unless you have pieces available trimmed from large sheets.

Concertina dividers are large strips of the above materials used to fold back and forth between pieces of food to separate them without the necessity to cut the divider into a number of small pieces. Greaseproof paper is quite satisfactory for this purpose and the method is particularly useful for pancakes, croquettes or sausages.

gradient inside the freezer. It causes oxidation which appears as patches of greyish discoloration, particularly on the surface of meat. Colour changes and fading of colour also occur when the temperature inside the freezer cabinet is allowed to fluctuate or rise above −18°C/0°F at any time. Exposure to light, particularly in retail cabinets, may be another cause, due to oxidation of the natural pigments in the food, and any packs affected in this way should be avoided.

HELPFUL HINTS: To prevent oxidation of food surfaces *inside* the pack (*e.g. avocado purée*) cover those likely to be affected with a layer of cling film. This will rise into the headspace as the food expands on freezing and will not disturb the seal. Certain fruits, particularly stone fruits, tend to rise in a

DOOR HANGING It is wise to make a firm decision on the site of an upright freezer before ordering because this will affect whether you require the door or doors to be hinged on the right or the left. Make sure that the supplier can alter this and enquire whether it could be changed if you move house.

Sheet divider, using odd pieces of foil.

DOOR STORAGE SPACE In some upright freezers there are narrow shelves attached to the inner side of the door enabling small items to be stored in a position of easy access. As there is likely to be a considerable fluctuation of temperature each time the door is opened in this storage area, it is advisable to use it for packs which contain food not easily damaged by semi-defrosting, or for small cartons which may be overlooked if put at the back of a freezer shelf.
See *UPRIGHT FREEZER.

DRAINAGE OUTLETS A feature available on some freezer models in the form of a drain plug for chest freezers and a flip-out drain spout for uprights which allows melting ice to escape into a container and makes the job of defrosting your freezer easier.

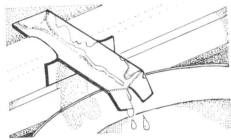

DRINKS Unless highly concentrated, the percentage of water in most drinks is too high to make them worthy of valuable freezer space. Carbonated drinks are not suitable because they contain carbon dioxide which will not freeze in a domestic freezer and therefore separates from the liquid.
See *JUICES, *GLASS CONTAINERS.

DRIP LOSS The loss of natural juices from food, particularly meat which has not been quickly frozen, during defrosting. Rapid freezing and slow thawing, preferably in the refrigerator, reduces drip loss to a minimum, or it can be entirely avoided by cooking meat from the frozen state.
See *DENATURATION OF PROTEINS, *ROASTING MEAT (from the frozen state).

DRIPPING Rendered down excess fat from meat. When you make a bulk purchase of meat, do not refuse the trimmings of fat. Have beef suet minced and keep this for suet pastry or render down all fat as follows. Have it roughly chopped up and gradually melt in a strong frying pan until as much liquid fat as possible has been extracted, straining off carefully into clean, shaped foil containers. Do not pour hot fat into polythene containers or bags. The scraps that remain may be covered with water and heated gently until all the fat has become liquid. Allow to cool so that the fat rises to the top of the water and sets. Remove the layer of fat, scrape all traces of sediment from the underside and discard, and pack for use in frying. Storage time 6 months.

DROP FRONT GRIDS Useful extras on upright freezers which retain packs safely on the shelves when the door is open. These are also described as slot-in pack retainers.
See *SHELVES.

DRUGGIST'S WRAP A method of wrapping meat or any other food of a regular shape which has a low water content and would not easily be damaged. Use a rectangular sheet of polythene, place the food in the centre and bring the two long sides together over the top. Fold down until tight against the contents, seal along this fold. Fold the short sides in to form points, bring in towards the centre and seal. Foil is equally suitable for this wrap and does not require sealing.

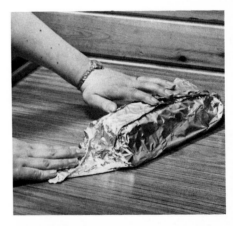

DRY ICE See *CARBON DIOXIDE.

DRY PACK To pack foods, especially fruit, without adding liquid or sugar. See *FRUIT PREPARATION AND PACKING.

DRY SUGAR PACK To pack foods in dry sugar. See *FRUIT PREPARATION AND PACKING.

DUCK A water bird suitable for freezing in any of the forms suggested for chicken. Ducklings are usually frozen split to serve two as the carcase is very bony and carries less flesh than that of a chicken. Allow extra weight per portion when preparing made-up dishes for the freezer in the proportion of a 2-kg/4½-lb duck to a 1·5-kg/3¼-lb chicken. Storage time 4–6 months, giblets 3 months.

See *POULTRY, *DEFROSTING.

NOTE: Freezing a stuffed duck reduces its storage time to 3 months and extra defrosting and cooking time must be allowed. It is unwise to freeze ducks with the giblets inside because this also reduces the storage time.

DUMPLINGS A mixture of flour, shredded suet and seasonings, made into a dough with water, then formed into balls. It is more satisfactory to prepare, open freeze and pack these separately from the stew they are to accompany, in convenient quantities, either in polythene bags or containers. These must be defrosted before they are cooked.

Fruit dumplings can be made with chopped fruit (*e.g. apricots*) or with the dumpling mixture surrounding a whole stoned fruit (*e.g. damsons*). These should be packed for freezing in the same way but cooked from the frozen state in fast boiling water for up to 1 hour, according to size. They may also be baked from frozen.

See *DEFROSTING.

ECONOMY The first aim in buying a freezer may be to shop in bulk and buy at lower prices to reduce shopping trips and to take advantage of seasonal gluts. Other less obvious economies can be effected. Bulk cooking reduces time spent in preparation and the cost of fuel. Leftovers which might otherwise be discarded may form the basis of good meals (*e.g. giblets from poultry and trimmings from vegetables for soup*). Savings may also be made in the economic use of packaging materials.

Economy in buying a freezer. If you wish to purchase the largest area of frozen food storage space for your money, the chest freezer still remains the best buy. This is because it is relatively cheaper to manufacture than the upright. If, however, space is so limited that you cannot accommodate a chest, it is cheaper to buy an upright with only one door and therefore only one freezing system, than a two-door upright with two completely separate compartments. A fridge-freezer with the freezing compartment situated above and the refrigerator compartment below is generally run from one freezing system. Although this may not be so convenient for daily use, it costs less to make than the fridge-freezer with the conventional arrangement of refrigerator above and freezer below, which necessitates two freezing systems.

Economy in running a freezer. Bearing in mind that a freezer uses anything from 1½ to 4 units of electricity per 28 litres/1 cubic foot per week according to size, you can keep running costs down by remembering these simple rules.

1. Do not site a freezer in a confined space or hot kitchen.

2. Do not open or close the door or lid more often than is strictly necessary and avoid leaving the freezer open for any length of time.

3. Defrost before any appreciable build-up of frost occurs as this raises the running costs.

4. Keep the freezer at least three-quarters full, unless deliberately running down stocks, as empty space costs more to keep cold than frozen food.

5. Do not from housewifely pride keep the temperature lower than is necessary for safe storage. Resist the temptation to reduce the temperature or turn on the fast freeze switch for small additions, especially if you are likely to forget that you must adjust this again as soon as possible.

6. It is a saving in the end to build up

gradually a stock of re-usable containers with their own seals. There is no doubt that the best of these are Tupperware containers. Each piece carries a 10-year guarantee, and with reasonable care the seal remains perfect and the containers continue to give good service even longer than that. Here is a case where an initially expensive investment proves its worth over the years. Shaped foil containers, again if treated carefully, can be used more than once for freezing, and small cream, yogurt and cottage cheese cartons may be used twice or even more times, although they are not in any way guaranteed and require to be covered with foil for re-use. Empty glass jars that have been freezer tested give good service, but I do not recommend using sheet foil or polythene bags for a second time for freezing, although they may be used for other domestic purposes.

See *PACKAGING.

Economy in stocking a freezer. Do not buy in bulk without careful thought as to whether you use sufficient of this commodity to warrant a big investment.

See *BULK BUYING.

EEL Fresh water fish not recommended for freezing as it is usually cooked and served cold, set in its own jelly which breaks down when frozen.

EGGS Hens' eggs are excellent for freezing in many forms. The eggs of other birds are not recommended for

freezing. Eggs in the shell would burst as the water content freezes and expands, so work carefully and break them one at a time into a cup and add to a bowl, checking that each one smells quite fresh. Beat very lightly, but not sufficiently to incorporate air. If the egg mixture is to be used for sweet dishes, add ½ teaspoon sugar per egg; if savoury add ¼ teaspoon salt per egg. Pack in small quantities allowing a headspace, and be sure to label the pack whether sweet or savoury. Small amounts can be frozen in ice cube trays or in the shaped side of absolutely clean, plastic egg boxes.

When the latter are fully frozen two halves can be taped together with a divider between the frozen surfaces. About 2 tablespoons of this mixture is the equivalent of 1 whole egg. Midget Tupperware tumblers hold the equivalent of 1 large egg, can be used as moulds and turned out when fully frozen. These frozen egg blocks can be stored in polythene bags and defrosted for use in cooking a few at a time as required.

Freezing separated eggs

1. Egg yolks should be lightly mixed with sugar or salt in the proportions of ½ teaspoon sugar or ¼ teaspoon salt to each 4 egg yolks. About 1 tablespoon thawed egg yolk equals 1 egg yolk.

2. Egg whites require nothing to be added to stabilise the mixture and are therefore equally suitable for sweet and savoury cooking. About 1 tablespoon thawed egg white equals 1 egg white.

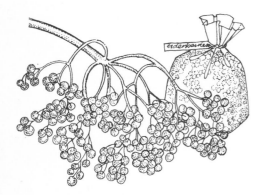

ELDERBERRY A wild berry fruit which can be gathered when in season, removed from the stalk and frozen in dry or sugar syrup pack, or as a purée. Elderberries can also be frozen and used later for making wine. Storage time in sugar or sugar syrup pack 10–12 months, dry without sugar and as purée 6–8 months.
See ★FRUIT PREPARATION AND PACKING, ★DEFROSTING.

ELECTRICAL INSTALLATION Make sure that the voltage which is shown on the freezer is the same as that of the circuit into which it will be plugged. Installation is by inserting a 3-pin 13 or 15 amp plug into an earthed socket at any suitable point on the wall, preferably easy of access. Avoid trailing flex as someone could trip over it and jerk out the plug. Also avoid using an adaptor as there is a possibility that this might be partially withdrawn from the socket breaking the connection. Although it may be unsightly, it is a safety precaution to cover the plug and switch with adhesive tape so that

it is not switched off by mistake. A lighting point would be quite unsuitable and if you are in any doubt have the supplier or qualified electrician approve the site. Most accidental disconnections occur if the electricity is switched off at the mains when the family goes on holiday. Do remember that the freezer must not be disconnected and if you have a modern fuse box you may choose to remove all the fuses except that for the freezer, or install the freezer on a separate circuit. Allow the freezer to run for several hours before putting in any foods; at least 2 hours for frozen food and 12 hours before adding fresh food to freeze down.
See ★BUYING A FREEZER.

EMERGENCIES These are panic situations caused either by power failures, mechanical breakdowns or accidental disconnections of the freezer.

1. Power failures may occur because of incidents beyond the control of the Electricity Board (*e.g. industrial disputes*) or within their control (*e.g. failure of a generator*). Sometimes this affects your rights under your insurance policy for compensation. In any event your best course is to place all items which defrost quickly (*e.g. ice cream*) in the coldest part of the freezer (if advance notice is given of a power cut). Then resist the temptation to open the freezer and check the condition of the food. A large quantity of frozen food tightly packed together will remain frozen longer than a small quantity of food spread about in a half-empty freezer. If you feel you must make a check, put a frozen tray of ice cubes just inside the freezer and open it only long enough to see whether the ice is beginning to melt.

2. Mechanical breakdowns are rare because the compressor unit is robust, but the bill for replacing the motor is substantial. As there is also the danger of loss of food in store if there is a mechanical breakdown, it is wise to have noted within sight of the freezer a

telephone number and address of some friend or retailer (*e.g. wholesale butcher*) who could offer temporary accommodation for your stock. Quick action is necessary so this may be even more important than being in contact with an engineer to effect repairs, but this contingency should be covered by arrangements at the time you purchase your freezer and as far as possible covered by your insurance policy.
3. Accidental disconnections are unfortunately not so rare emergencies as the first two mentioned above and in addition to making it extremely difficult to disconnect the freezer by accident, it is worth putting a small notice on the wall above the switch giving a reminder not to switch off. See* INSURANCE.

ENDIVE (US CURLY ENDIVE)
Salad vegetable with frilly curled leaves not suitable for freezing.

ENZYMES
Natural substances present in all foods which, after harvesting, continue to be active and work slowly, even after freezing. They cause notable deterioration in most vegetables unless inactivated by blanching. Otherwise they remain active to a certain extent, even at as low a temperature as −40°C/−40°F. Some vegetables, particularly of the Brassica family (*e.g. Brussels sprouts*), deteriorate very quickly when frozen without blanching as continuing enzyme activity affects colour, texture, flavour and even Vitamin C content.
NOTE: There are vegetables in which enzyme activity is virtually negligible (*e.g. carrots*). These may be safely frozen without blanching for short storage.

EQUIPMENT
Apart from packing and labelling materials, other pieces of equipment are required. Some, normally to be found in the kitchen, are indispensable. These include sharp knives for trimming, slicing, etc., bowls for washing and preparing fruit and vegetables and a large pan for blanching. If no special blanching basket is available a long handled metal colander or nylon muslin bag could be used instead. Most kitchens are equipped with clean tea towels and absorbent kitchen paper for draining blanched vegetables, and washable oven mitts which can be used to handle frozen food.

Specialised equipment should include at least one strong serrated knife for cutting frozen food or a set of special knives including a saw and a cleaver. Other useful items include a heat sealer, bag sealer, meat thermometer, freezer thermometer, vacuum pump, ice cream scoop and frost scraper. Some freezer owners might want to invest in open freezing trays that stack, rubberised ice ball or cube trays, ice cone or lolly moulds or a defrosting box. Flat packs or bottles filled with a chemical substance colder than ice are useful extras for transporting food in insulated bags. These can also be heated in boiling water to keep food hot in the same containers. See *PACKAGING, *THAWING BOX, *INSULATED CONTAINERS, *MEAT THERMOMETER.

EUTECTIC POINT As food freezes its water content is converted into ice. While this process is still incomplete, the natural salts present in the food become more and more concentrated in any water remaining unfrozen, until a point is reached when all the water and its soluble contents finally solidify together. This is known as the eutectic point which occurs below –18°C/0°F. Until this point is reached, enzymes have not passed into the range of minimal activity, and micro-organisms (although dormant and unable to reproduce) might be reawakened by a slight increase in temperature. Reduction to below the eutectic point should therefore be achieved as quickly as possible, and temperature fluctuations above it in storage are undesirable.

EVAPORATOR A system of coiled tubes through which the refrigerant liquid travels, boils and expands into a vapour, absorbing heat from the interior of the cabinet.

EXPANSION OF AIR Food which is sealed for freezing in airtight containers intended to be reheated (*e.g. boilable bags*) requires vacuum space within the pack to accommodate the expansion of hot air and steam. That is why the lids or seals of foil containers are recommended to be removed before placing in the oven. Boilable bags cannot be undone for reheating as water would enter the bag. So be sure to create a vacuum when packing. You will notice that after immersion in boiling water this compressed area will appear to swell. In fact no additional air is being introduced; the air trapped inside the bag is expanding as it heats. A boilable bag which is filled with food right up to the closure might split under the pressure of this expansion.

EXPANSION OF WATER All foods contain some percentage of water but certain foods contain a very high per-

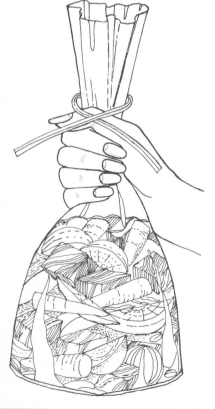

centage (*e.g. strawberries 90% water content*). Water expands by one-tenth of its total volume when it freezes and space must be allowed within the pack for this expansion. Liquid foods (*e.g. soup*) are often stored in tumblers and the surface area is relatively small, so a deep headspace must be allowed within the tumbler under the seal – approximately one-tenth of the height of the tumbler. If the liquid were frozen in a shallow container the surface area would be relatively much greater and the total increase in height caused by expansion would be more widely distributed, therefore requiring much less headspace – perhaps only one-twentieth of the height of the sides of the container. In solid foods like peas or strawberries, this expansion is taken up by the air spaces between the individual vegetables or berries, so no headspace is needed.

Containers which are too closely packed with liquid foods may expand sufficiently to split the container or force off the seal.
See *HEADSPACE.

FAN-COOLED FREEZER A model which has a fan situated behind a grille to disperse heat into the ambient atmosphere, usually to be found at the back or side of a chest, or the front of an upright. It is important to allow space adjacent to the grille so that heat may be easily dissipated.
NOTE: This type of freezer is noisier than the skin condenser type.
See *NOISE.

FAST FREEZING The reduction of food to the fully frozen state as quickly as possible. Damage is caused to food during freezing in two ways, both of which may be reduced by the speed at which it is frozen.
1. Damage by micro-organisms and enzymes. Unrefrigerated food may be warm. To become fully frozen it must be reduced to −18°C/0°F right through to the centre of the food. This involves passing through a wide temperature range during which several processes take place. At the top of the scale, bacterial growth is fast, so micro-organisms which produce moulds and food poisoning are busily multiplying, and enzyme activity is rapid. As the temperature of the food descends, these processes begin to slow down. First, micro-organisms begin to multiply more slowly (at around 5°C/41°F) then cease to multiply and become dormant. Enzymes continue in a state of slow activity even at temperatures as low as −40°C/−40°F which is lower than any temperature reduction possible to achieve with a domestic freezer. Obviously the more quickly food reaches the low temperature range at which bacterial growth gradually ceases and enzymes become almost inactive, the less the bacterial build-up and the decay caused by enzymes in the food.
2. Damage to cell structure. During the freezing process, the cell structure of food is damaged by the formation of ice crystals and by alterations in osmotic pressure. Water freezes at a higher temperature than other elements in food, 0°C/32°F. When ice forms, the food is by no means yet fully frozen. The zone of maximum crystal formation is between 0°C/32°F and −5°C/23°F and it is in passing through this zone while the other elements are still gradually freezing that most damage is caused. If this passage can be achieved within 1–2 hours per 450 g/1 lb according to the size and density of the food, damage is minimised. In slow freezing it might take as long as 6 hours per 450 g/1 lb for food to pass through this particular zone. See *CELL DAMAGE.

FAST FREEZING AT HOME Reduce temperature inside the freezer cabinet before adding fresh food to be frozen down. This does not apply to small single items (*e.g. a cake*). Throw the fast freeze switch or adjust the numbered dial according to your model of freezer about 2 hours before adding the food. This overrides the thermostat and causes the motor to function continuously, thus achieving the lowest temperature of which your freezer is capable. For this reason it is important to remember to reverse the fast freeze switch or alter the dial again as soon as the food is frozen, or you may be unnecessarily straining the freezer motor and wasting electricity.

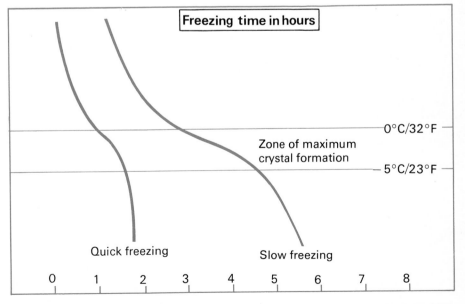

FATS AND OILS All fats, both animal and vegetable, can be frozen but animal fats tend to become rancid after prolonged storage. Solid fats in the form of butter and lard freeze well; salted butter has a shorter storage life than unsalted. Bulk purchases of meat usually provide excess fat which can be rendered down to make dripping. White vegetable fats and margarine keep even longer and can be bought in bulk to save shopping expeditions. There is no point in freezing vegetable oils in bulk but a small amount of oil added to cooked pasta keeps the strands separate. Storage times unsalted butter 6 months, salted butter 3 months, dripping 6 months, white vegetable fat and margarine 12 months.
See *BUTTER, *DRIPPING.

FENNEL A plant of which the feathery foliage may be frozen as a herb and the bulbous root as a vegetable. Storage time 10–12 months.
See *HERBS, *VEGETABLE PREPARATION AND PACKING, *DEFROSTING.

FIG Pear-shaped fruit with many seeds suitable for freezing whole or peeled in syrup pack. Storage time in syrup pack 10–12 months, without sugar 6–8 months.
See *FRUIT PREPARATION AND PACKING, *DEFROSTING.

FILLINGS Both sweet and savoury fillings freeze well providing they do not have too high a water content. Savoury mixtures made with a basis of thick sauce can be frozen separately in bags and thawed and used to complete the dish (*e.g. vol au vent*) when required. This applies particularly to a large *vol au vent* case.
Moist sandwich fillings freeze well (with a few exceptions, *e.g. salads, hard-boiled eggs*) in made-up sandwiches.
Buttercream cake fillings freeze well in layer cakes. Other cake fillings are better frozen separately and added at serving time.
Fresh cream cake fillings are better combined with a little sifted icing sugar and layered with jam rather than fresh fruit. As the cake thaws, juices will run from the fruit and stain the cream, spoiling the appearance.

FISH Freshwater varieties are rarely available except to enthusiastic fishermen. Varieties include pike, brill, bream, bass, perch, dace, chubb, tench; but only trout, salmon trout and salmon are really worth freezing. Freshness is essential so freeze down within 12 hours of the catch. Storage time 3–4 months. Sea fish freeze well whole, filleted or portioned raw, or cooked with a small amount of liquor or sauce to keep them moist. For storage times see individual entries.
See *FISH PREPARATION AND PACKING, *DEFROSTING.

Fish Preparation and Packing

Fish/Season	Preparation	Packing
White flat fish		
Plaice (all year)	Whole fish: Remove head, fins, tail and scales and gut. Wash well. Open freeze on a baking tray for 2 hours. Dip fish in a bowl of iced water until a film of ice forms. Return to the freezer for 30 minutes, then repeat dipping process until ice is 5 mm/$\frac{1}{4}$ inch thick.	Foil or polythene bags
	Fillets: Dip in a salt solution — 1 teaspoon salt: 600 ml/ 1 pint water. Drain well.	Polythene bags with dividers
Skate (October—April)	Freeze the wings as for fillets of plaice.	Foil with dividers
Sole (all year — best April—January)	As plaice	As plaice
Turbot (all year — best April—July)	As plaice	Foil with dividers
White round fish		
Cod (all year — best October—April)	Freeze in either fillets or steaks. Dip in a salt solution (as plaice). Drain well.	Polythene bags with dividers
Haddock (all year)	Freeze fillets — dip in a salt solution (as plaice) and drain well.	As cod
Hake (all year — best July—March)	Freeze in either fillets or cutlets. Dip in a salt solution (as plaice) and drain well.	As cod
Halibut (August—April)	Freeze steaks/cutlets as for cod.	As cod
Whiting (all year)	Whole fish: Remove head, fins and tail and gut. Wash well. Open freeze on a baking tray for 2 hours. Dip fish in a bowl of iced water until a film of ice forms. Return to the freezer for 30 minutes, then repeat dipping process until ice is 5 mm/$\frac{1}{4}$ inch thick.	Foil or polythene bags
	Fillets: Freeze as for cod.	As cod
Oily fish		
Herrings (all year — best May—March)	Fillet and dip in ascorbic acid solution — 1 teaspoon ascorbic acid: 600 ml/1 pint water. Drain well.	Polythene bags with dividers
Mackerel (all year)	As herrings	As herrings
Salmon (best May—July)	If salmon is small, it can be frozen whole. Remove head, fins, tail and scales and gut. Wash well. Open freeze on a baking tray for 2 hours, dip fish in a bowl of iced water until a film of ice forms. Return to freezer for 30 minutes, then repeat dipping process until ice is 5 mm/$\frac{1}{4}$ inch thick.	Foil or polythene bags
	If salmon is large, cut into steaks and dip into ascorbic acid solution (as herrings).	Polythene bags with dividers
Sprats (all year — best November—March)	As herrings	Polythene bags with dividers
Trout (all year) Sea or Salmon Trout (May—July)	As salmon	As salmon
Whitebait (February—July)	Freeze whole, wash and dip in ascorbic acid solution (as herrings). Drain well.	Polythene bags
Shellfish		
Crab (May—September)	Kill and bring to the boil in salted water or court boullion. Allow 15 minutes per 1 lb. Drain, open and remove flesh, taking care to discard small sac behind the head and spongy grey gills, the 'dead men's fingers'.	Either combine white and dark meat or pack separately in polythene containers

Fish/Season	Preparation	Packing
Lobster (all year – but best March–October)	Kill and bring to the boil in salted water or court bouillon. Allow 20 minutes for a 450-g/1-lb lobster, 30 minutes for a 700-g/1½-lb lobster, 45 minutes for a 1-kg/2-lb lobster. Drain and remove flesh, taking care to remove small stomach bag in head, the gills and dark intestinal vein down tail.	Polythene containers
Mussels (October–March)	Make sure they are alive with tightly closed shells – discard any open ones. Wash, scrub and remove beard. Cook in white wine or stock.	With cooking liquor, in polythene containers
Oysters (September–April)	Remove from shells, dip in salted water and drain.	With liquor from the shells, in polythene containers
Prawns (all year)	Cook in boiling salted water for 3–5 minutes. Cool quickly and drain well. Peel.	Polythene bags
Dublin Bay prawns Scampi (all year – best May–November)	Cook in boiling salted water for 10–15 minutes. Cool quickly and drain well. Shell.	Polythene bags
Scallops (October–March)	To open shells, place alive in a hot oven. Scrape away beard and black thread. Dip in salted water and drain.	With liquor from shells in polythene bags
Shrimps (all year)	Cook in boiling salted water as for prawns.	Polythene bags

NOTE: Avoid cross-contamination of other foods in the freezer by enclosing fish and shellfish packs in a large polythene container or batching bag.

FLAG LABELS See *LABELLING.

FLANS Most pastry flans can be frozen fully cooked complete with the filling. It is also useful to freeze empty cases, both cooked and uncooked, as occasionally the filling will not stand freezing (*e.g. fresh fruit with a jam glaze*) or the filling requires no cooking (*e.g. lemon curd*). Unbaked flan cases are useful to have in store because you can make up fillings in quantity at a time when you are not busy making pastry. When freezing uncooked pastry and filling together, it is advisable to brush the interior with beaten egg white to prevent pastry becoming soggy. Non-pastry flans are usually sweet, made from either sponge mixture; biscuit crumbs, sugar and butter; breakfast cereals coated in various sweet mixtures; or meringue. Freezability depends on the delicacy of the flan case. Meringue cases are so delicate that they are better frozen without any filling, protected by a polythene bag slipped inside a cardboard cake box or in a rigid-based polythene container.

See *PASTRY, *DEFROSTING.
NOTE: One packet of large foil flan dishes can be used to make 10 shaped pastry cases which are open frozen, then removed from the foil dishes and stacked with dividers in one or two packs. The same flan dishes can be used to open freeze fillings in shapes ready for removal and packing, and the dishes themselves are still capable of further use. Flan cases can be moulded round the base of an existing foil flan dish to make a larger size.

FLAVOUR Freezing, compared with other methods of food preservation which include cooking (such as canning), is best for preserving the natural flavour of food. It will not, however, improve it. The condition of the food to be frozen is of vital importance. Given the proper conditions of careful preparation, freezing and storing, good quality produce will retain its flavour for at least as long as the recommended storage time. Delicate flavours tend to fade and highly seasoned flavours to intensify. Herbs may develop a musty off-flavour in time.

Blackberry freezer jam (page 163)

Apricot and raspberry topping (page 163)

FLAVOURINGS Synthetic flavourings sometimes become too strong if used in frozen foods. Reduce the quantity you normally use by about half. Vanilla essence tends to become very pungent and is better imparted by using sugar flavoured by dry storage with vanilla pods. Natural fruit flavourings tend to fade slightly.

FLOUR All flour is suitable for freezing in made-up dishes, but where it is used as a thickening agent for sauces it may tend to separate on defrosting. The sauce can usually be reconstituted if it is possible to whisk it, but if this is not possible it is advisable to use cornflour instead. Remember that you will require to use only half the quantity of cornflour to achieve the same result. Alternatively, the dish can be frozen without thickening and *beurre manié* stirred in and cooked after the dish has defrosted.
NOTE: *Beurre manié* is a combination of softened butter and plain flour in the proportions of 20 g/¾ oz flour to 25 g/1 oz butter formed into small dice.

FLOW FREEZING A further development of blast freezing, in which the actual product (*e.g. peas, beans*) is suspended without any packaging and carried forward in a tunnel by an upward stream of refrigerated air. Each single item is individually quick frozen and the resulting product is free-flowing. Typical freezing time is 10–20 minutes.

FLOWERS Although many flowers have been tested for freezing in bloom, only the rose seems to be satisfactory.
Buds which are just opening should be cut and placed for several hours up to their necks in water or the stems may collapse when defrosted. There are two methods for preparing them.
1. Lay them in a shallow polythene container, pour in 2·5 cm/1 inch water and open freeze until partially frozen. Add sufficient water to cover the flowers completely and freeze. To use,

thaw at room temperature and arrange. They will open more quickly than if freshly picked.
2. Wrap each stem separately in foil, crimping it together above the head at one end and the cut stem tip at the other. The pack will be tube shaped. Pack a number of these tubes closely together in a polythene container and freeze. This method makes it easier to defrost and arrange the flowers as they need not be fully thawed out first.
Large blooms can be frozen in small foil pudding basins or Tupperware refrigerator bowls. To remove, dip the container in hot water until it releases the contents which can be piled up in a shallow glass bowl to make a table centrepiece or put in finger bowls.
Petals can be frozen and used decoratively in the same way as blooms.

FLUIDISED BED FREEZING See *BLAST FREEZING.

FOOD PRESERVATION From the earliest recorded times, man has had to preserve food. Some of the oldest methods are still used today. These include drying, salting and smoking. The Romans froze their food in vast underground ice vaults, using ice brought down from high mountains. In the 18th century work was done at various Scottish universities to produce 'man-made cold'. This work continued and in the 19th century an ice-making machine was jointly invented by an Englishman and an American (who was actually granted a British patent). However, none of the attempts to employ mixtures of salt, or calcium chloride brines and ice for the quick freezing of food proved commercially viable until in the early 1920's the name Birdseye emerged as the pioneer of quick freezing. Clarence Birdseye, an American naturalist and fur trapper, observed that fish frozen in the extreme cold of winter was more palatable than that frozen in autumn. Experiments showed that quick preparation and fast freezing fol-

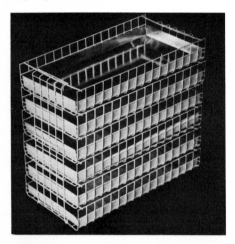

A pack of six individual locking free-flow trays by Hamster.

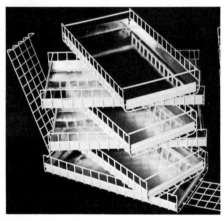

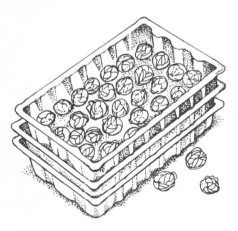

lowed by storage at a temperature below freezing point produced the best results. Food preserved at its peak of freshness by modern freezing methods not only tastes more like fresh food than that preserved by heat processes, but often has a greater nutritional value than the same food which has passed this peak.

FOUR-STAR SYMBOL See *BUY-ING A FREEZER.

FREE-FLOW FREEZING A method which prevents single items of food from sticking together when frozen and forming a solid block. By spreading out small items (*e.g. peas, cauliflower florets*) so that they are not touching on trays or racks, each item forms its own overcoat of frost, enabling you to pack when fully frozen in convenient portions which remain free flowing so that you may tip out small quantities at a time. The food also freezes more quickly as greater surface areas are exposed to cold air.

FREE-FLOW TRAYS Shallow trays which stack to make a unit easy to handle and which exploit freezer space to the utmost are available in the following forms:
1. Shallow wire mesh trays, plastic coated, with a non-stick lining; the pack of six locks together and they are made in two sizes to give 0·45 square metres/5 square feet or 0·8 square metres/9 square feet of level freezing area.
2. Polythene-coated wire mesh trays with aluminium foil-coated card liners supplied for fitting if required. Sold in sets of six which stack on each other and can be locked together. The locking clip can be removed if the trays are required for use separately in a front opening freezer. The small size trays are each 42 by 20 by 35·5 cm/16½ by 8 by 14 inches high, giving a total area of 0·45 square metres/5 square feet, and the popular size trays, which fit most freezers, are 47 by 30 by 35·5 cm/18½

by 12 by 14 inches high, a total area of 0·8 square metres/8·75 square feet.
3. Fast-freezing trays of plastic which stack one on top of the other when in use. A set of five gives 0·33 square metres/3⅓ square feet of level freezing area. These trays are not so durable but are relatively inexpensive, and they have the advantage that a special grooving allows them to be reversed to fit snugly one inside the other for compact storage when not in use.

FREEZER BURN This is apparent on the surface of frozen food, especially meat, as greyish-white patches. These marks are caused by dehydration of inadequately wrapped food, resulting in oxidation. Prolonged exposure to cold, dry air permits oxygen to penetrate the food tissues. The outer layer then becomes oxidised, and in the case of fat it rapidly becomes rancid. If the food is not badly affected, exposure to moist conditions such as cooking in liquid, may make these changes unnoticeable.

FREEZER CARE All new freezers should be wiped out with a clean damp cloth and allowed to dry before switching on. If your freezer has a temperature control dial, check with the salesman that it has been set for normal conditions and whether you may need to adjust it yourself. It is wise to switch on the empty freezer overnight before putting in food stocks, but try to make your first addition a substantial one as it is uneconomical to run a freezer more than half empty. Frost may build up quickly at first but providing the seal on the door or lid is completely effective this will not become excessive for at least 4 months in an upright model, or 10 months in a chest model. Although a few scratches will not affect the mechanical operation of the freezer, the exterior should be cleaned and occasionally polished with white furniture cream. This requires to be done more frequently in a damp ambient atmosphere to prevent rusting. Dust any grilles occasionally so that the passage of warm air is not obstructed by fluff and dirt. If food with a strong odour has been open frozen or packed in a material which is not entirely moisture-vapour-proof, there may be quite an unpleasant smell inside the cabinet. In the latter case, remove and re-pack the offending food and use it up as soon as possible. The only entirely satisfactory method of dealing with this problem is to defrost the freezer completely and clean the inside with a solution of 1 tablespoon bicarbonate of soda and 300 ml/½ pint vinegar to 4½ litres/ 1 gallon water. All vegetables of the Brassica family (*e.g. Brussels sprouts*) are particular offenders.

FREEZER CENTRES Shops which cater particularly for the needs of freezer owners. Some multiple firms with many branches offer the following comprehensive service.

1. A range of freezers at very competitive prices complete with hire purchase facilities if these are required, insurance and service, and a budget account system.

2. A wide selection of frozen foods, including medium and large size packs. This selection includes unusual gourmet foods and prepared dishes, not readily available elsewhere.

3. Grocery lines which can be purchased in bulk at the same time as stocks of frozen food. This is a useful service because when you have formed the habit of shopping less frequently for your frozen foods it is convenient also to buy other items in bulk.

4. Multiple firms frequently have their own brand names and have foods specially grown and packed for them, for example, the Co-op. Freezer centres exist throughout the country selling their own brand of freezers as well as food.

5. A choice of accessories for freezing at home, books on the subject and freezer record books.

6. Large insulated bags into which your purchases are packed are supplied at a nominal sum. These give protection for about 3 hours, and can be used again.

7. The advice of a trained home economist on freezing problems and evening sessions which customers are invited to attend for talks about freezing techniques.

NOTE: Much smaller establishments consisting of one branch only describe themselves as freezer centres but obviously do not offer all these facilities.

FREEZER CONTENTS RECORD Sometimes called a freezer log, this may take the form of a book, card index, magnetic wall chart or part of a diary. However good your memory, you may frequently have to search through your stocks of food to find a particular item unless you do keep some record of contents. Whatever form the record takes, it should be kept with a pen or pencil attached, close to the freezer. Every member of the family who uses the freezer ought to know how to use the record. Most freezer owners choose to keep a book. Four columns are necessary on each page, which should be headed: Date in, Description of pack, Number of packs, Shelf or basket. Indicate the number of packs by separate strokes which can be crossed through when a pack is removed. If you require a more specific record, further columns can be added to indicate the weight of each pack and the date by which it should be used.

Keeping a record has a further important bonus. It will show, after a time, which foods are most popular and which were not really worth the effort of freezing.

FREEZER SITE Before buying a freezer, consider whether it can be negotiated through any doorways, up or down any staircases en route for the chosen site, and remember that an

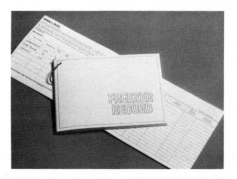

adequate power supply and socket must be available.

In addition, the following factors must be taken into account.

Weight. If the site is on an upper floor, or in an old house, make sure that the floor will be able to support the very considerable loaded weight of the freezer. For example, a 270-litre/9·5-cubic feet chest freezer which weights 82 kg/180 lb unloaded, may weigh as much as 243 kg/532 lb when fully loaded.

Accessibility. The most accessible place is undoubtedly the kitchen, and if yours is large enough for it to be installed away from direct heat (*e.g. well away from the cooker*) this is the obvious choice. Make sure that it is easy to open the door which can be hung either right or left handed. Ideally, the freezer should not stand in direct sunlight or in a steamy atmosphere, but an extractor fan would probably dispose of the latter problem. For this reason a utility room containing a boiler, washing machine, etc. or a very small kitchen might not be suitable. Good circulation of air round the freezer is essential, but before relegating it to an outhouse bear in mind the disadvantage of having to go outside in bad weather for some small item.

Damp Freezer Sites. If the only possible site for your freezer is in a garage, cellar, or other situation where the surrounding atmosphere is always likely to be damp, the best choice

would be a freezer with a skin condenser. If the freezer is of the fan-cooled condenser type it would be inclined to form rust on all exposed metal surfaces because of condensation. Good air circulation under the base is essential, especially in a garage because cars will inevitably be driven in hot, frequently wet, and will add to the condensation problem. If possible retain the wooden block on which the freezer is delivered, or place four short lengths of plank under the corners. This raises the height of the freezer, causing problems for the petite. Some chest freezers are slightly lower than others and at least one upright model has the compressor unit situated on top of the storage cabinet, making it easier to reach inside.

Do not try to protect the exterior with a rug or tarpaulin as this may only trap moisture and prevent the motor from working properly. If the top of a chest freezer is likely to be used as a working surface it is a good idea to protect it with Formica or laminate. Freezers can also be effectively under-sealed with any water-based bitumen emulsion, but it is advisable to underseal newly-purchased freezers only.
HELPFUL HINT: If the site is ill-lit, keep a torch handy.

FREEZER STORAGE NEEDS Various factors affect the capacity which should be chosen to suit your requirements. Most manufacturers advise 60–100 litres/2–3·5 cubic feet for each member of the household. If, however, you will be able to freeze your own garden produce and expect to make large bulk purchases, you are more likely to need 100–115 litres/3·5–4 cubic feet capacity per person. There may also be some special bonus, such as a regular catch of fresh fish or a present of game, which require freezer space. Also you may wish to prepare in advance for entertaining on a large scale. All these considerations may make it advisable for you to decide on a larger model.

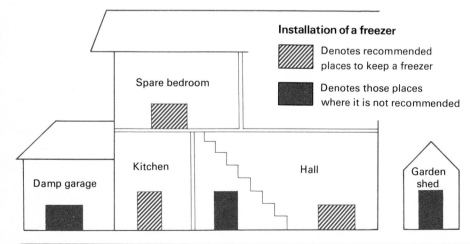

Installation of a freezer

Denotes recommended places to keep a freezer

Denotes those places where it is not recommended

Spare bedroom

Damp garage

Kitchen

Hall

Garden shed

FREEZER TEMPERATURE The regular maintenance temperature of your freezer should not rise above −21°C/ −5°F. Temporary fluctuations caused by the addition of fresh food can be discounted.
See *ECONOMY.

FREEZER TYPES These include the chest, large one-door upright, small one-door upright with working surface, roll-away small one-door upright which can be kept under a working surface, two-door upright, refrigerator/freezer and small top-of-the-cabinet freezer, side-by-side freezer/ refrigerator. Some refrigerators also have a freezer section with its own separate door within the cabinet. Some, but not all, upright freezers have door storage space.

FREEZING CYCLE See *COMPRESSOR, *CONDENSER, *EVAPORATOR.

FRONT SHELF FLAPS These prevent loss of cold air in upright freezers when the door is opened. They also act as pack retainers and are usually spring-mounted.

FROST-FREE FREEZERS In these freezers a radiation coil (similar to that of a car) is concealed behind the cabinet lining. A fan circulates air across the coil and refrigerates the air causing moisture to collect as frost. As the motor runs, a defrosting timer also operates and about every 6 hours the machine goes into a 25-minute defrost period. Water runs into a tray and the circulation of air results in subsequent water evaporation.

Fruit Growing Guide

Fruit	Varieties recommended	Harvesting hints
Apples (cooking)	Bramley's Seedling, Arthur Turner, George Neal, Wellington, Golden Noble, Encore.	Hold the apple and give a slight twist; if the stalk parts readily from the spur the apple is ready to pick.
Blackberries	Oregon Thornless.	Use best ripe but firm fruit.
Blackcurrants	Wellington XXX, Baldwin, Amos Black.	Pick the sprigs when the berries are ripe but firm.
Gooseberries	Careless, Lancashire Lad.	Slightly under-ripe fruit freezes the best.
Loganberries	LY59.	Pick on a dry day when ripe but still firm. If fruit is damp mildew will set in very quickly.
Melon	Ogen, Charantais, Sweetheart F_1, Golden Crispy F_1.	Pick when ripe but still firm.
Pears	Williams' Bon Chrétien, Conference.	Pick for freezing when slightly under-ripe.
Plums	Victoria, Jefferson, Greengage.	Allow to develop to the fully ripe stage for the best flavour when most varieties will part readily from the stalks. Do not pick if fruit is wet.
Raspberries	Glen Cova, Malling Admiral, Lloyd George.	As loganberries. Pick fruit leaving the plug behind on the plant.
Redcurrants	Laxton's No. 1, Wilson's Long Bunch.	Pick the whole sprigs a few days after the currants have coloured.
Rhubarb	The Sutton, Hawke's Champagne, Timperley Early, Victoria.	When picking rhubarb, pull the stems rather than cut them. Spread the cropping evenly over all the plants and stop pulling in late July.
Strawberries	Cambridge Rival, Royal Sovereign, Templar.	Pick dry fruit, with the plug still attached.

Fruit Preparation and Packing

Since fruit can be prepared in so many ways and in different forms for freezing, considerable space is devoted to making this entry as complete as possible. General directions are given here and special hints which apply to a particular fruit are given under its own name.

Sugar syrup

The choice of strength for the syrup depends on two facts. One, whether the flavour of the fruit is very delicate and may be overwhelmed by a strong syrup. Two, whether the fruit is sour and may be improved by mellowing in a heavy syrup. A medium heavy syrup is suitable for most fruits.

Solution	Sugar	Water	Strength
10%	50 g/2 oz	600 ml/1 pint	very thin
20%	100 g/4 oz	600 ml/1 pint	thin
30%	200 g/7 oz	600 ml/1 pint	medium thin
40%	300 g/11 oz	600 ml/1 pint	medium heavy
50%	450 g/1 lb	600 ml/1 pint	heavy
60%	700 g/1 lb 9 oz	600 ml/1 pint	very heavy

Method	Suitable fruit	Preparation and packing	Uses
OPEN FREEZING	Berry fruits which are delicate and require quick freezing because of their high water content, or fruits not needing sugar. Suitable: strawberries, raspberries, cranberries, blackberries, loganberries.	Wash fruit only if necessary, drain, hull afterwards. Spread out on clean baking trays or fast freeze trays and freeze, uncovered, for 1–2 hours until hard. Pack quickly before a bloom appears on the fruit in shallow polythene containers, with foil dividers between layers, to prevent lower layers of fruit becoming crushed as they defrost. If packed in bags, tip into flat dish before thawing. As fruit is packed frozen, leave no headspace.	As fresh fruit. Serve while still chilled to preserve a firm texture.
DRY SUGAR PACK	Berry fruits with a skin, but also high juice content; other juicy fruits. Suitable: currants, gooseberries, rhubarb intended for cooking, pineapple, melon, citrus fruits.	Prepare fruits and spoon alternate layers of fruit and sugar into polythene bags or containers. Or place all the prepared fruit and sugar in a bowl, turn until lightly coated. Allow $\frac{1}{4}$ weight of sugar to weight of fruit, slightly more if fruit is sour. Allow on average a 1-cm/$\frac{1}{2}$-inch headspace, more for small fruit (*e.g. currants*). Use granulated or castor sugar; icing sugar if a smooth syrup is liked. Dry packing of these fruits is possible without sugar if they are required for recipes unsweetened.	Soufflés, sorbets, ice cream, pies, flans, gâteaux, garnishes.
SUGAR SYRUP PACK	Stone fruits, and those which discolour easily. Suitable: apples, pears, peaches, apricots, damsons, figs, citrus fruits, grapes, plums, melon and pineapple.	Prepare fruit according to chart below. Apples, pears, peaches, apricots, sprinkled with lemon juice before freezing; or add $\frac{1}{2}$ teaspoon ascorbic acid crystals to each 600 ml/1 pint hot sugar syrup. Ensure crystals are fully dissolved when syrup is cold. Chill in refrigerator. Pack prepared fruit into containers half-filled with syrup or pour over sufficient to just cover fruit. Leave a 1-cm/$\frac{1}{2}$-inch headspace, and cover with a piece of crumpled foil, pressed lightly on to fruit, to keep it under the syrup, then seal.	Pies, fools, soufflés, sorbets, sauces.
PUREE PACK	Any fruit which can be stewed and made into a purée with or without sugar; apples, plums, damsons. Delicate fruits which can be puréed without cooking; peaches, strawberries, raspberries.	Use the minimum amount of water, about 4 tablespoons to each 450 g/1 lb prepared fruit. Cook to a pulp over gentle heat. Liquidise or sieve if necessary, cool quickly. Pack into containers with 1 cm/$\frac{1}{2}$ inch headspace.	Pies, fools, soufflés, sorbets, sauces.

Fruit	Preparation	Packing
APPLES (cooking) Available: all year	Peel, core and slice into cold salted water. Blanch 1 minute or steam blanch over boiling water 2 minutes. Freeze dry in dry sugar or syrup pack. Can be frozen as purée after cooking with or without sugar, sieve or blend and cool. Especially useful for apple sauce or baby food.	Polythene bags or polythene containers
APRICOTS Available: May–September	Freeze whole, or halved and stoned or sliced, in syrup pack; add ascorbic acid.	Polythene containers
BILBERRIES Available: July/August BLACKBERRIES Available: July–October	Wash fruit, if necessary, and drain, then remove hulls. Freeze dry in dry sugar or syrup pack. Can be frozen as purée, with or without sugar. Choose firm, dry fruit.	Polythene containers
CHERRIES Available: June–August	Remove stalks, wash, drain and stone. Open freeze then pack dry, in dry sugar or syrup pack. White cherries freeze best in syrup. Red cherries freeze better than black.	Polythene bags
COCONUT Available: all year	Shred, add coconut milk. When using, pour off milk. Can be toasted.	Polythene containers
CRANBERRIES Available: October–February	Remove stalks, wash and drain. Open freeze and pack dry or in syrup pack. Can be frozen as sauce.	Polythene containers or polythene bags
CURRANTS – black, red or white Available: June–August	Sprigs – wash, drain, open freeze then pack in dry sugar pack. Or, top and tail and freeze whole, with or without sugar, or purée with sugar and little or no water.	Polythene bags or polythene containers
DAMSONS Available: July–October	Wipe the skins, halve and stone. Freeze in syrup pack or as cooked purée, with or without sugar.	Polythene containers
FIGS Available: August–December	Wash gently, leave whole and freeze wrapped individually, or peel and freeze in syrup pack.	Foil Polythene containers
GOOSEBERRIES Available: May–August	Wash, dry, top and tail. Freeze in dry sugar or syrup pack. Slightly under-ripe fruit freezes best.	Polythene bags or polythene containers
GRAPEFRUIT Available: all year	Wash, peel, segment or slice. Open freeze segments then pack in dry sugar or syrup pack. Juice can be frozen and packed as ice cubes. Grate zest and mix with sugar then freeze.	Polythene containers
GRAPES Available: all year	Remove stalks, halve and remove seeds. Peel, if liked. Freeze dry or in syrup pack. Seedless grapes can be frozen whole in syrup pack.	Polythene containers
GREENGAGES Available: August	Freeze whole, or halve and stone. Freeze dry or in syrup pack.	Polythene containers
LEMONS/LIMES Available: all year	Leave whole, or slice or segment, and freeze in dry sugar or syrup pack. Open freeze lemon slices and pack dry for drinks. Juice can be frozen and packed as ice cubes. Grate zest and mix with sugar then freeze.	Polythene bags or polythene containers
LOGANBERRIES Available: June–September	Wash only if necessary, drain, then hull. Open freeze and pack dry or purée with or without sugar. Pick on a dry day when ripe but firm. Mildew develops within hours on wet fruit.	Polythene containers

Fruit	Preparation	Packing
MANGOES Available: January–September	Peel, halve and stone, slice and freeze in syrup pack with ascorbic acid.	Polythene containers
MELONS Available: all year	Cut flesh into cubes or slices, or scoop into balls. Freeze in dry sugar or syrup pack.	Polythene containers
ORANGES Available: all year	Segment or slice: freeze in dry sugar or syrup pack. Juice can be frozen and packed as ice cubes. Grate zest and mix with sugar then freeze. In season, freeze Seville oranges whole and make marmalade later.	Polythene containers Polythene bags
PEACHES Available: June–August	Skin, halve and stone. Freeze halved or sliced in syrup pack with ascorbic acid. Can be frozen as purée with lemon juice and sugar. For a special occasion, serve still slightly iced and flamed with brandy.	Polythene containers
PEARS Available: June–August	Peel, core and slice. Poach in boiling syrup 1½ minutes. Drain, cool and freeze with syrup, or prepare straight into cold syrup with ascorbic acid. Choose perfect, slightly under-ripe fruit.	Polythene containers
PINEAPPLE Available: all year	Peel, core and slice, dice or crush. Freeze slices in layers with dividers. Freeze in dry sugar or syrup pack.	Polythene containers
PLUMS Available: July–October	Wash, halve and stone. Freeze in dry sugar or syrup pack. Can be frozen as cooked purée, with or without sugar.	Polythene containers
RASPBERRIES Available: August–September	Wash only if necessary, drain and then hull. Open freeze and pack dry in dry sugar pack. Can be frozen as purée, with or without sugar. Pick on a dry day when ripe but firm. Mildew develops within hours on wet fruit.	Polythene containers
RHUBARB Available: March–June	Wash, trim and cut into 2·5-cm/1-inch lengths, blanch in boiling water for 1 minute, and cool. Freeze in dry sugar or syrup pack. Can be frozen as cooked purée, with or without sugar. Blanching is necessary as rhubarb is the stem of the plant not the fruit.	Polythene containers
STRAWBERRIES Available: June–August	Wash only if necessary, drain and then hull. Open freeze and pack dry in dry sugar or syrup pack. Can be frozen as purée, with or without sugar. Choose firm, dry fruit.	Polythene containers

GAME All game deteriorates rapidly, but tends to be tough unless hung (with one exception, rabbit, especially domestic rabbits reared for eating). All shot should be carefully removed before preparation. Be particularly careful to prevent flies from settling on the game while it is hanging.

Feathered game. Pluck and draw waterbirds as soon as possible to prevent the flesh from having a 'fishy' flavour. Other feathered game can be frozen in feather and undrawn if you are short of time, but plucking and drawing after defrosting is rather an unpleasant task.

Large furred game. The preparation of large game meats such as venison is similar to that for beef and is best undertaken by a butcher who will joint it and pack it ready for freezing. Otherwise, the animal should be beheaded, bled, skinned and eviscerated (or drawn). Hang in a cool place for at least 5 days, or as long as 10 days in cold weather. Large or small joints should be frozen as for beef. Large joints of venison are 'saddle' and 'haunch' which will probably weigh too much, unless divided, to cook for one meal. If you have it, the liver can be used combined with other kinds of liver, to make a game pâté. Game meat is very strong tasting and, for this reason, poorer cuts which are not suitable for roasting may be minced or used in stews or pies combined with other meats.

Small furred game. Hares and rabbits should be prepared for freezing as soon as possible after killing. Behead and hang up to bleed for up to 24 hours in a cool place before skinning and eviscerating (or drawing). Wash, drain

French oven-steamed chicken (page 239)

Chicken Kiev (page 239)

Tandoori chicken (page 232)

Quick paella (page 236)

and wipe dry with kitchen paper. If preferred, hang the hare for 5–7 days to develop a 'gamey' flavour. Joint, if liked, and wrap each portion closely in cling film to prevent dehydration as there is little fat on either rabbit or hare. The hare's blood can be saved for cooking it later as jugged hare. It should be frozen separately, with a good pinch of salt, in a polythene container.

GARLIC Dried bulb with exceptionally pungent flavour composed of a number of 'cloves', each one with papery light brown skin. Use sparingly as the flavour tends to become over-accentuated or slightly musty during frozen storage. It is safer to use garlic salt or garlic granules as a flavouring, or add crushed cloves on reheating.

GARNISHES To save time, prepare certain garnishes for savoury dishes at your leisure and freeze them in small portions to be produced when required. Those which freeze well include prawns, shelled or in the shell, croûtons, pastry fleurons, neatly diced blanched carrot, buttered almonds, chopped herbs, lemon and lime slices and savoury butters. All these should be stored in small containers for quick defrosting. Storage time – see individual entries.

GELATINE An almost tasteless organic substance which sets liquids solid. If it is added to foods with a high water content, it tends to separate out on freezing and cannot be reconstituted, giving a granular texture to jellies. Milk jellies made with evaporated or condensed milk do not separate, and gelatine can be added to rich mixtures (*e.g. soufflés, chilled cheesecakes*) successfully.

GIBLETS These usually include the neck, liver, heart and gizzard of birds. Remove any surplus fat, wash very carefully and dry on kitchen paper before packing, discarding any portion of the liver which is tinged with green from the gall. For storage times see *CHICKEN, *DUCK, etc.

GLACÉ FRUITS Some of these may be left over after Christmas. They freeze well if removed from their box and wrapped individually in cling film then packed together in a rigid-based container. Candied peel and angelica may also be frozen in the same way. Storage time 1 year.

GLASS CONTAINERS Jars with wide mouths and screw tops are useful containers for freezing, but since glass may shatter when reduced to a low temperature it is advisable to test the containers first. Fill with water leaving a good headspace for expansion. Replace the screw top and seal the filled jar in a polythene bag. Place in the freezer for several days. If the jar remains intact it is suitable for use as a freezer container without having to overwrap it.

GLAZE Whole fish and large fish fillets can be coated in an ice glaze to seal in the flavour. Open freeze until solid, have ready a bowl of iced water and dip the frozen fish up and down, holding it by the tail, until a visible coating of ice forms. Either place on a wire rack over the solid freezing tray or invert a freezer basket over it and peg the fish tails to the grid, making sure that the heads do not touch the solid tray underneath. Return to the freezer. When the glaze is solid, after about 30 minutes, repeat the dipping process if necessary. Individual fish or fillets may then be packed together using dividers so that single portions may easily be removed.
See *FISH PREPARATION AND PACKING.

GOOSE Like duck, goose is a fatty bird with a large bony structure and low proportion of meat to the size of the carcase. Although rarely available, goose freezes well but for a shorter period than turkey because of the fat content. It is not suitable to be frozen stuffed. Storage time 4–6 months.
See *POULTRY, *DEFROSTING.

GOOSEBERRY Berry fruit of a shrub which freezes well whole on its own or in dry sugar or syrup pack, cooked in the form of purée or in made-up dishes. Storage time in sugar or sugar syrup pack 9–12 months, dry without sugar and as purée 6–8 months.
See *FRUIT PREPARATION AND PACKING, *DEFROSTING.
NOTE: Gooseberries sometimes have a brownish yellow colour on defrosting which can be corrected by adding a few drops of green food colouring after cooking. However, do not add colouring before freezing.

GRAPE Pulpy smooth-skinned fruit which grows in clusters on vines and is suitable for freezing whole in dry pack, halved and with the pips removed in a syrup pack, and in made-up sweet or savoury dishes.

Small seedless grapes can also be frozen whole in syrup. If peeled grapes are required, dry and peel after freezing. Storage time in sugar or sugar syrup pack 9–12 months, dry without sugar 6–8 months.
See *FRUIT PREPARATION AND PACKING, *DEFROSTING.

GRAPEFRUIT Large, roundish yellow-skinned citrus fruit suitable for freezing in sections, in the form of juice or in made-up dishes. Storage time in sugar or sugar syrup pack 9–12 months, as juices 4–6 months.
See *CITRUS FRUIT, *FRUIT PREPARATION AND PACKING, *DEFROSTING.

GRAVY Make all gravies slightly thinner than usual as they tend to be thicker on defrosting. Cornflour as a thickening agent is less likely to result in a gravy which curdles or separates on reheating. Potato flour (the basis of a popular commercial gravy powder) is also suitable. Sliced cooked meat which might tend to dry out (*e.g. lean topside of beef*) keeps moist if covered with a layer of gravy. Meat stock may be used for the same purpose. Small quantities of left-over gravy frozen in small containers are useful to add to soups and casseroles, or to reheat to serve with roast meats where the pan juices are being reserved for another purpose.

GREENGAGE Stone fruit suitable for freezing halved and with the stones removed, cooked in the form of purée, or as part of a made-up dish. Storage time in sugar or sugar syrup pack 9–12 months, dry without sugar and as purée 6–8 months.
See *FRUIT PREPARATION AND PACKING, *DISCOLORATION, *DEFROSTING.

GROUSE Small game bird suitable for freezing. Season August to beginning of December. Storage time 6 months. See *GAME, *DEFROSTING.
NOTE: Capercailzie is a species of grouse.

HADDOCK Lean round fish of the same family as cod suitable for freezing raw whole or in portions, coated in breadcrumbs or batter, or cooked in made-up dishes. Storage time 6 months, in breadcrumbs or batter 3 months.
See *FISH PREPARATION AND PACKING, *DEFROSTING.

HAKE Lean round fish of the same family as cod suitable for freezing raw whole or in portions, coated in breadcrumbs or batter, or cooked in made-up dishes. Storage time 6 months, in breadcrumbs or batter 3 months.
See *FISH PREPARATION AND PACKING, *DEFROSTING.

HALIBUT Lean flat fish suitable for freezing raw, coated in breadcrumbs or batter, or cooked in made-up dishes. Storage time 6 months, in breadcrumbs or batter 3 months.
See *FISH PREPARATION AND PACKING, *DEFROSTING.

HARE Small furred game with a very pronounced flavour. Must be well hung or frozen jointed in a marinade. Season August to the end of March. Storage time 6 months.
See *GAME.

HEADSPACE The space left empty between the surface of the food and the underside of the seal to allow for the water content of the food to expand as it freezes.
See *EXPANSION OF WATER.

HEART Internal organ which therefore does not have as long a storage life as other meat, but is suitable for freezing raw or cooked in the form of a casserole. Stuffing reduces the storage life even further. Storage time raw 2–3 months, stuffed 1 month.
See *OFFAL, *DEFROSTING.

HEAT SEALER An electrical device which generates heat through two Teflon-coated bars causing polythene sheets to melt and weld together without sticking to the source of heat. They can be adjusted for the length of time the heat is generated according to the polythene thickness. Useful for making bags from sleeve polythene.

HERBS Plants of which the leaves, some stalks, stems and seeds are used for flavouring foods. Those with woody stems, such as rosemary, can be washed, shaken dry and frozen on the stem and wrapped individually in foil, or their leaves may be rubbed off when frozen and packed in polythene bags. Alternatively, wash and chop the herbs and pack into ice-cube trays. Cover with water, freeze and then pack the cubes into polythene bags. These cubes can be used in soups, stews, sauces, etc.

Cubes of chopped mint in vinegar with castor sugar make excellent mint sauce with the addition of a little boiling water. Or the chopped mint may be frozen in sugar syrup. To serve, thaw the cubes and add a little vinegar. (For mint sauce, select young shoots with full flavour.)

All green herbs retain a bright colour if blanched for 1 minute before freezing.

Cooked plaice with parsley sauce packed in a bag ready for heat sealing.

and refrigerating defects. But read the guarantee carefully as it might cover the provision of new parts but not labour, and remember that it does not cover replacement of the contents if spoiled through breakdown of the freezer. You should insure against this contingency. If the freezer is manufactured abroad, it is particularly important to make sure that the guarantee can be implemented without delay if spare parts are required.
See *INSURANCE.

HERRING Oily round fish of the same family as sardines and pilchards, suitable for freezing raw, soused or in made-up dishes; also smoked. Storage time 3–4 months.
See *FISH PREPARATION AND PACKING, *DEFROSTING.

HIRE PURCHASE Buying a freezer by instalments over a period of time eventually costs more than paying cash, but if it enables you to stock the freezer with frozen food immediately, this is an advantage. It almost always ensures that you will receive good after-sales service, and you may be able to make a package deal – that is, regular single payments which cover the purchase price of the freezer, insurance against loss of contents or damage to the freezer itself, and any necessary repairs. A large multiple firm such as Bejam Group Ltd. arranges insurance for a nominal sum for the first year and a reasonable amount for successive years, covering service, loss of food other than by your own negligence, and even offers a budget account system for the purchase of frozen food. This means you have only one regular all-in payment to remember each month, or it can be made by bankers' order.

Guarantee. Most freezer manufacturers give a 1-year guarantee on a new machine which covers all mechanical

HORSERADISH Plant of which only the pungent root is edible. Freeze peeled and grated, moistened with a little white vinegar for making into horseradish cream later. Mix in the proportions of 1 teaspoon of grated horseradish to 1 tablespoon of lightly whipped cream with seasoning to taste. Storage time 10–12 months.
See *DEFROSTING.

HYGIENE It is absolutely essential that the highest standards of hygiene are observed in the preparation, storage and thawing of frozen food, otherwise there may be a danger to health. The multiplication of harmful bacteria takes place at the highest rate in circumstances frequently to be found in the kitchen, a warm moist atmosphere with temporary storage in a dark place such as inside the oven. The transfer of contamination by unwashed hands and kitchen utensils, even so-called 'cleaning' and 'drying' materials such as plastic sponges and tea towels, is unseen and therefore not always appreciated. It is particularly dangerous to allow cooked and uncooked meat, and utensils used for preparing them, to come into contact. Food which is hot should be rapidly cooled, and handled as little as possible during packing. An excellent safety rule for the handling of cooked food is that it should be kept cool, clean and covered.
See *CONTAMINATION.

ICE CREAM Commercial or home-made ice creams are 'naturals' for freezer storage but require to be placed where they are not subjected to fluctuations in temperature. Do not be dismayed if you find the home-made ice cream costly by comparison with the commercial product, as the latter rarely contains dairy cream, always an expensive ingredient. Many varieties can be made, and even combined to be frozen in moulds for special occasions. Ice cream turns out easily from a loose-bottomed cake tin, or if the base of the mould is dipped in hot water for a few seconds. Those ice creams marketed as being easy to scoop when taken straight from the freezer are whipped to incorporate air, and being sold by volume not weight they occupy more space for the same weight in solid block form. They are relatively expensive but the convenience may outweigh the cost consideration. Commercial ice creams are also now packed in long 'sliceable' blocks so that they are easy to cut into portions.

Re-usable containers with drop-in refill packs are popular, and so are square 1-litre/35-fl oz and 2-litre/70-fl oz packs, although these containers do not subsequently give an airtight seal. Storage time 3 months.

ICE CRYSTALS These vary in size depending upon the rate of freezing. Fast freezing produces smaller ice crystals and thus a better quality frozen product. Slow freezing or poor storage conditions, with temperature fluctuations or a fixed temperature slightly above rather than below freezing point may result in crystals increasing in size.

ICE CUBES A plentiful supply of ice cubes can be made in trays, turned out and quickly sealed in polythene bags for short-term storage in the freezer. Do not allow the cubes to begin melting before you return them to the freezer, otherwise they will stick together in the bag. These are particu-

larly useful during the summer for cold drinks, for parties and for fast cooling of blanched vegetables before packing.

Flavoured ice cubes can be made with fruit juices or flavouring essences, and look extremely pretty when added to drinks. A peppermint-flavoured cube can be tinted pale green with food colouring, for instance. Maraschino cherries, olives and tiny slivers of lemon rind can be frozen in cubes for use in cocktails. Very concentrated chicken and meat stock can be frozen to make bouillon cubes, as can concentrated fish stock for cooking, but keep a separate tray for this purpose. Chopped mint and other herbs can be frozen in cubes with or without finely chopped onion for use in savoury cooking and to make mint sauce. Strong coffee in cubes makes excellent iced coffee.

Iced lollies made at home may be preferable to the commercial product because you can choose the ingredients to suit the child's diet. Unsweetened fruit juices and low calorie fruit drinks make almost calorie-free ice lollies for young or old with a weight problem. Some lolly moulds have re-usable sticks and others are intended to be used with throw-away sticks. Storage time plain ice cubes 1 month, flavoured ice cubes and ice lollies 2 months.
See *COFFEE.

Three different flavours from a selection of individual chocolate-covered ice creams by Wall's.

I

ICINGS Those which contain no fat have a tendency to 'sweat' and remain damp on the surface for some time after thawing. This applies particularly to royal icing and glacé icing, but is less noticeable on moulded plastic icing. Butter cream and fudge icings are more satisfactory, but all iced cakes appear better after at least 24 hours in a warm dry atmosphere than they do immediately after thawing. Chocolate icings made of melted chocolate, or containing a high proportion of melted chocolate, lose their shiny texture and tend to dry out with grey patches.
See *CAKES.
NOTE: American frosting, or cooked icing, provides the best result of any white icing but is not suitable for piping or formal decoration.

IMMERSION FREEZING Commercial quick freezing by immersing the product (*e.g. prepacked poultry*) in a refrigerated liquid. It may also be achieved by immersing the product (*e.g. peas*), without prepacking, directly into a refrigerant, such as Freon. Cryogenic freezing is the generic term for an alternative method in which the chemical employed is sprayed on the food in the form of a gas (*e.g. nitrogen*) while it is being conveyed on a belt through a tunnel. Typical freezing time is measured in seconds.

INDICATOR PANEL A modern freezer is usually supplied with an indicator panel which gives the following information at a glance.
1. A light indicator showing that the freezer is properly connected to the electrical supply and therefore the thermostat is working to maintain automatic temperature control.
2. A second light indicator, usually red, which only comes on if the temperature inside the freezer cabinet rises above that at which the thermostat is set.
3. A third light indicator, which

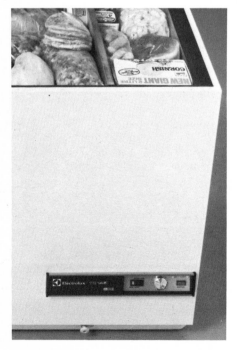

shows when the fast freeze switch is operating.
4. Some upright freezers also have a dial which may be set to control the maintenance temperature within a limited range.
5. Some freezers also have a switch operating a condensation guard which can be left on permanently if the freezer is sited in a damp place or during a period of the year when the site is particularly damp. This device keeps the exterior surface of a freezer warm to prevent condensation.

INSTALLATION OF A FREEZER
Providing that you have chosen a site for the freezer with professional advice if necessary, and taken the same precaution over the electrical installation, you may still be faced with a few problems unless you ensure that they are dealt with before delivery.

Ask to have the freezer put on test run before delivery to make sure that it is not faulty. Enquire about the delivery arrangements as sometimes the freezer is dumped from the van and not even conveyed to the site you have chosen. Even unpacking such a heavy piece of equipment and putting it into position can be a major operation. If you are in any doubt about the procedure (which should include washing out the inside of the cabinet and drying thoroughly before plugging in and switching on), find out beforehand or ask the advice of the delivery men.
See *BUYING A FREEZER.

INSULATED CONTAINERS Freezer centres often provide stout paper sacks which will keep food from thawing during transport for at least two hours, either free or at a nominal charge. Bejam Group Ltd. charge a few pence for a double-thickness strong, paper sack called 'Carrycold'. These are suitable for heavy loads to be put in the back of a car. If you frequently need to transport frozen food by hand, there are insulated boxes made of extended polystyrene which are light in themselves. Although not covered on the outside by a rigid plastic skin they stand up to a lot of work if not overloaded. The smaller sizes can be carried by a webbing handle (which tends to pull out if the box is overloaded), but there is a large size with straight sides and recessed finger inserts measuring 45·5 cm/18 inches long, 35·5 cm/14 inches wide and 34 cm/13·5 inches deep. This size container will hold up to 13·5 kg/30 lb frozen food.

There are also various insulated freezer bags which fold almost flat when not in use and wipe clean both inside and out. These come in sizes from 24 to 27 litres/0·85 to 0·95 cubic feet and have an insulating filling between the outer bag and lining. They zip close with an interlocking strap handle above and are very hardwearing if care is taken not to puncture the material. Insulated containers have other uses besides, for shopping and straightforward transport. Hot food can be taken out for a day's fishing, the bag emptied and leftovers put in a polythene bag to avoid contamination, and the space filled with the catch (in a separate polythene batch bag) to keep it cool on the journey home. Special chemical packed envelopes are available which can either be frozen and put in with frozen food to lengthen the period of preservation, or heated in boiling water and used to help keep food hot.
HELPFUL HINT: Assemble all your insulated containers when defrosting the freezer and use them to hold frozen stock without harm.

INSULATION The earlier models of freezers wasted much storage space because of the insulation required between the outer and inner shells. The latest models owe their reduced bulk to modern improvements in this field. Materials such as asbestos, cork and fibreglass have been used for insulating freezers, but they are now mostly insulated with polymethane pumped in liquid form between the

walls. This expands to a foam which fills the space completely, is particularly effective and allows freezers to maintain their low temperature levels for long periods even during power cuts.
NOTE: Do not try to insulate the exterior yourself by covering it with a rug, heavy polythene sheeting or tarpaulin, as this may only trap moisture and might prevent the motor from functioning properly.

INSURANCE This is a highly complicated question, involving both the freezer and the food inside it, which may be ruined by a mechanical breakdown. It is easy to accept an additional charge on your household insurance policy to cover food spoilage, but this usually works out at far more than the comprehensive insurance arranged by brokers specialising in freezer insurance. A typical specialised protection plan for a freezer up to ten years old covers food spoilage up to a substantial sum, covers labour and parts on repairs, finds the engineer and pays the bill. More complicated plans pay a sum for alternative freezer hire or space in another freezer, and do not limit the age of your freezer. Read the small print on any policy carefully and know what is covered.

Three important points
1. Your plan may provide or insist on regular routine maintenance. Such maintenance is rarely needed or improves the machine's performance.
2. Your plan may limit repairs to exterior damage and may not cover internal damage such as accidentally breaking the inner lining.
3. Food cover should include failure of fuses or switches linking the machine to the electricity supply, breakdown of the freezer due to failure of any component and failure of the public electricity supply due to accidental causes, as distinct from labour disputes and consequent power cuts. Damage by refrigerant leakage should also be covered.

Bejam's 'Carrycold' insulated containers.

INTERLEAVING This process prevents foods from sticking together when frozen and makes it possible to remove single items without defrosting a complete pack. It may be carried out by using single dividers, or by concertina folding back and forth of a long strip between single items.
See *DIVIDERS.

INTERNAL LIGHT Not all freezers have an internal light, so it is a useful extra if your freezer is to be situated in a dark place.

INTERNAL LININGS There are three types for freezer cabinets.
1. Rigidised aluminium.
2. Moulded PVC, easy to keep clean.
3. Enamelled steel, stronger than moulded PVC.

JAMS Since jams made by the conventional method store well without freezing, the only jams recommended for the freezer are uncooked jams and those set with flavoured gelatine.
See *UNCOOKED FREEZER JAMS.

JELLIES See *GELATINE.

JUICES Natural fruit and vegetable juices – the latter can be extracted by special attachment to an electric food mixer – are suitable for freezing in small containers or ice cube trays for use in drinks or cooking. Storage time fruit juices 4–6 months, vegetable juices 3 months.

KALE Leafy green plant of the Brassica family which can be frozen blanched after discarding the tough main stem. Treat in the same way as Brussels sprouts regarding packing as the flavour is very strong. Storage time 10–12 months.
See *VEGETABLE PREPARATION AND PACKING, *DEFROSTING.

KEBABS Skewers threaded with small cubes of meat and other foods which are grilled and usually served on rice. The meat requires to be very tender as the cooking time is short and less tender cuts of meat are suitable if prepared and frozen in a marinade, as this has a tenderising action. To save time on defrosting, all the ingredients can be cut to the correct size and frozen together in the marinade. Other suitable ingredients for threading on the skewers are mushrooms, pieces of bamboo shoot, small onions, pieces of red or green sweet peppers, water chestnuts and large pineapple cubes. Storage time 3 months.
See *MARINADES.

KIDNEY Internal organ which therefore does not have as long a storage life as other meat, but is suitable for freezing raw or cooked as part of a made-up dish. Storage time 2–3 months.
See *OFFAL, *DEFROSTING.

KNIVES Really sharp knives which are purpose-designed are invaluable to prepare food, particularly meat, for the freezer. A comprehensive selection of such knives is now available, including a meat cleaver, saw, boning knife and butcher's knife together with serrated knives, Teflon-coated or not, which even make it possible to cut through fully frozen foods with reasonable ease. Some are serrated on both cutting edges. These knives are extremely sharp and should be used and stored with special care, if possible in protective sheaths. An electric carving knife is useful for foods with an open texture (*e.g. bread*) but cannot be expected to slice frozen bread.
NOTE: If a cutting board is likely to slip, put a folded tea towel between the board and the working surface.

KOHLRABI Plant of the Brassica family of which the stem swells above ground into an edible bulb-like formation. Very small ones are suitable for freezing whole, larger ones need to be diced. Storage time 10–12 months.
See *VEGETABLE PREPARATION AND PACKING, *DEFROSTING.

Above: Brisket of beef (page 150). Below: Stuffed cheese pancakes (page 151)

Above: Gammon steaks with plum sauce (page 169). Below: Piggy in the bag (page 169)

LABELLING Some method of identifying the contents of packs is essential because frozen food soon becomes anonymous. There are a number of suitable methods.

1. Stick-on labels must be self-adhesive or they will peel off the packs. These labels come in various sizes, shapes and colours. Plain large white ones are useful if you require to write full defrosting and serving instructions on them; some freezer owners also prefer to know the exact date when the pack was frozen. Different coloured labels can be used for colour coding (i.e. if you pack all your meat supplies in one large container, you can put all your cuts of beef in blue bags and all cuts of lamb in red bags).

Tupperware labels are printed in various colours on white and marked with the foods 'Food' and 'Use by'. The backing sheet indicates storage times. Self-adhesive labels should be affixed to the side of packs for storage in upright freezers, on top for chest freezers. Press them in place on empty polythene bags before filling rather than on a pack filled with knobbly food or on a frozen pack. Peel the labels off while the container is dry.

2. Flag labels are made of paper with a twist tie or in plastic with a pull through sealing device. The latter are re-usable, but require a chinagraph pencil.

3. Punch printed labels made with a Dymo machine are self-adhesive and the printing is legible at a considerable distance, useful if you are short-sighted. Some polythene bags have a label area on which to write the contents. See *PACKAGING, *CHINAGRAPH PENCILS.

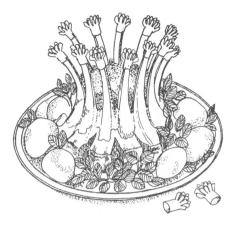

LAMB This represents one of the most useful of all purchases for the freezer as even a small family will soon use up a side of lamb and even a whole lamb is not an unmanageable quantity. It provides a good selection of roasting, grilling, frying and stewing cuts, with very little waste. Like beef, large packs of preferred cuts are available at a slight reduction per kg/lb, or single items (*e.g. shoulders*) ready frozen and each separately wrapped, at an economy price. As the cuts are known by different names in various parts of the country, the following guide to bulk buying lamb is given with some alternative names although these will not cover all local variations.

LAMB

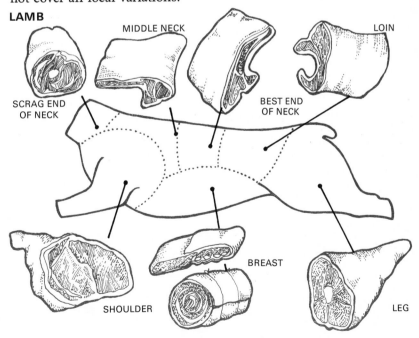

SCRAG END OF NECK

MIDDLE NECK

BEST END OF NECK

LOIN

SHOULDER

BREAST

LEG

HALF A LAMB

Approximate weight: English lamb
6–10 kg/14–22 lb
New Zealand lamb
4–8 kg/8–17 lb
Percentage of bone and fat to be expected: 30–33%

Cuts included	Possible alternative names	Preparation	Suitable cooking method
Leg – fillet end	Gigot, Gigot chops	Joint on bone, boneless slices, cubes	Roasting, grilling, frying
– shank end		Joint on bone, cubes	Braising, stewing
Loin	Double loin	Joint on bone, boned and rolled, chops and chump chops	Roasting, grilling, frying
Shoulder	Fore shoulder	Joint on bone, boned for stuffing, cubes	Roasting, grilling, frying
Best end of neck	Loin	Joint on bone, boned and rolled, cutlets, noisettes	Roasting, grilling, frying
Breast	Flank	Joint on bone, boned and rolled or left flat	Slow roasting, pot roasting, stewing
Middle neck	Back rib	Cut between bones into 'chops'	Stewing
Scrag end of neck	Neck	Cut between bones into 'chops'	Stewing

Special occasion roasts:

'Crown' — two best ends of neck, trimmed and tied into a circle

'Guard of honour' — two best ends of neck, trimmed and with the bones interlaced

'Saddle' — whole back of lamb extending from the best end of neck to the end of the loin, including the kidneys

LARGE PACKS Large frozen food packs are bound to exceed your requirements for one serving. If the pack is in the form of a polythene bag it is easy to remove the quantity required and then reseal close to the surface of the food that is left. If it is in the form of a cardboard carton, it is better to divide the contents the first time you open it into convenient portions and pack these separately. It is unwise to leave a half-empty carton in the freezer because the contents are damaged and space is wasted.

LAYERED STORAGE Delicate foods which are packed in layers tend to squash and bruise the bottom layer while defrosting. To spread the weight as equally as possible, use shallow containers with a wide base and place foil dividers (which are reasonably strong and rigid) between the layers to prevent the upper layers from sinking as the food defrosts.

LEEK Edible plant of the lily family, similar in flavour to the onion but having a cylindrical bulb. A good vegetable to freeze sliced and sautéed in butter for soups and stews or cooked as part of a made-up dish. Storage time 10–12 months.
See *VEGETABLE PREPARATION AND PACKING, *DEFROSTING.

LEFTOVERS Small quantities of cooked food should be treated with great care as they have been exposed to some measure of contamination. If more than sufficient for one meal has been prepared, it is much safer to deal with the surplus in this way.
1. Slices of cake should be sealed in cling film and placed together in a bag or polythene container.
2. A portion of a made-up dish (*e.g. spaghetti bolognese*) should be removed to a container before the dish is served, if this is possible. In any case, leftover food should be cooled and

covered quickly before freezing.

Party leftovers may include nuts, potato crisps and olives. Providing they are still in half-used packs and have not been exposed to the air in dishes for hours, both nuts and crisps can be frozen quite successfully. Olives should be rinsed thoroughly in cold water and frozen in small containers. They will not remain fresh as long as in the original brine but will keep in the refrigerator for a couple of days after defrosting.

LEMON A Yellow glossy-skinned citrus fruit suitable for freezing in many forms including neat lemon slices to use for garnishing. Pack these with dividers in polythene containers. Storage time in sugar or sugar syrup pack 9–12 months, dry without sugar 6–8 months, juice or zest 4–6 months. See *CITRUS FRUITS, *FRUIT PREPARATION AND PACKING, *DEFROSTING.
HELPFUL HINT: Do not discard squeezed lemon halves. These can be frozen individually packed in cling film for adding to curries or stews. If not previously grated, the zest can easily be removed from the frozen lemon half.

LETTUCE A salad vegetable with large succulent leaves unsuitable for freezing raw. It can be frozen cooked, usually in the form of a soup. Surplus lettuce hearts can be blanched and frozen to combine with frozen peas *à la française* later. Storage time 10–12 months.
See *VEGETABLE PREPARATION AND PACKING.

LIGHT Commercially frozen foods packed in transparent plastic and stocked in open retail cabinets are sometimes exposed to light which activates photo-sensitive enzyme reactions, which in turn produce colour and flavour changes. This particularly applies to vegetables such as peas, but does not affect frozen food in opaque bags or waxed cardboard cartons.

LIME A small green or greenish-yellow glossy-skinned citrus fruit which can be used in all the same ways as a lemon. Storage time as lemons. See *CITRUS FRUIT, *LEMON, *FRUIT PREPARATION AND PACKING, *DEFROSTING.

LIVER An internal organ which therefore does not have as long a storage life as other meat, but is suitable for freezing raw or cooked as part of a made-up dish. Storage time 2–3 months.
See *OFFAL, *DEFROSTING.

LOCKS If your freezer is sited sufficiently far from the kitchen to be out of sight and earshot a lock is a necessary safety device. Children have been known to open a freezer, climb inside and shut the lid by accident; and reasonable protection is needed against theft from a fully stocked freezer cabinet. If you are in any doubt, make sure that your insurance covers you against loss of frozen food by theft, but a lock will usually deter thieves.

LOGANBERRY Soft berry fruit of a plant which bears the fruit on canes. Suitable for freezing in dry pack, dry sugar pack or as purée. Also suitable for making uncooked freezer jam. Storage time in dry sugar pack 9–12 months, without sugar and as purée 6–8 months.
See *FRUIT PREPARATION AND PACKING, *UNCOOKED FREEZER JAMS, *DEFROSTING.

Freeze left-over mince in foil containers. Pipe on a potato topping after defrosting.

M

Young's smoked fillets of mackerel.

MACKEREL Oily round fish with distinctive wavy cross markings. Mackerel are suitable for freezing raw whole. Commercially frozen smoked mackerel fillets are now available, which are delicious as an hors d'oeuvre. Storage time 3–4 months. See *FISH PREPARATION AND PACKING, *DEFROSTING.

MARGARINE See *FATS AND OILS.

MARINADES Highly seasoned liquids in which fish, meat or game are placed before cooking. These impregnate the food with various flavours and also make it more tender. A mixture of oil, wine or vinegar and seasonings is generally used. Prepared foods such as diced meat for kebabs should be refrigerated for at least 24 hours in the marinade before being frozen. Or, the marinade may be frozen separately, thawed out and used when required with fresh food. Storage time 3 months.
See *KEBABS.

MARKING Some forms of writing tend to fade when reduced to sub-zero temperatures, but in addition to chinagraph pencils, wax crayons, felt tip pens and ballpoint (for short-term storage) are all useful. You can write directly on the white cardboard surface of the lid supplied with shaped foil containers. Some mail order firms supply extra lids for this purpose as the dishes are re-usable. It is possible to write on polythene containers but it is easy to smudge the writing and sometimes difficult to remove the marks.

MARROW (US SQUASH) Vegetable marrows are actually the fruit of a creeping plant of the same family as cucumber but eaten as a vegetable. Marrow is suitable for freezing as blanched rings or large dice, or cooked whole and stuffed. Storage time 10–12 months.
See *VEGETABLE PREPARATION AND PACKING, *DEFROSTING.

MARZIPAN This cooked form of almond paste freezes well as part of a cake (*e.g. Simnel cake*) but in the form of blocks it crumbles and is difficult to work with when thawed. If you have time to spare, it is worth making some small moulded decorations to open freeze and then pack carefully to avoid damage, for later use. Unpack and put in place while still frozen. Storage time for decorations 3 months.

MATURING This is important to develop the full flavour and produce the right texture in some foods.
1. Meat, notably beef, is hung for varying periods of time to mature before freezing, or it may be rather tough and tasteless.
2. Game is hung for the same purpose in some cases until natural processes of decay are well advanced.
3. Food frozen in marinades requires refrigerated storage in the marinade before freezing, to allow the liquid to penetrate the tissues.
4. Some cakes and puddings including fats and oils, especially rich fruit mixtures, need to mellow sealed at room temperature in an airtight containers for anything from a few days to 2 weeks.
5. Some uncooked cakes and desserts (*e.g. summer pudding*) also require to stand before freezing.

MAYONNAISE An emulsion combining oil, egg yolks and seasonings which does not freeze well as the ingredients separate when thawed. A little mayonnaise may be used with other ingredients in a sandwich filling.

MEAT BUYING Experience in bulk buying meat soon shows that there may be pitfalls to avoid.
1. Remember that the price quoted is on the gross weight of big buys such as a forequarter of beef or side of pork. By the time all unusable bone and fat is removed the weight loss may be as high as 25–30% of that total, thus

increasing the price per kg/lb for usable meat considerably. However, fat may be rendered down for dripping and bones used to to make stock.

2. You must be prepared to devote a large amount of freezer space to a bulk purchase, and this may not be convenient.

3. Although it may not have occurred to you to ask your supplier to freeze down the meat for you, he will be able to do this efficiently if you request it and you will not have the trouble of keeping a large amount of meat in prime condition while you freeze it down in batches.

4. Always take the trouble to discuss your exact requirements and see that a note is made of them in order to have the meat butchered and bagged in the way that suits you best. It is a great advantage, for which you should not have to pay, to have such joints as a breast of lamb, boned, rolled and tied if you ask for this to be done. It is an easy matter for a butcher to score pork roasting joints, but tricky for the housewife.

5. Consider having joints boned, especially beef, as far as possible. They take up less space and sharp bones either have to be padded or tend to pierce the pack, damaging other items when you re-arrange the contents of your freezer.

6. Try to resist the temptation to use up all the choice cuts from a mixed pack first, condemning your family to live on stews for weeks before you can afford to invest again in roasting joints and other prime cuts.

MEAT PACKING Lamb, beef and pork are all excellent freezables dealt with under their specific headings. The instructions for packing meat differ according to whether the meat is to be frozen in joints, in small cuts or minced, but since oxygen coming into contact with meat surfaces causes oxidation, and meat expands so little on freezing, the closer the wrap the better.

To freeze joints, wrap as closely as possible, especially awkward shaped joints. Mould the joint in foil or cling film, or in sheet polythene using the butcher's wrap, taping in every corner which might hold an air pocket. If the joint has a bony piece which is not essential for roasting, cut it off first using a serrated knife or saw designed for the purpose.

Check the size of the piece of wrapping material you will need to enclose the joint completely before cutting it from the roll. Place the joint in the centre and mould in one side first. A joint such as a leg of lamb should be placed diagonally, and the wrap big enough to fold up over the knuckle end. Smooth the wrapping closely against the surface of the meat and aim to achieve a smooth shaped parcel with no sharp corners to pierce other packs.

To freeze small cuts, place a number of items together (in meal-sized quantities if preferred), using dividers so that you can separate them even when frozen. Mould as closely as possible in foil or cling film, pack in sheet polythene using the druggist's wrap or in polythene bags. The dividers should be large enough to fold over any bony parts of the meat to avoid these piercing the wrap. Alternatively, mould small cuts individually in foil or cling film and pack together in a large polythene container or batching bag.

To freeze minced meat, divide the meat into convenient quantities (*e.g. 500 g/1–1¼ lb*) and pack in foil, cling film or polythene bags. Or, season the mince, add chopped onion, then form into shapes for frying as beefburgers (hamburgers) or meat balls. There is a mini press available for forming your own shapes. Treat these as 'small cuts' and pack in polythene containers with dividers. Minced meat, because of the number of exposed cut surfaces, has a shorter storage life than other cuts.
See *BEEF, *LAMB, *PORK, *VEAL, *KNIVES.

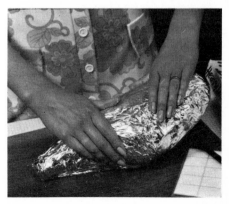

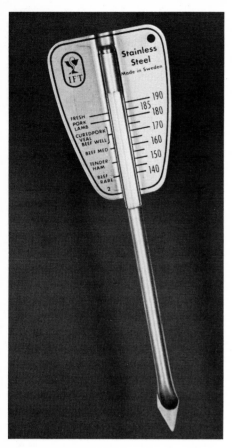

MEAT THERMOMETER A thermometer with a temperature dial at one end and spike at the other. It is not easy to judge when roasting joints are cooked, especially when an allowance must be made for thawing, if cooking a joint from the frozen state. A meat thermometer should be inserted into the thickest part of the joint, about half an hour before the time at which you expect the joint will be ready. Take care that it does not touch a bone, and that the dial is in a position easy for you to read without removing the roasting tin from the oven. When the indicator reaches the correct temperature this means that the meat is cooked to the extent you require and eliminates the necessity for other tests. Most American housewives regard this as an essential piece of equipment. Here is a chart of the recommended temperatures for different cooked meats.

Meat	Recommended temperature
Poultry	88°C/190°F
Fresh pork	88°C/190°F
Lamb	82°C/180°F
Cured pork	77°C/170°F
Veal	77°C/170°F
Beef – well done	77°C/170°F
Beef – medium	68°C/155°F
Beef – rare	60°C/140°F

MELON Fruit of a creeping plant belonging to the same family as cucumber and marrow. Melons are suitable for freezing sliced, diced, or scooped into balls in dry sugar or sugar syrup pack. Storage time in sugar or sugar syrup pack 9–12 months.
See *FRUIT PREPARATION AND PACKING, *DEFROSTING.

MERINGUES These are a useful standby for desserts with a long storage life, in the freezer or in an airtight tin, and should always be stored unfilled. Open freeze before packing and sealing, preferably in a rigid container as they are very fragile. If packed in polythene bags, do not draw out the

air with a pump as the meringues may collapse. Freeze large meringue cases in the same way. They require hardly any defrosting as they contain such a high percentage of sugar and are therefore particularly useful for parties. Storage time 4–6 months.
See *DEFROSTING.

MICRO-ORGANISMS All foods contain micro-organisms such as bacteria, yeasts and moulds, often in large numbers. Not all are harmful, some are useful and a few foods depend for their very existence on micro-organisms (*e.g. yogurt*). Freezing does not destroy micro-organisms as heat does, so avoid leaving food intended for freezing in warm, dark, moist conditions which encourage existing bacteria to thrive. They are invisible to the naked eye, often impossible to detect by taste or smell.

MICROWAVE COOKING This works on the principle of high frequency. Microwaves agitate the water molecules which are contained in all foods, causing them to jostle together thus producing energy. It is this energy in the form of heat which thaws, reheats or cooks frozen food in a very short time. The microwaves must penetrate the food from all angles and they pass through materials such as glass, china, plastic and paper leaving them cool. The advantages are chiefly the following.
1. Even the densest of foods (*e.g. a large beef joint*) can be defrosted and cooked in minutes rather than in hours. Foods of lighter texture seem to defrost and reheat or cook in a flash – a frozen bread roll can be thawed in 10 seconds.
2. Washing up and preparation work at the interim stage between the freezer and the table are practically eliminated. Combined cooking and reheating operations to produce a complete meal can take place in the oven in minutes.

The microwave oven is an excellent

investment, especially for freezer owners, providing one allows for certain limitations in its use.

1. Joints of meat, poultry, steaks and chops, will not brown on the outside unless the cooker has its own 'micro-browner'.

2. Cakes cook so quickly that the outside does not have time to turn golden or brown in the usual way.

3. Foods that require steam from the inside to cook and heat from the outside to make them crisp (*e.g. Yorkshire pudding*) are not satisfactory.

4. Tough cuts of meat and elderly birds, suitable for stewing or braising, will not cook satisfactorily. However, cooked dishes of this kind can be thawed and reheated in a microwave oven.

NOTE: Some microwave ovens are equipped with a special defrost cycle which causes food to defrost evenly throughout. However, any domestic microwave oven can be used for defrosting.

MICROWAVE DEFROSTING
This can be done most effectively in a domestic microwave oven. The best results are obtained by defrosting in stages, especially for meat, poultry and fish. The process is as follows:

Place the food to be defrosted uncovered on a suitable plate in the oven and switch on for a period of 5 minutes. Allow to 'rest' for 1½ minutes, then switch on for a further period of 5 minutes. The 'resting' period is necessary to allow the heat to penetrate evenly, without cooking the outer surface of the food before the centre is fully thawed. Foods with low density, such as bread, will be fully defrosted in 3 minutes. Cakes will require 5 minutes heat, 1½ minutes 'rest', then a further 2–5 minutes heat, according to the size of the cake.

A joint of meat weighing 1·5 kg/3 lb can be defrosted by this method, allowing slightly longer rest periods, in 3 stages totalling 15 minutes heating and 10 minutes rest. It can then be

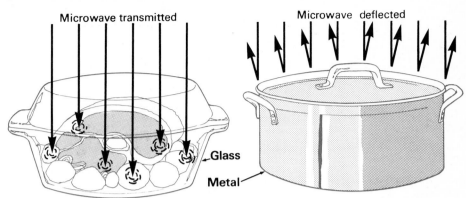

Microwave transmitted   Microwave deflected

Glass

Metal

cooked in 3 stages, totalling 15 minutes heating and 10 minutes 'rest'. This 'rest' time can be utilised for cooking vegetables to accompany it. The cost of fuel will be low, as the oven is only in operation throughout defrosting and cooking for 30 minutes. To prevent uneven-shaped joints from overcooking in parts, cover protruding portions (*e.g. bone of leg of lamb*) with a strip of aluminium foil.

MILK With daily milk deliveries there is no point in keeping a stock of milk in the freezer but it is useful in an emergency to be able to produce a small quantity at short notice. Homogenised milk only should be frozen. Freeze in a carton or polythene tumbler, never in the glass bottle in which it was delivered. Storage time 3 months.
See *DAIRY PRODUCE, *DEFROSTING.

MINCEMEAT It is not necessary to freeze mincemeat made by a classic recipe with suet, but an uncooked mincemeat made with fresh fruit and melted butter freezes very well. The combination of fruits may be varied but the basic requirement is melted butter instead of suet, lemon juice instead of alcohol and a mixture of dried fruits such as raisins and sultanas, with fresh fruits such as chopped apple and grapes. Use brown sugar rather than white sugar and allow the mincemeat to mature in the container for 24 hours before freezing. Storage time 6 months.
See *DEFROSTING.

All foods are capable of absorbing microwaves which cause molecular friction, thus generating heat. However, the transmission of the microwave energy will be deflected if metal containers are used, preventing the food from being heated and possibly damaging the power unit of the oven.

MIXED VEGETABLES Sales at a comparatively high price in freezer centres prove the usefulness of bags of mixed diced root vegetables. Whenever you have time, or a surplus of any particular vegetable, dice and blanch a few. (Blanching is unnecessary if the packs are for short storage.) Pack as available, combining parsnips, turnips, carrots and onions. Celery and fennel can be added with advantage, and the outer stalks of these vegetables, otherwise often discarded, are best used in this way. A bag of mixed vegetables added to meat together with stock makes a stew or, if added to stock alone, a soup. Roughly chopped parsley and other fresh sweet herbs can be added to the pack – even the odd quarter or slice of lemon. These 'stew packs' cost little to assemble and freeze and are invaluable when one is particularly busy.

Mixed summer vegetable packs. These are worth preparing when various home-grown vegetables become available at different times, or cannot be bought together at their cheapest. Prepare the vegetables as they come to hand and store in small containers. Then, when the full range is in store make up combined packs of selections such as sliced runner beans, diced carrots and turnips, sweet corn kernels and peas. Prepared mixtures of vegetables for *ratatouille* also freeze well. Storage time blanched 10–12 months, unblanched 3 months.
See ★DEFROSTING.

MOISTURE-VAPOUR-PROOF Term applied to packaging materials which are not permeable by moisture vapour and are essential to protect frozen foods from the effects of oxidation and dehydration.
See ★PACKAGING.

MONOSODIUM GLUTAMATE A chemical product sold under various trade names (*e.g. Accent*) which may be used alone or with other seasonings in the form of a savoury salt. It may be added to foods before cooking to improve their flavour. Subsequent freezing does not alter its effect in any way.

MOULD Growths of minute fungi associated with decay which can cause spoilage in many foods, some within hours (*e.g. raspberries*). Moulds are not destroyed by freezing as they are by cooking but remain dormant.

MOUSSES Very delicate dishes made with eggs and/or cream and flavoured with fruit, fish or vegetables, sometimes with gelatine added. If possible freeze them in the dishes from which they will be served, so as not to spoil their appearance or disturb the texture when thawed. Storage time 3 months.
See ★DEFROSTING.

MUSHROOM Edible fleshy fungi suitable for freezing without blanching but best lightly sautéed in butter. Do not freeze field mushrooms as it is difficult to know how old they are; they usually turn a very dark colour on cooking and discolour other ingredients in a dish. It is also easy to confuse poisonous fungi with those safe to eat. Storage time 3 months, sautéed 6 months.
See ★VEGETABLE PREPARATION AND PACKING, ★DEFROSTING.

MUSSEL Small hinged mollusc which is only suitable for freezing in the cooked form with its cooking liquid and preferably without its shell. Mussels must always be purchased alive and there are two ways to check that they are safe to eat.
1. Before cooking, tap each mussel sharply with a spoon. The shell should close. Discard any that remain open.
2. Alternatively, live mussels should open during cooking. Discard any that do not. Storage time 1 month.
See ★FISH PREPARATION AND PACKING, ★DEFROSTING.

NECTARINE Stone fruit which is a smooth-skinned type of peach and which usually needs covering with boiling water for 1 minute to loosen the skin for peeling. Nectarines are suitable for freezing in syrup pack and as purée with sugar and lemon juice. The flesh discolours when cut and exposed to the air so prepare straight into sugar syrup or add ascorbic acid to pack. Storage time in sugar syrup pack 10–12 months, as purée 6–8 months. See *FRUIT PREPARATION AND PACKING, *DISCOLORATION, *DEFROSTING.

NITROGEN A chemical stored in its liquid form under pressure and vaporised in a tunnel through which food passes, providing a very fast commercial method of freezing. See *IMMERSION FREEZING.

NOISE This is measured in decibels and prolonged exposure to noise levels in excess of 80 decibels is a health hazard. For instance, the blast of a car horn produces about 120 decibels. Freezers produce noise, when the motor is functioning, of between 60 and 70 decibels. The fan assisted type is noisier than the condenser type, something to bear in mind if the freezer is not sited in a room where you can close the door on it. A third type, the static machine, has a decibel level midway between the other two types.

NON-FREEZABLES There are virtually no foods which cannot be frozen in *some* form. The following categories present special problems.
1. Foods with a high water content, particularly salad vegetables, which are normally only eaten raw. This high water content causes their texture to become limp through cell damage during freezing and cannot be restored. Lettuce, cucumber and other salad greens can all be frozen in a cooked form where the change in texture is not noticeable.
2. Dairy foods with a high water content (*e.g. single cream*), where the fat separates out on freezing in the form of globules which tend to agglomerate and cannot be reconstituted to give the same consistency later. Homogenised milk is an exception because of the breaking down and distribution of the fat globules.
3. Eggs, which can only be frozen whole if cooked commercially because the albumen (white) freezes at a different temperature from the yolk and thaws with an unpleasant rubbery texture. Cooked egg in made-up dishes (*e.g. cakes*) and raw eggs in various forms can be frozen, but not whole in the shell.
4. Emulsions (*e.g. mayonnaise*), which tend to separate and cannot be homogenised again.

NON-STICK TRAYS Food that is open frozen is sometimes difficult to remove from the tray for packing. Some surfaces are coated or impregnated with Teflon or a silicone glaze, and food is easily moved by sliding a spatula, dipped in hot water, under it. Non-stick parchment does not even require this treatment, and used as a lining paper makes any tray non-stick. It can be wiped, with disposable kitchen paper damped with hot water, for re-use.

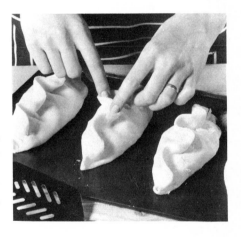

NUTRITIONAL VALUES If care is taken in the choice, preparation, packing and storage of foods for freezing, their nutritional value may be *for all practical purposes* as high as those normally bought and served fresh. In fact, vegetables which have passed through the market on their way to a retailer may be several days old and have lost possibly half their Vitamin C content. Vegetables harvested and frozen almost immediately lose very little.

Fat content, especially of meat, is the only constituent of food which changes perceptibly and loses some nutritional quality. After long storage animal fats evenually tend to become rancid and oxidised, which results in some loss of Vitamin A.

Mineral content, again especially with meat, may be affected because some loss of mineral elements occurs on thawing when there is a noticeable 'drip loss'. With other foods, as with fruits, this may be contained in a syrup and the loss therefore is negligible. If frozen vegetables are cooked without thawing in very little fast boiling water, or with no water added, for only the recommended time, the loss of minerals will be hardly greater than that from fresh vegetables.

NUTS The kernels of most nuts freeze well when removed from the shells. Some have a tough inner skin and are better blanched to remove this before freezing. Where the skin is not tough (*e.g. hazel nuts*) the kernel is chopped or ground, or left whole with the skin on. Flaked or split almonds or whole almonds, with the skin or blanched, are all freezable, and any blanched nuts can be gently tossed in butter until light brown then frozen salted or unsalted for party use. Chestnuts are the only exception, as these require to be cooked, shelled and skinned before freezing in any form. Mixed nuts may be worth freezing if you have not sufficient of one kind to make a pack. Storage time uncooked 1 year, browned in butter 6 months, with salt 4 months.

OFFAL Liver, heart and kidney can be frozen raw or cooked, but brains, sweetbreads and tripe are better frozen cooked because of the problems of discoloration. No offal has a long storage life. Treat as follows:

Liver, heart and kidney. If not to be immediately prepared for freezing in a cooked form (*e.g. liver pâté*) or cooked to make a strong stock for freezing, wash well, removing any green parts, dry on soft kitchen paper and pack in small quantities.

Brains, sweetbreads and tripe. Blanch according to kind, adding either lemon juice or vinegar to the blanching water. If not immediately to be prepared for freezing in a cooked form (*e.g. tripe and onions*), freeze in a little chicken stock to keep moist and cover the exposed surface of the blanched offal with cling film to exclude air. Storage time 3 months.
See *DEFROSTING.

OKRA Edible seed pod of a plant of the mallow family suitable for freezing blanched. Storage time 3 months.
See *VEGETABLE PREPARATION AND PACKING, *DEFROSTING.

OLIVE Small oval fruit of a Mediterranean tree, eaten pickled in brine. Olives are available green with the stone removed and the centre stuffed, usually with red pimiento, or black, when they are often referred to as 'ripe' olives. Unopened jars of olives store well in a cupboard but it is possible to freeze the olives in small quantities once the jar has been opened. Rinse in cold water and pack in polythene containers. However, the olives will not keep long after defrosting and should be stored in the refrigerator. Storage time 3 months.
See *DEFROSTING.

ONION A plant of the lily family of which the succulent bulb is edible. Onions are suitable for freezing blanched for long-term storage or unblanched for short-term storage. Because of their strong smell, onions must be carefully sealed in airtight packs – preferably double polythene bags which can be discarded after use – otherwise they can cause contamination of other foods in the freezer. Storage time blanched 10–12 months, unblanched 3 months.
See *VEGETABLE PREPARATION AND PACKING, *OVERWRAPS, *DEFROSTING.

OPEN FREEZING A fast method of freezing food before packing it for storage. It has the following advantages:

1. Vegetables (*e.g. peas*) and fruits (*e.g. raspberries*) remain free flowing, as each pea or raspberry is separately frozen. The food to be frozen should be spread out on trays so that the items do not touch, to permit the free passage of cold air all round them.

2. Foods with a high water content and delicate cell structure (*e.g. strawberries*) freeze comparatively quickly when spread out rather than closely packed, and this minimises undesirable changes in cell structure.

3. Foods which might be easily damaged by pressure (*e.g. decorated cakes*) are open frozen until firm enough to pack safely. It is also important to unpack them while frozen to avoid damage during defrosting.

See *FREE-FLOW TRAYS.

ORANGE Deep golden citrus fruit of which there are two kinds, sweet and bitter. The latter is used in making marmalade and other preserves. There are also small fruited decorative oranges which are not edible. Sweet oranges are suitable for freezing in many forms; segmented in syrup, in dry sugar pack or whole for future use in cooking.

Seville oranges are deep golden bitter oranges used in making marmalade and other preserves. Suitable for freezing whole for preserve making later. Storage time in sugar or sugar syrup pack 9–12 months, juices 4–6 months, whole Seville oranges 6 months.

See *CITRUS FRUIT, *FRUIT PREPARATION AND PACKING, *DEFROSTING.

OVERLOADING The addition of too much fresh food to be frozen down at one time. This usually means adding more than 10% of the total capacity of the freezer, resulting in slow temperature reduction and slow freezing of the new additions. This may be disregarded in the unusual circumstance

that the freezer is functioning practically empty. In this case it would be reasonable to bring the freezer's contents up to half the total capacity.

Close packing is another form of overloading. Shelves or baskets filled with cube-shaped packs, all touching, do not permit useful finger spaces or sufficiently free circulation of air.

OVERWRAPS Additional covering to the basic moisture-vapour-proof wrap or container. These are usually needed for foods of uneven shape with sharp pointed projections (*e.g. meat bones*) which tend to pierce their covering and damage other packs. The damage goes unnoticed until punctured packs are defrosted. Any material used as a second wrap or overwrap should be strong but not necessarily freezer proof (*e.g. cardboard carton, stockinette sleeve*) and sufficiently clean to be hygienic providing it does not come into contact with the food.

Throw-away overwraps are advisable if foods are so strongly flavoured that they can permeate even a moisture-vapour-proof wrap or container to the extent of causing cross flavours or an unpleasant smell in the freezer; this second wrapping must also be moisture-vapour-proof.

OXIDATION The effect of oxygen through the action of enzymes on all food. By oxidation fat goes rancid, ascorbic acid breaks down, discoloration by browning accelerates. The effects of freezer burn in animal tissue are particularly noticeable because severe dehydration of the surface of the meat produces an open texture which permits oxygen to penetrate the tissue.

OYSTER Hinged mollusc which is suitable for freezing raw with its shell liquid and without its shell, or as part of a made-up dish. Storage time 1–2 months.

See *FISH PREPARATION AND PACKING, *DEFROSTING.

Open freezing and packing strawberries. Speed is essential to prevent the fruit from partially defrosting during the packing process.

P

PACKAGING   To give adequate protection against the extremely cold dry air of the freezer, all food must be sealed into an air-tight wrapping or container made of moisture-vapour-proof material. This requirement is essential because we preserve food in the freezer for far longer and at a far lower temperature than by any other method. Here is a detailed description of the various wrappings and containers available.

Polythene containers.   Must be able to withstand sub-zero temperatures without splitting or warping. Tupperware containers are not only guaranteed for 10 years' use, but proof against reduction to –57°C/–70°F. Cheaper containers may split or warp after one use, so that the lid which gives an airtight seal is never again a perfect fit. The seal should make the container airtight.

Coloured polythene containers. An aid to easy identification without getting at close range to the label. Coloured lids are helpful but it is better for the container itself to be coloured. Use warm colours for fruit and sweet sauces, cool colours for vegetables and savoury sauces for example.

Polythene bags.   Must be of thick gauge (200–250) to be moisture-vapour-proof. To give them an airtight seal it is necessary to close them with a tightly tied plastic- or paper-coated wire tie (twist ties) or with freezer tape. Ordinary clear adhesive tape is not suitable because it peels off at low temperatures. Gussetted bags can be filled to make a square-standing pack, sealed with a twist tie, freezer tape or simply tied in a knot. Plain bags can be sealed in any of these ways, or across the open end with a heat sealer. These packs can be laid flat and stack very conveniently, rather like commercial packs. For fish and other relatively long thin items of food such as French loaves, there are bags of the correct shape, large size 25 by 75 cm/10 by 30 inches, smaller size 12·5 by 45 cm/5 by 18 inches.

Coloured polythene bags.   These come in six different colours and are useful in that you can create your own colour code when using them. Once you have decided that you use green for vegetables, white for fruit and black for the dog's dinners, it is no particular disadvantage that the packs are opaque. But for those who have a phobia about it, there are 'stripey bags' in various sizes, which have alternate stripes of clear and coloured polythene. Batching bags permit a number of similar items to be packed together. In this case it is really better to use clear polythene bags inside the batching bag, or for example use a large red bag for meat, and inside package beef in small red bags, pork in white, lamb in blue and so on.

Boilable bags.   These come in various types (see ★BOILABLE BAGS). Vegetables can be blanched in the bags but it is a lengthy process and generally proves unsatisfactory. Cooked foods, blanched vegetables and raw smoked fish have all given good results in these bags, although it is a wise precaution to pack a number of them all together in some container for protection against damage in the freezer. A special advantage, for example with vegetables, is that if they are packed with a knob of butter and a little seasoning, there is no loss of the moisture and nutrient elements at the reheating stage, because they do not come into direct contact with boiling water. If carefully handled and washed, the bags can often be used more than once. Intrepid freezer addicts may like to experiment with the blanching-freezing-reheating process; such experiments are all part of the fun of owning a freezer.

Sheet wrapping.   Available in useful rolls which come in varying lengths and widths.
1. Polythene sheeting which needs sealing with freezer tape.
2. Cling film which comes in two thicknesses, one for very short-term storage, and freezer wrap for long-term

storage. This is good for items which need close wrapping and are irregular in shape. Being transparent it permits easy recognition of the contents and requires no sealing.

3. Heavy gauge aluminium freezer foil makes a self-sealing close wrap and ordinary kitchen foil (used double) is also suitable for the same purpose. Foil has the advantage that it needs no freezer tape if the edges are crimped together or smoothed close to the surface; in fact an entirely airtight and watertight pack can be achieved with sheet foil. Another use is to line a favourite container, such as a pretty ovenproof casserole, or a family-size saucepan with a good heavy base. Foil can be moulded to fit the container, filled with a cooked stew, and the surplus foil brought together in the centre when the contents are semi-frozen, to make a compactly-shaped pack. The advantage of this is that if the frozen pack is held under warm running water for a short time, the foil can be peeled off and the frozen food fits neatly into the casserole for oven heating, or the saucepan for top-of-the-cooker heating. I also use foil freezer bags successfully for curries and stews. They are not cheap, and in my experience can only be used once. Then you must handle them adroitly as they tend to disintegrate if handled carelessly when lifted out of the saucepan after reheating.

NOTE: Sheet foil has another bonus; because it is so strong a narrow strip folded and placed under any item in a deep container helps you to lift it out by the protruding ends.

Shaped foil containers. These now come in many shapes and sizes. They are useful for freezing cooked dishes to be reheated in the oven. Some have covers supplied which must be removed before the containers are put in the oven. Foil pie plates, in which pastry can be frozen and then cooked, are also extremely handy. Sturdy shaped foil dishes can be sterilised in boiling water.

Waxed cartons. The original cartons which came with separate lids required to be taped round to be sealed, but the latest cartons are designed with self-closing tops. Allow a 10% headspace for expansion when freezing liquids in these cartons, and cool food, otherwise there may be a tendency for the wax to melt. Sizes range from 0·5–1 litre/1–1¾ pints.

Gussetted bags, polythene- and foil-lined. A pack which can make an almost square shape without the use of a pre-former. There is a space on which to write the contents, but the information could be altered if the pack is used a second time. With care, they may be re-usable and, as when using waxed cartons, food must be really cool before placing in a polythene-lined bag. Sealing is achieved by folding down the top over a long twist tie and folding the ends. Sizes range between 1–2 litres/1¾–3½ pints.

Aluminium boxes and glass jars. These are, after long experience, my least favourite containers although I do use them. Aluminium boxes have to be taped round completely, but they do conduct heat rapidly and freeze and thaw contents quickly. Jars with straight necks and screw tops are the best, but they should always be tested to see if they would shatter when reduced to a low temperature.
See *GLASS CONTAINERS.

Pyrosil. A toughened ceramic which withstands freezing, oven cooking or cooking over direct heat, straight from the freezer. Marvellous for a dinner party dish prepared a few days ahead to come smartly to the table.
See *LABELLING, *BAG SEALER, *ADHESIVE FREEZER TAPE, *HEAT SEALER.

NOTE: Re-using bought yogurt and cream cartons after the contents have been eaten can only be recommended if they are very thoroughly washed, rinsed and dried. In most cases a cap of foil smoothed very closely down the sides of the container gives a better seal than re-using a snap-on lid.

Above: A Bettafreez foil-lined bag.
Below: Thorpac waxed containers.

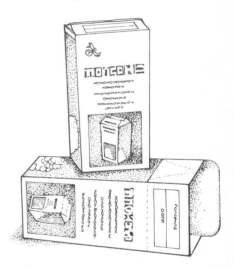

PACKED MEALS If some members of the family frequently take packed meals to school or to work, or on picnics, it is useful to have these prepared and labelled either with the contents or the name of the person for whom they are intended. Rigid-based containers are the most suitable, and the Tupperware Double Diner has a movable divider to provide two separate compartments. Cooked chicken portions, sausages, pasties and small meat pies are all popular. If including sandwiches, make them up into meal-sized packs, seal in cling film and place in the container. Other items for inclusion might be wedges of cake, jam tarts or mince pies, fruit or savoury flans, or cheese, also wrapped in cling film, or buttered scones, home-made biscuits and flapjacks and small cakes such as rock cakes. When the container is taken from the freezer it can be opened and a piece of fresh fruit or salad vegetables added to fill any spare corners. Chocolate biscuits in their bought wrappings can be placed in the pack before freezing to save time. Storage time 1 month. See *SANDWICHES.

PACKING FACE-TO-FACE A number of flat packs can be quickly assembled for freezing by placing a divider over the exposed surface of the food. A method of saving time and some packaging material when dealing with a number of small flat packs (*e.g. pies*). Open freeze, then place a divider over the exposed surface of one pack and reverse another on to it. Tape together to seal. One item only can be removed as required leaving the other sealed with the divider.

PACKING YOUR FREEZER Packing food into the freezer requires some expertise to make the best use of space, and the method depends largely upon your type of freezer.

Upright freezers usually have the least accessible shelf at the top which should be left for reserve supplies unless it is a tall model with only one door, in which case the top shelf may not be suitable for long-term storage. Shelves which form part of the evaporator system are immovable, and if those shelves which can be moved do not permit you to create a space large enough for big awkwardly shaped packs, the best place for these is usually at the bottom. Keep small packs on the shelves which are close together and do not pack them too closely. Small spaces between packs facilitate removal and permit air to circulate. Labels should be at the side of the pack so that they are easily visible. See *UPRIGHT FREEZER.

Chest freezers should be packed in three layers.

1. The bottom layer is best reserved for large containers such as coloured batching bags, polythene shopping bags or cardboard cartons each containing a number of packs intended for long-term storage and all clearly labelled on top with the contents. This is the place for your bulk supplies.

2. The middle layer should be occupied by numbered baskets or other containers with contents identified by colour and/or labels on top (*e.g. Basket 2, Cakes*). These baskets or containers are best kept for staple foods with a relatively long storage life, including a few packs of fresh meat, vegetables, and all your cooked dishes.

3. The top layer should consist of sliding baskets with a space left through which the middle layer is visible. They should contain foods with short storage life and those frequently required. These may vary according to your family catering pattern but might include bread and items for emergency meals (*e.g. pizzas*) which can quickly be cooked or reheated from the frozen state, or quickly defrosted (*e.g. sandwiches*), or eaten frozen (*e.g. ice cream*).

NOTE: Both upright and chest freezers can be fully equipped with made-to-measure Hamster storage baskets, which preclude the necessity for any other bulk containers. To economise on the purchase of baskets or to divide space to suit your needs, 'L' shaped freezer dividers could also be used.

PANCAKES All pancakes freeze well, especially those made from an enriched batter. Cool and freeze in piles with dividers, then seal in polythene bags. Thaw at room temperature for about 1 hour before reheating. Spread out on baking trays covered with foil in a hot oven or refry quickly, one at a time, in a very lightly oiled pan for about 30 seconds on each side.
Stuffed pancakes rolled round a savoury filling can be packed side-by-side in a shallow foil container, covered with sauce and stored ready to reheat from the frozen state with a sprinkling of grated cheese, or with toasted breadcrumbs and butter.
Layered pancakes can be built up with a savoury or sweet sauce between the layers but require to be defrosted for several hours at room temperature before reheating, or they may remain frozen in the centre. Serve cut into wedges.
Folded pancakes can be thinly spread with a sweet or savoury filling, folded in four and frozen overlapping in a shallow foil container with a complementary sauce. Reheat as for stuffed pancakes.

PARSNIP Creamy white root vegetable with a sweet flavour suitable for freezing blanched or as a cooked purée with butter. Storage time 10–12 months, as a purée 6–8 months.

See *VEGETABLE PREPARATION AND PACKING, *DEFROSTING.

PARTRIDGE Small game bird suitable for freezing. Season September to January. Storage time 6 months.
See *GAME, *DEFROSTING.

PASTA Cooked pasta is suitable for freezing on its own or layered with a rich sauce. Alternatively, the sauce should be put into the container and the pasta turned all at once into the centre, forcing the sauce up round it. This is easier than putting in the pasta first and trying to pour the filling round the outside.

The top layer of pasta exposed tends to dry out in freezing, so cover it with cling film. If reheating in the oven, replace this cover with foil and only remove to brown with a sprinkling of grated cheese or breadcrumbs and a little butter. If the pasta is to be frozen alone, make sure that it is only just cooked, rinse under cold running water after draining to prevent it from continuing to cook in its own heat and drain well again. Coat the strands with a little oil to keep them separate. Defrost by turning into fast boiling water, leave only until the water comes to the boil again, drain immediately and serve. Storage time plain cooked pasta 3 months.

PASTRY All pastries are suitable for freezing unbaked, baked and in the form of made-up dishes. Hot water crust is the only exception; it should not be frozen unbaked.

1. Shortcrust, flaky, rough puff and puff pastries can all be treated as follows:

Make up the pastry to your usual recipe and freeze unbaked. Shape quantities suitable for individual dishes into rolls or cubes, mould in foil or cling film and freeze. Do not attempt to freeze in large portions which will take a long time to thaw out and will not handle well. Defrost pastry in the refrigerator, only sufficiently to make it easy to roll out. Uncooked shapes for flans, pie lids, tarts, *vol au vent* cases, etc. may be open frozen then packed with dividers, if necessary in polythene containers to protect them from damage. Baked pastry items are fragile so should always be open frozen and packed for storage with care.

2. Hot water crust may be frozen baked in the form of pies but due to the high fat content it is only suitable for short-term storage, and hard-boiled eggs should be omitted from meat fillings. Storage time plain unbaked pastry 2–3 months, made-up pastry dishes baked or unbaked 4–6 months, baked hot water crust pies up to 1 month.
See *DEFROSTING, *DUMPLINGS, *CHOUX PASTRY, *FLANS, *PUDDINGS (sweet and savoury suet puddings).

PÂTÉS Fish, meat and poultry pâtés freeze extremely well and can be packed in various ways. For everyday use, a loaf shape is the most useful. Slices can be cut off as required, or the pâté can be chilled, cut into slices and repacked in shape with dividers so that portions can be easily removed in the frozen state. Or, the pâté can be packed in individual containers or ramekins ready to serve for parties. Large round dishes in which commercially-made pâtés are often sold are not as convenient for serving.

PEA Edible seed of a climbing plant, or in the case of the mangetout pea, the immature pod including the seeds. Peas are very good for freezing, blanched, for long-term storage and unblanched for short-term. Storage time, including mangetout, blanched 10–12 months, unblanched 3 months. See *VEGETABLE PREPARATION AND PACKING, *DEFROSTING, *GROWING GUIDE.

PEACH Stone fruit with downy skin, suitable for freezing in a sugar syrup pack or as purée. The flesh of peaches discolours when cut and exposed to the air, so prepare straight into sugar syrup or add ascorbic acid to pack. Storage time in sugar syrup pack 9–12 months, as purée 6–8 months.
See *FRUIT PREPARATION AND PACKING, *DISCOLORATION, *DEFROSTING.

PEAR Hard fruit, rounded but becoming smaller towards the stem end. Pears are suitable for freezing if poached in sugar syrup then drained and packed with the cold syrup. Or, as the flesh discolours when cut and exposed to the air, prepare straight into sugar syrup and add ascorbic acid. Pears can be frozen as part of a made-up dish or in recipes where the poaching liquid is well coloured (*e.g. with red wine*). Storage time in sugar syrup 9–12 months.
See *FRUIT PREPARATION AND PACKING, *DISCOLORATION, *DEFROSTING.

Preparing pears into sugar syrup and ascorbic acid, and packing with crumpled foil to keep them under the surface of the syrup.

Strawberry sorbet (page 166)

Strawberry Pavlova (page 165)

PECTIN A setting agent used in jams made with fruits which have a naturally low pectin content or for uncooked freezer jams. Over-ripe fruit is often low in pectin, which is available commercially in 240 ml/8 fl oz bottles. See *UNCOOKED FREEZER JAMS.

PEPPERS A species of capsicum of which the fruit is green or red. Large sweet peppers, and the red Spanish variety called pimientos, are quite mild in flavour and used as a vegetable, cooked or raw. (Pimientos are often green or yellow if unripe.) Small hot green or red peppers are used whole as a flavouring, then removed. Sweet peppers are suitable for freezing blanched, in cooked dishes and unblanched for short-term storage. The dried berries are used either whole (black pepper) or ground (white pepper). The flavour of hot peppers and dried berries tends to become stronger during frozen storage. Storage time blanched 10–12 months, unblanched 3 months.
See *VEGETABLE PREPARATION AND PACKING, *DEFROSTING.

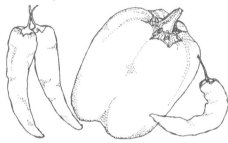

PERMEABILITY Some materials (*e.g. cellophane*) are permeable by vapours though not necessarily by liquids, and allow moisture and flavour to be drawn out through them from the food inside the pack. Such materials are unsuitable for freezer use.

Cell walls are permeable by the solutions inside the cells themselves and also the solutions between the cells. Damage to the texture of frozen food often results from cell walls with a delicate structure becoming completely permeable.
See *CELL DAMAGE (osmotic pressure).

PHEASANT Game bird suitable for freezing, which is traditionally served roasted and decorated with the tail feathers of the cock which should be reserved after plucking for this purpose. Season October to January. Storage time 6 months.
See *GAME, *DEFROSTING.

PIES Uncooked deep dish or double crust pastry pies are better packed without a steam vent as this allows dehydration of the filling. Cut a slit, or several if necessary, in the pastry when required to be cooked. Defrost and bake in a hot oven (220°C, 425°F, Gas Mark 7) allowing about 15–20 minutes extra baking time. This depends on the filling, which should be either uncooked raw fruit, or a savoury filling such as cooked meat or chicken in a thick sauce.
Baked pies should be defrosted before reheating as the long exposure to oven heat required to defrost and reheat tends to dry out the pastry. Storage time baked and unbaked 4–6 months. See *PASTRY.

PIGEON Small game bird which is more common and less expensive than others. Pigeons are best frozen cooked in casseroles and pies, or raw for roasting if they have plump breasts (the only part tender enough to eat when roasted). Season: Almost all year round; best August to October. Storage time 6 months.
See *GAME, *DEFROSTING.

PINEAPPLE Edible juicy fruit of a tropical plant. The pineapple is in fact a large collective fruit rising from a spike or head of flowers and crowned with spiky leaves. Pineapple is suitable for freezing sliced, diced or crushed on its own in dry sugar or sugar syrup pack. Storage time in sugar or sugar syrup pack 9–12 months, without sugar and crushed 6–8 months.
See *FRUIT PREPARATION AND PACKING, *DEFROSTING.

PIZZA An Italian dish with a basis of white bread dough and a savoury topping. Pizzas are excellent for freezing because they defrost and cook in a short space of time in a hot oven and make a convenient main meal or snack meal. Home-made pizzas should be baked complete with the topping, then open frozen, packed in polythene bags or individually wrapped. Reheat from frozen on baking trays in a hot oven (220°C, 425°F, Gas Mark 7) for 15–25 minutes depending on size. Storage time 3 months.

PLAICE Lean flat fish suitable for freezing raw whole or as fillets, coated in breadcrumbs or batter, or cooked in made-up dishes. Storage time 6 months, in breadcrumbs or batter 3 months.
See *FISH PREPARATION AND PACKING, *DEFROSTING.

PLATE FREEZING The first commercial method of quick freezing in which the prepacked food is kept in contact under pressure with plates behind which a refrigerating medium (generally ammonia) circulates. A typical freezing time would be about 1 hour.

PLATE MEALS Portions of cooked food with appropriate vegetables comprising a complete meal, frozen in shaped foil plates. Some are available made specially for the purpose with three separate sections. The food should be well spread out to fill the sections and planned so that it will all defrost and reheat in about the same time. The filled plate should be covered with foil well crimped over the edges and clearly labelled with the contents. The plates can be placed straight from the freezer into a moderately hot oven (200°C, 400°F, Gas Mark 6) for 30 minutes to defrost and reheat. Here are some suggestions.
1. Sliced roast meat covered with gravy, blanched Brussels sprouts, lightly boiled new potatoes. Place a small nut of butter on the potatoes and on the sprouts.
2. Baked fillet of white fish covered with cheese sauce, creamy mashed potatoes and green peas. Place a small nut of butter and some chopped mint on the peas.
3. Casserole of ox or lambs' kidneys, cooked rice and sliced blanched carrots. Place a small nut of butter and a little chopped parsley on the carrots.
4. Boned and sliced cooked chicken covered with gravy, cooked noodles and chopped spinach. Place a small nut of butter on the noodles and sprinkle with Parmesan cheese. Storage time 4–6 months.
NOTE: It is inadvisable to add stuffing to poultry, or any single item (*e.g. whole chicken drumsticks*) which would take longer to defrost and reheat than the rest of the meal.

PLUM Stone fruit of the same family as the cherry but with an oval shape and an oval stone. There are many varieties – red, yellow and purple. Plums are suitable for freezing halved and with the stones removed in dry sugar or sugar syrup pack and as a cooked purée. The flesh discolours when cut and exposed to the air but this is only a problem with the light coloured varieties – discoloration is masked when red or purple plums are cooked. Prepare plums straight into a sugar syrup or add ascorbic acid to the pack. Storage time in sugar or sugar syrup pack 9–12 months, as purée 6–8 months.
See *FRUIT PREPARATION AND PACKING, *DISCOLORATION, *DEFROSTING.

POLYTHENE All transparent plastic food wraps and bags are referred to as polythene but in fact they are made of various materials. Most are either made of polyethylene (PE) or polyvinylchloride (PVC). Cling film is made of polyvinylidene chloride (PVDC). Some sheet wraps have excellent self-cling properties. Heavy gauge cling film (sometimes described as double thickness) gives longer protection than light gauge.

PORK A whole pig makes a large bulk purchase, and as pork does not have as long a storage life as other meats, a side is probably as much as the average family will require at one time. It provides a good selection of roasting, grilling and frying cuts, but with more waste than lamb. Cuts which are used for stewing from other animals can be used for roasting (*e.g. belly*). Like beef, large packs of preferred cuts are available at a slight reduction per kg/lb, or single items (*e.g. legs*) usually sold divided into two or three roasting joints, at an economy price. As the cuts are known by different names in various parts of the country, the following guide to bulk buying pork is given with some alternative names although these do not pretend to cover all local variations.

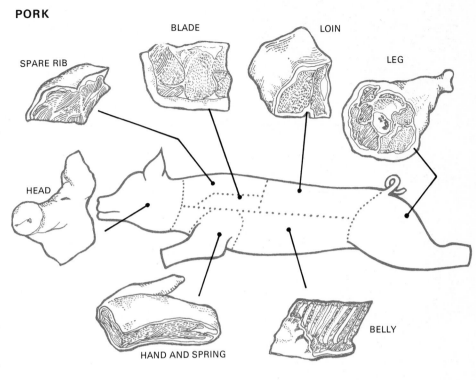

PORK

SPARE RIB
BLADE
LOIN
LEG
HEAD
HAND AND SPRING
BELLY

Cuts included	Possible alternative names	Preparation	Suitable cooking method
Leg – fillet end	Gammon	Joint on bone or boned for stuffing, slices	Roasting, frying
– knuckle end	Gigot	Joint on bone or boned for stuffing	Roasting
Loin	Middle	Joints on bone or boned and rolled, chump and middle loin chops, loin cutlets	Roasting, grilling
Tenderloin	Fillet	Whole or sliced (in small pigs left attached to loin)	Grilling, frying
Blade	Back rib	Joints on bone or boned for stuffing, cubes	Roasting, stewing and in pies
Spare rib	Back rib	Joints on bone or boned for stuffing, cutlets, cubes	Roasting, stewing and in pies
Belly	Flank	Joint (lean end), slices, mince	Roasting, grilling and minced in terrines and pâtés
Hand and spring	Fore shoulder	Joints (hand and shank ends), on the bone or boned for stuffing, cubes	Slow roasting, stewing; can be pickled for boiling
Head		Best chopped in two or three pieces	Boiling (brawn)

SIDE OF PORK
Approximate weight: 18–27 kg/40–60 lb
Percentage of bone and fat to be expected: 25–30%

POTATO Root vegetable with white flesh and brown papery skin. A less well-known variety is the sweet potato with yellower flesh and harder skin. Potatoes are suitable for freezing blanched in water or fat for frying, roasted, creamed as duchesse potato for piping or as croquettes. Piped potato rosettes can be frozen on a baking tray then loosened with a warm spatula and packed in bags. Storage time 4–6 months.
See *VEGETABLE PREPARATION AND PACKING, *DEFROSTING.
NOTE: Small new potatoes may be almost fully cooked by boiling in lightly salted water and frozen whole with chopped mint and a little melted butter. They can then be defrosted and reheated without adding any water.

POULTRY Chicken, duck, turkey and goose are all freezable and dealt with under their specific headings. The instructions for packing poultry differ according to whether the bird is to be frozen whole, halved or in portions.
1. To freeze whole, clean the bird, tie the legs together with string, press the wings close to the body. The leg bones which protrude may puncture the wrapping, so pad them with caps of foil or greaseproof paper. The prepared bird can be moulded in foil or cling film, or packed in a gussetted polythene bag.
2. To freeze in halves, which saves freezer space, lay the bird on one side, and cut from the neck to the tail, as closely as possible along both sides of the backbone. Take out the neck and backbone. Lay the bird on its breast, pull it open and cut along the inside of the breastbone. Pack the halves together, dividing them with foil or separately. The giblets can be frozen in bags, but it is more sensible to make strong stock from them for freezing, with the exception of the livers, which can be used for pâté.
3. To freeze in portions, joint carefully and make stock from the carcases

and trimmings, rather than cut the bird in four with poultry scissors. Ready-frozen portions are properly jointed, and suppliers of frozen food will do so on request. After jointing, wash the portions and dry them. The easiest way to protect portions is to mould them individually in foil or cling film, and pack all together in a large polythene container.
NOTE: If you are killing your own poultry, starve the birds for 24 hours before killing but give them plenty of water to drink. They should be plucked immediately after killing while they are still warm. It is easier to pluck ducks or geese if they are plunged into boiling water for 2–3 minutes. The birds should then be hung by the feet in a cool place for at least 24 hours. Heavier birds, i.e. over 2·25 kg/5 lb, can be hung for 48 hours for a more mature flavour.

POWER CUTS It is possible that your freezer will be disconnected at some time by an electrical power cut, but most unlikely that this will last long enough to damage your stock of frozen food. Seek information on how long the cut is likely to last – if the worst happens, your insurance should cover the loss, but it may exclude power cuts due to such causes as industrial disputes.
See *EMERGENCIES, *INSURANCE.

PRAWN Small crustacean which is suitable for freezing, if very fresh, raw or cooked, with or without its shell. Prawns can also be frozen as part of a made-up dish. Storage time raw 1 month, cooked 3 months.
See *FISH PREPARATION AND PACKING, *DEFROSTING.

PRE-FORMED 'BRICKS' To pack a king-size casserole in three equal portions (or in two large portions and two small ones), line a large roasting tin with foil. Pour in the stew when it is cool, making sure that the foil comes just above the level of the stew, and place in the freezer until partially frozen. Remove the pack from the pan which has been used as the pre-former, divide the stew into three portions with a large serrated knife and, if liked, the third portion into two small ones. Wrap each separately in cling film or foil.

NOTE: It is often convenient to freeze a small portion of cooked food to serve just two members of the family, although the usual meal-sized portion is to serve four.

PRE-FORMED PACKS Food can often be stored in convenient shapes for stacking, and also to replace in useful dishes for eventual serving, by lining the container with a gussetted polythene bag, cling film or foil.

1. To make handy square or oblong packs, line a sugar carton and pour in the food, which should be cold, allowing a small headspace. Freeze, remove bag or shape from pre-former and seal. The food can easily be removed from the pack if it is held for a few seconds under running water.

2. Food you wish to serve in a dish which is too useful to be banished to the freezer can be frozen inside the dish lined with foil. Allow sufficient extra foil when lining the dish to bring in and crimp together to seal after freezing. Remove the shaped pack from the dish for storage. When the pack is removed from the freezer, peel off the foil and place in the serving dish. This is particularly useful for cooked casseroles.

PRESSURE BLANCHING A method which can be used for blanching vegetables. Follow the chart given here, remembering that pressure must be quickly reduced and the lid removed, or the vegetables will be overcooked. Most other vegetables require between 1 and 2 minutes to pressure blanch.

Vegetable	Blanching time (minutes)
Artichokes	1
Asparagus	To pressure only
Broad beans	1
French/Runner beans	To pressure only
Beetroot – small (fully cooked)	10
Broccoli	1
Brussels sprouts – small	1
Carrots	2
Cauliflower florets	1
Celery – cut	1
Leeks	1
Parsnips	1
Peas	1
Potatoes – new	2
Spinach	To pressure only
Swede – diced	1
Sweet corn	2
Turnips – diced	2

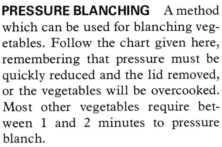

1. Put trivet into pressure cooker and add 600 ml/1 pint boiling water.
2. Fill cooker with prepared vegetables no more than two-thirds full.
3. Bring to high pressure (15 lb), allow blanching time according to chart, reduce pressure and remove cover. Lift out vegetables with a slotted draining spoon, cool and pack.

PRESSURE COOKING For dishes which require long cooking, especially steamed puddings, the pressure cooker can be used to save time. Here are the special instructions for defrosting and cooking, or defrosting and reheating, medium-sized (scant 1-litre/1½-pint basin) sponge and suet puddings from the frozen state.

1. Sponge puddings frozen uncooked should be covered with double greaseproof paper. (If using foil, cook for a further 5 minutes at pressure.) Follow manufacturer's instructions but add an extra 150 ml/¼ pint water to cooker. Stand pudding on trivet and steam for an extra 10 minutes. Bring to low pressure and cook for an extra 10 minutes. Reduce pressure at room temperature.

2. Sponge puddings frozen cooked should be covered as above. Add an extra 450 ml/¾ pint water to cooker, stand pudding on trivet and bring to high pressure. Cook for 25 minutes and reduce pressure with cold water.

3. Suet puddings frozen uncooked (except those with a raw savoury filling) should be covered as above. Add an extra 150 ml/¼ pint water to cooker, stand pudding on trivet and steam for an extra 15 minutes. Bring to low pressure and cook for an extra 10–15 minutes, depending on type of pudding. Reduce pressure at room temperature.

See *PUDDINGS.

PUDDINGS Sponge puddings and suet puddings freeze well, cooked or uncooked, but milk puddings (*e.g. semolina*) and custard puddings (*e.g. Queen of puddings*) or any others with a high milk content, tend to separate. Rich rice puddings to be served either hot or cold (*e.g. rice imperatrice*) are quite satisfactory and so are sweet pasta puddings (*e.g. noodle kugel*). Providing the proportion of milk, and therefore of water, is low, there is no problem.

Sponge puddings can be frozen cooked or uncooked. The measured amount of mixture for the pudding should be turned into a greased vinyl-lined pudding basin, boilable plastic or china basin (if you can part with these). Cover ready for cooking and freeze. To serve, cook from the frozen state allowing 30 minutes extra boiling or steaming time for the mixture to defrost, or use a pressure cooker.

Summer puddings should be completely defrosted in the refrigerator overnight and turned out in the usual way.

Sweet suet puddings can be frozen cooked or uncooked. The pudding should be made up in the usual way. Allow 45 minutes additional boiling or steaming time for the mixture to defrost. Puddings frozen raw can also be cooked from the frozen state in a pressure cooker.

Savoury suet puddings should always be frozen either completely cooked or with a cooked filling inside raw pastry. Allow 45 minutes additional boiling or steaming time for the mixture to defrost. As with sweet puddings, raw savoury puddings can be cooked from frozen in a pressure cooker.

Roly poly puddings, made of suet pastry, both sweet and savoury, can be fully prepared and frozen, then cooked in the oven from the frozen state, uncovered. Increase usual baking time by 15 minutes. To reheat cooked and frozen roly poly puddings, increase baking time by 10 minutes. Storage time sponge or suet puddings 4–6 months.

See *PRESSURE COOKING.

HELPFUL HINT: Eve's pudding can be prepared in a large shaped foil container with raw fruit under the

sponge mixture, sealed and frozen. To cook, remove the cover and bake from the frozen state allowing 30 minutes extra cooking time.

PUMPERNICKEL Coarse and sour-tasting bread made with wholemeal rye flour suitable for freezing, combined with various fillings, as sandwiches. Storage time as sandwiches 4 months.
See *SANDWICHES, *DEFROSTING.

PUMPKIN Fruit of a creeping plant of the gourd family, of which the flesh is suitable for freezing in the form of cooked purée, or in made-up dishes such as sweet pie fillings or savoury soups. Storage time 10–12 months.
See *VEGETABLE PREPARATION AND PACKING, *DEFROSTING.

PUNCH LABELS   See *LABELLING.

PURÉES Many foods can be reduced to a purée which occupies little space in the freezer and can be increased in volume by the addition of liquid after thawing (*e.g. soups*). Freezing purées of suitable foods (*e.g. fruit, vegetables*) makes good sense because it eliminates a messy stage of preparation when time is often precious, just before serving, as well as saving space. NOTE: Many fruits with pips or seeds make a rather gritty purée in an electric blender, but are tiresome to sieve. It is worth using the blender first then quickly passing the purée through a sieve to remove the pips. Fruit often needs no cooking but can be reduced to a raw purée. To make a smooth sweetened purée use icing rather than castor or granulated sugar.

QUICK FREEZING The zone of maximum ice formation (for most products between –1°C and –5°C/30°F and 23°F) is passed through extremely quickly and the temperature finally reduced to and then maintained at –18°C/0°F or colder. This cannot be achieved by domestic food freezers but is achieved industrially.
See *PLATE FREEZING, *BLAST FREEZING, *IMMERSION FREEZING.

RABBIT Small furred game which does not require to be hung before freezing. Domestic rabbits bred for the table have a very delicate flavour similar to chicken. Storage time 3 months.
See *GAME, *DEFROSTING.

RANCIDITY A condition caused by exposure of fat to air, allowing the surface to become desiccated by dehydration and oxygen to penetrate the food tissues. After defrosting, it is recognisable by an unpleasant stale smell or taste. The presence of salt in the fat speeds up rancidity.
See *OXIDATION.

RASPBERRY Soft berry fruit of a plant which bears the fruit on canes. Suitable for freezing in dry pack, dry sugar pack or as purée. Also suitable for making uncooked freezer jam. Storage time in dry sugar pack 9–12 months, dry without sugar and as purée 6–8 months.
See *FRUIT PREPARATION AND PACKING, *UNCOOKED FREEZER JAMS, *DEFROSTING.

Using the seal of the container to cut out shapes of foil for dividers.

REDCURRANT See *CURRANTS.

REFREEZING There is a great deal of doubt in many minds about the safety of refreezing food which has already been frozen once and partially or completely thawed. Whether or not to refreeze depends entirely on the circumstances and extent of thawing. The following guide lines may prove useful.

1. Foods (*e.g. ice cream*), which lose their consistency completely when thawed, will obviously not be suitable for refreezing.

2. Foods which have been exposed to a hot atmosphere for a considerable time after being fully thawed, would be as suspect as fresh food exposed to contamination and deterioration in these circumstances, but there is an added danger – bacteria do multiply more quickly in food after it has been frozen than before.

3. Food which has thawed in the refrigerator and thus never reached the temperature at which bacterial activity is intense, will probably be quite *safe* to refreeze providing the texture and appearance have not suffered.

4. Food which has thawed, covered, has at least not been exposed to additional contamination and is more suitable for refreezing than food which has been thawed uncovered.

5. For the most rigid adherence to safety rules, it is preferable that some ice crystals should remain in the food.

Scientific safety. No mysterious change of a chemical nature occurs when frozen food thaws, making it necessary either to eat it at once or to throw it away.

See *CONTAMINATION, *HYGIENE.

REFRIGERATOR/FREEZER Where available floor space is small, both appliances can be accommodated by

stacking. This may be achieved by buying a single appliance described as a refrigerator/freezer, or by buying a matching refrigerator and freezer made by the same manufacturer, who also supplies a stacking unit. The refrigerator is usually mounted above the freezer for easy access.

See *BUYING A FREEZER.

REHEATING There are several ways of reheating cooked foods, both from the frozen state and after thawing.

1. In the freezing container, by oven heat.

2. In the case of solid foods, placed either wrapped or unwrapped on a baking tray, by oven heat.

3. Turned out into a saucepan, by direct heat.

4. Turned out into a double boiler.

5. Unwrapped and cooked under the grill.

If time permits and the texture of the food will not be harmed, it is always safer to thaw slowly in the refrigerator, where temperatures never reach the zone of intense bacterial activity, and reheat when fully thawed. Quick thawing at room temperature involves exposing food to renewed bacterial activity for a period which is often difficult to calculate. Reheating direct from frozen lessens any such risk providing the food is thawed as speedily as possible, quickly brought to a temperature high enough to destroy harmful organisms and held there for at least 10 minutes. In any case it is never wise merely to warm cooked food which has been prepared some time previously.

REMOVALS Before moving, check that the plug of your freezer will fit the new socket and if necessary be ready to change it. If the move is likely to take less than 12 hours it should be possible to move the freezer with its contents intact. First check with the removers and make sure that they can handle the loaded weight. If this is no problem set the fast freeze switch 24

Crab bisque with avocado (page 242); Crab mousse (page 182)

Turkey in cream sauce with grapes (page 167)

Turkey salamagundy (page 167)

Turkey, ham and mushroom pie (page 168)

hours before the move, lock if possible and make sure that the lid or door(s) cannot be opened by accident. Ensure that the freezer is the last item to be loaded and the first to be put into the new house where it should be connected at once.

If the removers are unable to manage the loaded freezer try to reduce stocks as far as possible, sort out the freezer and defrost it just before moving day. Order dry ice and, at the last possible moment, pack the food into insulated bags or into tea chests with some well-protected dry ice. Unload the freezer and food immediately on arrival. Connect the freezer, check that it is functioning properly, leave on fast freeze and return the food to it as quickly as possible.

When the move is likely to take several days it is advisable to reduce the stock completely or sell the freezer with the house, otherwise it will be necessary to hire cold storage space.

If you are likely to have to move frequently it is much better to buy your freezer from the Electricity Board or an organisation such as the Co-op with retail outlets and service facilities throughout the country, whom you may call on in an emergency.

RHUBARB The edible stalks of a plant which grow from a crown. (The leaves themselves are poisonous.) Rhubarb is suitable for freezing blanched, in sugar syrup pack, in uncooked freezer jam or in made-up dishes. Blanching is necessary because rhubarb is the stalk of the plant, not the fruit. Do not use metal containers for any prepared dish with rhubarb, which is very acid. Storage time in sugar syrup pack 9–12 months. See *FRUIT PREPARATION AND PACKING, *UNCOOKED FREEZER JAMS, *DEFROSTING.

RICE Contrary to old-fashioned misconceptions, cooked rice on its own or in made-up dishes freezes extremely well. It should be cooked by your pre-ferred method until only just tender and the grains well separated. Place in polythene bags when completely cold and seal close to the surface allowing no appreciable headspace. Rice can be reheated for serving in three ways.

1. Turn from the bag while still frozen into a saucepan of boiling, lightly salted water. Bring back to the boil, breaking up gently, and immediately strain through a colander. Place the colander over the empty saucepan and cover the rice with the saucepan lid. After 1 minute, shake gently to fluff up the rice.

2. Allow the bag of rice to defrost at room temperature for 1 hour. Turn into a non-stick saucepan, add 1 tablespoon water and cover the pan. Place over moderate heat, shaking gently occasionally, for about 5 minutes. A little more water may be necessary if the rice can absorb it without becoming sticky.

3. Defrost the rice as above, spread out in a shallow ovenproof dish, dot with butter, cover with foil and reheat in a moderate oven (160°C, 325°F, Gas Mark 3) for 20 minutes. This is an ideal method if you are using the oven for the main dish.

4. Made-up dishes (*e.g. risotto*) should be defrosted and reheated, covered either by methods 2 or 3 above. Storage time plain cooked rice 4–6 months, in made-up dishes 3 months.

ROASTING MEAT Joints can be thawed slowly overnight in the refrigerator (for very large joints, at room temperature) and then roasted in the usual way. Meat thawed slowly is generally considered to be juicier than if thawed rapidly. This is because there is a longer period in which the juices withdrawn from the tissues during freezing, usually called 'drip loss', can be reabsorbed. 'Drip loss' can be entirely avoided by roasting joints and grilling small cuts such as steaks and chops from the frozen state. Roasting from frozen is expensive unless you can fully utilise the oven space.

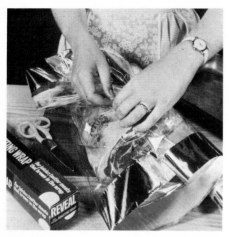

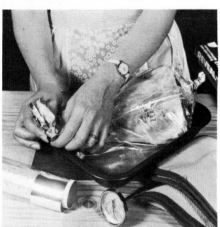

Roasting meat from the frozen state
BEEF
Prime roasting cuts. Weigh joint, preheat oven to moderately hot (200°C, 400°F, Gas Mark 6), place joint in a roasting tin in the oven for 10 minutes to seal the meat. Cover with a dome of foil, reduce temperature to moderate, (180°C, 350°F, Gas Mark 4) and allow 1 hour per 450 g/1 lb from this point. Towards the end of cooking time, insert a meat thermometer to the centre of the joint, check from then onwards every 10 minutes until temperature reaches 60°C/140°F for rare, 68°C/155°F for medium and 77°C/170°F for well done.

Medium roasting cuts. Weigh joint, preheat oven to moderate (180°C, 350°F, Gas Mark 4), place joint in dimpled roaster or roasting bag and roast for 1 hour per 450 g/1 lb. Towards the end of cooking time, insert a meat thermometer to the centre of the joint, if necessary plunging through the bag above the level of the juices. Check from then onwards as above.

LAMB
Weigh joint, preheat oven to moderate (160°C, 325°F, Gas Mark 3), place joint in roasting tin and cover with a dome of foil. Allow 45 minutes per 450 g/1 lb. About 45 minutes before you expect the joint to be cooked, insert a meat thermometer and remove foil. Continue roasting until temperature reaches 82°C/180°F. For those who like lamb slightly pink, 77°C/170°F.

PORK
Joints required with crackling. Weigh joint, preheat oven to moderately hot (200°C, 400°F, Gas Mark 6), place joint in roasting tin in oven for 20 minutes. Cover with a dome of foil and proceed as for beef prime cuts until thermometer registers 88°C/190°F.

Joints from which skin has been removed. Proceed as for beef prime cuts until thermometer registers 88°C/190°F.

Small joints. Those weighing less than 1·5 kg/3 lb are not very satisfactory, but do require cooking by the same calculation of 1 hour per 450 g/1 lb as for large joints. The criterion should always be the temperature of the joint, which is why it is advisable to start checking the temperature 45 minutes to 1 hour before you expect the joint to be done.

ROASTING WRAPS Bags made from polyester film or foil-edged sheet wrapping which withstands oven heat as well as being moisture-vapour-proof at low temperatures. The foil edges on the sheet wrapping can be crimped together to make an airtight pack. Food sealed in bags made of this material can be defrosted and reheated or defrosted and cooked in boiling water or exposed to direct oven heat providing the temperature does not exceed 200°C (400°F, Gas Mark 6). The material has a tendency to melt at very high oven temperatures. The advantage is that all juices are retained within the pack and the contents, especially meat, remain moist and tender. Joints can be roasted from frozen enclosed in these bags or in sheet wrapping and the following chart is recommended:

Minutes per 450 g/1 lb – oven setting 190°C, 375°F, Gas Mark 5

	over 2 kg/4½ lb	under 2 kg/4½ lb
Beef		
choice cuts	40	45
second quality cuts	45	50
Lamb	45	50
Pork	55	60
Veal	45	50

Poultry must be fully defrosted before cooking and is therefore not included in the chart. Spread the breast with a little softened butter before sealing it into the bag or wrap to prevent the skin from sticking to the material while cooking.

HELPFUL HINTS: After cooking, open the pack or slit the bag as soon as possible and pour off and reserve the juices to prevent steam from making the surface of the food soggy. Use the juices to make gravy. There is no need to snip the corner off the bag (sometimes recommended to accommodate the expansion of hot air inside the pack), but there is no harm in piercing the wrap by inserting a meat thermometer above the level of the juices. If surplus air is excluded when the pack is made, there is no danger of the wrap bursting during cooking.

ROLLAWAY FREEZERS Heavy or awkwardly sited freezers are mounted on castors to make opening them easier. A small chest model may actually fit under a working surface, and can be pulled out to open and close the lid. This makes it possible to have a chest freezer without sacrificing any working surface against the wall, in a small kitchen or pantry. A pair of rollers can be fitted to an existing freezer. They do not damage the floor having three sets of wheels to distribute the weight and a safety brake which makes it easy to control even a heavy freezer when you pull it away from the wall. They can be adjusted from 53 cm/21 inches to 80 cm/32 inches and will move 455 kg/1,000 lb. One wing nut locks the rollers at the correct length for your freezer. There is also a smaller size suitable for freezers weighing up to 272 kg/600 lb.

RUNNING COSTS Since maintenance costs little, the main expense connected with running your freezer is its consumption of electricity. Estimates vary from 1½ to as high as 4 units per 28·3 litres/1 cubic foot per week. To keep this cost as low as possible remember that the number of times a day you open the freezer affects the consumption, especially if it is sited in a warm kitchen, and the amount of electricity used may vary at different times of the year. Obviously if you keep a preponderance of short storage items and frequently freeze down fresh food this may increase the running cost.
See *ECONOMY.

SAFETY Like other pieces of electrical domestic equipment, the freezer must conform to certain safety rules. It must, by law, be connected to an earthed socket in a suitable electrical system. The wires are coloured in accordance with the following code and should be connected to the corresponding terminals in the plug.

Green and yellow Earth (E)
Blue Neutral (N)
Brown Live (L)

NOTE: If you own a disused freezer (or refrigerator) keep it safely locked, or remove the lid or doors. A child or pet might accidentally be trapped and suffocate.

SALADS Green salad vegetables and tomatoes do not freeze well in the raw state because of their high water content. Rice or pasta salads with such ingredients as cooked peas, raw mild onion, chopped sweet peppers and French dressing freeze fairly well. Fresh fruit salads freeze well in a syrup pack. Storage time rice or pasta salads 2 months, fresh fruit 10–12 months.

SALMON Oily round fish suitable for freezing raw whole or if large enough as steaks, and as part of made-up dishes. Storage time 3–4 months.

See *FISH PREPARATION AND PACKING, *DEFROSTING.

SALMON TROUT Oily round fish suitable for freezing raw whole or if big enough as steaks, and as part of made-up dishes. Commercially frozen pink trout now available as small whole fish (around 1 kg/2-2¼ lb) have the same texture and flavour as salmon trout. Storage time 3–4 months.

See *FISH PREPARATION AND PACKING, *DEFROSTING.

SANDWICHES Most families require a regular supply of sandwiches or at least some for special occasions such as summer picnics or entertaining. All kinds of sandwiches freeze well for short periods providing the filling is suitable. Hard-boiled eggs and moist salad vegetables, or mixtures including a high proportion of mayonnaise, are not suitable. Sandwiches can be made from white, brown, wholemeal or fancy continental breads. The bread should be spread out to the edges with softened butter or margarine to prevent the filling from sinking into the bread as the sandwiches thaw. Prepare in bulk. For sandwich meals, make up mixed packs with dividers to prevent cross-flavouring. Sandwiches with strongly

flavoured fillings should be separately wrapped in freezer film. This is especially important if the sandwiches are to be made up in lunch boxes with other frozen foods (*e.g. rock cakes*). Label sandwich packs clearly with the contents to make sure that anyone who removes a pack chooses one with fillings he or she will enjoy. All sandwiches defrost within 1 hour if spread out, or 2–4 hours if in a pack.

Fancy sandwiches include pinwheel, club and chessboard varieties. All are better frozen uncut and sliced when partly defrosted for serving. A whole sandwich loaf can be assembled, complete with cream cheese frosting, and frozen like a cake.

Open sandwiches are better piped with softened cream cheese for decoration than with mayonnaise. Open freeze for 30 minutes only, then pack in layers with dividers covering the top layer with cling film, but preferably in a shallow container with no more than two layers. Unwrap while still frozen and defrost at room temperature.

Toasted open sandwiches should be made with bread lightly toasted on one side only and spread on the other with well seasoned savoury mixture (*e.g. cheese sauce sprinkled with crumbled cooked bacon*). Cool, open freeze for 30 minutes only, then pack in foil or cling film. Unwrap while still frozen and place under a hot grill to defrost and complete cooking.

Fried sandwiches are made in the usual way with processed cheese or some other cheese which melts easily as part of the filling. Wrap as for toasted sandwiches. Shallow fry from the frozen state in a mixture of butter and oil until golden brown on both sides. Storage time 4 months.

See *PACKED MEALS.

SARDINE Small oily round fish of the same family as herring, only available in cans or imported from Mediterranean waters. Fresh sardines, frozen, are available commercially in 450 g/1 lb packs.

SAUCES All the following sauces freeze well. Basic sauces are always in demand and if made in quantity some can be divided to produce a number of classic variations.

Savoury sauces
1. White (béchamel) sauce – cheese, parsley, shrimp or prawn, caper, mushroom, anchovy; and such French sauces as *suprême*, *aurore* and *soubise*.
2. Brown (espagnole) sauce – Reform, piquant, and such classic French sauces as *bigarade* and *Robert*.
3. Tomato sauce – such classic Italian sauces as *Milanese* and *bolognese*.
4. Spicy sauces such as curry, barbecue and mustard.

Mayonnaise and hollandaise sauce do not freeze well.

Sweet sauces
These may be made to serve hot or cold. Many rich sweet sauces remain slightly viscous at low temperatures because of the high sugar content.
1. Sweet white sauce – vanilla, coffee, chocolate, butterscotch. By adding other essences and the appropriate food colourings (very sparingly) you can make lemon, orange, almond, raspberry, strawberry, banana, coconut, brandy or rum.
2. Rich sweet sauces (not based on cornflour and milk) – chocolate, butterscotch, caramel.
3. Fruit sauces (based on fruit purées) – raspberry, blackcurrant, strawberry, plum, damson, etc.
4. Hard sauces – brandy, rum and Cumberland butters.

SAUSAGE PRODUCTS Fresh sausage meat and sausages which contain a high fat content and seasoning freeze successfully for short-term storage only. A great variety of cooked sausage products (delicatessen, charcuterie) also freeze well. Those which are unsmoked (*e.g. liver sausage*) store better than smoked (*e.g. salami*). Because of their short storage life, sausage stuffings, like savoury rice stuffings,

should not be put inside poultry or boned joints as this reduces the storage life of the meat to that of the stuffing. Storage time raw 12 months, cooked 3 months, sausage stuffings 2 months.
See *DEFROSTING.
HELPFUL HINT: sausages can be fried or grilled from the frozen state, therefore it is time-saving to freeze them with concertina dividers so that a quantity can quickly be removed from the pack.

SCALLOP Hinged mollusc with white flesh and coral coloured roe which freezes well raw if very fresh for short storage out of the shell. Scallops can also be frozen cooked as part of a made-up dish and are available commercially frozen without the shells. Storage time 1–2 months.
See *FISH PREPARATION AND PACKING, *DEFROSTING.
NOTE: The deep scallop shells can be scrubbed clean and sterilised by boiling for use as freezer containers for made-up fish dishes. These can be reheated straight from the freezer and can then appear on the table. Fish and

shell-fish mixtures in rich sauces, piped with potato and open frozen, need only be covered with moulded foil or cling film which is removed before the filled shells go into the oven or under the grill.

SCAMPI/DUBLIN BAY PRAWNS
Largest of the small crustaceans which are suitable for freezing if very fresh, raw or cooked, shelled or unshelled. They can also be frozen as part of a made-up dish. Storage time raw 1 month, cooked 3 months.
See *FISH PREPARATION AND PACKING, *DEFROSTING.

SEASONAL PLANS
At different times of the year, most freezer owners find they wish to devote time to preparing special products for freezing and will allow space in the freezer to accommodate them.
Spring. Eggs, including pullets' eggs, become plentiful and this is the time to make fruit curds, meringue baskets, mousses, sponge sandwich layers, sponge puddings and pancakes. Poultry from the farm may include spring chickens and pullets at a reasonable price. Try to make barbecue sauce and a good supply of sandwiches ready for picnics.
Summer. Soft fruit is in abundance and can be bought cheaply if a freak of the weather provides a glut. Store it on its own in dry sugar, or sugar syrup pack, as purée sauce and uncooked jam to last the whole year through. Also take advantage of an overflowing market to make fruit and vegetable chutneys, relishes and sauces which require freezer rather than pantry storage. Fish and shellfish are available in great variety, and as well as being good in made-up dishes, combine with avocados and other freezables to make light cold dishes (*e.g. crab and avocado mousse*).
Autumn. Vegetables are at their peak, another freezable of which you can pack a year's supply. Tomatoes are really in season and the late ones are

good for tomato sauce, tomato curd and uncooked chutneys. Furred and feathered game appears on the scene and country dwellers may have enough to freeze some down.
Winter. This is the time to make concentrated soups and vegetable purées, as root vegetables come into their own. Use them also in economical meat stews and casserole dishes. With poultry becoming more expensive towards Christmas, meat may be a better bargain. Most housewives reserve freezer space to cook ahead for Christmas, and a little for the abundance of citrus fruits coming early in the New Year to store in dry sugar or sugar syrup pack, as juice, grated zest or even whole bitter oranges for preserve making later.

SEASONING
See *HERBS, *SPICES.

SECONDHAND FREEZERS
As you are unlikely to receive any kind of enforceable guarantee from the vendor, this is very much a matter of luck if you buy privately. A reconditioned freezer from a firm which specialises in supplying secondhand domestic equipment should have a specific guarantee, however limited. In either case, the arrangement of future service is important, otherwise you will have nowhere to turn if the freezer breaks down unless you take out a service insurance contract at the time you buy it. Perhaps more satisfactory is the deal you get from a firm such as Buyers and Sellers Ltd. of London. They specialise in shop-soiled and blemished freezers, usually only scratched or dented, sold at prices considerably lower than the recommended retail price. In every case the damage is only superficial, and the machine is in working order complete with manufacturer's guarantee of sale. You should visit the company's premises to choose from current stock. They deliver anywhere in the country, but purchasers living at a distance have to pay a delivery charge.

SEVILLE ORANGE See *ORANGE, *CITRUS FRUIT, *DEFROSTING.

SHELVES Only available in upright freezers and some which form part of the evaporator system are always immovable. The other shelves can usually be rearranged to give deep storage space where required. Some shelves are fitted with spring loaded front flaps or slot-in pack retainers. See *UPRIGHT FREEZER.
NOTE: If you try to shut the door without returning the pack retainer to position you may damage the freezer, or, you may think you have shut the door and when you turn away from it the magnetic seal is unable to hold the door closed. Make sure you always return pack retainers to their slots after use.

SHERBETS Frozen desserts made with milk, or a mixture of milk and single cream, with fruit juice, sometimes including gelatine or beaten egg whites. They are less rich than ice creams but more satisfying than sorbets and have a relatively long freezer storage life. Storage time 3 months.

SHRIMP Tiny crustacean which is suitable for freezing if very fresh or cooked, shelled or unshelled. Shrimps can also be frozen as part of a made-up dish, or potted and covered with a layer of melted butter. Storage time raw 1 month, cooked 3 months.
See *FISH PREPARATION AND PACKING, *DEFROSTING.

SIEVES Nylon and metal sieves can be used when preparing food for the freezer but they must be washed with great care as any trace of food adhering to the mesh may harbour bacteria. Metal sieves should not be used for acid foods. If sieving food intended for babies, place the sieve beforehand in a solution made with sterilising tablets.

SKATE Lean flat fish suitable for freezing raw in portions as 'wings' on the bone, or in made-up dishes. Storage time 6 months.
See *FISH PREPARATION AND PACKING, *DEFROSTING.

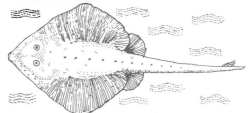

SLICED COOKED MEATS Providing the meat is not dry when sliced, it will store well even packed without dividers and the slices can easily be separated when fully defrosted. Sliced tongue tends to fall to pieces after defrosting. If packing a large quantity from which you may wish to remove part, either use dividers between the slices or make up a number of small packs sealed in foil or cling film and put together in one container. Sliced chicken or turkey meat, or any poultry of which the flesh is dry, should be sprinkled with a little chicken stock before being packed.
Meat to serve hot should be packed in shaped foil trays and covered with sauce or gravy, then reheated, still covered, to prevent drying out. Storage time 3–4 months.
See *PLATE MEALS, *DEFROSTING.
NOTE: Take particular care to use a really clean knife when carving cold meat for freezing.

SLOW FREEZING The speed of freezing normally achieved in a domestic food freezer where the transition from water to ice takes place over many hours. Some foods (*e.g. meat*) are not noticeably affected by the rate of freezing; for others (*e.g. ice cream*) quick freezing gives a markedly superior result.

SOLE Lean flat fish suitable for freezing raw, whole or as fillets, or cooked in made-up dishes. Storage time 6 months.
See *FISH PREPARATION AND PACKING, *DEFROSTING.

SOLID ICE PACK See *GLAZE.

SORBETS Frozen desserts made with fruit purée or juice, beaten egg whites and sometimes gelatine added. Sorbets are sufficiently light and refreshing to be served as a separate course in the middle of an elaborate menu. Storage time 3 months.

SORTING SHELVES Racks which hook on to the outer rim of a chest freezer which are useful if there is no working surface near by. When planning a site for your chest freezer, it is easy to overlook the fact that once the lid is open there is nowhere to place items which must be kept level until arranged in their storage position.

SOUFFLÉS Savoury or sweet mixtures which are served hot or cold. Hot cooked soufflés cannot be frozen but the mixture can be made up to the point of adding the stiffly beaten egg whites and then frozen so that it can be defrosted, the egg whites added and baked off when required. Cold soufflés set with gelatine freeze very well when completed. It is usual to pin a cuff of non-stick parchment, foil or oiled greaseproof paper round the soufflé dish and pour in the mixture before it sets so that it rises above the edge of the dish. Freeze with the cuff still in position and peel it off as soon as the

soufflé has been removed from the freezer and before it begins to thaw. It is better to add the final decorations, such as chopped nuts round the sides and piped cream rosettes on top, just before serving.

SOUPS Concentrated soups take up less space in the freezer and can be brought back to the right consistency by adding stock, milk and water, milk or cream at reheating time. This helps to thaw the soup without risk of burning and reheat it quickly.

It is a great asset to use a liquidiser or Mouli vegetable mill, rather than pressing vegetables through a sieve. But this process is frequently necessary to remove fragments of skin, seeds and coarse fibres (*e.g. celery soup*).

Cooked vegetable purées can be used to make soups by the addition of any of the liquids mentioned above with seasoning to taste. For special occasions the soups can be garnished at serving time with a swirl of cream, croûtons, etc., all of which can come from the freezer.

Uncooked vegetable purées, including tomato, cucumber and avocado, can be used to make both hot and cold soups. Tomato purée, however, seems to have a richer flavour if cooked for a short while before sieving.

Clear soups can be frozen but unless very much reduced they waste valuable freezer space. Soups with meat, poultry or game in them are usually highly seasoned and best for short-term storage only. Fish and shellfish soups also have a limited storage life. Storage time cooked vegetable soups 6–8 months, uncooked vegetable soups and meat, poultry, game and fish soups 3 months.
See *PURÉES, *DEFROSTING.

Soup with fenugreek (page 230); Crispy pancakes with bean sprouts (page 229)

Vegetable pie with potato pastry (page 264); Country pie (page 265)

SOYA PROTEIN A product of the soya bean plant which is particularly rich in vegetable protein and has recently been used to produce meat substitutes and extenders. Although you can grow the plant yourself and eat the beans, it is not yet possible to produce these derivatives at home. Both these products freeze well without any alteration in flavour or texture and have as long a storage life as cooked meat. Storage time 3 months.

SPICES Pungent or aromatic substances of vegetable origin used dry in cooking as seasonings or preservatives. Use sparingly as the flavour seems to intensify on freezing.

SPINACH Plant with succulent green leaves suitable for freezing blanched for long-term storage, unblanched for short-term storage, or cooked in made-up dishes. Blanched spinach can be packed in a much smaller space than unblanched spinach. Storage time blanched 10–12 months, as pureé or chopped 6–8 months, unblanched 3 months.
See *VEGETABLE PREPARATION AND PACKING, *DEFROSTING.

SPRAT Small oily round fish similar to herring, suitable for freezing whole. When defrosted, dry carefully on soft kitchen paper and coat before frying. Storage time 3–4 months.
See *FISH PREPARATION AND PACKING, *DEFROSTING.

STAR MARKINGS There is considerable confusion about the frozen food storage compartments of refrigerators as many refrigerator owners feel that these are in effect small freezers. In fact the markings shown below indicate only their capacity to store ready-frozen food for various lengths of time and they are not capable of freezing down fresh food quickly enough to produce a satisfactory result, with the exception of ice cream.
See *TEMPERATURE CHART.

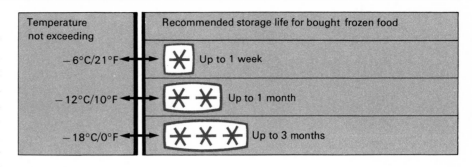

Temperature not exceeding	Recommended storage life for bought frozen food
−6°C/21°F ✱	Up to 1 week
−12°C/10°F ✱✱	Up to 1 month
−18°C/0°F ✱✱✱	Up to 3 months

NOTE: the Four-Star Symbol is the only one which denotes a freezer.
See *BUYING A FREEZER.

STEWS See *CASSEROLES, *PREFORMED PACKS.

STOCK Meat, poultry or fish stocks can be made with surplus bones from a bulk purchase, carcases of birds or heads, bones and trimmings of fish. They take up valuable freezer space unless well reduced but can be frozen in ice cube trays and the cubes packed in polythene bags. Tupperware midgets hold a good quantity of reduced stock to improve a soup or stew. Add frozen cubes straight to the pan. Storage time 3 months.

STORAGE TIMES See individual items.

STRAWBERRY Soft berry fruit which grows from the crown of the plant having very delicate cell structure and high water content. Strawberries are suitable for freezing whole in dry sugar or sugar syrup pack, without sugar, as purée in uncooked freezer jam or as part of a made-up dish. When frozen whole they loose their texture on defrosting and are best eaten while still chilled. If combined with cooked fruit such as rhubarb, both the appearance and texture are similar to canned strawberries. Storage time in sugar or sugar syrup pack 9–12 months, dry without sugar and as a purée 6–8 months.
See *FRUIT PREPARATION AND PACKING, *UNCOOKED FREEZER JAMS, *DEFROSTING.

STUFFINGS Those made with bread have a short storage life, especially if highly seasoned. Rice and sausage meat stuffing mixtures have a longer storage life but the same disadvantage exists, that stuffed joints and poultry take a long time to cook through to the centre and the stuffing may not be cooked by the time the flesh is ready. Savoury bread stuffings are better formed into small balls, frozen in bags and cooked separately in the oven with the roast. Freeze prepared stuffing mixtures in polythene bags. Storage time bread stuffings 1 month, other stuffings 2 months.

SUET When bulk buying beef ask to have the suet, which you do not intend to render down to make dripping, shredded and packed in polythene bags. It can be used for suet pastry, pudding crust, suet puddings, cobbler scones, mincemeat, gingerbread, and even pancakes if a suitable recipe is used. Storage time 3 months.
See *DEFROSTING.

SUGAR SYRUP As well as being used for packing fruit, it can be flavoured with spirits or fortified wines while hot and used to enrich cakes (*e.g. savarin*). Pour the syrup over the cake while it is still warm and allow to soak in before freezing.
Syrup pack. To pack fruit especially those which discolour easily, in sugar syrup. See *FRUIT PREPARATION AND PACKING.

SWEDE A yellow root vegetable which is a variety of turnip. Swedes are suitable for freezing blanched, or as a fully cooked purée with butter. Storage time 10–12 months, as a purée 6–8 months.
See *VEGETABLE PREPARATION AND PACKING, *DEFROSTING.

SWEETBREAD An internal organ (pancreas) which requires blanching before cooking. Storage time 3 months.
See *OFFAL, *DEFROSTING.

SWEETS Home-made candies and other sweetmeats freeze well and can be made for festivities, or to give as presents, well ahead of time when you are not too busy. If a number of varieties are prepared they can be placed in paper sweet cases and made up into mixed packs for gifts. Toffee and fudge mixtures can be poured into buttered shallow foil trays, marked when partially set and frozen in these containers. Foil trays are also easy to present attractively as the selection of sweets can be covered with cling film and decorated with a ribbon bow. Because of their high sugar content, sweets defrost very quickly. Storage time 6 months.
See *DEFROSTING.

TEABREADS See ⋆CAKES.

TEMPERATURE CHART The range of temperatures involved in reducing food from room temperature to the very low temperatures employed for industrial quick freezing cover a wide range, as shown below.

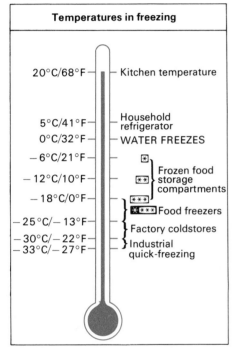

Temperatures in freezing

20°C/68°F	Kitchen temperature
5°C/41°F	Household refrigerator
0°C/32°F	WATER FREEZES
−6°C/21°F	⊡ Frozen food storage compartments
−12°C/10°F	⊡⊡
−18°C/0°F	⊡⊡⊡
	⊡⊡⊡⊡ Food freezers
−25°C/−13°F	Factory coldstores
−30°C/−22°F	Industrial quick-freezing
−33°C/−27°F	

TEMPERATURE GRADIENT The flow of air which enters the freezer when it is opened causes changes of temperature in one part of the freezer resulting in slight dehydration of any inadequately protected foods and this produces water vapour. When the temperature inside the cabinet drops again this vapour is deposited on the interior walls or shelves as frost. A rapid build-up of frost is often caused by having a number of badly protected packs in the freezer.

TEMPERATURE REGULATOR See ⋆DIAL SETTING, ⋆ECONOMY.

TERRINES See ⋆PÂTÉS.

TEXTURE Cooked foods with a high water content frequently have a granular texture after defrosting. This is particularly noticeable in dishes to be served cold, but creams and mousses with gelatine used as a setting agent are smooth providing sufficient gelatine is used to ensure a really firm set. Foods which are not cooked (*e.g. some berries*) which also have a high water content, lose their crispness of texture when completely thawed, although the effect can be somewhat disguised by serving them while still partially frozen, or in a syrup. Salad greens lose their original crisp texture very noticeably.

THAWING BOX A plastic box with a transparent ventilated top, allowing the circulation of air at room temperature. The food sits on a perforated tray so that juices from it drain into the base from which they may be easily poured away.

THERMAL CONDUCTIVITY The ease and speed with which heat passes through any material. Oddly enough frozen food is a better heat conductor than thawed food. The outside of the food freezes first and the most difficult heat to be extracted – that at the centre – passes comparatively swiftly to the outside through already-frozen tissue which has high thermal conductivity.

If thawing is carried out by the reverse process, by contact with warm air or placing the food in warm water, even while still protected by a bag or container, the outside of the food thaws first. Now comes the obstacle. The heat required to thaw the centre has to pass with difficulty through a comparatively inefficient heat transfer medium-thawed tissue. The process takes a long time and the outside of the food may reach and pass the temperature at which bacteria reactivate and multiply while the centre of the food is still frozen solid. There are therefore several good arguments for roasting meat from the frozen state. The heat in the oven passes more quickly to the centre of the joint through frozen tissue than it would do through thawed tissue, and the cold 'core of resistance'

at the centre defrosts more quickly because it is not surrounded by a 'baffle' of poor thermal conductivity: rather like a tea cosy over a teapot. Now for the return journey. Cold from the centre is quickly conveyed out to the surface of the meat. There the temperature is too high for bacteria to flourish – in fact survive at all. This method does not take that much longer than roasting in the usual way.

THERMOMETER A freezer thermometer indicates a different range of temperatures than that shown on an oven thermometer or a meat thermometer. It is a useful gadget to own so that you can adjust the freezer temperature control if necessary.

THROW-AWAY CONTAINERS Food which contaminates the wrapping or container so that it is difficult to remove the smell by washing (*e.g. sliced onion, curry sauce*) could well be stored in yogurt or cream cartons. Since they cannot be provided with a completely airtight seal and are not entirely moisture-vapour-proof, such packs will certainly need an overwrap.

TOMATO Fruit of a plant, usually red but occasionally yellow, which is treated as a vegetable. Tomatoes are suitable for freezing as a cooked purée or as part of a made-up dish. Whole tomatoes can be frozen but are only suitable for use in cooking. The texture when defrosted is too soft for salad use. Storage time 10–12 months.
See *VEGETABLE PREPARATION AND PACKING, *DEFROSTING.

HELPFUL HINT: Tomatoes frozen whole can be halved while still semi-frozen and grilled. The skins of frozen tomatoes can easily be slipped off under running water.

TONGUE An organ which comes under the heading of offal, usually pickled, but as the meat has a very soft texture when cooked it needs freezing in thick slices, if not whole. Storage time 3 months.
See *OFFAL, *DEFROSTING.

TRIPE Muscular lining of the compound stomach of a cow. The preferred cut is honeycomb; other types are described as the blanket, monk's head and book, coming from the parts of the stomach which suggest the names from the shape. Tripe requires blanching before cooking.
See *OFFAL, *DEFROSTING.

TROUT Oily round fish suitable for freezing raw whole or as part of made-up dishes. Pink trout are now available commercially frozen as small whole fish (about 1 kg/2–2¼ lb) and have the same texture and flavour as salmon trout. Storage time 3–4 months.
See *FISH PREPARATION AND PACKING, *DEFROSTING.

TUPPERWARE The largest range of shapes, sizes and colours in polythene containers with airtight seals, of a particularly high quality capable of being reduced to –57°C/–70°F without damage. The range includes unusual shapes such as parfait dishes and fluted moulds, easy to turn out. These containers carry a 10-year guarantee and, although relatively expensive to buy initially, most freezer owners find them an excellent investment. Only available through Tupperware parties; details of local distributors can be found in the yellow pages of telephone directories.
See ★PACKAGING.

TURBOT Large lean flat fish suitable for freezing raw as steaks or fillets, or cooked in made-up dishes.
See ★FISH PREPARATION AND PACKING, ★DEFROSTING.

TURKEY Largest of the white-fleshed poultry and as versatile as chicken, freezes well whole or jointed, raw or cooked, and in made-up dishes. General rules applying to chicken also apply to turkey. Storage time 12 months, giblets 3 months. See ★POULTRY, ★CHICKEN, ★DEFROSTING.

TURNIP White root vegetable which is suitable for freezing blanched, or as a fully cooked purée with butter. Storage time 10–12 months, as a purée 6–8 months.
See ★VEGETABLE PREPARATION AND PACKING, ★DEFROSTING.

UNBLANCHED VEGETABLES Certain vegetables marked thus ★ in the Vegetable Preparation and Packing Chart are suitable for short-term storage without blanching. Remember that when required to serve, these will need the full amount of cooking time compared with blanched vegetables which are frequently almost fully cooked and merely require to be defrosted and reheated. Storage time 3 months.
See ★VEGETABLE PREPARATION AND PACKING.

UNCOOKED FREEZER JAMS Only suitable for storage in the freezer. These jams would soon deteriorate if transferred to a larder shelf, so pack them in small quantities and keep them in the refrigerator after opening. Fresh berry fruits such as blackberries, blackcurrants, loganberries, redcurrants and strawberries are suitable for making uncooked freezer jam.

To each 1 kg/2 lb of fruit in a bowl, add 1·5 kg/3½ lb castor sugar and 4 tablespoons lemon juice. Stir well and leave to stand until the sugar has completely dissolved, which may take from 20 minutes to 2 hours. Add 250 ml/scant ½ pint commercial pectin and stir until beginning to set. This may be delayed overnight, but if necessary leave at warm room temperature in the bowl. Pack in small quantities in polythene containers. This type of jam defrosts within 30 minutes but retains its easy spreading consistency. Storage time 12 months.
HELPFUL HINT: Fruit and sugar allowed to stand together overnight can be brought to the boil, removed from the heat and set by stirring in the appropriate fruit-flavoured jelly cubes.

Allow 1 packet jelly to 1·5 kg/3 lb fruit, such as rhubarb mixed with red berries, and 450 g/1 lb sugar. The same defrosting and storage rules apply as for uncooked freezer jams.

UPRIGHT FREEZER Shaped like a cupboard with a front hinged door or two hinged doors, controls on the front panel and ventilation grid on the back. Available in sizes from 120–600 litres/4–20 cubic feet. It requires little floor space, is particularly suitable for a kitchen site but requires defrosting about twice a year, unless automatic. Smaller freestanding models, placed on or under a working surface, are available in one or two sizes up to 60 litres/2 cubic feet. Large uprights when fully loaded place exceptional stress on the floor area they occupy. Some shelves are adjustable but none to the extent of accommodating large uneven shaped packs easily. Some models include pull-out baskets or have drawers instead of some shelves and baskets. Those shelves which are made up of evaporator coils are immovable and the evaporator system is not enclosed. Packs placed on these shelves freeze down fastest. Door storage space enables small items to be kept handy but exposure to fluctuations in temperature restrict the choice of foods which can be kept in this storage area. Great care must be taken not to hamper the closure of the door by inserting packs that are slightly too large in this storage area. Accessibility is the greatest advantage except in the case of very tall uprights where you may have to climb on a stool to reach items at the back of the top shelf.

NOTE: A problem sometimes arises with a tall upright freezer which has only one door. The top shelf may be unsuitable for long-term storage of frozen food. Above the recommended load level it is advisable to store bread and other baked foods such as plain cakes (which are little affected by fluctuations in temperature) or items you expect to use up in a short time (*e.g. packs of sandwiches*).

Side-by side freezer/refrigerator.
Matching upright units designed to make the best use of cold, chilled and frozen storage. The freezer has many extras, including a flip-out spout to aid defrosting. The refrigerator has both a cold zone for unfrozen food storage and a chilled zone suitable for storing drinks, etc. The capacity of each zone can be varied by moving the special 'cold shield' shelf.

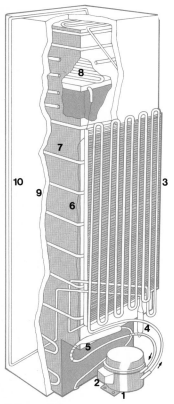

1 Compressor
2 Relay-combination
3 Condenser
4 Dryer
5 Collection bottle
6 Capillary
7 Evaporator
8 Evaporator plate
9 Insulation
10 Hot gas pass

Vegetable Growing Guide

Vegetable	Varieties	Sowing, transplanting and harvesting times	Harvesting hints
Artichokes Globe	Grande Beurre.	Sow: late spring Harvest: July—September the following year.	Cut heads when plump, but still young and tender. The scales should still be tight.
Jerusalem	White Skinned.	Sow: early spring Harvest: following autumn/winter	Pick when stems and foliage die and turn brown in autumn. Freeze immediately as they lose flavour if kept.
Asparagus	Connover's Colossal, Brocks Imperial F_1.	Sow: April/May Harvest: after bed has been established for 3 years	Cut when asparagus spears are 10 cm/4 inches high and 5—10 mm/$\frac{1}{4}$—$\frac{1}{2}$ inch diameter. Using a sharp knife cut the shoots about 7·5 cm/3 inches below the soil. Do not continue cutting after mid June.
Aubergine	Burpee Hybrid F_1, Early Long Purple.	Sow: February under glass Harvest: August onwards	Pick while bloom is still on the skin. As the shine goes it becomes bitter.
Beans Broad	Imperial Green Longpod, Masterpiece, Meteor, Imperial Green Windsor, Imperial White Windsor, The Sutton, Dreadnought, Express.	Sow: March/April Harvest: June—August	Pick when young, before a black eye has formed on the seeds within the bean pod; otherwise the skin could become tough.
French	Kentucky Wonder, Blue Lake White Seeded, The Prince, Masterpiece, Tendergreen, Cordon, Romano, Kinghorn Wax.	Sow: April/May Harvest: July—October	Pick when young and freeze whole.
Mung (bean sprouts)		Grow on damp towelling or in a jar. Allow 5—8 days to sprout.	Cut with scissors when 5 cm/2 inches long.
Runner	Kelvedon Marvel, Prize-winner, Achievement, Streamline.	Sow: May/June Harvest: August—October	Pick frequently during cropping. Beans should be flat and tender and snap when broken.
Beetroot	Early Bunch, Globe, Detroit Little Ball, Boltardy, Early Model, Mono King Emperor. Snowhite (white beetroot)	Sow: March—June Harvest: June—September	Globe and Detroit varieties produce golf-ball size beets — ideal for freezing. Take care not to bruise or damage roots when lifting. Use leafy tops and cook as a green vegetable.

Vegetable	Varieties	Sowing, transplanting and harvesting times	Harvesting hints
Broccoli	Green Comet F_1, Premium Crop F_1, Express Corona F_1, Early Purple Sprouting, Christmas Purple Sprouting.	Sow: April/May Transplant: June/July Harvest: September–February	Cut shoots with about 10–13 cm/4–5 inches of stem. Tie in bunches and cook like asparagus. The heads should be firm and picked before the flower buds open.
Brussels Sprouts	Peer Gynt F_1, Roodnerf Stiekema Early, Roodnerf Seven Hills, Achilles F_1, Cambridge No. 5, Citadel F_1, Lindo.	Sow: March/April Transplant: May/June Harvest: September–March	Pick when sprouts are the size of a walnut starting from the bottom of the stem. Use the tops as cabbage after all the sprouts have been harvested.
Cabbage summer autumn/winter spring	Greyhound, May Star F_1, June Star F_1. January King, Hidena, Winnigstadt, Winter White. Wheelers' Imperial, Spring-tide, Flower of Spring, Blood Red.	Sow: March Transplant: May. Sow: March–May Transplant: June Harvest: autumn/winter Sow: July/August Transplant: September/October Harvest: Spring	Mix the varieties sown so cabbages can be harvested throughout the year. Pick when crisp and young.
Carrots	Nantes Champion Scarlet Horn, Chantenay Red Cored, Amsterdam Forcing.	Sow: March–July Harvest: May–October	If freezing whole pull when finger length.
Cauliflower summer winter	Snowball, All the Year Round, Kangaroo, Barrier Reef, South Pacific. Snow's Winter White, Armado April.	Sow: March/April Transplant: April/May Harvest: September onwards Sow: April/May Transplant: June/July Harvest: December onwards	Cut heads when small. Freeze the florets only. Use thick white stem to make soup.
Celeriac	Globus.	Sow: March (under glass) Transplant: May Harvest: September onwards	Leave in the soil until required but lift all roots before frost.
Celery	New Dwarf White, Giant Pink, Giant Red.	Sow: February–April (under glass) Transplant: May/June Harvest: September–November	
Corn-on-the-cob	First of All, North Star F_1, John Innes Hybrid F_1, Earliking F_1, Kelvedon Glory F_1, Early Xtra Sweet F_1, Honey Dew F_1, Polar Vee F_1, Northern Belle F_1, Honey and Cream F_1.	Sow: April (under glass) Transplant: May/June Harvest: August/September	Pick when young and yellow. Test for ripeness when silks wither and press seeds – the contents should be like thick cream. Freeze as soon as possible after picking.
Courgettes	True French, Green Bush Improved, Green Bush F_1, Aristocrat F_1, Golden Courgette F_1.	Sow: April (under glass), May Transplant: June Harvest: July/August	Pick when approximately 10 cm/4 inches long if freezing whole.
Cucumber	Telegraph (Frame), Conqueror (Frame), Butcher's Disease Resisting (Frame), Burpee Hybrid (Ridge).	Sow: Frame varieties – January–May (under glass) Ridge varieties – May Harvest: July–September	Cut as soon as they reach the required size.
Fennel	Sweet Florence.	Sow: April Harvest: late summer	Pull when bulbs are the size of a tennis ball.
Kale	Tall Green Curled, Fribor F_1.	Sow: April/May Harvest: November onwards	Cut the outer leaves as they mature.

Vegetable	Varieties	Sowing, transplanting and harvesting times	Harvesting hints
Kohlrabi	White Vienna, Earliest Purple.	Sow: April–August Harvest: July–November	Cut when the bulb stems are like medium-sized apples.
Leeks	Musselburgh, Prizetaker.	Sow: March Transplant: June Harvest: October–May	Lift the leeks when they reach a suitable size.
Marrow	Long Green Trailing, White Bush, Golden Delicious, Vegetable Spaghetti.	Sow: April (under glass), May Transplant: June Harvest: August onwards	Cut when still young before outer skin hardens.
Onions	Bedfordshire Champion, Ailsa Craig. Autumn Queen, Reliance, Solidity. Onion sets – Stuttgarter Giant.	Sow: January (under glass), March/April Sow: September Transplant: March Plant: March/April Harvest: June onwards	When the tops of the plants bend over and growth is slower, lift bulbs out. Dry in the sun.
Parsnips	Offenham, Improved Hollow Crown.	Sow: March–May Harvest: September onwards	Leave in the soil until required.
Peas	Early Onward, Little Marvel, Kelvedon Wonder, Onward, Show Perfection, Hurst Green Shaft.	Sow: March–June Harvest: June–October	Pick when the pods are just filled. The peas should be bright green and the pods break easily when a little pressure is applied.
Mangetout peas	Carouby de Maussane, Dwarf Sweet Gem, Oregon Sugar Pod, Dwarf de Grace.	Sow: March–June Harvest: July onwards	Pick when peas can just be felt in the pods and before they are too large.
Peppers (Capsicums)	Slim Pim F_1, New Ace F_1, Canape F_1.	Sow: March (under glass) Transplant: May/June Harvest: August onwards	Small long peppers, pick when 6 cm/$2\frac{1}{2}$ inches long. Pick all peppers when green or red but still firm.
Potatoes early	Epicure, Sharpe's Express, Home Guard.	Plant: March Harvest: June/July	Lift when the potatoes are large enough, usually when they begin to flower.
mid-season and late	Majestic, King Edward VII.	Plant: April Harvest: August–October	
Pumpkins	Hundredweight, Hubbard Squash Golden, Ornamental.	Sow: May (under glass) Plant: June Harvest: September	Allow to ripen on the plant before lifting.
Salsify	Sutton's Giant, Mammoth Sandwich Island.	Sow: April/May Harvest: October onwards	Avoid damage to the roots when lifting or 'bleeding' may occur.
Scorzonera (black-rooted salsify)	Russian Giant.	Sow: April/May Harvest: October onwards	Lift for use as required.
Seakale	Lily white.	Sow: March Harvest: Following February/March	The heads should snap off when 15–22.5 cm/6–9 inches high by lightly bending.
Seakale beet	Vintage Green F_1.	Sow: May–July Harvest: July onwards	Pick the leaves a few at a time from each plant. The fleshy white midrib may be cooked and eaten separately.
Spinach	Greenmarket, Longstanding Round.	Sow: March–July (summer varieties) August/September (winter varieties) Harvest: 8–11 weeks after sowing	Leaves should be picked when fresh and bright in colour, a few leaves at a time being taken from each plant.
Tomatoes	Potentate, Moneymaker, Sugarplum (Gardener's Delight), Outdoor Girl, Tiny Tim, Yellow Perfection.	Sow: March or early April (under glass) Harvest: July–October	Pick when fully-coloured and ripe.

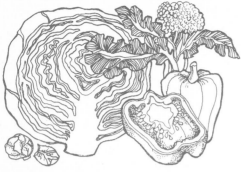

Vegetable Preparation and Packing

Most vegetables keep well for a full year. For long-term freezing, blanching is the all-important step, as it virtually halts the enzyme action which causes spoilage. Vegetables, unlike fruit, are a non-acidic food and once picked start to deteriorate, even in the frozen state. Brussels sprouts, for instance, show an appreciable deterioration after a week of frozen storage if they are not blanched. Certain vegetables, marked thus *, are suitable for short-term storage without blanching. For blanching instructions see *BLANCHING.

Vegetable	Preparation	Blanching time	Packing
ARTICHOKES			
Globe	Remove outer leaves, trim tops, wash well. Add lemon juice to blanching water.	7–10 minutes	Polythene bags
Jerusalem	Cook and freeze as purée for soups.	Boil 30 minutes	Polythene containers
ASPARAGUS (Buy at their cheapest – use stalk trimmings for soup)	Wash, trim, blanch and grade. Pack all lying in one direction.	Thin stems 2 minutes; thick stems 4 minutes.	Rectangular polythene containers
AUBERGINES	Peel, cut into 2·5-cm/1-inch slices. Blanch, cool and pack in layers with dividers.	4 minutes	Polythene containers
AVOCADOS	Most successful as purée with seasoning and lemon juice added.		Polythene containers, cling film over surface to prevent discoloration
BEANS			
Broad	Pod, grade and blanch.	3 minutes	Polythene bags
French*	Top and tail, slice or leave whole. Blanch. Or, freeze young, tender beans whole unblanched; store 3 months only.	3 minutes	Polythene bags
Mung (bean sprouts)	Freeze beans whole unblanched.		Polythene bags
Runner	Trim, slice thickly and blanch.	2 minutes	Polythene bags
BEETROOT	Cook until tender, cool, peel, slice or dice. Tiny ones can be cooked, peeled and frozen whole.	Boil 40–50 minutes	Polythene containers
BROCCOLI	Select compact heads with tender stalks. Trim, wash in salted water, blanch, drain well. Pack tips to stalks.	3–5 minutes, depending on size	Polythene bags, overwrap
BRUSSELS SPROUTS	Select firm, tight, small evenly sized sprouts. Peel, trim and wash thoroughly. Blanch.	3–5 minutes	Polythene bags, overwrap
CABBAGE	Select firm, crisp cabbage. Shred coarsely or cut into wedges, blanch, drain well.	1½ or 4 minutes	Polythene bags, overwrap
CARROTS*	Trim, peel or scrape, wash and slice or dice. Blanch. Freeze young carrots whole unblanched; store 3 months only.	4 minutes	Polythene bags
CAULIFLOWER*	Choose tight, white heads with no blemishes. Trim to small florets. Wash and blanch in salted water, drain well. Open freeze. Store 3 months only.	3 minutes	Polythene bags
CELERIAC	Wash, peel, slice and steam over boiling water until almost tender, or cut into matchstick lengths and blanch for use in salads, such as *Céleri remoulade*.	Steam 25 minutes; blanch 1 minute	Polythene containers
CELERY (use only for cooked dishes)	Trim, scrub and cut into 2·5-cm/1-inch lengths. Blanch.	3 minutes	Polythene containers

Vegetable	Preparation	Blanching time	Packing
CHICORY (use in cooked dishes or with white sauces)	Remove outer leaves, add lemon juice to blanching water.	2 minutes	Polythene bags
CORN-ON-THE-COB (Do not freeze late-season cobs)	Select young, pale yellow kernels. Remove husks and silks, wash, blanch, cool and dry. Or, when cooked, scrape off kernels and open freeze.	4–8 minutes depending on size.	Individually in cling film, then in polythene containers. Defrost before cooking. Polythene bags
COURGETTES*	Wash, trim into 5-mm–1-cm/¼–½-inch slices, blanch or sauté in butter. Freeze whole unblanched; store 3 months only.	1 minute	Polythene containers
Stuffed	Halve and blanch courgettes before stuffing.	2 minutes	
CUCUMBER (Not suitable to serve raw)	Peel, grate or liquidise for use in soups or mousses. Can also be frozen diced, lightly sautéed in butter to serve as a hot vegetable.		Polythene containers Polythene containers
FENNEL (Not suitable to serve raw)	Trim, wash, cut into ½–1-cm/¼–½-inch slices. Blanch.	3 minutes	Polythene bags
KALE	Wash, discard tough main stem, blanch.	2 minutes	Polythene bags
KOHLRABI	Trim, wash, peel and dice. Blanch, open freeze. Very small ones can be trimmed, scrubbed, blanched and frozen whole.	2 minutes 3 minutes	Polythene bags Polythene bags
LEEKS (Use in cooked dishes or with white sauces)	Remove tops, roots and stalks. Cut into 1-cm/½-inch slices. Sauté in butter, 3–4 minutes.		Polythene containers
MARROW	Use small young marrow. Peel, cut into 2·5-cm/1-inch rings and remove seeds. Blanch.	3 minutes	Polythene containers
Vegetable spaghetti	Peel, cut into thick rings, remove seeds and blanch.	3 minutes	Polythene containers
MUSHROOMS	Wash and freeze small button mushrooms unblanched; store 3 months only. For longer storage; wash, drain and sauté whole button mushrooms, or sliced larger ones, in butter for 1 minute. Store 6 months only.		Polythene containers
OKRA	Remove stems and blanch.	3–4 minutes depending on size	Polythene containers
ONIONS*	Peel, slice or chop and blanch. Button onions can be blanched whole. Freeze chopped onion unblanched; store 3 months only.	2 minutes	Double polythene bags or extra throw-away overwrap
PARSNIPS	Trim, peel, slice or dice, blanch, cool and drain. Can also be frozen after cooking as a purée with butter.	2 minutes	Polythene bags
PEAS* (Open freezing ensures free-flow packs)	Select young peas, shell and grade. Blanch. Open freeze. Or, freeze peas unblanched; store 3 months only. Trim ends, blanch.	1 minute	Polythene bags
Mangetout		2–3 minutes	Polythene bags
PEPPERS*	Wash, remove stems, pips and pith. Cut in halves, slices or strips. Blanch. Freeze sliced unblanched; store 3 months only.	3 minutes	Polythene containers
POTATOES new	Scrape, cook until just tender.		Polythene bags
chip	Prepare chips and part fry: 2 minutes.		
roast	Peel, cut into even sized pieces, bring to boil in salted water, drain, shake dry. Coat with oil or dripping and slightly under-roast.	Roast 1 hour	Polythene bags
POTATOES (cont.)			

Vegetable	Preparation	Blanching time	Packing
duchesse	Peel, slice and boil until tender. Mash with butter, eggs, seasonings. Pipe out on baking trays, open freeze, pack with dividers.	Boil 10 minutes	Polythene containers
croquette	Cook and mash as above. Make croquettes, coat in egg and breadcrumbs, open freeze.	Boil 10 minutes	Polythene containers
PUMPKIN	Peel, slice, remove seeds. Steam until tender and mash.	Steam 35–40 minutes	Polythene containers
SALSIFY	Scrub, blanch then cut in 5-cm/2-inch lengths and peel while warm.	2 minutes	Polythene bags
SCORZONERA (black rooted salsify)	Treat as salsify.		
SEAKALE	Wash, trim and blanch. Pack all lying in one direction.	4 minutes	Rectangular polythene containers
SEAKALE BEET	Wash, strip green part of leaf, blanch, press out excess water. Central ribs can be treated as celery. Cut into 5-cm/2-inch lengths. Blanch.	2 minutes 3 minutes	Polythene containers Polythene containers
SPINACH	Select young leaves, trim and wash well. Blanch and press out excess water. Wash spinach and freeze unblanched; store 3 months only.		Polythene containers Tightly packed in polythene bags
SWEDES	Trim, peel and dice. Blanch. Can be frozen after cooking puréed with butter.	3 minutes. Boil 30–40 minutes	Polythene bags. Polythene containers
TOMATOES* (Suitable for cooking only)	Wipe, remove stem and freeze whole, unblanched; store 3 months only. Can also be frozen as purée; skin, simmer 5 minutes, rub through sieve, cool.		Polythene bags Polythene containers
TURNIPS	Trim, peel and dice. Blanch. Can also be frozen after cooking as a purée with butter. Tiny turnips can be frozen whole, blanched.	3 minutes Boil 30 minutes 3 minutes	Polythene bags Polythene containers Polythene bags

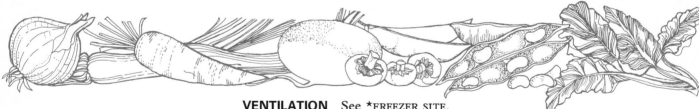

VENTILATION See *FREEZER SITE.

VITAMIN C The chief sources of Vitamin C are fruit and vegetables. Considerable loss of this very important vitamin occurs during the lapse of time from harvesting to consumption in the fresh state, or from harvesting to freezing. If the handling process includes preparation, blanching, freezing, defrosting and subsequent cooking, the loss of Vitamin C is bound to be great. Enzymes in plant cells cause a chemical action when cells are ruptured by chopping or cooking, which destroys Vitamin C.

The following rules should be observed.
1. Do not keep fruit and vegetables waiting any longer before freezing than is absolutely necessary.
2. Do not handle or chop fruit and vegetables more than is essential.
3. Add ascorbic acid to replace lost Vitamin C if desired.
NOTE: Other vitamins necessary to a balanced diet are not so much affected by preparation and cooking.
See *ASCORBIC ACID.

VITAMINS See *NUTRITIONAL VALUES.

WATER ICES These are the most simple frozen desserts which can be elaborated to make sherbets and sorbets. Storage time 6 months.
See *SHERBETS, *SORBETS.

WATER VAPOUR This vapour, to use a technical expression, 'sublimes' to form frost when exposed to an extremely cold temperature. Sublimation is the process of a solid going directly to a gas or a gas going to a solid (*i.e. missing out the liquid phase*). When it is very cold, gaseous water vapour goes straight to ice; that is frost. The frost visible inside a pack of frozen food is caused by the sublimation of the moisture in the food by the cold air inside the pack. Warm air which enters the freezer loses its water vapour content in the sublimation of frost on the walls or shelves.

WHITEBAIT Tiny oily round fish of the same family as herring and sardine. Whitebait are frozen whole. When defrosted, dry carefully on soft kitchen paper before coating in seasoned flour and deep-frying. Storage time 3–4 months.
See *FISH PREPARATION AND PACKING, *DEFROSTING.

WHITECURRANT See *CURRANTS.

WHITING Lean round fish suitable for freezing raw, whole or as fillets, or cooked in made-up dishes. Storage time 6 months.
See *FISH PREPARATION AND PACKING, *DEFROSTING.

WILD FRUIT Some wild fruit is suitable for making jellies or wines, although too bitter or hard to serve as a dessert fruit. If it is not convenient to use it for either of these purposes when it is in season, it should be carefully cleaned and frozen in dry pack for use later. Storage time 6–8 months.
See *DEFROSTING.

WINE Small quantities which were previously thrown away, or stored with difficulty in the refrigerator for a short time can be frozen for use later in cooking or in marinades. Do not mix red and white wines; freeze separately in small polythene containers. For very small amounts, Tupperware midget tumblers are ideal.

Another way to use up the leftovers is to add them to dishes for freezing. Red wines to bolognese or tomato sauce, to beef stews or pork terrines, for instance; white wines to delicate sauces, ice creams and sorbets.

YEAST A living organism which acts as a raising agent. It is not destroyed by cold as it is by heat, but gradually loses strength in storage. Pack moulded in small blocks suitable for one bake. If necessary it can be grated while still frozen to hasten defrosting. Storage time 3 months.
See *BREAD, *DEFROSTING.

YOGURT Although yogurt can be frozen, it will undergo a slight separation and need vigorous stirring on defrosting to counteract this. Commercially frozen yogurt contains a stabiliser which makes this reconstitution unnecessary. Yogurt containing fruit has less of a tendency to separate than natural yogurt, which is more successfully frozen in made-up dishes. Storage time 1 month.
See *DAIRY PRODUCE, *DEFROSTING.

ZONE OF CELL DAMAGE See *CELL DAMAGE.

Useful facts and figures

Liquid measures

Fluid ounces	Recommended millilitres
5 ($\frac{1}{4}$ pint)	150
9	250
10 ($\frac{1}{2}$ pint)	300
18	500
20 (1 pint)	600
35 (1$\frac{3}{4}$ pints)	1 000 (1 litre)

NOTE: For quantities of 1$\frac{3}{4}$ pints and over, litres and fractions of a litre have been used.

Notes on metrication

In this book quantities are given in both imperial and metric measures. Exact conversion from imperial to metric measures does not usually give very convenient working quantities and so the metric measures have been rounded off into units of 25.

Solid measures

Ounces	Approx. g to nearest whole figure	Recommended conversion to nearest unit of 25
1	28	25
2	57	50
3	85	75
4	113	100
5	142	150
6	170	175
7	198	200
8	227	225
9	255	250
10	283	275
11	312	300
12	340	350
13	368	375
14	396	400
15	425	425
16 (1 lb)	454	450

NOTE: When converting quantities over 16 oz (1 lb), first add the appropriate figures in the centre column, *then* adjust to the nearest unit of 25. As a general guide, 1 kg (1 000 g) equals 2·2 lb or about 2 lb 3 oz. This method of conversion gives good results in nearly all cases, but in certain cake recipes a more accurate conversion is necessary (or the liquid in the metric recipe must be reduced slightly) to produce a balanced recipe.

Metric capacity of freezers

The metric capacity of freezers is measured in litres. To convert cubic feet to litres multiply by 28·3.

Notes for American users

Each recipe in this book has an American column giving US cup measures for the ingredients. The American pint equals 16 fluid ounces whereas the British pint measures 20 fluid ounces.

Spoon measures

All spoon measures given in this book are level unless otherwise indicated.

Oven temperature chart

	Electricity °C	°F	Gas Mark
Very cool	110	225	$\frac{1}{4}$
	120	250	$\frac{1}{2}$
Cool	140	275	1
	150	300	2
Moderate	160	325	3
	180	350	4
Moderately hot	190	375	5
	200	400	6
Hot	220	425	7
	230	450	8
Very hot	240	475	9

Part II

Freezing for
Your Family Lifestyle

Young Couple Both Out at Work

Building up for the future may take a bit of self-discipline, but it is a time you can really enjoy providing you budget sensibly. It pays to stop and think carefully before you rush into making any major purchase; large pieces of domestic equipment for the kitchen are expensive. But today most young couples put a refrigerator only second in priority to a cooker, and the swing is more and more towards a refrigerator with a four-star freezer section, rather than just a frozen food storage compartment.

This means that right from the start you can have the benefits of freezer ownership, admittedly on a small scale. It requires more cash in hand than you will probably want to spend to buy frozen food in bulk. But as the family unit is small, it is more economic to purchase items like chicken and certain cuts of meat when they are on 'special offer'. Then you can make up a favourite recipe in sufficient quantity to serve you both more than once and provide an easy meal for entertaining. That's what freezing is all about.

When you get tired of commercial packs, no matter how convenient they are, it is nice to know that you can try your hand at more creative cooking. Without spending a fortune on the food or needing complicated utensils, you can become quite an accomplished cook. A small blender and hand mixer are great time-savers and they ought to be well up on your 'nice-to-have' list, but you could manage with a Mouli-grinder and a strong right arm. Let the electric carving knife wait until later if necessary!

The recipes in this section are tailored to fit your needs which are probably, in order of importance, as follows:
1. Since your budget would be seriously upset by failures, the recipes must be easy to follow and sure to succeed.
2. The ingredients must be realistically priced and generally available. (Anyone can make a delicious mousse with a jugful of double cream, a balloon glass of brandy and two cups of fresh mango pulp. The cost and the dubious possibility of finding ripe fresh mangoes in your local store would make such a recipe a non-starter.)
3. People who go to work early and come home tired consider their leisure time to be precious. You don't really want to waste hours patiently peeling pistachio nuts, so the recipes here are streamlined to the shortest possible preparation span.
4. Finding space is a problem for food that requires lots of it. A delicate meringue gâteau might take up half your entire freezer space, whereas a loaf-shaped cake takes comparatively little.

Although frozen pastry and cakes are so readily available, it would be a pity to decide out of hand that you are never going to make these yourself. The simple flaky pastry and basic sandwich cake mixture I have purposely included in this section are planned to give the inexperienced cook a confident introduction to the joys of baking.

Freezing part of a favourite dish for future entertaining

Dinner party for four – before and after. Grapefruit and mint sorbets, New Zealand guard of honour, duchesse potato nests, apricot cream gâteau (pages 142–143)

Liver pasta bake and liver burgers

METRIC/IMPERIAL	AMERICAN
450 g/ 1 lb ox liver	1 lb beef liver
1 large onion	1 large onion
225 g/8 oz sausage meat	½ lb sausage meat
75 g/3 oz dried breadcrumbs	¾ cup dry breadcrumbs
1 large egg	1 large egg
1 teaspoon salt	1 teaspoon salt
pinch pepper	pinch pepper
¼ teaspoon dried marjoram	¼ teaspoon dried marjoram
2 tablespoons chopped parsley	3 tablespoons chopped parsley
1 tablespoon ketchup	1 tablespoon ketchup
150 ml/¼ pint beef stock or tomato juice	⅔ cup beef stock or tomato juice
350 g/12 oz cooked pasta	¾ lb cooked pasta
50 g/2 oz butter	¼ cup butter
when serving:	*when serving:*
4 rashers streaky bacon	4 bacon slices

Blanch the liver in boiling water for 5 minutes. Drain thoroughly and discard the blanching liquid. Mince the liver and onion and stir in the remaining ingredients, mixing thoroughly. Divide into 3 portions.

Liver pasta bake: Take 2 portions of the mixture and use each to press against the base and sides of a 450-g/1-lb foil loaf-shaped container. Fill the centres with the cooked pasta and top with the butter.

To freeze: Cover with lid. Seal and label.

To serve: Defrost at room temperature and then bake in a moderate oven (180°C, 350°F, Gas Mark 4) for 45 minutes. Serve with a green salad.

Liver burgers: Shape the remaining meat mixture into 4 large flat cakes.

To freeze: Pack with dividers. Seal and label.

To serve: Wrap a rasher of bacon around each frozen burger and place in a shallow baking tin. Bake in a moderately hot oven (200°C, 400°F, Gas Mark 6) for 30–40 minutes until the bacon is crisp.

Makes: 2 bakes/4 servings.

　　　　4 liver burgers.

Storage time: 3–4 months.

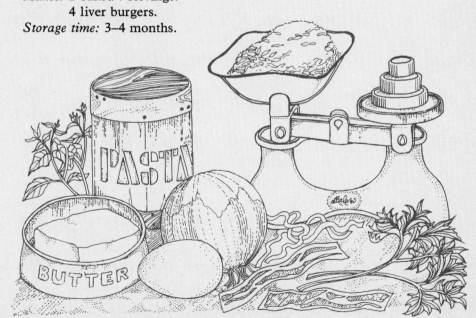

Individual meat loaves

METRIC/IMPERIAL	AMERICAN
700 g/1½ lb minced beef	1½ lb ground beef
2 tablespoons minced onion	3 tablespoons minced onion
2 tablespoons chopped green pepper	3 tablespoons chopped green pepper
100 g/4 oz dried white breadcrumbs	1 cup dry white breadcrumbs
½ teaspoon salt	½ teaspoon salt
¼ teaspoon pepper	¼ teaspoon pepper
½ teaspoon dry mustard	½ teaspoon dry mustard
1 egg	1 egg
3 tablespoons ketchup	¼ cup ketchup
2 teaspoons prepared horseradish sauce	2 teaspoons prepared horseradish sauce
150 ml/¼ pint beef stock	⅔ cup beef stock

Mix all the ingredients together in a large bowl. Shape into 6 small loaves. Place in a greased shallow baking dish so that the sides touch. Bake in a moderate oven (180°C, 350°F, Gas Mark 4) for 1 hour. Cool.
To freeze: Pack individually. Seal and label.
To serve: Unwrap the loaves and place still frozen in a greased shallow baking dish. Bake in a moderately hot oven (200°C, 400°F, Gas Mark 6) for 30 minutes. If desired, brush the top of each loaf with ketchup 10 minutes before the end of the reheating time.
Serves: 6.
Storage time: 4–6 months.

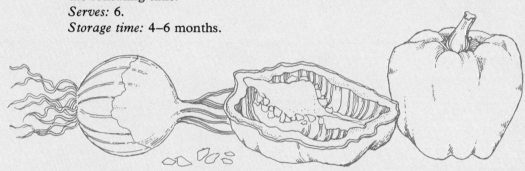

Dress-ups from the Freezer for Individual Meat Loaves and Sausages
Lift simple meat loaves or sausages into an entirely different class by serving one of these interesting accompaniments. The quantities are sufficient to serve 8, or can be cooled and frozen in polythene bags (or boilable bags) in portions to suit your own requirements.

French purée de petits pois: Strip the outside leaves from a large lettuce and wash well. With scissors, snip up 4 or 5 spring onions rather too large for the salad bowl. Put the leaves and onions to cook gently with 25 g/1 oz/2 tablespoons butter in a covered pan until limp. Add 450 g/1 lb frozen peas, cover again and place over high heat until the peas are defrosted. Turn into a blender and liquidise to a purée with 4 tablespoons (US ⅓ cup) of milk. Season generously with salt, pepper, 1 teaspoon of sugar and 2 tablespoons (US 3 tablespoons) mint sauce from a jar (or 3 teaspoons freshly made mint sauce). Reheat, beat well with a fork and allow to 'dry off' to a thick purée over the heat. Serve on the side.

Bali-Bali sauce: Turn a small 225-g/8-oz can of drained pineapple pieces into a saucepan. Add 2 tablespoons (US 3 tablespoons) crunchy peanut butter. (If you use the smooth kind, add only 1 tablespoon of peanut butter and 1 tablespoon salted peanuts.) Add 1 teaspoon turmeric, ½ teaspoon powdered coriander, and cook, stirring, for 2 minutes. Moisten 1 teaspoon cornflour with some of the pineapple juice, add to the mixture, stir well, then add the remaining juice. Cook over low heat so that the mixture just bubbles, until very thick and smooth. Taste for seasoning and add salt if necessary.

Golden onion sauce: Chop 2 large onions finely and fry in 2 tablespoons (US 3 tablespoons) oil until soft and just turning golden brown. Drain. Melt 50 g/2 oz/¼ cup butter in a saucepan and stir in 40 g/1½ oz/6 tablespoons flour until blended. Gradually add 600 ml/1 pint/2½ cups of milk and bring to the boil, stirring constantly. Cook for 2 minutes. Season generously with salt, pepper and ground nutmeg and stir in the cooked onion. Taste and adjust seasoning.

Cooking Main Dishes in Quantity
Although you certainly will not want to eat curry every few days until all the portions frozen are used up, it is a good idea to try a slightly exotic recipe like this one. If you reserve sufficient to make a large 'brick' to serve 6, you can offer it to friends and you will still have 3 small portions for yourselves. Next time you decide to give an hour to cooking a more elaborate dish than usual in quantity, try an entirely different recipe which allows you to ring the changes, serving a curry 'brick' one day and if you wish, a much milder dish the next. A suitable recipe I would recommend for this treatment is the mild Gingered beef curry (see page 230).

Madras lamb curry

METRIC/IMPERIAL	AMERICAN
1·75 kg/4 lb lean shoulder of lamb	4 lb lean lamb shoulder
1 large onion	1 large onion
6 tablespoons cooking oil	½ cup cooking oil
3 teaspoons cumin seeds	1 tablespoon cumin seeds
½ teaspoon ground cinnamon	½ teaspoon ground cinnamon
¼ teaspoon ground cloves	¼ teaspoon ground cloves
½ teaspoon ground ginger	½ teaspoon ground ginger
2 cloves garlic	2 cloves garlic
3 tablespoons curry powder	¼ cup curry powder
1 tablespoon paprika	1 tablespoon paprika
½ teaspoon chilli powder	½ teaspoon chili powder
450 g/1 lb fresh tomatoes	1 lb fresh tomatoes
600 ml/1 pint water	2½ cups water
1 tablespoon cardamom seeds	1 tablespoon cardamom seeds

Dice the lamb into 1-cm/½-inch cubes. Slice the onion and sauté in the oil until lightly browned. Add the cumin seeds, cinnamon, cloves and ginger. Crush the garlic and fry with the onions, curry powder, paprika and chilli powder for 3–4 minutes. Add the meat and sauté until well browned. Peel and chop the tomatoes and add to the meat mixture with the water. Sprinkle the cardamom seeds on top. Cover and simmer gently for 1½ hours. Add more water during cooking if necessary. Cool.
To freeze: Pack in convenient quantities. Seal and label.
To serve: Turn frozen curry into a saucepan, add a small amount of water, cover and reheat gently to boiling point, stirring frequently. Serve with rice, poppadums, mango chutney, grated coconut and sliced bananas.
Serves: 12.
Storage time: 4–6 months.

Never-fail flaky pastry

METRIC/IMPERIAL	AMERICAN
600 g/1¼ lb plain flour	5 cups all-purpose flour
1 teaspoon salt	1 teaspoon salt
225 g/8 oz margarine	1 cup margarine
225 g/8 oz lard	1 cup shortening
1 egg	1 egg
2 tablespoons white vinegar	3 tablespoons white vinegar
175 ml/6 fl oz water	¾ cup water

Sift the flour and salt into a large bowl. Rub the lard into the flour until the mixture resembles coarse breadcrumbs. Beat the egg lightly with the vinegar and water. Add the liquid to the flour and fat mixture, tossing lightly with a fork until a soft dough forms.
To freeze: Pack in convenient quantities. Seal and label.
To serve: Defrost only sufficiently to enable you to roll out.
Makes: 1·25 kg/2½ lb pastry.
Storage time: 4–6 months.

Pork pot pies

METRIC/IMPERIAL	AMERICAN
450 ml/¾ pint beef stock	2 cups beef stock
½ teaspoon salt	½ teaspoon salt
½ teaspoon dried basil	½ teaspoon dried basil
1 medium onion	1 medium onion
2 large carrots	2 large carrots
1 stick celery	1 stalk celery
50 g/2 oz plain flour	½ cup all-purpose flour
3 tablespoons water	¼ cup water
450 g/1 lb cooked pork or lamb	1 lb cooked pork or lamb
225 g/8 oz frozen peas	½ lb frozen peas
1 quantity Never-fail flaky pastry (see above)	1 quantity Never-fail flaky pastry (see above)

Pour the beef stock into a large saucepan and add the salt and basil. Chop the onion, carrots and celery. Add to the beef stock and simmer for 30 minutes. Mix the flour and water to a smooth paste and slowly stir into the vegetable-stock mixture. Cook and stir over medium heat until thickened. Cool quickly by putting the pan in iced water. Cut the meat into bite-sized pieces. Divide the meat and frozen peas between 12 individual shaped foil pie dishes. Spoon the thickened sauce and vegetables over the meat and peas. Defrost the pastry, roll out and use to cover the pies. Trim the edges and crimp well.
To freeze: Open freeze then cover. Seal and label.
To serve: Unwrap and make 3 or 4 slits in the pastry top. Bake from frozen in a moderately hot oven (200°C, 400°F, Gas Mark 6) for 35–40 minutes.
Makes: 12 individual pies.
Storage time: 4–6 months.

Chicken pot pies

METRIC/IMPERIAL
75 g/3 oz chicken fat or butter
50 g/2 oz plain flour
1 teaspoon salt
pinch white pepper
300 ml/½ pint chicken stock
300 ml/½ pint milk
450 g/1 lb cooked chicken, diced
225 g/8 oz frozen mixed vegetables
1 quantity Never-fail flaky pastry
  (see page 140)

AMERICAN
6 tablespoons chicken fat or butter
½ cup all-purpose flour
1 teaspoon salt
pinch white pepper
1¼ cups chicken stock
1¼ cups milk
1 lb cooked chicken, diced
½ lb frozen mixed vegetables
1 quantity Never-fail flaky pastry
  (see page 140)

Melt the fat in a large saucepan. Stir in the flour, salt and pepper. Cook for 1 minute, then gradually stir in the chicken stock and milk. Cook and stir over low heat until thickened. Remove from the heat and cool quickly. Divide the diced cooked chicken and frozen mixed vegetables between 12 individual shaped foil pie dishes. Spoon the thickened sauce over the chicken and vegetables. Defrost the pastry, roll out and use to cover the pies. Trim the edges and crimp well.
To freeze: Open freeze then cover. Seal and label.
To serve: Unwrap and make 3 or 4 slits in the pastry top. Bake from frozen in a moderately hot oven (200°C, 400°F, Gas Mark 6) for 35–40 minutes.
Makes: 12 individual pies.
Storage time: 4–6 months.

Frozen ambrosia

METRIC/IMPERIAL
250 ml/8 fl oz pineapple juice
450 ml/¾ pint unsweetened orange juice
6 tablespoons lemon juice
200 g/7 oz icing sugar
2 (64-g/2¼-oz) packets dessert topping mix
when serving:
150 ml/¼ pint double cream
little desiccated coconut

AMERICAN
1 cup pineapple juice
2 cups unsweetened orange juice
½ cup lemon juice
1½ cups confectioners' sugar
2 (2¼-oz) packages dessert topping mix
when serving:
⅔ cup heavy cream
little shredded coconut

Mix the fruit juices with the icing sugar until the sugar dissolves. Pour into 12 individual foil or polythene moulds, filling each one about half full. Prepare the dessert topping mix according to the packet directions. Spoon whipped topping mix on top of the fruit juice, but do not combine with it.
To freeze: Open freeze until firm. Seal and label.
To serve: Unmould on serving plates. Whip the cream and use to pipe decorations on each serving. Sprinkle with desiccated coconut.
Serves: 12.
Storage time: 4–6 months.

Menu

Grapefruit and mint sorbets

METRIC/IMPERIAL
175 g/6 oz sugar
150 ml/¼ pint water
2 grapefruit
small bunch fresh mint
2 egg whites
when serving:
sprigs fresh mint

AMERICAN
¾ cup sugar
⅔ cup water
2 grapefruit
small bunch fresh mint
2 egg whites
when serving:
sprigs fresh mint

Dissolve the sugar in the water over gentle heat then boil for 3 minutes. Cool. Cut the grapefruit in half and carefully scoop out the flesh, keeping the shells intact and discarding any pith or pips. Strip the mint leaves from the stalks and wash them. Place the mint leaves and grapefruit flesh in a blender, pour over the syrup and liquidise until smooth. Pour into a shallow container and freeze until mushy. Meanwhile, vandyke the edges of the grapefruit shells (i.e. cut out a series of small Vs) with a sharp knife. Liquidise the grapefruit mixture again and fold in the stiffly beaten egg whites. Spoon some of the sorbet into the prepared grapefruit shells and the remainder into a small polythene container.
To freeze: Seal container and freeze. Open freeze grapefruit shells until firm then cover. Seal and label.
To serve: Unpack the grapefruit halves and scoop extra sorbet on top of each one. Decorate each one with a tiny sprig of mint and allow to soften in the refrigerator for 10 minutes before serving.
Makes: 8 servings/4 in shells.
Storage time: 4–6 months.

New Zealand guard of honour

METRIC/IMPERIAL
2 best ends of neck of lamb, each with 6
  bones
when serving:
salt and pepper to taste
sprigs parsley

AMERICAN
2 racks of lamb, each with 6 bones
when serving:
salt and pepper to taste
sprigs parsley

Remove the chine bone from each joint and clean the bone tips of 3·5 cm/1½ inches of fat. The butcher may be prepared to do this for you but he will probably charge for the service. Press the two joints together, crossing the bones in the centre. Pad the bones with crumpled foil to avoid puncturing the pack.
To freeze: Cover with cling film. Seal and label.
To serve: Defrost and remove wrapping, but leave foil pads on the bone ends. Place the joint in a well greased roasting tin and sprinkle with salt and pepper. Roast in a moderate oven (180°C, 350°F, Gas Mark 4) for 30–35 minutes per 450 g/1 lb. Serve on a hot dish, surrounded by the potato nests and peas. Garnish with sprigs of parsley.
Serves: 4–5.
Storage time: 4–6 months.

Duchesse potato nests

METRIC/IMPERIAL	AMERICAN
1·75 kg/4 lb potatoes	4 lb potatoes
100 g/4 oz butter	½ cup butter
2 eggs	2 eggs
½ teaspoon ground nutmeg	½ teaspoon ground nutmeg
salt and pepper to taste	salt and pepper to taste
when serving:	*when serving:*
little beaten egg	little beaten egg
50 g/2 oz frozen peas per nest	2 oz frozen peas per nest

Peel and slice the potatoes. Cook in boiling salted water until tender, then drain well and mash thoroughly. Beat in the butter, eggs and seasonings. Pipe the potato mixture in the form of nests on to non-stick baking trays, or on to baking trays lined with non-stick parchment or greased foil.

To freeze: Open freeze until solid then pack in foil containers. Seal and label.

To serve: Uncover and brush the required number of frozen nests with beaten egg. Reheat in a moderately hot oven (200°C, 400°F, Gas Mark 6) for 25 minutes. If you are using the oven for another purpose the nests can be reheated at a moderate temperature (180°C, 350°F, Gas Mark 4) for 30 minutes, or in a hot oven (220°C, 425°F, Gas Mark 7) for 20 minutes. Meanwhile, cook the peas in very little boiling salted water until tender, drain and use to fill the nests.

Storage time: 4–6 months.

Apricot cream gâteau

METRIC/IMPERIAL	AMERICAN
175 g/6 oz self-raising flour	1½ cups all-purpose flour sifted with 1½ teaspoons baking powder
pinch salt	pinch salt
175 g/6 oz butter	¾ cup butter
175 g/6 oz castor sugar	¾ cup sugar
3 eggs	3 eggs
300 ml/½ pint double cream	1¼ cups heavy cream
10 canned apricot halves	10 canned apricot halves
5 glacé cherries and angelica	5 candied cherries and angelica
1 packet orange quick-setting jelly	1 package orange quick-setting jello

Sift the flour and salt. Cream together the butter and sugar until light and fluffy and beat in the eggs, one at a time. Fold in the flour. Place the mixture in a greased and floured 1-kg/2-lb loaf tin and bake in a moderate oven (160°C, 325°F, Gas Mark 3) for 45–50 minutes. Cool on a wire rack. Split the cake in half. Whip the cream and use one-third to sandwich the two layers of cake together. Spread a little cream evenly around the sides of the cake. Drain the apricots well and arrange them on top of the cake, placing the cherries in between with small spikes of angelica. Make up the jelly as directed on the packet, and when just setting use to glaze the fruit. Allow to set. Pipe the remaining cream to decorate the top of the gâteau.

To freeze: Open freeze on a rigid base. Cover with container. Seal and label.

To serve: Keep covered and defrost in the refrigerator overnight, or at room temperature for 3 hours.

Serves: 5–6.

Storage time: 4–6 months.

Small Family Living in Town

A home in town usually has the advantages of shopping facilities, amusements and public transport close by, but is sometimes restricted in space for the family to expand. Every cupboard is carefully counted by architects when they design buildings for super-expensive urban sites! The kitchen often does double duty as dining-room, and the housewife is more likely than her country cousin to go out to work at least part of the day.

As always when space is limited, it has to be allocated carefully to major pieces of domestic equipment. Here is the ideal situation for a fridge/freezer, which stacks one essential item on top of the other, using the minimum of floor space. Since time is also precious, you really cannot do without either of these, the busy housewife's best friends.

If you live in a flat, the kitchen is often the only possible home for the freezer, as you are less likely to have easy access to a garage than the house-dweller, and there is no upstairs room where the noise of the freezer motor running will not be heard. Neither, of course, do you have that useful cupboard space under the stairs. One of your problems may be your inability to buy frozen food in bulk, for lack of space to store it. Shopping just has to be a little more frequent in your case, but at least it is simple to find a choice of good suppliers within easy reach. It is even practical for you to shop around and compare prices and special offers to get the best bargains available. A balance of storage space which gives you slightly more refrigerated storage but at least 142 litres/5 cubic foot of frozen food storage would be your minimum requirement.

Often it is difficult to get the whole family to sit down together and mealtimes have to be staggered to fit in with mother's working day, father's arrival home from the office and children's tea after school. Keeping the freezer stocked with home-cooked food is sometimes a struggle since time to cook for it has to be found. But if you make a strict study, you will find the occasional cook-in pays dividends.

Be enterprising in using special packaging that saves time and trouble by taking food straight from the freezer to the cooker. Food packed in roasting film goes into the oven, or packed in boilable bags goes straight into a pan of boiling water on top of the cooker.

Your parties are unlikely to be huge affairs – there is simply no room to hold a banquet in the average town home. So go Continental with an occasional wine and cheese party, or, to be more original, choose the food and drink of another country. For you I have suggested a German beer and pumpernickel party based on purchases from the delicatessen counter. Just freeze the traditional layered cheese sandwiches and piped canapés ahead of time.

In Part III of this book there are many suggestions for food to please the children, including dishes they can take out of the freezer and get ready to eat themselves, but be extra careful over labelling; use big labels and write clear serving directions on them for the kids.

144

Iced lollies – an instant success with children of all ages

German-style buffet party – creamy canapés, fried cheese balls, salami cornets, blue cheese dip, pumpernickel cheese towers (pages 154–155)

146

Left: High rise puffs (page 150). Below: Cider spiced gammon with cranberried apples (opposite)

148

Cider spiced gammon with cranberried apples

(Illustrated opposite)

METRIC/IMPERIAL

1·5 kg/3 lb middle gammon joint
about 600 ml/1 pint cider
about 600 ml/1 pint water
2 bay leaves
8 peppercorns
3 whole allspice
sprig thyme
bouquet garni
4 tablespoons demerara sugar
cranberried apples:
150 ml/¼ pint cider vinegar
75 g/3 oz brown sugar
100 g/4 oz granulated sugar
1 teaspoon mixed pickling spices
4 tablespoons water
4 tablespoons cranberry jelly
6 small dessert apples
1 teaspoon arrowroot
when serving:
sprigs parsley

AMERICAN

3 lb ham steak or butt
2½ cups cider
2½ cups water
2 bay leaves
8 peppercorns
3 whole allspice
sprig thyme
bouquet garni
⅓ cup brown sugar
cranberried apples:
⅔ cup cider vinegar
6 tablespoons brown sugar
½ cup granulated sugar
1 teaspoon mixed pickling spices
⅓ cup water
⅓ cup cranberry jelly
6 small dessert apples
1 teaspoon arrowroot
when serving:
sprigs parsley

Place the joint in plain cold water, bring to the boil, drain and cover with the cider and water mixture. Add the spices and herbs and bring to the boil again. Cover the pan and simmer gently for 20 minutes per 450 g/1 lb plus 20 minutes over. Top up during cooking with more water if necessary. When the joint is cooked, drain and allow to cool slightly before stripping off the rind. Score the fat into large diamonds. Press the demerara sugar into the fat and bake in a hot oven (220°C, 425°F, Gas Mark 7) for about 10 minutes, until lightly browned. While the joint is cooking make the cranberried apples. Mix together the vinegar, sugars, pickling spices and water and simmer for 5 minutes. Add the cranberry jelly and stir until completely melted. Peel the apples, leaving the stalks on, and poach gently in the spiced syrup until tender but still retaining their shape. Carefully remove with a slotted draining spoon. Moisten the arrowroot with 2 teaspoons water and add to the remaining syrup. Bring to the boil, stirring constantly, until the sauce is clear and shiny. Place the gammon on a hot serving dish, surround with the apples and spoon over a little cranberry sauce. Garnish with parsley sprigs. Serve the remaining sauce separately.
To freeze left-over ham: Cool quickly, cut into neat dice and pack in polythene containers. Seal and label.
To serve: Defrost the sealed pack in the refrigerator overnight.
Serves: 8–10, hot or cold.
Storage time: 2 months.
NOTE: The pickled cranberry sauce stores well in the freezer but the pickling spices should therefore be tied in muslin and removed before the sauce is frozen down. When using, bring the defrosted sauce back to the boil, stirring briskly until smooth.
Variation: Pickled peaches can be prepared in a similar manner. Use canned peach halves, omit the cranberry jelly, reduce the amount of granulated sugar to 75 g/3 oz/6 tablespoons and substitute 4 tablespoons (US ⅓ cup) syrup from the canned peaches for the water. Serve the peaches round the joint and, if liked, spoon a little cranberry jelly into each one.

High rise puffs

(Illustrated on page 148)

METRIC/IMPERIAL	AMERICAN
100 g/4 oz plain flour	1 cup all-purpose flour
pinch salt	pinch salt
2 eggs	2 eggs
300 ml/½ pint milk and water, mixed	1¼ cups milk and water, mixed
pinch dried mixed herbs	pinch dried mixed herbs
when serving:	*when serving:*
4 teaspoons oil	4 teaspoons oil
50–75 g/2–3 oz chopped ham, defrosted	⅓ cup chopped ham, defrosted
24 blanched almonds	24 blanched almonds

Place the flour and salt in a mixing bowl. Make a well in the centre and drop in the eggs. Gradually add the milk liquid and beat well until smooth. Stir in the mixed herbs and allow to stand for 10 minutes.

To freeze: Pack allowing headspace. Seal and label.

To serve: Defrost at room temperature for 3 hours. Pour ½ teaspoon oil into each of 8 Yorkshire pudding tins, 10 cm/4 inches in diameter, and heat in a hot oven (220°C, 425°F, Gas Mark 7) for 10 minutes. Meanwhile, beat the batter. Remove the tins from the oven and divide the batter among them. Sprinkle 1 tablespoon of ham and 3 almonds in the centre of each and bake for 15–20 minutes until well risen and golden brown. Serve immediately.

Makes: 8 puffs.

Storage time: 4–6 months.

Ways with Roasting Film: Excellent for large joints in the lower price bracket because cooking by this method retains juices and keeps them moist. Also for reheating parcels of cooked food.

Brisket of beef

(Illustrated on page 77)

METRIC/IMPERIAL	AMERICAN
25 g/1 oz butter	2 tablespoons butter
1 tablespoon oil	1 tablespoon oil
about 1·5-kg/3-lb joint of unsalted rolled brisket	about 3-lb joint unsalted rolled brisket
salt and pepper to taste	salt and pepper to taste
when serving:	*when serving:*
450 g/1 lb potato, diced	1 lb potato, diced
350 g/12 oz turnip, diced	¾ lb turnip, diced
350 g/12 oz carrot, sliced	¾ lb carrot, sliced
2 small onions, sliced	2 small onions, sliced
1 stick celery, sliced	1 stalk celery, sliced
salt and pepper to taste	salt and pepper to taste

Heat the butter and oil and use to brown the joint all over. Sprinkle with salt and pepper and allow to cool.

To freeze: Place the joint on a sheet of roasting film, bring the plain edges together over the top and fold down two or three times. Crimp the foil edges together to seal. Label.

To serve: Defrost the sealed pack in the refrigerator overnight then place in a roasting tin, making sure the foil seals are as high as possible. Cook in a moderate oven (170°C, 325°F, Gas Mark 3) for 2½–3 hours. The prepared vegetables can be cooked together with a little seasoning in a small roasting bag placed in the oven with the joint for about 30 minutes, or in a little lightly salted water in a saucepan on top of the cooker. Make a bed of vegetables on a hot serving dish and serve the joint on top.

Serves: 6–8.

Storage time: 4–6 months.

Stuffed cheese pancakes

(Illustrated on page 77)

METRIC/IMPERIAL	AMERICAN
225 g/8 oz plain flour	2 cups all-purpose flour
1 teaspoon dry mustard	1 teaspoon dry mustard
½ teaspoon salt	½ teaspoon salt
¼ teaspoon pepper	¼ teaspoon pepper
100 g/4 oz hard cheese, grated	1 cup grated hard cheese
2 eggs	2 eggs
25 g/1 oz butter, melted	2 tablespoons melted butter
600 ml/1 pint milk	2½ cups milk
oil for frying	oil for frying

suggested fillings:

1. Cooked minced beef bound with thick brown gravy
2. Cooked minced beef mixed with finely diced pickled beetroot
3. Chopped cooked chicken in saffron-flavoured savoury white sauce
4. Flaked tuna mixed with diced cooked potato and chopped parsley

suggested fillings:

1. Cooked ground beef bound with thick brown gravy
2. Cooked ground beef mixed with finely diced pickled beets
3. Chopped cooked chicken in saffron-flavored savory white sauce
4. Flaked tuna mixed with diced cooked potato and chopped parsley

Sift together the flour, mustard and salt and pepper. Add the grated cheese and make a well in the centre. Mix together the eggs, melted butter and the milk and add to the dry ingredients, beating well until smooth. Allow to stand for 30 minutes. Beat up the batter again. Heat a very little oil in a small frying pan and fry the pancakes on both sides until golden brown. Stack the cooked pancakes with dividers and cool. When cold, stuff with one of the suggested fillings.

To freeze: Make up the filled pancakes into packs of convenient quantities, mixing the flavours if you wish. If liked, decorate the top of each pancake with a few chopped vegetables. Place the pancakes on a sheet of roasting film, bring the plain edges together over the top and fold down two or three times. Crimp the foil edges together to seal. Label.

To serve: Defrost the sealed pack in the refrigerator overnight then place in a roasting tin and reheat in a moderately hot oven (190°C, 375°F, Gas Mark 5) for 15–20 minutes.

Makes: 20 pancakes.

Storage time: 4–6 months.

Ways with Boilable Bags: A selection of foods frozen in these bags can be immersed in boiling water in one pan straight from the freezer. With care they can be washed and used again and you don't even have a dirty saucepan.

Smoked cod in orange sauce

(Illustrated on page 17)

METRIC/IMPERIAL	AMERICAN
450 g/1 lb smoked cod fillet	1 lb smoked cod fillet
600 ml/1 pint milk	2½ cups milk
40 g/1½ oz butter	3 tablespoons butter
40 g/1½ oz flour	6 tablespoons flour
pinch ground nutmeg	pinch ground nutmeg
grated zest and juice of 1 orange	grated rind and juice of 1 orange
salt and pepper to taste	salt and pepper to taste
when serving:	*when serving:*
450 g/1 lb frozen carrot slices	1 lb frozen carrot slices
450 g/1 lb frozen cauliflower florets	1 lb frozen cauliflower florets
little grated orange zest	little grated orange rind

Cut the fish into large chunks. Cover with water, bring to the boil, drain off and discard the water. Pour over the milk and simmer gently, covered, for about 10 minutes, until the fish is tender. Melt the butter in a clean saucepan and stir in the flour. Gradually add the strained milk from cooking the fish and bring to the boil, stirring all the time. Add the nutmeg and the orange zest and juice, stir well and cook for 2 minutes. Season to taste with pepper and salt if necessary. Place the fish with the sauce in a boilable bag and allow to cool.
To freeze: Press out excess air; fasten the seal above your clenched hand to create a vacuum to allow air inside the bag to expand as food reheats. Label.
To serve: Place the bag, still frozen, in a large saucepan of boiling water, together with a boilable bag containing the frozen blanched carrot slices and one containing the frozen blanched cauliflower florets. Bring back to the boil and simmer for 30 minutes. Arrange alternate piles of carrot and cauliflower round the edge of a hot serving dish and pour the cod and sauce into the centre. Garnish the vegetables with a sprinkling of grated orange zest.
Serves: 4.
Storage time: 3–4 months.

How to make iced lollies

Diluted lime cordial, orange squash and lemon squash will make refreshing lollies for the children, but here are some more exciting ideas for you to try.

Fruity orange: Put a fresh orange slice into each mould and cover with diluted orange squash.

Harlequin: Make up some diluted lemon squash, fill the bases of the moulds with a little and freeze. Colour a little more squash red with food colouring and add a layer to the moulds, tilting them to one side. Freeze until firm then top up with green coloured squash.

Blackcurrant blush: Add sufficient blackcurrant syrup to milk to flavour it well and give a good colour.

Easy Creamy Sweets: One to take out of the freezer the night before, and the other just before the meal if you cannot plan ahead, so you are never at a loss for a really glamorous finale.

Lemon refrigerated cheesecake

METRIC/IMPERIAL	AMERICAN
100 g/4 oz digestive biscuits	¼ lb graham crackers
50–75 g/2–3 oz margarine	4–6 tablespoons margarine
25 g/1 oz soft brown sugar	2 tablespoons soft brown sugar
225 g/8 oz full fat soft cheese	½ lb full fat soft cheese
75 g/3 oz castor sugar	6 tablespoons granulated sugar
2 eggs, separated	2 eggs, separated
1 (175-ml/6-fl oz) carton lemon yogurt	¾ cup lemon yogurt
juice and grated zest of ½ lemon	juice and grated rind of ½ lemon
15 g/½ oz gelatine	2 envelopes gelatin
4 tablespoons water	⅓ cup water
150 ml/¼ pint double cream	⅔ cup heavy cream

Crush the biscuits finely. Melt the margarine and the brown sugar together and stir in the biscuit crumbs. Press the mixture into the base of a greased 20-cm/8-inch or 23-cm/9-inch cake tin with a loose bottom and chill. Cream the cheese and castor sugar until smooth. Gradually add the egg yolks, yogurt and the lemon zest and juice. Dissolve the gelatine in the water, in a basin over a pan of hot water. Cool slightly and add to the creamed mixture, blending thoroughly. Lightly whip the cream. Whisk the egg whites until they stand in soft peaks and fold carefully into the mixture with the cream. Pour over the prepared base and chill until firm.
To freeze: Open freeze and then dip the tin in hot water. Remove the cheesecake to a foil plate or serving dish. Wrap closely. Seal and label.
To serve: Unwrap while still frozen and defrost in the refrigerator overnight.
Makes: 1 cheesecake/6–8 servings.
Storage time : 4–6 months.

Marshmallow coffee mousse

(Illustrated on page 36)

METRIC/IMPERIAL	AMERICAN
600 ml/1 pint milk	2½ cups milk
1 packet coffee blancmange	1 package coffee blancmange
2 tablespoons very strong black coffee	3 tablespoons very strong black coffee
225 g/8 oz marshmallows	½ lb marshmallows
2 egg whites	2 egg whites

Make up the blancmange as directed on the packet, blending the powder with the coffee instead of the equivalent amount of milk. Allow to cool and thicken. Melt the marshmallows in a basin over a pan of hot water and stir into the coffee mixture. Beat the egg whites until stiff and fold in gently. Pour into individual glasses or into shaped foil trays and allow to set.
To freeze: Cover glasses with cling film or foil and smooth down edges. Cover trays with lids or foil. Seal and label.
To serve: Uncover individual glasses and allow to defrost at room temperature for 1 hour. Decorate each with a rosette of whipped cream and toasted flaked almonds. Or, scoop from the trays into glass dishes.
Serves: 4–6.
Storage time: 4–6 months.
NOTE: To make Marshmallow chocolate mousse use a chocolate flavoured blancmange and melt 25 g/1 oz plain chocolate with the marshmallows.

Menu

German-style buffet party for twelve
(Illustrated on pages 146–147)
Mellow blue cheese dip, with fingers
of Westphalia Farmbread, pickled
gherkins and onions
Cheeseboard with smoked processed
cheeses and Emmenthal, with
Bavarian sweet mustard and
Melba toast
Cornets of Westphalian salami piped
with cream cheese
Pumpernickel cheese towers
Fried cheese balls
Creamy canapés with cucumber,
radish and tomato toppings
Light German beer

Blue cheese dip

METRIC/IMPERIAL	AMERICAN
450 g/1 lb blue cheese	1 lb blue cheese
1 tablespoon grated onion	1 tablespoon grated onion
1 tablespoon chopped parsley	1 tablespoon chopped parsley
150 ml/¼ pint soured cream	⅔ cup sour cream
salt and pepper to taste	salt and pepper to taste

Crumble the blue cheese into a bowl and mash with a fork. Gradually add the remaining ingredients, mixing until well combined.
To freeze: Pack in convenient quantities. Seal and label.
To serve: Defrost at room temperature for 3–4 hours, depending on size of pack. Beat well and pile into a serving dish.
Serves: 8–10.
Storage time: 4–6 months.

Salami cornets

METRIC/IMPERIAL	AMERICAN
12 slices salami	12 slices salami
100 g/4 oz cream cheese	¼ lb cream cheese
4 tablespoons double cream	⅓ cup heavy cream
salt and pepper to taste	salt and pepper to taste
when serving:	*when serving:*
12 slices ham sausage	12 slices ham sausage
few slices gherkin	few slices sweet dill pickle

Remove rind and cut in towards the centre of each slice of salami. Roll round to form a cornet and secure with a cocktail stick. Beat together the cream cheese and the cream. Season and place in a piping bag fitted with a star tube. Pipe a swirl of creamy mixture into each cornet.
To freeze: Arrange in a shallow rigid-based container and cover the uneven surfaces lightly with cling film. Seal and label.
To serve: Partially defrost in the container, remove the seal and cling film and arrange on a board. Place rolled slices of ham sausage between the cornets and just before serving remove the cocktail sticks and garnish each cornet with a piece of gherkin.
Serves: 12.
Storage time: 3 months.

Pumpernickel cheese towers

METRIC/IMPERIAL
1 packet dark pumpernickel
50 g/2 oz butter
1 (90-g/3½-oz) packet horseradish cheese
  spread
1 (90-g/3½-oz) packet smoked cheese
  slices
when serving:
cucumber slices
radishes

AMERICAN
1 package dark pumpernickel
¼ cup butter
½ cup horseradish cheese spread
3½ oz smoked cheese slices
when serving:
cucumber slices
radishes

Separate the pumpernickel slices and butter them. Spread very lightly with horseradish cheese spread and cover with cheese slices. Build up four layers and press under a weight. Cut each four-layer sandwich into 6 portions.
To freeze: Pack in foil. Seal and label.
To serve: Defrost in the pack overnight. At serving time, stand each tower on a cucumber slice and top with a radish spiked on a wooden cocktail stick and pressed into the centre.
Serves: 12.
Storage time: 4–6 months.

Fried cheese balls

METRIC/IMPERIAL
450 g/1 lb cream cheese
1 teaspoon grated onion
2–3 tablespoons fresh white breadcrumbs
salt and pepper to taste
chopped almonds for coating
when serving:
oil for frying

AMERICAN
1 lb cream cheese
1 teaspoon grated onion
3–4 tablespoons fresh white breadcrumbs
salt and pepper to taste
chopped almonds for coating
when serving:
oil for frying

Combine the cream cheese, onion, breadcrumbs and seasoning and mix well. Form into balls the size of a walnut and toss in chopped almonds. Chill well.
To freeze: Pack in layers with dividers. Seal and label.
To serve: Fry from the frozen state in deep hot oil until golden brown.
Makes: 20–24 cheese balls.
Storage time: 4–6 months.

Large Family Living in the Country

How could a family like yours get the best out of life without the help of a freezer? With fresh food of all descriptions literally at your door and the possibility of growing so much garden produce, the bigger the freezer for you the better. Space in a country kitchen is not likely to be so jealously allocated as it is in town but if your kitchen is not spacious enough to accommodate a large chest freezer, a garage, pantry, or even a barn ought to take care of it. About 400 litres/14 cubic feet of storage space would not be too much for your needs, and with a large family you should go for a bigger one still, unless you intend to join the growing band of two-freezer families.

Your freezer is unlikely to become a vast store cupboard for commercial packs, so you ought to consider carefully the arguments for and against blanching vegetables; experiment with identified packs to be used up quickly on which you have skipped blanching. You will also get more value from knowing how to utilise the fruit which crops particularly well. In a good apple year there is quite a risk of a family rebellion against 'apples with everything'. When the carrot harvest is twice as heavy as last year's, yet another way to serve them is a godsend. Making imaginative use of home produce is a great part of the freezer art for the country family. The barter system for items you would prefer to have instead rarely works in the country because everyone in the neighbourhood has the same surplus to dispose of.

Children are staunch supporters of 'pudding', the indispensable second course which must be sweet, whether it is baked and served hot or frozen and served cold. They also love bread and butter, especially with fresh fruit preserves from the freezer, as much as you like the same jams with hot crusty rolls.

You may not visit the freezer centre for fruit or vegetables, but to cater for quite a few people you will probably bulk buy your meat and poultry and financially these will be your big investment. Buying straight from the farm, however, may not prove to be such an economy as you suppose when you first see a tempting notice near the farmyard gate, 'Chickens by the case', quoting a very low price. It is likely the chickens will be plucked but not drawn, unless you arrange with the farmer to make them 'oven-ready' and this service is not usually included in the price. Problems also arise in buying meat direct from a farm because butchering is a specialised job, requiring more expertise than plucking a bird.

In Part III, Freezing for Everyone, you will find bulk cooking chains for breads, sausages, meat, poultry and cakes. The recipes in your section are planned to help a country family take advantage of their enviable rural surroundings, as follows:

1. Savoury and sweet ways with apples.
2. Lots of ideas for using short-season fruits.
3. Suggestions for family meals from a roast turkey, which could be adapted to use with chicken, plus enterprising ideas with roasting bags.
4. The sort of informal party to give in a large room or outside in the garden.

A family in the country can freeze bumper crops of fruit and vegetables for use throughout the year

Eve's pudding (page 162); Late summer pudding (page 160); Apple and peach turnovers (page 161)

Apple muesli

METRIC/IMPERIAL	AMERICAN
4 tablespoons rolled oats	⅓ cup rolled oats
2 tablespoons lemon juice	3 tablespoons lemon juice
4 tablespoons sweetened condensed milk	⅓ cup sweetened condensed milk
3 large apples	3 large apples
50 g/2 oz hazel nuts, finely chopped	½ cup finely chopped hazel nuts

Mix the rolled oats with the lemon juice and condensed milk. Allow to stand for 1 hour. Grate the apples into the rolled oat mixture and add the chopped hazel nuts.
To freeze: Pack in convenient quantities. Seal and label.
To serve: Defrost at room temperature for 1–2 hours or overnight in the refrigerator. Serve as a breakfast cereal or for dessert.
Serves: 4
Storage time: 4–6 months.

Dapple mince

METRIC/IMPERIAL	AMERICAN
2 slices rye or wholemeal bread	2 slices rye or wholemeal bread
2 tablespoons oil	3 tablespoons oil
225 g/8 oz onions, finely chopped	½ lb onions, finely chopped
700 g/1½ lb minced beef	1½ lb ground beef
½ teaspoon dried marjoram	½ teaspoon dried marjoram
pinch ground cloves	pinch ground cloves
pinch ground allspice	pinch ground allspice
salt and pepper to taste	salt and pepper to taste
1 tablespoon flour	2 tablespoons flour
350 g/12 oz cooking apples, peeled and diced	¾ lb baking apples, peeled and diced
1 beef stock cube	1 beef bouillon cube

Remove the crusts from the bread and cut into small pieces. Crumble the bread to make crumbs. Heat the oil in a large saucepan, fry the crust pieces and reserve. Sauté the onions in the pan until softened. Add the meat and cook, stirring, until it changes colour. Sprinkle over the herbs, spices, seasonings and flour and stir until well blended. Add the diced apple and mix in lightly. Place half the meat mixture in a shaped foil dish, cover with the breadcrumbs, then with the remaining meat mixture. Make up the stock cube with 150 ml/¼ pint/⅔ cup boiling water, pour over the meat mixture and top with the fried crust pieces. Cool.
To freeze: Cover with lid or foil. Seal and label.
To serve: Defrost in the refrigerator overnight and then uncover and place in a moderately hot oven (200°C, 400°F, Gas Mark 6) for 30 minutes.
Serves: 6.
Storage time: 4–6 months.

Lamb apple and ginger curry

METRIC/IMPERIAL	AMERICAN
2 tablespoons oil	3 tablespoons oil
450 g/1 lb boned lamb, diced	1 lb boned lamb, diced
1 large onion, chopped	1 large onion, chopped
2 teaspoons cornflour	2 teaspoons cornstarch
2 teaspoons ground turmeric	2 teaspoons ground turmeric
salt to taste	salt to taste
1 tablespoon curry powder	1 tablespoon curry powder
1 large cooking apple	1 large baking apple
grated zest and juice of ½ lemon	grated rind and juice of ½ lemon
2 tablespoons sultanas	3 tablespoons seedless white raisins
4 pieces stem ginger, chopped	4 pieces preserved ginger, chopped
2 tablespoons ginger syrup from the jar	3 tablespoons ginger syrup from the jar
1 chicken stock cube	1 chicken bouillon cube
150 ml/¼ pint natural yogurt	⅔ cup unflavored yogurt

Heat the oil and use to fry the meat quickly until brown on all sides. Remove and keep hot. Sauté the onion in the remaining oil until soft but not brown. Replace the meat and sprinkle in the cornflour, turmeric, salt and curry powder. Mix well and cook gently for 2 minutes. Peel and dice the apple and stir into the pan with the lemon zest and juice, sultanas, ginger and ginger syrup. Make up the stock cube with 150 ml/¼ pint/⅔ cup boiling water, add to the mixture and bring to the boil. Cover the pan, reduce the heat and simmer gently for 30 minutes, or until the meat is tender. Add the yogurt, taste and adjust the seasoning. Cool.
To freeze: Pack in convenient quantities. Seal and label.
To serve: Reheat the frozen curry in a pan, stirring frequently.
Serves: 6.
Storage time: 3 months.
NOTE: This is rather a mild curry so increase the curry powder if you prefer.

Late summer pudding

(Illustrated on page 158)

METRIC/IMPERIAL	AMERICAN
12–16 thin slices white bread	12–16 thin slices white bread
1·25 kg/2½ lb raspberries and blackberries mixed	2½ lb raspberries and blackberries mixed
1 kg/2 lb cooking apples	2 lb baking apples
sugar to taste	sugar to taste

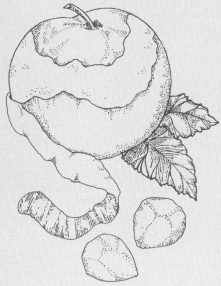

Remove the crusts from the bread slices and line 2 700-g/1½-lb foil pudding basins with the bread, reserving some for the tops. Keep a few raspberries for decoration if desired and place the remainder in a saucepan with the blackberries. Peel, core and slice the apples and add to the pan with sugar to taste. Simmer until the fruit is soft. Divide the fruit mixture between the lined basins and top with the reserved bread. Cover with lids and seal. Place weights on top of the puddings and chill in the refrigerator overnight.
To freeze: Recheck seals and label. Freeze extra raspberries separately.
To serve: While still frozen, turn out on a serving dish and defrost at room temperature for 4 hours. Decorate with the reserved raspberries.
Makes: 2 puddings/12 servings.
Storage time: 4–6 months.

Apple cake

METRIC/IMPERIAL
275 g/10 oz self-raising flour
1 teaspoon salt
1 teaspoon ground mixed spice
100 g/4 oz butter
225 g/8 oz castor sugar
1 egg, lightly beaten
1 teaspoon vanilla essence
450 g/1 lb apples, peeled and grated
½ teaspoon caraway seeds

AMERICAN
2½ cups all-purpose flour sifted with 2½
    teaspoons baking powder
1 teaspoon salt
1 teaspoon ground mixed spice
½ cup butter
1 cup sugar
1 egg, lightly beaten
1 teaspoon vanilla extract
1 lb apples, peeled and grated
½ teaspoon caraway seeds

Sift the flour with the salt and spice. Cream the butter and sugar until light and fluffy. Gradually beat in the egg and vanilla essence. Stir in the grated apple and fold in the flour. Place in a greased and lined 18-cm/7-inch square or 20-cm/8-inch round cake tin, smooth the top and sprinkle with the caraway seeds. Bake in a moderate oven (180°C, 350°F, Gas Mark 4) for 1¼ hours, or until a skewer inserted in the cake comes out clean. Leave in the tin for 5 minutes then cool on a wire rack.
To freeze: Wrap closely. Seal and label.
To serve: Defrost, still wrapped, at room temperature for 4 hours.
Storage time: 4–6 months.

Apple and peach turnovers

(Illustrated on page 158)

METRIC/IMPERIAL
700 g/1½ lb shortcrust pastry
700 g/1½ lb cooking apples, peeled, cored
    and sliced
4 medium peaches
¼ teaspoon ground nutmeg
grated zest of 1 lemon
sugar to taste
beaten egg white to glaze
castor sugar to sprinkle

AMERICAN
1½ lb basic pie dough
1½ lb baking apples, peeled, cored and
    sliced
4 medium peaches
¼ teaspoon ground nutmeg
grated rind of 1 lemon
sugar to taste
beaten egg white to glaze
sugar to sprinkle

Roll out the pastry on a lightly floured board and cut into rounds 13 cm/5 inches in diameter. Peel and stone the peaches, chop roughly and mix at once with the sliced apple, nutmeg, lemon zest and sufficient sugar to sweeten, according to the tartness of the cooking apples. Place a little of the fruit mixture in the centre of each pastry circle. Dampen the edges, fold over and seal well, fluting the edges with finger and thumb. Place on a baking tray and brush with lightly beaten egg white. Sprinkle with sugar and make a small vent in each turnover with a fine skewer. Bake in a moderately hot oven (200°C, 400°F, Gas Mark 6) for 20–30 minutes, until golden brown. Cool.
To freeze: Pack in layers with dividers. Seal and label.
To serve: Place still frozen in a moderately hot oven as above for 20 minutes.
To freeze unbaked: Open freeze then pack as above. Cook from frozen on a baking tray in a hot oven (220°C, 425°F, Gas Mark 7) for 30 minutes.
Makes: 16 turnovers.
Storage time: 4–6 months.

Eve's pudding

(Illustrated on page 158)

METRIC/IMPERIAL	AMERICAN
1·5 kg/3 lb cooking apples	3 lb baking apples
sugar to taste	sugar to taste
grated zest of 1 orange	grated rind of 1 orange
225 g/8 oz margarine	1 cup margarine
225 g/8 oz castor sugar	1 cup sugar
4 eggs	4 eggs
225 g/8 oz self-raising flour	2 cups all-purpose flour sifted with 2
when serving:	teaspoons baking powder
little castor sugar	*when serving:*
	little sugar

Peel, core and slice the apples and divide between 2 greased 6-portion shaped foil trays, about 15 cm/6 inches by 20 cm/8 inches. Sprinkle the apples with sugar to taste and the orange zest. Cream the margarine and sugar until light and fluffy. Lightly beat the eggs and gradually add to the creamed mixture, beating well all the time. Fold in the flour. Spread the mixture carefully over the apples, dividing it equally between the containers.
To freeze: Open freeze until solid, then cover with lids or foil. Seal and label.
To serve: Uncover and place still frozen in a moderately hot oven (190°C, 375°F, Gas Mark 5) for 50 minutes, until risen and golden brown on top. Sprinkle with sugar before serving.
Makes: 2 puddings/12 servings.
Storage time: 4–6 months.

Apple mint jelly

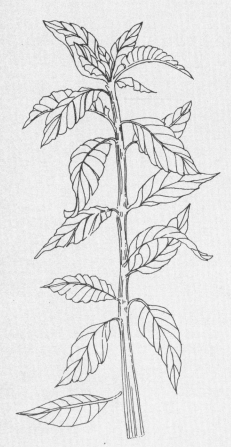

METRIC/IMPERIAL	AMERICAN
1 kg/2 lb cooking apples	2 lb baking apples
50 g/2 oz fresh mint leaves	2 oz fresh mint leaves
600 ml/1 pint water	2½ cups water
1·5 kg/3¼ lb sugar	6½ cups sugar
3 tablespoons lemon juice	¼ cup lemon juice
6 tablespoons liquid fruit pectin	½ cup liquid fruit pectin

Wash and cut up the apples roughly. Place in a large pan with the mint leaves, add the water and simmer, covered, for 20 minutes, until the apple is soft. Strain overnight through a fine cloth or jelly bag. Do not squeeze the bag or the jelly will be cloudy. If necessary, make the juice up to 900 ml/1½ pints/3¾ cups with water and pour into a preserving pan. Add the sugar and lemon juice and heat gently, stirring occasionally, until the sugar has dissolved. Bring quickly to a full rolling boil, stir in the pectin and boil rapidly for 1 minute, stirring occasionally. Add a few drops of green food colouring, just sufficient to tint the jelly pale green. Remove from the heat, skim if necessary and cool.
To freeze: Pour into small containers. Seal and label.
To serve: Defrost at room temperature for 30 minutes and if possible store in the refrigerator once opened.
Makes: 900 ml/1½ pints/3¾ cups.
Storage time: 12 months.
NOTE: I actually have some mint in my garden called Applemint which is ideal for this recipe, but any of the varieties usually grown are suitable.

A good crop should provide
sorbets, toppings for ice cream,
puddings, desserts and freezer jams to
see your family through the year.

Apricot and raspberry topping

(Illustrated on page 56)

METRIC/IMPERIAL	AMERICAN
450 g/1 lb apricots	1 lb apricots
450 g/1 lb raspberries	1 lb raspberries
300 g/11 oz sugar	scant ½ cup sugar
600 ml/1 pint water	2½ cups water

Stone and quarter the apricots. Mix gently with the raspberries and divide
among 2 or 3 polythene containers. Dissolve the sugar in the water over
moderate heat, then allow to boil steadily until reduced to about 600 ml/
1 pint/2½ cups. Cool the syrup and when completely cold pour over the fruit.
To freeze: Place crumpled foil on top of the fruit to keep it under the syrup. Seal
and label.
To serve: Defrost, spoon over ice cream and decorate with walnuts, or heat the
fruit in its syrup, thicken it slightly with arrowroot and use while still warm.
Makes: 1 litre/1¾ pints/4¼ cups topping.
Storage time: 4–6 months.

Blackberry freezer jam

(Illustrated on page 55)

METRIC/IMPERIAL	AMERICAN
1 kg/2 lb blackberries	2 lb blackberries
1·5 kg/3½ lb castor sugar	7 cups sugar
4 tablespoons lemon juice	⅓ cup lemon juice
250 ml/8 fl oz liquid fruit pectin	1 cup liquid fruit pectin

Place the prepared fruit, sugar and lemon juice in a bowl. Stir well and allow to
stand in a warm place until the sugar has completely dissolved. Stir in the pectin
and when the jam begins to set ladle into polythene or freezer-tested glass
containers.
To freeze: Seal and allow to stand in a warm place overnight. Check seal and
label.
To serve: Defrost at room temperature for about 30 minutes, depending on size
of container. Store in the refrigerator after defrosting.
Makes: About 2·5 kg/5½ lb jam.
Storage time: 12 months.
NOTE: To use as a filling for a sponge flan, pour in shortly before it is required
to be served to avoid colour from the fruit soaking into the sponge.

Raspberry and rhubarb freezer preserve

METRIC/IMPERIAL	AMERICAN
1 kg/2 lb rhubarb	2 lb rhubarb
450 g/1 lb sugar	2 cups sugar
½ teaspoon ground nutmeg	½ teaspoon ground nutmeg
450 g/1 lb raspberries	1 lb raspberries
1 (127-g/4½-oz) packet raspberry jelly	1 package raspberry jello

Cut the rhubarb into 2·5-cm/1-inch lengths and place in a large saucepan. Add the sugar and nutmeg, stir and allow to stand overnight. Add the raspberries and cook, stirring, until boiling. Remove from the heat. Break up the jelly tablet and stir into the fruit mixture until melted. Cool.
To freeze: Pour into polythene or freezer-tested glass containers. Seal and label.
To serve: Defrost at room temperature for about 30 minutes, depending on size of container. Store in the refrigerator after defrosting.
Makes: About 1·5 kg/3¼ lb preserve.
Storage time: 12 months.

Gingered rhubarb crumble

METRIC/IMPERIAL	AMERICAN
1 kg/2¼ lb rhubarb	2¼ lb rhubarb
100 g/4 oz castor sugar	½ cup granulated sugar
2 tablespoons water	3 tablespoons water
6 pieces stem ginger, chopped	6 pieces preserved ginger, chopped
2 tablespoons ginger syrup from the jar	3 tablespoons ginger syrup from the jar
225 g/8 oz plain flour	2 cups all-purpose flour
2 teaspoons ground ginger	2 teaspoons ground ginger
100 g/4 oz butter	½ cup butter
100 g/4 oz demerara sugar	½ cup brown sugar

Trim the rhubarb and cut into 2·5-cm/1-inch lengths. Place in a saucepan with the castor sugar and water. Cook gently until tender. Carefully stir in the chopped ginger and the syrup but try not to break up the fruit. Divide the mixture between 2 deep shaped foil containers and allow to cool. To make the crumble, sift the flour and ground ginger into a bowl and rub in the butter. Stir in the demerara sugar. Divide this mixture between the dishes, spooning evenly over the fruit. Firm the crumble mixture with the back of a metal spoon and smooth the tops.
To freeze: Cover with lid or foil. Seal and label.
To serve: Uncover and place the frozen crumble in a moderately hot oven (190°C, 375°F, Gas Mark 5) for 45–50 minutes.
Serves: 8.
Storage time: 4–6 months.

Loganberry fool

METRIC/IMPERIAL
1 kg/2¼ lb loganberries
100 g/4 oz soft brown sugar
300 ml/½ pint made custard
300 ml/½ pint double cream
when serving:
few toasted almonds, flaked

AMERICAN
2¼ lb loganberries
½ cup soft brown sugar
1¼ cups made custard
1¼ cups heavy cream
when serving:
few toasted flaked almonds

Place the loganberries in a saucepan with the sugar and cook gently, crushing with a wooden spoon, until soft. Mash well and push through a sieve. Stir the purée into the custard until well blended. Whip the cream until just thick and fold evenly into the fruit mixture.
To freeze: Divide between 8 individual containers, or 2 large containers. Seal and label.
To serve: Uncover and allow to defrost at room temperature for 2 hours if small, 4 hours if large. Decorate the surface with toasted flaked almonds.
Serves: 8.
Storage time: 4–6 months.

Strawberry Pavlova

(Illustrated on page 96)

METRIC/IMPERIAL
3 egg whites
175 /6 oz castor sugar
pinch salt
when serving:
150 ml/¼ pint double cream
225 g/8 oz frozen strawberries

AMERICAN
3 egg whites
¾ cup sugar
pinch salt
when serving:
⅔ cup heavy cream
½ lb frozen strawberries

Prepare a baking tray by covering with non-stick parchment. Draw a 20-cm/8-inch circle lightly on this and brush with oil. Whisk the egg whites in a bowl until they are stiff. Sprinkle in half the sugar and whisk until the mixture is as stiff as before. Using a metal tablespoon, gently fold in the remaining sugar with the salt. Spread one-third of the meringue mixture over the marked circle, keeping within the pencilled outline. Put the remaining mixture in a piping bag fitted with an open star tube and pipe rosettes round the edge of the meringue circle. Use the remaining meringue to pipe extra rosettes on another baking tray, lined in the same way, for decoration. Place in a very cool oven (110°C, 225°F, Gas Mark ¼) for 2–2½ hours, until completely dry, removing the separate rosettes first if necessary. Do not allow to become browned. Remove from the oven. Peel off the paper and cool the meringue case and rosettes on a wire rack.
To freeze: Pack in a rigid-based container. Seal and label.
To serve: Place the frozen Pavlova on a serving plate. Whip the cream until thick and partially defrost the strawberries. Spread half the cream in the meringue case, cover with a layer of halved strawberries, reserving the best-looking ones for the decoration, and cover with the remainder of the cream. Arrange the separate meringue rosettes on the cream and place the remaining strawberries gently in the centre. Serve at once before the strawberries thaw out fully.
Storage time: 3 months.
NOTE: The meringue case can be made ahead of time and frozen separately in a rigid-based polythene container, or stored 2–3 weeks in an airtight tin.

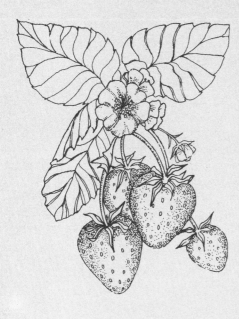

Strawberry and rhubarb double crust pie

METRIC/IMPERIAL	AMERICAN
700 g/1½ lb shortcrust pastry	1½ lb basic pie dough
1 kg/2¼ lb rhubarb	2¼ lb rhubarb
1 kg/2¼ lb strawberries	2¼ lb strawberries
350 g/12 oz sugar	1½ cups sugar
6 tablespoons cornflour	½ cup cornstarch
2 teaspoons finely grated orange zest	2 teaspoons finely grated orange rind
25 g/1 oz butter, melted	2 tablespoons melted butter
when serving:	*when serving:*
little castor sugar	little sugar

Roll out two-thirds of the pastry and use to line 2 deep 20-cm/8-inch or 23-cm/9-inch pie plates. Chill these while you make up the filling. Trim the rhubarb and cut into 1-cm/½-inch slices. Cut the strawberries into slices. Place the fruit, sugar, cornflour, orange zest and melted butter in a bowl and stir until well mixed. Allow to stand for 15 minutes then divide the fruit mixture between the pastry pie shells. Roll out the remaining pastry and make lids for the pies. Dampen the edges of the pastry and seal well, fluting the edges.
To freeze: Cover closely. Seal and label.
To serve: Uncover and cut three steam vents in the top of the frozen pies. Bake in a hot oven (220°C, 425°F, Gas Mark 7) for 20 minutes. Reduce heat to moderate (180°C, 350°F, Gas Mark 4) for a further 40–45 minutes and serve sprinkled with castor sugar.
Makes: 2 pies/12 servings.
Storage time: 4–6 months.

Strawberry sorbet

(Illustrated on page 95)

METRIC/IMPERIAL	AMERICAN
1 kg/2¼ lb strawberries	2¼ lb strawberries
juice of ½ lemon	juice of ½ lemon
juice of ½ orange	juice of ½ orange
225 g/8 oz sugar	1 cup sugar
150 ml/¼ pint water	⅔ cup water
2 egg whites	2 egg whites
when serving:	*when serving:*
strawberries or chopped nuts	strawberries or chopped nuts

Sieve the strawberries to make 600 ml/1 pint/2½ cups of purée and add the lemon and orange juices. Place the sugar and water in a saucepan and stir over low heat until the sugar has dissolved. Bring to the boil and continue boiling without stirring for 5 minutes, until a little cooled syrup forms a short thread between thumb and forefinger. Cool. When the syrup is cold, add to the strawberry mixture and pour into a shallow container and freeze until firm around the sides. Turn into a bowl and mash well until mushy. Beat the egg whites stiffly and fold into the frozen mixture until well blended.
To freeze: Pack in convenient quantities. Seal and label.
To serve: Place in the refrigerator for 30 minutes to soften slightly then scoop into glass dishes. Decorate with fresh strawberries if possible, or chopped nuts.
Makes: 900 ml/1½ pints/3¾ cups sorbet.
Storage time: 4–6 months.

Turkey in cream sauce with grapes

(Illustrated on page 106)

METRIC/IMPERIAL	AMERICAN
100 g/4 oz green grapes	¼ lb white grapes
1 tablespoon dry vermouth	1 tablespoon dry vermouth
300 ml/½ pint savoury white sauce	1¼ cups savory white sauce
4 tablespoons double cream	⅓ cup heavy cream
salt and pepper to taste	salt and pepper to taste
1 egg yolk	1 egg yolk
350 g/12 oz cooked turkey, diced	¾ lb cooked turkey, diced
2 teaspoons chopped tarragon	2 teaspoons chopped tarragon
2 teaspoons chopped mint	2 teaspoons chopped mint

Ways with Cooked Turkey: A big roast turkey should supply plenty of meat for a festive meal and sufficient frozen down to make three other dishes: 1) a mixture of brown and white meat diced in a delicious hot savoury; 2) delicate slices from the breast for a sumptuous salad; and 3) other pieces that are not so neat, diced to make a filling for a savoury pie to freeze down.

Peel the grapes and remove the pips. Place the peeled grapes in a small basin and pour over the vermouth. Allow to marinate for 1 hour if possible. Place the sauce in a pan and strain in the marinade. Heat gently to boiling point, add the cream, stir over gentle heat and adjust seasoning if necessary. Remove from the heat, whisk in the egg yolk then stir in the turkey. Reserve about 12 grapes and add the rest to the turkey mixture. Stir well and reheat without allowing to boil. Place the mixture in a serving dish, scatter the remaining grapes over the top and sprinkle the herbs round the edge of the dish.
Serves: 4.

Turkey salamagundy

(Illustrated on page 107)

METRIC/IMPERIAL	AMERICAN
2 hard-boiled eggs	2 hard-cooked eggs
2 spring onions	2 scallions
350 g/12 oz cooked turkey breast	¾ lb cooked turkey breast
4 tablespoons mayonnaise	⅓ cup mayonnaise
15-cm/6-inch length cucumber, sliced	6-inch length cucumber, sliced
1 small lettuce	1 small head lettuce
small bunch radishes, trimmed	small bunch radishes, trimmed
few sprigs watercress	few sprigs watercress
1 teaspoon chopped parsley	1 teaspoon chopped parsley

Shell the eggs, halve them, press the yolks through a sieve and chop the whites. Finely chop the white part of the spring onions. Slice the turkey thickly to display the brown skin on the edges of the slices. Trim the slices and combine the trimmings with the mayonnaise, chopped egg whites and onions. Pile up the mayonnaise mixture in the centre of a flat serving platter, surround with overlapping cucumber slices and top with the sieved egg yolk. Make a bed of lettuce leaves round the edge of the plate, arranging the turkey slices like the spokes of a wheel and propping up each slice on a radish. Garnish with remaining radishes, whole and sliced, sprigs of watercress and the chopped parsley.
Serves: 4.

Turkey, ham and mushroom pie

(Illustrated on page 108)

METRIC/IMPERIAL	AMERICAN
600–700 g/1¼–1½ lb cooked turkey and ham	1¼–1½ lb cooked turkey and ham
100 g/4 oz mushrooms, sliced	1 cup sliced mushrooms
3 tablespoons chopped parsley	¼ cup chopped parsley
300 ml/½ pint savoury white sauce	1¼ cups savory white sauce
1 (212-g/7½-oz) packet frozen puff pastry, defrosted	½ lb frozen puff paste, defrosted
when serving:	*when serving:*
little beaten egg	little beaten egg

Dice the meat and combine with the mushrooms, parsley and sauce. Place in a pie dish. Roll out the pastry and use to cover the pie. Decorate with pastry leaves made with the pastry trimmings. Mark a criss-cross design with a sharp knife on top of the pastry.
To freeze: Cover with foil. Seal and label.
To serve: Unwrap, brush with beaten egg and bake from the frozen state in a moderately hot oven (200°C, 400°F, Gas Mark 6) for 45 minutes.
Serves: 6.
Storage time: 4–6 months.

Carrot nuggets

METRIC/IMPERIAL	AMERICAN
3 medium carrots	3 medium carrots
350 g/12 oz brown sugar	1½ cups brown sugar
350 g/12 oz margarine	1½ cups margarine
2 eggs	2 eggs
1 teaspoon vanilla essence	1 teaspoon vanilla extract
1 tablespoon grated orange zest	1 tablespoon grated orange rind
3 tablespoons orange juice	¼ cup orange juice
2½ teaspoons baking powder	2½ teaspoons baking powder
450 g/1 lb wholewheat flour	1 lb wholewheat flour
50 g/2 oz nuts, chopped	½ cup chopped nuts

Finely dice the carrots. Cook in a small amount of boiling salted water until tender. Drain and allow to cool. Cream the brown sugar and margarine until light and fluffy. Beat in the eggs and vanilla essence. Add the remaining ingredients and the cooked carrots. Stir until well combined. Drop by spoonfuls on to a lightly greased baking tray. Bake in a moderate oven (170°C, 325°F, Gas Mark 3) for 20–25 minutes.
To freeze: Pack in convenient quantities. Seal and label.
To serve: Unpack and defrost at room temperature and spread out on a serving dish for 30 minutes.
Makes: 72 nuggets.
Storage time: 4–6 months.

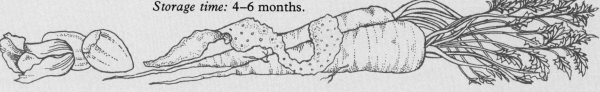

Roasting Bags for Freezer-to-oven Meals: It's a super convenience to whisk filled bags straight from the freezer into a roasting tin, and cook immediately or after defrosting, without having to handle the food or wash up afterwards.

Gammon steaks with plum sauce

(Illustrated on page 78)

METRIC/IMPERIAL	AMERICAN
75 g/3 oz sugar	6 tablespoons sugar
150 ml/¼ pint water	⅔ cup water
½ teaspoon ground cinnamon	½ teaspoon ground cinnamon
1 teaspoon tomato purée	1 teaspoon tomato paste
1 teaspoon vinegar	1 teaspoon vinegar
salt and pepper to taste	salt and pepper to taste
450 g/1 lb red plums	1 lb red plums
4 gammon steaks	4 ham steaks
1 tablespoon oil	1 tablespoon oil

Dissolve the sugar in the water over gentle heat then boil for 1 minute. Remove from the heat and stir in the cinnamon, tomato purée, vinegar and salt and pepper to taste. Halve and stone the plums, add to the pan and simmer gently until just tender. Cool. Derind the gammon steaks and snip the fat. Heat the oil and use to fry the steaks quickly for 1 minute on each side. Remove and cool. Pack each steak in a small roasting bag and pack the sauce in a similar bag.
To freeze: Remove excess air from bags. Seal and label.
To serve: Place all the bags in a roasting tin, making sure that the bottom edges are pointing upwards, and snip off 1 cm/½ inch from one corner of each of the four steak bags. Do not snip the sauce bag. Cook from the frozen state in a moderately hot oven (190°C, 375°F, Gas Mark 5) for about 45 minutes. Serve the steaks sprinkled with salt and black pepper and garnished with parsley. Spoon a little sauce on each steak and serve the remainder separately.
Storage time: 2 months.

Piggy in the bag

(Illustrated on page 78)

METRIC/IMPERIAL	AMERICAN
4 pork chops	4 pork chops
2 teaspoons made mustard	2 teaspoons made mustard
salt and pepper to taste	salt and pepper to taste
1 red sweet pepper	1 red sweet pepper
2 small tomatoes	2 small tomatoes
1 leek or 1 bunch spring onions	1 leek or 1 bunch scallions
3 rashers bacon	3 bacon slices
2 medium potatoes, sliced	2 medium potatoes, sliced

Spread the chops thinly on each side with mustard and season with salt and pepper. Deseed and chop the pepper, peel and slice the tomatoes and chop the leek or spring onions. Derind the bacon and cut into small pieces. Blanch the potato slices in boiling water for 1 minute then drain and place in a large roasting bag. Mix together the chopped pepper, tomato slices, chopped leek and the bacon. Arrange this mixture on the chops and lift them carefully into the bag on top of the potatoes.
To freeze: Remove excess air from the bag. Seal and label.
To serve: Defrost in the refrigerator then place the bag in a roasting tin with the bottom edges pointing upwards. Snip 1 cm/½ inch from one corner. Cook in a moderately hot oven (190°C, 375°F, Gas Mark 5) for about 45 minutes.
Storage time: 4–6 months.

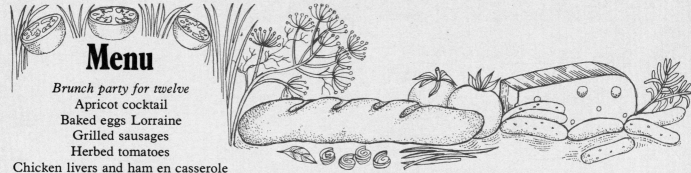

Menu

Brunch party for twelve
Apricot cocktail
Baked eggs Lorraine
Grilled sausages
Herbed tomatoes
Chicken livers and ham en casserole
Hot crusty bread
Almond French toast
Whipped strawberry butter
Refrigerator bran muffins
Butter curls   Blackberry freezer jam
Iced fruit bowl
Cremocha

Apricot cocktail

METRIC/IMPERIAL	AMERICAN
450 g/1 lb dried apricots	1 lb dried apricots
2 litres/3½ pints pineapple juice	4½ pints pineapple juice
150 ml/¼ pint lemon juice	⅔ cup lemon juice
when serving:	*when serving:*
granulated sugar	sugar
2 bananas, sliced	2 bananas, sliced
12 ice cubes	12 ice cubes

Place the apricots in a saucepan, cover with water and allow to stand overnight. Simmer the apricots in the soaking water until tender. Liquidise or press through a sieve and stir in the pineapple and lemon juices.
To freeze: Pack in polythene containers. Seal and label.
To serve: Defrost overnight in the refrigerator. Dip the rim of each serving glass in a small amount of the apricot cocktail and then in the sugar. Chill the sugar frosted glasses until required. At serving time, drop a few thin slices of banana and an ice cube in each glass and pour the apricot nectar over.
Serves: 12.
Storage time: 4–6 months.

Baked eggs Lorraine

METRIC/IMPERIAL	AMERICAN
12 rashers streaky bacon	12 bacon slices
100 g/4 oz Gruyère cheese	¼ lb Gruyère cheese
12 eggs	12 eggs
salt and pepper to taste	salt and pepper to taste
1 teaspoon chopped chives	1 teaspoon chopped chives
175 ml/6 fl oz single cream	¾ cup light cream

Cut the bacon into 1-cm/½-inch dice. Grill or fry the bacon pieces and drain on absorbent paper. Arrange the cooked bacon in a shallow lightly buttered ovenproof dish. Grate the cheese over the bacon. Break the eggs and arrange individually over the bacon and cheese mixture. Sprinkle with salt, pepper and the chopped chives. Pour the cream over the eggs. Bake in a moderate oven (180°C, 350°F, Gas Mark 4) for 15–20 minutes until the eggs are set. To serve, cut in squares, allowing 1 egg per person. Do not place on a warming tray, as this would overcook the eggs. This dish can stand at room temperature for up to 1 hour without loss of flavour. Serve with hot croissants.
Serves: 12.

Herbed tomatoes

METRIC/IMPERIAL
6 large tomatoes
25 g/1 oz butter, softened
4 tablespoons chopped fresh herbs

AMERICAN
6 large tomatoes
2 tablespoons softened butter
⅓ cup chopped fresh herbs

Cut each tomato in half and spread the cut side with butter. Sprinkle the herbs on top. Grill until just heated through.
Serves: 12.
NOTE: Any combination of herbs may be used – parsley, chives, tarragon, rosemary, dill, thyme, etc.

Chicken livers and ham en casserole

METRIC/IMPERIAL
1 kg/2 lb chicken livers
1 small onion
50 g/2 oz butter
300 ml/½ pint chicken stock
600 ml/1 pint milk
150 ml/¼ pint single cream
100 g/4 oz butter
50 g/2 oz plain flour
4 tablespoons sherry
4 tablespoons chopped parsley
¼ teaspoon Worcestershire sauce
450 g/1 lb cooked ham
salt and pepper to taste
when serving:
150 ml/¼ pint soured cream

AMERICAN
2 lb chicken livers
1 small onion
¼ cup butter
1¼ cups chicken stock
2½ cups milk
⅔ cup light cream
½ cup butter
½ cup all-purpose flour
⅓ cup sherry
⅓ cup chopped parsley
¼ teaspoon Worcestershire sauce
1 lb cooked ham
salt and pepper to taste
when serving:
⅔ cup sour cream

Cut the chicken livers in half and chop the onion finely. Fry the chicken livers and the onion in the butter until tender. Lift out the chicken livers and set aside. Stir the chicken stock, milk and single cream into the pan. Mix the butter with the flour and add in small pieces to the pan, whisking well until the sauce thickens. Stir in the sherry, parsley, chicken livers and Worcestershire sauce. Dice the ham and add to the chicken liver mixture. Season to taste with salt and pepper. Cool.
To freeze: Pack in convenient quantities. Seal and label.
To serve: Defrost overnight. Turn into a large chafing dish, stir in the soured cream and reheat to boiling point. Serve with melba toast.
Serves: 12.
Storage time: 2–3 months.

Almond French toast

METRIC/IMPERIAL	AMERICAN
3 eggs	3 eggs
pinch salt	pinch salt
3 tablespoons castor sugar	¼ cup sugar
300 ml/½ pint milk	1¼ cups milk
½ teaspoon almond essence	½ teaspoon almond extract
12 slices white bread	12 slices white bread

Beat the eggs, salt, sugar, milk and almond essence together. Dip the bread into the egg mixture, coating both sides of each slice. Place the bread slices on well buttered baking trays and bake in a hot oven (230°C, 450°F, Gas Mark 8) for 7 minutes, turn and bake until golden brown. Cool.
To freeze: Pack in layers in convenient quantities. Seal and label.
To serve: Reheat from frozen in a hot oven, as above, for 6–7 minutes. Serve hot with whipped strawberry butter or maple syrup.
Makes: 12 slices.
Storage time: 6 weeks.

Whipped strawberry butter

METRIC/IMPERIAL	AMERICAN
225 g/8 oz butter	1 cup butter
175 g/6 oz icing sugar	1⅓ cups confectioners' sugar
450 g/1 lb fresh or frozen strawberries	1 lb fresh or frozen strawberries

Beat the butter with the sugar until light and fluffy then beat in the strawberries.
To freeze: Pack in convenient quantities. Seal and label.
To serve: Defrost, beat until fluffy and spoon into a serving bowl. Chill until serving time.
Makes: 12.
Storage time: 4–6 months.
NOTE: If using frozen strawberries, defrost and drain well before using.

Refrigerator bran muffins

METRIC/IMPERIAL	AMERICAN
175 g/6 oz natural bran	6 oz natural bran
600 g/1¼ lb granulated sugar	2½ cups sugar
225 g/8 oz margarine	1 cup margarine
450 ml/¾ pint boiling water	2 cups boiling water
4 eggs	4 eggs
900 ml/1½ pints buttermilk	3¾ cups buttermilk
1 teaspoon salt	1 teaspoon salt
600 g/1¼ lb plain flour	5 cups all-purpose flour
4 teaspoons bicarbonate of soda	4 teaspoons baking soda
450 g/1 lb All-bran	1 lb All-bran

In a large bowl, mix the natural bran, sugar, margarine and boiling water. Allow to cool for a few minutes. Beat in the eggs, one at a time, stir in the buttermilk and salt. Sift the flour and bicarbonate of soda into a large bowl and stir in the All-bran. Make a well in the centre of the dry ingredients and pour in the buttermilk-bran mixture. Stir lightly until all the flour is moistened. To bake, fill greased deep bun tins two-thirds full and bake in a moderately hot oven (200°C, 400°F, Gas Mark 6) for 15–20 minutes. Cool.

To freeze: Pack in convenient quantities. Seal and label.

To serve: Defrost and then reheat in a moderately hot oven, as above, for 5 minutes. If required quickly, place still frozen and wrapped in foil in a hot oven (230°C, 450°F, Gas Mark 8) for 15 minutes.

Makes: 60 bran muffins.

Storage time: 6 months.

NOTE: The unbaked dough can be stored in the refrigerator in a tightly covered container for up to 2 months. Spoon out the quantity required and refrigerate the remainder. This recipe is a great help when you are planning a big party and the freezer is already filled to bursting point!

Iced fruit bowl

Fill a large punch bowl with fresh unpeeled apples, oranges, grapefruit, apricots, tangerines, plums, pears or any other fruit in season. At serving time, cover the fruit with water and add ice cubes.

Cremocha

METRIC/IMPERIAL	AMERICAN
25 g/1 oz instant coffee	½ cup instant coffee
2 tablespoons cocoa	3 tablespoons cocoa
4 tablespoons sugar	⅓ cup sugar
1 litre/1¾ pints water	4¼ cups water
450 ml/¾ pint milk	2 cups milk
150 ml/¼ pint single cream	⅔ cup light cream
½ teaspoon vanilla essence	½ teaspoon vanilla extract
300 ml/½ pint double cream	1¼ cups heavy cream
ground nutmeg or cinnamon	ground nutmeg or cinnamon

Mix the coffee, cocoa and sugar in a large saucepan. Stir in the water and bring to the boil. Reduce the heat and stir in the milk, single cream and vanilla essence. Keep warm. Whisk the double cream until stiff. Serve the Cremocha in coffee mugs, topped with a spoonful of whipped cream sprinkled with nutmeg or cinnamon.

Makes: 12 175-ml/6 fl-oz/¾-cup servings.

Sophisticated Couple with Gourmet Tastes

Your lifestyle probably involves more entertaining than most others and so you need plenty of freezer storage space to increase the pleasure of party giving. When meals are elaborate, or you are coping with a large number of guests, chilled storage space is important too. Fortunately you can enjoy such luxuries as a choice of temperature zones, special accommodation for slow thawing of frozen food and automatic defrosting all hidden away behind one door in an upright cabinet, side by side with a twin freezer. This kind of equipment is not cheap but many hostesses have told me they find it almost worth another pair of hands in the kitchen.

Around 283 litres/10 cubic feet of space to store frozen food sounds a lot, but not for those who frequently serve meals to a number of guests, or even regularly serve a number of courses. The matching larder fridge is bigger, but this would be a good investment if you have wine to chill and drinks to keep cold. Bottles are terribly space-consuming. A worthwhile exercise for you would be to stock up an 'ice-bank' in your freezer, so that plenty is always available. Choose ice cube makers with care so that they turn out with a twist of the wrist. If you transfer cubes to a large container without allowing them any opportunity to defrost slightly they do remain separate, but it's a disaster if your ice cube trays require a douse of water to release their contents. Crushed ice makes the most elegant setting for a starter that is intended to be served chilled and the effect can easily be obtained by placing one tiny glass container inside a slightly larger one, embedded in the ice.

Experience shows that a lot of time is saved in the end by allocating a definite container or shelf to the food you prepare for a particular occasion. It is not even necessary to label with such care if you know that the foil packs of fish and game pâtés are planned to accompany the bags of poppy-seed rolls. The unruffled hostess cannot afford a last-minute panic, searching through the shelves for one essential pack without which the table setting will be incomplete!

Planning a menu is an art in itself and one which needs practice to develop. To be too ambitious may be disastrous. But you can present an elaborate menu by enlisting the aid of your freezer. The secret is to plan ahead, dividing the work between items which can be prepared well in advance, those which can be frozen or refrigerated just beforehand and the few vital items which need your last-minute attention. By introducing a judicious blend of dishes which could not possibly be frozen (especially salads) you can avoid giving an impression that the meal emerged complete from the freezer's depths. For example, a scattering of fresh avocado slices on a shellfish bisque, or a tower of firm ripe strawberries on a snowy meringue gâteau.

The recipes in your section are planned to show how this effect can be achieved for a party out of doors and a dinner party by candlelight. To keep the changes ringing on simpler three-course menus you will find a choice of exotic starters and sweets.

174

Snowy meringue and fresh fruit make a dessert any hostess will be proud of

176

Barbecue party for eight

Menu

Barbecue party for eight
Lamb kebabs with orange spice sauce
Cutlets in lemon ginger marinade
Herby garlic bread
Baby beetroot in soured cream
Fruit in curry mayonnaise
Wine – Macon

Outdoor Entertaining: A sophisticated barbecue party for eight is often far more pleasant in summer than even the most beautifully served meal at the dining table.

Herby garlic bread

METRIC/IMPERIAL	AMERICAN
1 French loaf	1 French loaf
100 g/4 oz butter	½ cup butter
1 clove garlic, crushed	1 clove garlic, crushed
juice of ½ lemon	juice of ½ lemon
salt and black pepper to taste	salt and black pepper to taste
2 teaspoons chopped mint	2 teaspoons chopped mint
2 teaspoons chopped parsley	2 teaspoons chopped parsley
2 teaspoons chopped chives	2 teaspoons chopped chives
2 teaspoons chopped marjoram	2 teaspoons chopped marjoram

Cut the loaf into 1-cm/½-inch slices. Cream the remaining ingredients together and spread generously on the bread slices. Reshape into a loaf.
To freeze: Wrap in foil. Seal and label.
To serve: Place on the griddle or in the coals and allow 20 minutes for reheating if frozen, 10 minutes if defrosted.
Serves: 8.
Storage time: 2–4 weeks.
Variation: Place a slice of cheese between the bread slices when reshaping.

Lamb kebabs with orange spice sauce

METRIC/IMPERIAL	AMERICAN
2 green sweet peppers	2 green sweet peppers
450–700 g/1–1½ lb shoulder of lamb, defrosted and cubed	1–1½ lb lamb shoulder, defrosted and cubed
salt and pepper to taste	salt and pepper to taste
oil for brushing	oil for brushing
sauce:	*sauce:*
1 teaspoon made mustard	1 teaspoon made mustard
1 tablespoon cornflour	1 tablespoon cornstarch
2 tablespoons water	3 tablespoons water
175 g/6 oz soft brown sugar	¾ cup soft brown sugar
1 (178-ml/6¼-fl oz) can frozen concentrated orange juice	6 fl oz frozen concentrated orange juice
4 tablespoons Worcestershire sauce	⅓ cup Worcestershire sauce
juice of 1 lemon	juice of 1 lemon

Deseed and cut the peppers into small pieces. Thread the cubed lamb and pepper on to skewers, season with salt and pepper and brush with oil. Place over the barbecue (or under the grill) and cook for 10–15 minutes, turning occasionally. To make the sauce, blend together the mustard, cornflour and water and mix with all the other ingredients in a saucepan. Bring to the boil, stirring continuously. Simmer for 2 minutes and serve with the kebabs.
Serves: 8.
NOTE: The sauce can be made and frozen in advance. Defrost from the frozen state in a small pan.

Cutlets in lemon ginger marinade

METRIC/IMPERIAL
16 best end cutlets of lamb
marinade:
150 ml/¼ pint oil
grated zest of 2 lemons
4 tablespoons lemon juice
2 tablespoons brown sugar
3 teaspoons ground ginger
salt and pepper to taste

AMERICAN
16 rib lamb chops
marinade:
⅔ cup oil
grated rind of 2 lemons
⅓ cup lemon juice
3 tablespoons brown sugar
1 tablespoon ground ginger
salt and pepper to taste

Place the frozen chops in a shallow dish. Mix all the marinade ingredients together and pour over them. Leave for 3–4 hours, turning occasionally. Remove the cutlets and place over the barbecue (or under a hot grill) and cook for 15 minutes. Turn occasionally and baste with the marinade.
Serves: 8.
NOTE: To save time on the day of the party the defrosted cutlets can be refrozen in the marinade, or the marinade made up on its own and frozen in a small container.

Fruit in curry mayonnaise

METRIC/IMPERIAL
3 oranges
3 dessert apples
1 tablespoon lemon juice
75 g/3 oz walnuts, chopped
6 sticks celery, diced
2 tablespoons concentrated curry sauce
6 tablespoons mayonnaise

AMERICAN
3 oranges
3 dessert apples
1 tablespoon lemon juice
¾ cup chopped walnuts
6 stalks celery, diced
3 tablespoons concentrated curry sauce
½ cup mayonnaise

Peel the oranges and remove the pith. Segment but do this over a bowl to catch all the juice. Core and dice the apple without peeling and toss in the lemon juice to prevent discoloration. Mix the nuts with the orange segments and juice, the apple dice and celery dice and place on a serving dish. Blend together the curry sauce and mayonnaise and serve with the salad.
Serves: 8.

Baby beetroot in soured cream

METRIC/IMPERIAL
400 g/14 oz pickled baby beetroot
1 small onion, sliced
150 ml/¼ pint soured cream

AMERICAN
14 oz pickled baby beets
1 small onion, sliced
⅔ cup sour cream

Drain the beetroot and divide the onion slices into rings. Place these in a serving dish and spoon over the soured cream.
Serves: 8.
NOTE: If you use frozen baby beetroot, defrost and chop them before tossing in a little vinegar and well seasoned soured cream.

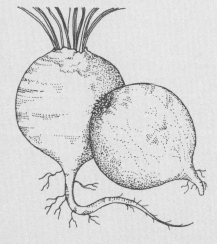

Menu

Dinner party for eight
Lobster shell soup
Polynesian stuffed veal
Spicy rice ring
Broad beans with celery
Spinach Caesar salad
Hot rolls with butter pats
Flaming pears Cardinal
Wine – Blanc de blanc, Sauternes
Cardamom coffee

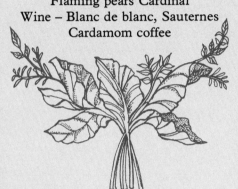

Indoor Entertaining: A dinner party for eight really displays your skill as a hostess but need take little time and effort on the day of the party if you use your freezer to its best advantage.

Lobster shell soup

METRIC/IMPERIAL	AMERICAN
1 boiled lobster, any weight	1 boiled lobster, any weight
750 ml/1¼ pints chicken stock	3 cups chicken stock
300 ml/½ pint dry white wine	1¼ cups dry white wine
450 ml/¾ pint tomato juice	2 cups tomato juice
bouquet garni	bouquet garni
salt and white pepper to taste	salt and white pepper to taste

Remove the meat from the lobster shell and slice into julienne strips. Place in the refrigerator. Break the lobster shell into pieces and place in a large saucepan with the chicken stock, white wine, tomato juice, bouquet garni and seasonings. Cover and simmer for 1 hour. Strain the soup, stir in the strips of lobster meat and cool.
To freeze: Pack in convenient quantities. Seal and label.
To serve: Reheat gently from frozen. Serve hot, garnished with croûtons or a spoonful of soured cream.
Serves: 8.
Storage time: 2–3 months.

Polynesian stuffed veal

METRIC/IMPERIAL	AMERICAN
2·75–3·5 kg/6–8 lb shoulder of veal, defrosted	6–8 lb shoulder of veal, defrosted
3 tablespoons lemon juice	¼ cup lemon juice
175 g/6 oz fresh seasoned breadcrumbs	3 cups fresh seasoned breadcrumbs
50 g/2 oz butter	¼ cup butter
1 (425-g/15-oz) can pineapple pieces	1 (16-oz) can pineapple pieces
50 g/2 oz walnuts, chopped	½ cup chopped walnuts
2 tablespoons chopped parsley	3 tablespoons chopped parsley
½ teaspoon ground ginger	½ teaspoon ground ginger
75 g/3 oz soft brown sugar	6 tablespoons soft brown sugar
orange slices	orange slices
sprigs fresh mint	sprigs fresh mint

Remove the bone from the shoulder of veal and brush the cavity with the lemon juice. Brown the breadcrumbs in the butter. Chop the pineapple pieces finely. Place the pineapple pulp in a sieve and allow to drain thoroughly. Mix the pineapple pulp with the chopped walnuts, parsley, ginger and brown sugar. Stir in the breadcrumbs. Stuff the cavity with the mixture and sew the edges securely together. Place the stuffed joint on a rack in a shallow roasting tin and roast in a moderate oven (160°C, 325°F, Gas Mark 3) allowing 35 minutes per 450 g/1 lb weight. Garnish with orange slices and sprigs of fresh mint. Allow to stand at room temperature for a few minutes to make carving easier.
Serves: 8, hot or cold.
NOTE: The joint can be stuffed before freezing but storage time is 3 months only. Defrost fully before roasting as above.

Spicy rice ring

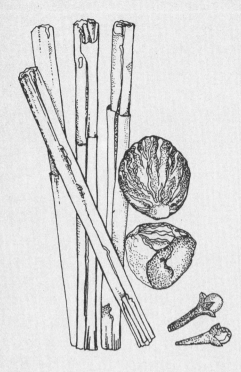

METRIC/IMPERIAL	AMERICAN
1 small onion	1 small onion
25 g/1 oz butter	2 tablespoons butter
350 g/12 oz long-grain rice	1½ cups long-grain rice
900 ml/1½ pints water	3¾ cups water
1 teaspoon salt	1 teaspoon salt
¼ teaspoon cinnamon	¼ teaspoon cinnamon
pinch ground nutmeg	pinch ground nutmeg
pinch ground cloves	pinch ground cloves
1½ tablespoons lemon juice	2 tablespoons lemon juice
100 g/4 oz seedless raisins	¾ cup seeded raisins

Chop the onion and sauté in the butter until soft. Stir in the rice and cook for 3 minutes. Stir in the water and salt. Bring to the boil, cover and simmer over low heat for 20 minutes or until the rice has absorbed all the liquid. Stir in the spices, lemon juice and raisins. Turn the rice mixture into a sieve and set over simmering water to keep hot. Cover. To serve, mound the rice around the edge of a hot serving plate and spoon the Broad beans with celery into the centre. *Serves: 8.*

Broad beans with celery

METRIC/IMPERIAL	AMERICAN
heart of celery	heart of celery
800 g/1¾ lb frozen broad beans	1¾ lb frozen lima beans
50 g/2 oz butter	¼ cup butter
¼ teaspoon dried rosemary	¼ teaspoon dried rosemary
¼ teaspoon white pepper	¼ teaspoon white pepper
3 tablespoons lemon juice	¼ cup lemon juice

Cut the celery diagonally in 1-cm/½-inch slices. Cook the beans and celery in a small amount of boiling salted water until just tender. Drain well. Melt the butter with the rosemary and pepper. Stir in the lemon juice. Drizzle the butter mixture over the vegetables. Spoon into the centre of the rice ring and garnish with a little chopped canned pimiento. *Serves: 8.*

Spinach Caesar salad

METRIC/IMPERIAL	AMERICAN
4 rashers streaky bacon	4 bacon slices
225 g/8 oz young spinach leaves	½ lb young spinach leaves
½ lettuce	½ head lettuce
225 g/8 oz mushrooms	½ lb mushrooms
1 lemon	1 lemon
150 ml/¼ pint olive oil	⅔ cup olive oil
4 tablespoons white wine vinegar	⅓ cup white wine vinegar
few drops Worcestershire sauce	few drops Worcestershire sauce
2 eggs, boiled for 1–1½ minutes	2 eggs, boiled for 1–1½ minutes
salt and black pepper to taste	salt and black pepper to taste
25 g/1 oz Parmesan cheese, grated	¼ cup grated Parmesan cheese

Cut the bacon rashers in half and stretch each slice by sliding the straight edge of a knife along it. Roll tightly and thread on a skewer. Grill until crisp, drain on absorbent paper and set aside. Tear the spinach leaves and lettuce leaves into bite-sized pieces and toss together in a large bowl. Slice the mushrooms into the bowl and squeeze over the lemon. Mix the olive oil and vinegar with the Worcestershire sauce. Just before serving, drizzle the dressing over the vegetables. Break in the eggs and toss lightly. Season with salt and pepper and sprinkle with Parmesan cheese. Lift out on to chilled salad plates and garnish with the bacon rolls.
Serves: 8.

Flaming pears Cardinal

METRIC/IMPERIAL	AMERICAN
16 canned pear halves	16 canned pear halves
syrup from the can	syrup from the can
450 g/1 lb cream cheese	1 lb cream cheese
2 tablespoons castor sugar	3 tablespoons sugar
50 g/2 oz walnuts, chopped	½ cup chopped walnuts
450 g/1 lb frozen raspberries	1 lb frozen raspberries
little icing sugar	little confectioners' sugar
6 tablespoons water	½ cup water
3 tablespoons cornflour	¼ cup cornstarch
when serving:	*when serving:*
3 tablespoons brandy	¼ cup brandy

Drain the pear halves, reserving the syrup. Beat the cream cheese with the sugar and enough of the syrup to give a spreading consistency. Stir in the chopped walnuts. Spread the cream cheese mixture on the cut side of each pear half, filling the cavity. Press 2 pear halves together. Thaw the raspberries and add icing sugar to taste. Blend the water and cornflour in a saucepan. Stir in the raspberries and cook over low heat until thickened. Press through a sieve and cool.
To freeze: Pack the filled pears in a container and cover exposed surfaces with cling film. Pack the raspberry sauce separately. Seal and label.
To serve: Defrost pears and sauce. Place a stuffed pear in each serving dish. Heat the raspberry sauce, stirring until hot and smooth. Keep the sauce warm in a chafing dish. At serving time, warm the brandy in a ladle, ignite and pour over the raspberry sauce. Spoon the flaming sauce over the filled pears.
Serves: 8.
Storage time: 4–6 months.

Cardamom coffee

Place 1 teaspoon ground cardamom or 1½ teaspoons cardamom seeds with the ground coffee and prepare in the usual way. Serve with lightly whipped double cream and soft brown sugar.

Exotic Starters: Always a good talking point to get your parties off to a sparkling start, so here are two unusual ones.

Curried banana and apple soup

METRIC/IMPERIAL	AMERICAN
4 apples	4 apples
2 large bananas	2 large bananas
1 small onion, quartered	1 small onion, quartered
222 g/8 oz cooked potato	1 cup cooked potato
4 teaspoons curry powder	1 tablespoon curry powder
1 litre/1¾ pints chicken stock	4¼ cups chicken stock
600 ml/1 pint milk or single cream	2½ cups milk or light cream
when serving:	*when serving:*
chopped chives	chopped chives

Peel and core the apples. Liquidise the apples, banana, onion and cooked potato in a blender until smooth. Pour into a saucepan and stir in the curry powder and chicken stock. Bring to the boil and simmer for 10 minutes, stirring frequently. Blend in the milk or cream and cool.
To freeze: Pack in convenient quantities. Seal and label.
To serve: Turn frozen soup into a saucepan and reheat gently to boiling point. Serve garnished with chopped chives. This soup is also delicious served cold.
Makes: About 2 litres/3½ pints/4½ pints.
Storage time: 4–6 months.

Crab mousse

(Illustrated on page 105)

METRIC/IMPERIAL	AMERICAN
15 g/½ oz gelatine	2 envelopes gelatin
175 g/6 oz cream cheese	6 oz cream cheese
150 ml/¼ pint mayonnaise	⅔ cup mayonnaise
1–2 tablespoons lemon juice	2–3 tablespoons lemon juice
2 tablespoons chopped parsley	3 tablespoons chopped parsley
2 (40-g/1½-oz) cans dressed crab	3 oz canned dressed crab
50 g/2 oz frozen crab meat, defrosted	2 oz frozen crab meat, defrosted
pinch salt	pinch salt
pinch pepper	pinch pepper
when serving:	*when serving:*
50 g/2 oz prawns	2 oz prawns
sprigs watercress	sprigs watercress

Dissolve the gelatine in 2 tablespoons (US 3 tablespoons) water in a basin over a pan of hot water. Cream the cheese until soft then gradually beat in the mayonnaise. Add the lemon juice, parsley and the crab and mix well. Taste and add salt and pepper. Stir in the gelatine and pour into a ring mould. Allow to set.
To freeze: Pack in the mould. Seal and label.
To serve: Unpack and dip the mould in hot water. Turn out on to a serving dish and defrost in the refrigerator for about 5 hours. Garnish with the prawns and watercress.
Serves: 6.
Storage time: 2–3 months.
NOTE: Make the mousse in the ring mould and freeze it specially for a party you are giving soon, or you can freeze it in individual soufflé dishes which you can take out as you require.

Couronne meringuée

METRIC/IMPERIAL	AMERICAN
3 egg whites	3 egg whites
½ teaspoon cream of tartar	½ teaspoon cream of tartar
75 g/3 oz castor sugar	6 tablespoons sugar
75 g/3 oz icing sugar, sifted	¾ cup sifted confectioners' sugar
cream ice filling:	*cream ice filling:*
2 egg yolks	2 egg yolks
2 eggs, separated	2 eggs, separated
50 g/2 oz sugar	¼ cup sugar
300 ml/½ pint milk	1¼ cups milk
½ teaspoon almond essence	½ teaspoon almond extract
50 g/2 oz toasted hazel nuts, chopped	⅓ cup chopped toasted hazel nuts
150 ml/¼ pint double cream	⅔ cup heavy cream
when serving:	*when serving:*
350 g/12 oz fresh strawberries	¾ lb fresh strawberries

Whip the egg whites with the cream of tartar and castor sugar until stiff and glossy. Fold in the icing sugar. Pipe or spread the mixture on to 2 baking trays lined with non-stick parchment to make a 23-cm/9-inch flat circle and a ring topped with rosettes. Bake in a cool oven (140°C, 275°F, Gas Mark 1) for 1½–2 hours, until dry. Cool. Meanwhile, whisk together the 4 egg yolks and remaining sugar. Gradually whisk in the milk and cook over boiling water until thickened. Cool, stirring frequently. Stir in the almond essence and the nuts and freeze until mushy. Turn into a bowl and beat until smooth. Lightly whip the cream and whisk the egg whites stiffly. Fold into the frozen custard and freeze until firm. Place the meringue circle on a plate, meringue crown on top and open freeze. When cream ice is ready, allow to soften only until it is possible to spoon it into the crown.
To freeze: Open freeze the filled meringue crown until the filling is solid.
To serve: Uncover and pile the strawberries on top. The dessert can stand at room temperature for 20 minutes, before the filling becomes too soft.
Serves: 8–10. Storage time: 3 months.

Café crème Royale

METRIC/IMPERIAL	AMERICAN
6 eggs, separated	6 eggs, separated
50 g/2 oz granulated sugar	¼ cup sugar
450 ml/¾ pint freshly made coffee	2 cups freshly made coffee
15 g/½ oz gelatine	2 envelopes gelatin
1½ tablespoons light rum	2 tablespoons light rum
100 g/4 oz castor sugar	½ cup sugar
150 ml/¼ pint double cream	⅔ cup heavy cream

Beat the egg yolks lightly in a basin, stir in the sugar, coffee and gelatine. Place over hot water and cook, stirring, until the mixture coats a wooden spoon. Remove from heat, add rum and chill until slightly thickened. Whisk the egg whites stiffly with the castor sugar, fold gently into the custard with the whipped cream. Spoon into a fancy mould and chill until set.
To freeze: Cover mould with foil. Seal and label.
To serve: Defrost in the refrigerator overnight and turn out on a plate.
Serves: 8. Storage time: 4–6 months.

Just a Couple Again

Life for the couple whose family have grown up and flown the nest is liable to be full of contrasts. There are quiet times when you are alone together and hectic ones when the children come to visit, sometimes with a noisy flock of grandchildren in tow. This may be the moment when you are getting rid of large pieces of domestic equipment you no longer need, and adjusting to life on a smaller scale again. Don't be tempted to convince yourself that you only need minimum freezer space because it is just for the two of you. One of the great pleasures of taking it easy and doing what you choose is that you have more time to prepare for guests, and leisure to enjoy their company. Even if you are unwilling to sacrifice any existing work surface in your kitchen, you can fit a neat little freezer under it. Or the freezer top can be part of the work surface. Either way, you will probably prefer an upright freezer to a chest, to avoid having problems lifting heavily-loaded freezer baskets.

Careful allocation of freezer space means that you always have a selection of cooked dishes ready to draw on when the weather discourages a shopping trip, and yet there is plenty of room left for the family's favourite cakes and biscuits. Unexpected talents may reveal themselves and there is great satisfaction in offering a gift you have cooked yourself. Or because you have time, patience and skill at your fingertips, you may be asked to provide some delicious speciality you excel in making for a wedding or christening. Here your freezer really comes into its own. You can cook calmly, dealing with intricate finishing touches well ahead of time.

Just because you have shed the old ties and responsibilities of a busy working life, other people are often inclined to think you must be at their beck and call in time of emergencies. Old friends, new neighbours and even far flung relatives may expect to be lent a hand and that may mean that one member of the family will have to leave the other to cater solo. This does not mean 'camping-out style' if you have an expertly stocked freezer.

Try to divide your precious freezer space between the breads, biscuits or cakes, and made-up dishes you two will want to eat daily, probably including lots of ready-frozen vegetables in small portions. A batch of rolls will more likely be useful to you than large loaves; and when you bake a cake it is a good idea to wrap and freeze it in wedges.

The recipes in your section are designed for a couple who enjoy eating on their own but spend a lot of time catering for others as well.
1. Interesting ways to cook universally popular chicken portions.
2. Biscuits and cakes to cook by the batch and produce to please both invited and unexpected guests.
3. Home-made sweetmeats easy to freeze and pack as gifts.
4. A luncheon party which could very well be given to celebrate a silver wedding, an engagement or exam success in the family – or just a gathering of cherished friends to exchange happy memories.

Home-made breads are always popular when the family comes to visit

Chocolate dips; Fudge brownies (page 190)

Home-made sweets – chocolate truffles, mocha fudge, coconut ice, pastel fondants, nutty toffee (page 191)

Chicken in cider and cream

Two ways with poached chicken portions

How to poach frozen chicken: Place 4 frozen chicken portions in a large saucepan with sufficient strong chicken stock just to cover. Bring to the boil, cover the pan and simmer gently for 1 hour. (Twenty minutes will be sufficient if the chicken is defrosted.) Allow to cool, remove the chicken and drain well back into the pan. Carefully remove the flesh from the bones and dice. Use immediately or freeze with a little of the stock to keep it moist.

Orange pimiento chicken: Grate the zest and squeeze the juice from 1 small orange. Dice the contents of a 70-g/2¾-oz can of red pimiento, heat with the juice from the can and the orange zest and juice. Stir in 4 tablespoons (US ⅓ cup) stock from the poached chicken and season to taste. Moisten 2 teaspoons cornflour with a little more chicken stock and use to thicken the sauce. Add the diced chicken from 2 portions and reheat gently to boiling point. Serve with mashed or tiny boiled new potatoes.
Serves: 2.

Spiced chicken with cucumber: Heat 1 tablespoon of oil and use to sauté 100 g/4 oz diced unpeeled cucumber until soft. Add the same quantity of drained canned pineapple pieces and 150 ml/¼ pint/⅔ cup stock from the poached chicken. Stir in 1 teaspoon vinegar and a pinch of ground ginger. Bring to the boil, stirring well, and season to taste. Add the diced chicken from 2 portions and reheat gently to boiling point. Serve with fluffy boiled rice or ribbon noodles.
Serves: 2.

Chicken in cider and cream

(Illustrated opposite)

METRIC/IMPERIAL	AMERICAN
1 medium onion	1 medium onion
2 dessert apples	2 dessert apples
25 g/1 oz butter	2 tablespoons butter
4 chicken portions	4 chicken portions
sprig fresh tarragon	sprig fresh tarragon
150 ml/¼ pint dry cider	⅔ cup dry cider
1 chicken stock cube	1 chicken bouillon cube
4 tablespoons single cream	⅓ cup light cream
salt and pepper to taste	salt and pepper to taste
1 teaspoon chopped parsley	1 teaspoon chopped parsley
few tarragon leaves	few tarragon leaves

Finely chop the onion and core and dice the apples. Melt the butter in a flameproof casserole or heavy saucepan, add the chicken portions and turn over medium heat until golden brown all over. Add the onion, apple and sprig of tarragon. Heat the cider just sufficiently to dissolve the stock cube in it and pour over the chicken. Cover and simmer gently for about 40 minutes, until the chicken juices are no longer pink when the flesh is tested with a skewer. Remove the chicken portions to a hot serving dish and keep warm. Stir the cream into the ingredients in the pan, taste and adjust the seasoning. Pour the sauce over the chicken and sprinkle with parsley and tarragon.
Serves: 4.

Fudge brownies

(Illustrated on page 186)

METRIC/IMPERIAL	AMERICAN
175 g/6 oz butter	¾ cup butter
2 tablespoons cocoa powder	3 tablespoons cocoa powder
175 g/6 oz castor sugar	¾ cup sugar
2 eggs	2 eggs
50 g/2 oz plain flour	½ cup all-purpose flour
50 g/2 oz walnuts, chopped	½ cup chopped walnuts

Melt one-third of the butter, stir in the cocoa until smooth and set aside. Cream the remaining butter with the sugar until light in colour. Gradually beat in the eggs, then fold in the sifted flour, the walnuts and cocoa mixture. Turn into a 17·5-cm/7-inch square greased and bottom-lined cake tin. Bake in a moderate oven (180°C, 350°F, Gas Mark 4) for about 45 minutes. Leave to cool in the tin. When cold, turn out and cut into 9 squares or bars.
To freeze: Pack in layers with dividers. Seal and label.
To serve: Arrange the brownies on a serving dish and defrost at room temperature for about 30 minutes. Serve sprinkled with icing sugar.
Makes: 9 squares or bars.
Storage time: 4–6 months.

Chocolate dips

(Illustrated on page 186)

METRIC/IMPERIAL	AMERICAN
175 g/6 oz butter	¾ cup butter
175 g/6 oz castor sugar	¾ cup sugar
1 egg	1 egg
2 teaspoons grated orange zest	2 teaspoons grated orange rind
350 g/12 oz plain flour	3 cups all-purpose flour
2 teaspoons baking powder	2 teaspoons baking powder
¾ teaspoon salt	¾ teaspoon salt
when serving:	*when serving:*
100 g/4 oz plain chocolate	4 squares semi-sweet chocolate
3 tablespoons water	¼ cup water
1 teaspoon salad oil	1 teaspoon salad oil
25 g/1 oz castor sugar	2 tablespoons sugar

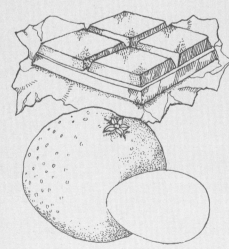

Cream the butter with the sugar until light and fluffy. Beat in the egg and orange zest. Sift the flour, baking powder and salt into the creamed mixture. Stir until well combined. Chill the dough in the refrigerator for 1 hour. Roll out on a lightly floured board to 3 mm/⅛ inch thickness. Cut the dough into small circles, squares, rectangles or other shapes with floured biscuit cutters and arrange on lightly greased baking trays. Bake in a moderately hot oven (190°C, 375°F, Gas Mark 5) for 10 minutes. Cool on a wire rack.
To freeze: Pack in convenient quantities. Seal and label.
To serve: Break the chocolate into small pieces and place in a pan with the water, oil and sugar. Stir constantly over low heat until the chocolate has melted and the mixture becomes smooth. Cool slightly then dip each frozen biscuit into it. For variety, dip only the corners or half of each biscuit into the chocolate.
Makes: 72 biscuits.
Storage time: 4–6 months.

Home-made Sweets Make Lovely Gifts: They look so good in the foil trays, just as they come from the freezer, or several varieties mixed and packed as assortments. (*Illustrated on page 187.*)

Mocha fudge

Place 50 g/2 oz/¼ cup margarine in a saucepan with 100 g/4 oz/4 squares plain chocolate, 1 tablespoon instant coffee and 3 tablespoons (US ¼ cup) evaporated milk. When melted add 450 g/1 lb/3½ cups sifted icing sugar and beat until smooth. Divide between two greased 15-cm/6-inch by 10-cm/4-inch shallow foil containers and cool. Cover with lid or foil and freeze. Allow 1 hour to defrost then cut each block into 24 2·5-cm/1-inch squares. *Storage time:* 4–6 months.

Coconut ice

Place 1 kg/2 lb/4 cups granulated sugar in a saucepan with 150 ml/¼ pint/⅔ cup each evaporated milk and water. Stir until the sugar dissolves then bring to the boil and simmer gently until a temperature of 116°C/240°F is reached, or when a little of the mixture dropped into cold water forms a soft ball. This takes about 1 hour. Remove from the heat and stir in 225 g/8 oz/2⅔ cups desiccated coconut and beat well. Pour half the mixture into an oiled 18-cm/7-inch square tin, colour the remainder pink and pour on top. Allow to set and mark into bars. Freeze in the tin or cut into 14 bars before freezing. Allow 1 hour to defrost. *Storage time:* 4–6 months.

Chocolate truffles

Melt 225 g/8 oz/8 squares plain chocolate in 2 tablespoons (US 3 tablespoons) strong black coffee in a basin over hot water. Remove from the heat and add to 100 g/4 oz/½ cup softened butter, beating well. Add an egg yolk and about 4 tablespoons (US ⅓ cup) evaporated milk, mix well then allow to harden in the refrigerator. Shape into about 30 balls the size of a walnut and toss in chocolate vermicelli. Chill until firm then pack in shallow foil containers and cover with lid or foil to freeze. Allow about 30 minutes to defrost and arrange in small paper sweet cases. *Storage time:* 4–6 months.

Nutty toffee

Place 225 g/8 oz/1 cup each butter and sugar in a saucepan with 2 tablespoons (US 3 tablespoons) evaporated milk and 4 tablespoons (US ⅓ cup) golden syrup. Stir until the sugar dissolves then bring to the boil and simmer gently until a temperature of 121°C/250°F is reached, or when a little of the mixture dropped into cold water forms a hard ball. This takes about 1¼ hours. Remove from the heat and stir in 50 g/2 oz/⅓ cup chopped peanuts. Beat until the mixture begins to thicken then pour into an oiled 15-cm/6-inch by 10-cm/4-inch shallow foil container and mark into 24 2·5-cm/1-inch squares before set. Cool then cover with lid or foil and freeze. Allow 1 hour to defrost then break into pieces. *Storage time:* 4–6 months.

Pastel fondants

Stir about 350 g/12 oz/2⅔ cups sifted icing sugar into 2 tablespoons (US 3 tablespoons) evaporated milk until the mixture is firm. Tint with food colourings, press into a fondant mat or form into balls. Dry for 24 hours and place in foil candy cups before freezing. *Makes:* About 25 fondants. *Storage time:* 4–6 months.

NOTE
Remove the saucepan from the heat when using the cold water test in order to avoid over-cooking the mixtures.

Menu

Luncheon party for eight
Iced lemon soup
Sesame crackers
Salmon loaf Wellington
Sauce piquant
Stuffed tomato towers
Frozen apple soufflés
Sugar crisps
Russian tea

Iced lemon soup

METRIC/IMPERIAL	AMERICAN
1 small onion	1 small onion
50 g/2 oz butter	¼ cup butter
25 g/1 oz plain flour	¼ cup all-purpose flour
1·75 litres/3 pints chicken stock	7½ cups chicken stock
1 large lemon	1 large lemon
4 egg yolks	4 egg yolks
when serving:	*when serving:*
crushed ice	crushed ice
4½ tablespoons double cream	⅓ cup heavy cream
25 g/1 oz toasted almonds, flaked	¼ cup toasted flaked almonds

Chop the onion very finely and sauté in the butter until limp, but not brown. Stir in the flour and cook for 1 minute. Gradually blend in the stock. Bring to the boil, cover and simmer for 10 minutes. Grate the zest from the lemon and squeeze the juice. Stir these into the soup and simmer for a further 5 minutes. Beat the egg yolks lightly. Stir in a little of the hot soup, then add this mixture to the soup in the pan, stirring constantly. Reheat but do not boil. Cool.
To freeze: Pack in convenient quantities. Seal and label.
To serve: Defrost overnight in the refrigerator. Spoon a little crushed ice into each soup bowl and pour over the soup. Whisk the cream lightly and float a spoonful on top of each bowl of soup. Sprinkle with toasted flaked almonds and serve with sesame crackers.
Sesame crackers: Place cream crackers on an ungreased baking tray and brush with melted butter. Sprinkle with sesame seeds. Bake in a moderate oven (180°C, 350°F, Gas Mark 4) for 5 minutes until crisp.
Storage time: 4–6 months.

Salmon loaf Wellington

METRIC/IMPERIAL	AMERICAN
225 g/8 oz plain flour	2 cups all-purpose flour
¾ teaspoon salt	¾ teaspoon salt
175 g/6 oz cottage cheese	6 oz cottage cheese
175 g/6 oz margarine	¾ cup margarine
1½ tablespoons cold water	2 tablespoons cold water
1 medium onion	1 medium onion
1 medium carrot	1 medium carrot
1 stick celery	1 stalk celery
50 g/2 oz butter	¼ cup butter
100 g/4 oz mushrooms, sliced	1 cup sliced mushrooms
1½ tablespoons lemon juice	2 tablespoons lemon juice
1 teaspoon salt	1 teaspoon salt
½ teaspoon dried dill weed	½ teaspoon dried dill weed
¼ teaspoon pepper	¼ teaspoon pepper
700 g/1½ lb cooked or canned salmon	1½ lb cooked or canned salmon
6 tablespoons soured cream	½ cup sour cream
50 g/2 oz soft white breadcrumbs	1 cup soft white breadcrumbs
15 g/½ oz butter, melted	1 tablespoon melted butter

To make the pastry, sift the flour and salt into a bowl. Rub the cottage cheese and margarine into the flour until the mixture resembles fine breadcrumbs. Sprinkle

with the cold water and mix lightly. Form the dough into a ball and chill for 1 hour. Meanwhile, prepare the filling. Chop the onion, carrot and celery very finely. Sauté in the butter until soft. Add the mushrooms, lemon juice and seasonings. Cover and cook for 2–3 minutes. Remove from the heat and stir in the boned and flaked salmon, the soured cream and breadcrumbs. Taste and check the seasoning. On a lightly floured board, roll out the chilled pastry dough into a rectangle 8 mm/⅓ inch thick. Spoon the salmon mixture into the middle of the pastry and pat into a loaf shape. Fold the sides of the pastry over the salmon, moisten the edges with water and pinch to seal. Place the loaf, seam side down, on an ungreased baking tray and brush with the melted butter. Decorate the top of the loaf with pastry leaves and petals made from the pastry trimmings. Pierce the top to allow the steam to escape. Bake in a moderately hot oven (190°C, 375°F, Gas Mark 5) for 40–45 minutes, until golden. Cool.
To freeze: Wrap closely. Seal and label.
To serve: Defrost and then reheat in a moderate oven (180°C, 350°F, Gas Mark 4) for 30 minutes. Transfer the loaf to a heated serving plate, slice and serve with Sauce piquant (see below).
Storage time: 3–4 months.

Sauce piquant

METRIC/IMPERIAL	AMERICAN
1 small dill pickled cucumber	1 small dill pickle
3 tablespoons chopped onion	¼ cup chopped onion
2 tablespoons chopped parsley	3 tablespoons chopped parsley
300 ml/½ pint mayonnaise	1¼ cups mayonnaise
4 drops Worcestershire sauce	4 drops Worcestershire sauce
2 tablespoons ketchup	3 tablespoons ketchup
1 teaspoon curry powder	1 teaspoon curry powder
¼ teaspoon paprika	¼ teaspoon paprika
½ teaspoon salt	½ teaspoon salt

Chop the dill pickle finely and mix with the remaining ingredients. Chill for several hours to blend flavours.
Makes: 450 ml/¾ pint/2 cups sauce.

Stuffed tomato towers

METRIC/IMPERIAL	AMERICAN
8 large tomatoes	8 large tomatoes
450 g/1 lb cooked or canned asparagus tips	1 lb cooked or canned asparagus tips
1½ tablespoons salad oil	2 tablespoons salad oil
2 teaspoons wine vinegar	2 teaspoons wine vinegar
pinch salt	pinch salt
pinch pepper	pinch pepper
pinch dried basil	pinch dried basil
8 lettuce cups	8 lettuce cups
16 black olives to garnish	16 ripe olives to garnish

Remove a thin slice from one end of each tomato. Then cut each tomato into 4 slices. Mash the asparagus tips with the oil, vinegar and seasonings until the mixture is a thick paste. Spread thickly on one side of each tomato slice. Re-assemble each tomato and place in a lettuce cup. Garnish and chill.

Frozen apple soufflé

METRIC/IMPERIAL	AMERICAN
4 egg yolks	4 egg yolks
225 g/8 oz granulated sugar	1 cup sugar
15 g/½ oz gelatine	2 envelopes gelatin
pinch salt	pinch salt
300 ml/½ pint single cream	1¼ cups light cream
450 ml/¾ pint unsweetened apple purée	2 cups unsweetened applesauce
150 ml/¼ pint double cream	⅔ cup heavy cream
when serving:	*when serving:*
150 ml/¼ pint double cream	⅔ cup heavy cream
about 50 g/2 oz nuts, finely chopped	½ cup finely chopped nuts
8 cherries with stems	8 cherries with stems

Beat the egg yolks over hot water until they become very light. Gradually whisk in the sugar, gelatine and salt. Heat the single cream and apple purée together, then gradually stir this mixture into the whipped eggs and sugar. Continue to stir over hot water until thick and smooth. Cool. Whisk the double cream until thick and fold into the apple custard. Tie a 5-cm/2-inch band of greaseproof paper around 8 individual soufflé dishes. Spoon in the apple mixture.
To freeze: Open freeze then cover with foil and smooth down the edges. Place all together in a large rigid container. Seal and label.
To serve: Allow to soften in the refrigerator for 1 hour. Carefully remove the paper collars. Whip the cream until thick and spread a little around the exposed sides of the soufflé. Press the chopped nuts against the cream. Use remaining cream to pipe a rosette on top of each soufflé. Decorate with the cherries.
Storage time: 4–6 months.

Sugar crisps

METRIC/IMPERIAL	AMERICAN
225 g/8 oz granulated sugar	1 cup sugar
100 g/4 oz butter	½ cup butter
2 egg yolks	2 egg yolks
100 g/4 oz plain flour	1 cup all-purpose flour
pinch salt	pinch salt
½ teaspoon cream of tartar	½ teaspoon cream of tartar
¼ teaspoon almond essence	¼ teaspoon almond extract

Cream the sugar with the butter until light. Beat in the egg yolks. Sift the flour, salt and cream of tartar into the creamed mixture. Stir in the almond essence. Form the dough into small balls. Place well apart on ungreased baking trays and bake in a cool oven (150°C, 300°F, Gas Mark 2) for 25–30 minutes. The biscuits will flatten and sugar crystals will appear on top. Cool on a wire rack.
To freeze: Pack in layers with dividers. Seal and label.
To serve: Unpack, spread on serving plates and defrost at room temperature.
Makes: About 24 biscuits.
Storage time: 4–6 months.
Russian tea: Mix 2 teaspoons each orange zest, lemon zest and sugar. Allow to stand overnight. Mix with 2 tablespoons (US 3 tablespoons) tea leaves and place in a warmed teapot. Pour over boiling water and steep for 5 minutes. Strain into small cups and serve with sugar.

Part III

*Freezing
for Everyone*

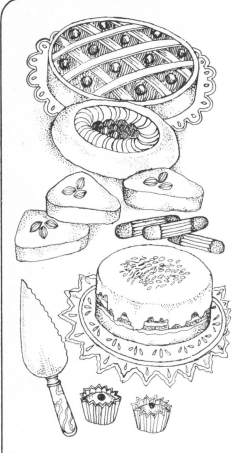

Bulk Cooking the Easy Way

Owning a freezer opens up a vast new range of possibilities in cooking. You can prepare a specific dish in a large quantity and freeze several portions; there is no need to bore the family by serving the same dish day after day until it is used up. The time and trouble saved in completing all the preparation and cooking pays off, providing the dish is a favourite which will always be welcomed when it appears on the table. This means, of course, you should try it out at least once, and make sure there is a satisfactory family reaction before you give it the 'king-size' treatment. Many housewives have told me this is the biggest boon of all to them of freezer ownership.

The 'chain' method is particularly useful for those who like a lot of variety. For instance, a staple food such as minced beef can be used from scratch, or prepared up to a certain point to make a basic mix. A few extra ingredients combined with portions of this produce a great many different dishes with very little extra trouble. Some families welcome a frequent reappearance of the well-loved favourites, others prefer more variations on a theme, and for them 'chain' cooking is the answer.

Once you have learned how to exploit your freezer's capabilities, you will certainly be ready to experiment with 'batch' cooking. This is a little more complicated, but is based on the idea of allocating a couple of hours, or perhaps longer, to preparing and cooking a number of related dishes, to build up your stores of frozen food. The aim here is to use the oven and the top of your cooker without wasting heat, and to spend your time economically. If the work plan is designed to keep you busy throughout your batch cooking session, it is amazing how many completed dishes you will have to show for your efforts; for example, a batch bake of small cakes, which produces 98 assorted items in about 2 hours. This would make tea-time a pleasure for many weeks to come, or could reduce your catering requirements for a big party to virtually nil. Imagine the satisfaction of entertaining all the members of your club to tea, with nothing to do but set out this selection of cakes on your prettiest plates and make several big pots of tea!

Some care is needed in working out a programme for cooking in quantity which is realistic in relation to the utensils you possess and your oven capacity. The investment in extra sandwich cake tins and baking trays is well worth while, or you may have to think ahead and borrow these. This is one of the best reasons for arranging to cook in bulk for your freezer in partnership with another enthusiast, so that you can pool your resources. Plan the shopping, check the utensils available and the capacity of your cooker and make out the work plan so that there are no awkward gaps when the oven is choc-a-bloc, or dishes ready to cook which should really not be delayed, and there are no forward preparations to be carried out which have not been planned for. Sometimes, just by looking through the work plan and adjusting it you can avoid such awkward

Caramelled oranges (page 241); Pavlova mincemeat baskets (page 222); Lattice
mincemeat tart (page 222)

Cider Christmas cake (page 219)

contingencies. If you have never attempted bulk cooking before but think it would be both interesting and rewarding, try out a simple plan first. Make up a big quantity of pastry, reserving some at the 'breadcrumb' stage for crumbles, bake off a number of tarts with different sweet fillings while a couple of covered meat casseroles cook away gently in the bottom of the oven. You could then have two 8-portion meat casserole dishes ready to transfer when cold to the freezer, two bags of crumble mixture to use up later with fruit, and four assorted tarts. Even if you serve four portions of the casserole and one of the tarts the same day, your freezaway bonus will still be: 3 main meal dishes; 3 sweet tarts; 2 pastry crumbles.

Sausage selection

By investing time and effort in preparing these dishes in king-size quantities, you can always have a main dish ready to take from the freezer, based on the succulent sausage. You could make all the five recipes in this 'batch' cook with large or small sausages if you prefer to buy them in bulk. Three of the recipes can be baked while you are preparing the other two on top of the cooker.

Salsicce al vino rosso

(*Illustrated on page 215*)

METRIC/IMPERIAL	AMERICAN
1 kg/2 lb large pork and beef sausages	2 lb large pork or beef sausages
about 2 tablespoons oil	3 tablespoons oil
450 g/1 lb pasta shells or bows	1 lb pasta shells or bows
salt and pepper	salt and pepper
sauce:	*sauce:*
1 large red sweet pepper	1 large red sweet pepper
1 large mild onion	1 large mild onion
1 tablespoon flour	1 tablespoon flour
1 teaspoon dried oregano	1 teaspoon dried oregano
1 teaspoon paprika	1 teaspoon paprika pepper
salt and pepper	salt and pepper
450 ml/¾ pint robust red wine	2 cups robust red wine
2 teaspoons tomato purée	2 teaspoons tomato paste
½ teaspoon sugar	½ teaspoon sugar
1 (396-g/14-oz) can tomatoes	14 oz canned tomatoes

Cook the sausages gently in 1 tablespoon of the oil in a frying pan for about 15 minutes, until golden brown all over. If necessary, cook in two batches. Remove and keep warm. To make the sauce, deseed and chop the pepper and finely chop the onion. Cook the pepper and onion in the fat remaining in the pan, adding a little extra oil if necessary, until soft but not brown. Stir in the flour. Add the herbs, paprika, salt and pepper to taste, the wine, tomato purée, sugar and the tomatoes with their juice. Stir well, bring to the boil and simmer gently until the mixture is reduced by about half. Taste and adjust the seasoning. Return the sausages to the pan and reheat in the sauce. Meanwhile, cook the pasta in plenty of boiling salted water for about 10 minutes, until just tender. Drain well, stir in the remaining oil and season with salt and pepper to taste.
To freeze: Spoon the sausages and sauce round the edge of 2 lightly oiled shaped foil containers, ensuring that you have an equal number of sausages in each.

Divide the pasta equally and pile in the centre of the containers. Cool. Seal and label.

To serve: Defrost, remove lid and cover container with foil. Reheat in a moderately hot oven (200°C, 400°F, Gas Mark 6) for 25–30 minutes. If liked, the surface of the pasta can be thickly sprinkled with grated cheese, the foil lightly laid on top and the dish reheated as above.

Serves: 8.

Storage time: 2–3 months.

Chicken 'n' chipolata drumsticks

(Illustrated on page 215)

METRIC/IMPERIAL	AMERICAN
16 chicken drumsticks	16 chicken drumsticks
16 pork chipolata sausages	16 pork link sausages
2 tablespoons seasoned flour	3 tablespoons seasoned flour
2 eggs, beaten	2 eggs, beaten
1 tablespoon milk	1 tablespoon milk
1 packet sage and onion stuffing mix	1 package sage and onion stuffing mix
oil for frying	oil for frying

Bone the drumsticks carefully, place 1 chipolata sausage inside each and remould into shape. (If liked, insert a 5-cm/2-inch length of macaroni into one end of each to simulate the bone.) Roll the stuffed drumsticks in the seasoned flour. Beat together the eggs and milk and use to coat the prepared drumsticks generously. Roll the coated drumsticks in the dry stuffing mix, making sure each one is completely covered. Fry, turning frequently, for 20 minutes, until light golden brown all over. Drain well on kitchen paper and cool.

To freeze: Pack in layers with dividers, or use one long sheet of interleaving paper as a concertina divider. Seal and label.

To serve: Defrost the desired quantity of drumsticks and re-fry until rich golden brown, or bake in a moderately hot oven (200°C, 400°F, Gas Mark 6) for 15 minutes. Garnish with lemon wedges and sprigs of parsley.

Makes: 16 stuffed drumsticks/8 servings.

Storage time: 2–3 months.

NOTE: If intended to be eaten cold, the stuffed drumsticks can be fully cooked until rich golden brown before freezing.

Bangers in blankets

(Illustrated on page 215)

METRIC/IMPERIAL	AMERICAN
2 rounded tablespoons peanut butter	3 rounded tablespoons peanut butter
2 rounded tablespoons French mustard	3 rounded tablespoons French mustard
1 large white thin-sliced loaf (very fresh and moist)	1 large white thin-sliced loaf (very fresh and moist)
32 pork or beef chipolata sausages	32 pork or beef link sausages
25 g/1 oz butter, melted	2 tablespoons melted butter

Blend together the peanut butter and mustard and warm slightly to make spreading easier. Remove the crusts from 16 slices of bread and spread with the

mixture. Cut each slice in half and wrap around a sausage, pressing the roll between the hands to make the bread adhere. Repeat with the remaining bread and sausages. Arrange the blanketed sausages, close together side by side (with the joins underneath), on a baking tray lined with foil. Brush the tops of the rolls with the melted butter. Bake in a moderately hot oven (200°C, 400°F, Gas Mark 6) for 25 minutes. Remove from the oven and drain off any surplus fat. Cool.
To freeze: Either make into one foil parcel, or cut through the foil base in the middle and make into two parcels. Seal and label.
To serve: Reheat the parcel from the frozen state in a moderately hot oven as above for 25–30 minutes. Open the parcel for the last 5 minutes to allow the tops to brown. Garnish with tomato wedges and sprigs of watercress.
Makes: 32 blanketed sausages/8 servings.
Storage time: 2–3 months.

Sausage and cheese en croûte

(*Illustrated on page 215*)

METRIC/IMPERIAL	AMERICAN
8 processed cheese slices	8 processed cheese slices
16 large pork sausages	16 large pork sausages
450 g/1 lb frozen puff pastry, defrosted	1 lb frozen puff paste, defrosted
1 egg, beaten	1 egg, beaten

Divide each slice of processed cheese in half. Wrap a piece of cheese round each sausage, securing with a wooden cocktail stick. Place on a baking tray and bake in a hot oven (220°, 425°F, Gas Mark 7) for about 10 minutes, or until the cheese begins to melt. Remove the baking tray from the oven and take out the cocktail sticks. Meanwhile, roll out the pastry thinly to a rectangle 40 cm/16 inches by 25 cm/10 inches and cut into 16 2·5-cm/1-inch wide strips. Allow the sausages to cool slightly. Beat the egg with 1 tablespoon water to make an eggwash and use to brush along one long edge of each pastry strip. Wind a pastry strip round each sausage, pressing the dampened edge to seal firmly. Replace on the baking tray and brush the tops with the remaining eggwash. Return to the oven and bake for about 20 minutes, until the pastry is well risen and golden brown. Cool.
To freeze: Pack in layers with dividers. Seal and label.
To serve: Defrost and place the desired quantity on a baking tray. Reheat in a moderately hot oven (200°C, 400°F, Gas Mark 6) for 15 minutes.
Makes: 16 wrapped sausages/8 servings.
Storage time: 2–3 months.

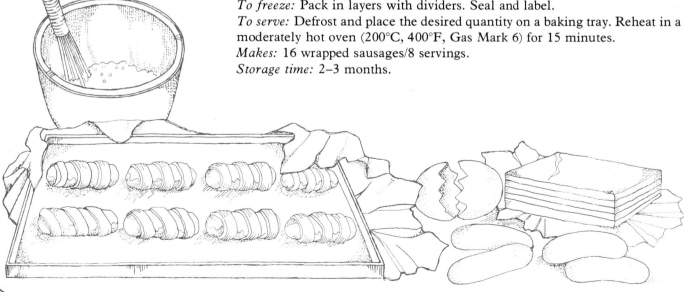

Savoury sausage roly-poly

METRIC/IMPERIAL	AMERICAN
2 medium cooking apples	2 medium baking apples
450 g/1 lb sausage meat	1 lb sausage meat
2 tablespoons chopped onion	3 tablespoons chopped onion
1 teaspoon dried mixed herbs	1 teaspoon dried mixed herbs
for the suet crust pastry:	*for the suet crust pastry:*
450 g/1 lb plain flour	4 cups all-purpose flour
1 teaspoon salt	1 teaspoon salt
4 teaspoons baking powder	4 teaspoons baking powder
225 g/8 oz shredded suet	½ lb shredded suet
cold water to mix	cold water to mix
when serving:	*when serving:*
little beaten egg	little beaten egg

Peel, core and chop the apple, add it to the sausage meat with the onion and herbs and mix well. Sift the flour with the salt and baking powder, mix in the suet lightly and stir in sufficient cold water to make a soft but not sticky dough. Roll out on a well-floured board into two rectangles, each 23 cm/9 inches by 18 cm/7 inches and about 5 mm/¼ inch thick. Divide the sausage mixture in half and spread over the pastry, leaving a 2·5-cm/1-inch border all round. Damp the borders lightly and roll up the pastry like a Swiss roll. Seal the ends and the joins. Line 2 large loaf tins with long strips of foil or pure vegetable parchment, the width of the base. Place the rolls in the tins (joins underneath) and make 3 or 4 slits in the top of each to allow the steam to escape. Bake in a moderately hot oven (200°C, 400 F, Gas Mark 6) for 20 minutes. Remove from the tins and cool.
To freeze: Wrap separately in foil. Seal and label.
To serve: Defrost, brush over with beaten egg and place on a baking tray. Bake in a moderately hot oven for 30–35 minutes, until golden brown.
Makes: 2 roly-polys/8 servings.
Storage time: 2–3 months.

A bulk buy of mince

Even if you prefer buying meat direct from a butcher rather than a freezer centre, you can get a special price on minced beef if you buy it in a large quantity. The saving may only represent the difference between the price of 'best' mince and the price of the cheaper quality, but it is a saving worth having. The aim is to produce 52 portions from 4·5 kg/10 lb of minced beef, as follows:
Curried croquettes 16 portions
Beef pockets 12 portions
Beef and cheese roll 8 portions
Moussaka 16 portions
It is always wise to keep an eye on the seesaw of meat prices. At times it might be almost as economical as minced pork or lamb, which would be equally delicious in these or similar recipes. Using this 'chain' as an example, it is easy to invent others based on diced stewing beef, lamb or pork. For example, if the butcher dices your purchase of pork meat small, part of it can be used to produce a Pork, onion and apple filling for pies and savoury puddings; part with tomato purée and paprika to produce Hungarian goulash; and part with onion, bamboo shoots and water chestnuts to produce Pork with Chinese vegetables.

Curried croquettes

METRIC/IMPERIAL	AMERICAN
2 (227-g/8-oz) packets frozen savoury rice	2 (8-oz) packages frozen savory rice
50 g/2 oz seedless raisins, chopped	⅓ cup chopped seeded raisins
2 large onions, grated	2 large onions, grated
3 tablespoons curry powder	¼ cup curry powder
1·5 kg/3 lb minced beef	3 lb ground beef
4 eggs, beaten	4 eggs, beaten
seasoned flour for coating	seasoned flour for coating
oil for frying	oil for frying
when serving:	*when serving:*
oil for frying	oil for frying

Cook the rice according to the directions on the packet, then cool. Mix with the chopped raisins, onion, curry powder, minced beef and sufficient beaten egg to make a firm mixture. Form into about 48 small croquettes, coat in seasoned flour and fry in hot oil, turning frequently until brown on all sides. Cool.
To freeze: Pack in layers with dividers. Seal and label.
To serve: Fry from the frozen state in deep hot oil for 5–6 minutes.
Serves: 16.
Storage time: 4–6 months.

Beef pockets

METRIC/IMPERIAL	AMERICAN
1 large onion, grated	1 large onion, grated
4 teaspoons ground coriander	4 teaspoons ground coriander
oil for frying	oil for frying
1 kg/2 lb minced beef, cooked	2 lb ground beef, cooked
salt and pepper to taste	salt and pepper to taste
150 ml/¼ pint sherry	⅔ cup sherry
4 tablespoons chutney	⅓ cup chutney
1 kg/2 lb suet crust pastry	2 lb suet crust pastry
(see *Savoury sausage roly-poly, page 202*)	(see *Savoury sausage roly-poly, page 202*)

First make the filling. Fry the onion and coriander in 1 tablespoon of oil for about 3–5 minutes. Add the cooked minced beef and stir over heat for a further 5 minutes. Add salt, pepper, sherry and chutney and mix well. Cool. Roll out the pastry and cut into small rounds with a pastry cutter. Place a small amount of filling in the centre of each round, damp the edges and bring up to seal into a pastry shape.
To freeze: Pack in layers with dividers. Seal and label.
To serve: Deep-fry the pasties from the frozen state in hot oil for about 10–15 minutes, until the pastry is cooked and the filling hot. Serve hot or cold.
Serves: 12.
Storage time: 3–4 months.

Beef and cheese roll

METRIC/IMPERIAL	AMERICAN
1 large onion	1 large onion
4 tablespoons oil	⅓ cup oil
1 kg/2 lb minced beef	2 lb ground beef
4 tablespoons tomato ketchup	⅓ cup tomato ketchup
2 teaspoons salt	2 teaspoons salt
¼ teaspoon cayenne pepper	¼ teaspoon cayenne pepper
700 g/1½ lb shortcrust pastry, defrosted	1½ lb basic pie dough, defrosted
225 g/8 oz crumbly white cheese	½ lb crumbly white cheese
beaten egg to glaze	beaten egg to glaze

Chop the onion finely, fry in the oil for a few minutes until transparent, add the beef, ketchup, salt and cayenne pepper and stir until the meat changes colour. Cool. Meanwhile, divide the pastry in half and roll out each piece thinly to make a large rectangle. Spread the cool filling over the rectangles to within 1 cm/½ inch of the edges, sprinkle over the crumbled cheese and roll up like Swiss rolls. Dampen the pastry edges and seal firmly together. Place on greased baking trays with the seals underneath, brush with beaten egg and bake in a moderately hot oven (200°C, 400°F, Gas Mark 6) for 30 minutes, then reduce heat to moderate (180°C, 350°F, Gas Mark 4) for a further 15 minutes. Protect the rolls with foil if necessary to prevent overbrowning. Cool.
To freeze: Wrap in foil. Seal and label.
To serve: Place still wrapped and frozen in a moderately hot oven (190°C, 375°F, Gas Mark 5) for 30 minutes. Unwrap and return to the oven for a further 10 minutes to crisp the pastry.
Makes: 2 rolls/8 servings.
Storage time: 4–6 months.

Moussaka

METRIC/IMPERIAL	AMERICAN
4 large onions, chopped	4 large onions, chopped
300 ml/½ pint oil	1¼ cups oil
1·5 kg/3 lb minced beef	3 lb ground beef
3 tablespoons tomato purée	¼ cup tomato paste
generous litre/2 pints water	5 cups water
salt and pepper to taste	salt and pepper to taste
4 large aubergines	4 large eggplants
350 g/12 oz cheese, grated	3 cups grated cheese
when serving (for each moussaka):	*when serving (for each moussaka):*
25 g/1 oz butter	2 tablespoons butter
25 g/1 oz flour	¼ cup flour
300 ml/½ pint milk	1¼ cups milk
salt and pepper to taste	salt and pepper to taste
25 g/1 oz cheese, grated	¼ cup grated cheese

Fry the onion in 1 tablespoon of the oil until soft but not browned. Add the meat and fry quickly for 5 minutes, stirring well. Stir in the tomato purée and water. Bring to the boil, cover and simmer for 10 minutes. Check the seasoning and add salt and pepper to taste. Slice the aubergines thinly. Heat the remaining oil in a large frying pan and fry the aubergine slices until golden brown, turning them once. Drain well. Grease 4 large shaped foil containers. Place a layer of aubergine slices in the bottom of each, sprinkle with half the cheese, cover with another layer of aubergine slices and finally the remainder of the cheese. Top with the meat mixture and any remaining aubergine slices.

To freeze: Cover with lid or foil. Seal and label.

To serve: Place still frozen in a moderately hot oven (190°C, 375°F, Gas Mark 5) for 1½ hours. Meanwhile, make the sauce. Melt the butter in a saucepan and stir in the flour. Cook over gentle heat for 1 minute. Gradually add the milk, beating well, and bring to the boil, stirring constantly until the sauce thickens. Season to taste and pour over the prepared moussaka. Sprinkle with the cheese and return to the oven for about 20 minutes, until golden brown.

Makes: 4 moussakas/16 portions.

Storage time: 4–6 months.

Basic meatballs with sauces

METRIC/IMPERIAL	AMERICAN
5 slices bread	5 slices bread
300 ml/½ pint milk	1¼ cups milk
2 eggs, beaten	2 eggs, beaten
700 g/1½ lb minced beef	1½ lb ground beef
225 g/8 oz minced pork	½ lb ground pork
1 small onion	1 small onion
1½ teaspoons salt	1½ teaspoons salt
¼ teaspoon pepper	¼ teaspoon pepper
3 tablespoons cooking oil	¼ cup cooking oil

Soak the bread in the milk. Stir in the beaten eggs, minced beef and minced pork. Grate or mince the onion and add to the meat mixture with the salt and pepper. Heat the oil in a large frying pan. Shape the meat mixture into 2·5-cm/1-inch balls. Brown in the hot oil. Drain on kitchen paper and cool.

To freeze: Pack in convenient quantities. Seal and label.

To serve: Simmer the frozen meatballs in one of the following sauces until heated through.

Serves: 12.

Storage time: 3 months.

Swedish meatball sauce:

(*Illustrated on page 38*)

METRIC/IMPERIAL	AMERICAN
50 g/2 oz beef dripping	¼ cup beef drippings
25 g/1 oz plain flour	¼ cup all-purpose flour
pinch ground ginger	pinch ground ginger
pinch ground nutmeg	pinch ground nutmeg
300 ml/½ pint beef stock	1¼ cups beef stock
2 tablespoons very strong coffee	3 tablespoons very strong coffee

Melt the dripping in a saucepan. Stir in the flour, ginger and nutmeg. Gradually add the beef stock and cook, stirring constantly, until slightly thickened. Stir in the coffee. Add the frozen meatballs and heat through. Serve with buttered noodles.

Barbecue sauce:

METRIC/IMPERIAL	AMERICAN
100 g/4 oz butter	½ cup butter
150 ml/¼ pint white vinegar	⅔ cup white vinegar
150 ml/¼ pint water	⅔ cup water
1 teaspoon dry mustard	1 teaspoon dry mustard
2 tablespoons grated onion	3 tablespoons grated onion
2 teaspoons granulated sugar	2 teaspoons sugar
1 tablespoon Worcestershire sauce	1 tablespoon Worcestershire sauce
150 ml/¼ pint tomato ketchup	⅔ cup tomato ketchup
1 tablespoon lemon juice	1 tablespoon lemon juice
½ clove garlic	½ clove garlic

Simmer all the ingredients together for 1 hour to blend the flavours. Remove the clove of garlic. Add the meatballs and simmer until heated through.

Pineapple and green sweet pepper sauce:

METRIC/IMPERIAL	AMERICAN
3 tablespoons white vinegar	¼ cup white vinegar
100 g/4 oz granulated sugar	½ cup sugar
2 tablespoons soya sauce	3 tablespoons soy sauce
½ teaspoon salt	½ teaspoon salt
1 green sweet pepper	1 green sweet pepper
1 (425-g/15-oz) can pineapple pieces	15 oz canned pineapple pieces
2 tablespoons cornflour	3 tablespoons cornstarch
300 ml/½ pint beef stock	1¼ cups beef stock

Mix the vinegar, sugar, soya sauce and salt in a small saucepan. Deseed and chop the green pepper and drain the pineapple pieces, reserving the juice. Add the juice to the vinegar liquid and simmer for 10 minutes. Moisten the cornflour with a little cold water to form a smooth paste. Stir into the hot liquid. Add the chopped green pepper, pineapple pieces and beef stock. Add the frozen meatballs and simmer for 30 minutes or until heated through. Serve with fluffy boiled rice.

Mushroom sauce: Simmer the meatballs in canned cream of mushroom soup. Add a few drops of soya sauce. Heat through and serve with brown rice and green beans. Sprinkle flaked almonds over the meatballs in sauce.

NOTE: All these sauces can be made up and frozen in polythene containers.

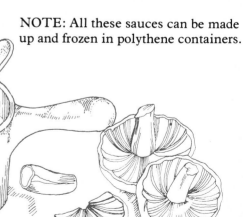

Pâte brisée

METRIC/IMPERIAL	AMERICAN
175 g/6 oz butter	¾ cup butter
50 g/2 oz lard	¼ cup shortening
450 g/1 lb plain flour	4 cups all-purpose flour
100 g/4 oz castor sugar	½ cup sugar
2 egg yolks (keep whites for macaroons)	2 egg yolks (keep whites for macaroons)
5 tablespoons water	6 tablespoons water

Rub the fats into the flour, stir in the sugar and bind the mixture with the egg yolks and water. Roll out thinly and use to line 36 fluted tartlet tins. Prick the base of each pastry case with a fork.

Basic filling

METRIC/IMPERIAL	AMERICAN
225 g/8 oz butter	1 cup butter
225 g/8 oz castor sugar	1 cup sugar
4 eggs, beaten	4 eggs, beaten

Cream together the butter and sugar until light and fluffy. Gradually add the beaten egg and continue beating until smooth. Divide the mixture into 2 equal portions.

Almandine tarts: Add 100 g/4 oz/1 cup ground almonds, 25 g/1 oz/¼ cup plain flour and a few drops of almond essence to 1 portion of the filling mix, folding in until well blended. Place a spoonful of the mixture into 18 pastry cases and bake in a moderately hot oven (200°C, 400°F, Gas Mark 6) for 15 minutes, until well risen and firm to the touch. Heat 4 tablespoons (US ⅓ cup) apricot jam with 1 teaspoon of lemon juice until melted, then sieve. Brush the warm tarts with the glaze. Lightly toast 100 g/4 oz/1 cup flaked almonds and sprinkle evenly over.

Orange tarts: Add 2 tablespoons (US 3 tablespoons) bitter chunky marmalade, 50 g/2 oz/½ cup self-raising flour, 25 g/1 oz/¼ cup ground almonds and the finely grated zest of 2 large oranges to the remaining portion of filling mix, folding in until well blended. Place a small spoonful of marmalade in the bases of the remaining 18 pastry cases and cover with a spoonful of the marmalade mixture. Bake in a moderately hot oven (190°C, 375°F, Gas Mark 5) for 15 minutes, until well risen and firm to the touch. Cool. Meanwhile, sieve 100 g/4 oz/1 cup icing sugar and beat in 1 tablespoon of warm water and 1–2 drops of orange food colouring. Swirl a small circle of icing in the centre of each tart and allow to set.

Macaroons: Whisk the 2 egg whites until stiff, add 75 g/3 oz/¾ cup castor sugar and whisk again until a very stiff mixture has been formed. Fold in a further 75 g/3 oz/¾ cup castor sugar, 100 g/4 oz/1 cup ground almonds and 1 teaspoon almond essence. Place the mixture in a piping bag fitted with a 1-cm/½-inch plain nozzle and pipe, or spoon, the mixture on to non-stick baking trays or trays lined with non-stick parchment or greased foil. Allow plenty of space between each for spreading. Top each macaroon with a flaked almond and bake in a moderate oven (180°C, 350°F, Gas Mark 4) for 15–20 minutes, until they are just turning colour. Allow to cool before removing from the trays.

Basic Victoria sandwich mixture

METRIC/IMPERIAL
450 g/1 lb butter
450 g/1 lb castor sugar
450 g/1 lb self-raising flour
8 eggs

AMERICAN
2 cups butter
2 cups sugar
4 cups all-purpose flour sifted with 4
    teaspoons baking powder
8 eggs

Cream together the butter and sugar until light and fluffy. Add the eggs one at a time and keep beating until the mixture is smooth. Add 1–2 tablespoons of flour with the last egg if the mixture shows signs of curdling. Fold in the flour and divide the mixture into 4 equal portions.

Chocolate mint cup cakes: Take 1 portion of the mixture and divide into two equal quantities. Colour one with 2–3 drops of green food colouring and to the other add 1 level tablespoon sifted cocoa powder and a few drops of gravy browning to give a rich chocolate brown colour. Have ready 12 paper cake cases on a baking tray and place a generous teaspoon of the chocolate mixture, and one of the green mixture, side by side, in each paper case. Bake in a moderately hot oven (190°C, 375°F, Gas Mark 5) for 20 minutes. Cool. Meanwhile, melt 100 g/4 oz plain chocolate and spread a layer over the top of each cup cake. Allow to set. Cream together 100 g/4 oz/½ cup butter and 225 g/8 oz/2 cups sifted icing sugar until smooth. Beat in a few drops of peppermint essence and tint pale green with green food colouring. Place the mixture in a piping bag fitted with a small star nozzle and pipe a rosette in the centre of each cake.
Variation: To make mocha cup cakes, instead of green colouring add 1 teaspoon instant coffee dissolved in 2 teaspoons boiling water to part of the mixture and colour the butter cream for piping with coffee in the same way.

Battenburg fancies: Take 1 portion of the mixture and colour pale pink with red food colouring. Grease and line 4 450-g/1-lb loaf tins. Divide the pink mixture between 2 of the prepared tins. Take a further portion of the basic mixture and add ½ teaspoon vanilla essence. Divide between the remaining 2 tins. Level the tops and bake in a moderately hot oven (190°C, 375°F, Gas Mark 5) for 25 minutes, or until well risen and firm to the touch. Cool on a wire rack. When cold, cut each cake in half across the top. Turn cut edges uppermost and cut diagonally in two. Place one pink and one vanilla cake together diagonally so that a square is formed and cut each square into approximately 5 slices. Cream together 100 g/4 oz/½ cup butter and 225 g/8 oz/2 cups sifted icing sugar until smooth. Sandwich the pieces of cake together with butter cream and re-form the slice. Coat the edges in butter cream and roll in desiccated coconut.

Nut and raisin cup cakes: Take the remaining portion of basic mixture and fold in 50 g/2 oz 'Nuts and Raisins' from a mixed packet (rub the skins from the nuts and chop them first). Have ready 12 paper cake cases on a baking tray and place a generous teaspoon of the mixture in each one. Bake in a moderately hot oven (190°C, 375°F, Gas Mark 5) for 20 minutes. Cool. Sift 100 g/4 oz/1 cup icing sugar and beat in 1 tablespoon of warm water until smooth. Swirl a small circle of icing in the centre of each cake and top with a quartered glacé cherry.

To freeze: All of these decorated cakes, except the macaroons, are best open frozen on baking trays and then packed in layers in rigid-based containers with dividers. Seal and label.

To serve: Remove from the freezer, immediately unpack and place on a serving plate to defrost without damage. Allow about 1 hour at room temperature for defrosting.

Makes: 18 Almandine tarts, 18 Orange tarts, 18 Macaroons, 12 Chocolate mint cup cakes, 20 Battenburg fancies, 12 Nut and raisin cup cakes.

Storage time: 4–6 months.

NOTE: If you are transporting some of the goodies, perhaps to a friend's house for a party, use non-stick parchment dividers. This will prevent the decorations from sticking to the dividers if they defrost even slightly.

Holiday biscuits

METRIC/IMPERIAL	AMERICAN
450 g/1 lb margarine	2 cups margarine
600 g/1¼ lb granulated sugar	2½ cups sugar
3 medium eggs	3 medium eggs
75 ml/3 fl oz single cream	3 fl oz light cream
3 teaspoons vanilla essence	3 teaspoons vanilla extract
700 g/1½ lb plain flour	6 cups all-purpose flour
25 g/1 oz baking powder	1 oz baking powder
2 teaspoons salt	2 teaspoons salt

Cream the margarine with the sugar until light. Beat in the eggs, cream and vanilla essence. Sift the flour, baking powder and salt into the creamed mixture. Stir until well blended. Divide the dough into 6 portions and flavour as directed below. Drop by small spoonfuls on to lightly greased baking trays and flatten with a fork. Bake in a moderately hot oven (200°C, 400°F, Gas Mark 6) for 10–12 minutes. Cool on a wire rack.

Variations:

Plain: Sprinkle the top of each unbaked biscuit with coloured sugar or finely chopped nuts.

Orange-nut: Add 15 g/½ oz grated orange zest and 25 g/1 oz finely chopped walnuts.

Chocolate-nut: Melt 25 g/1 oz cooking chocolate with 2 teaspoons milk. Cool and stir into the batter. Fold in 25 g/1 oz chopped nuts.

Mincemeat: Add 75 g/3 oz prepared mincemeat.

Coconut: Add 50 g/2 oz desiccated coconut. Brush the tops with egg white and sprinkle with coloured coconut.

Fruit: Add 50 g/2 oz chopped candied peel, chopped sultanas or raisins.

Coffee (*Illustrated on page 35*): Substitute the same quantity of coffee essence for the vanilla essence. Sprinkle with icing sugar.

To freeze: Pack in suitable quantities in layers with dividers. Seal and label.

To serve: Defrost spread out on a plate for 30 minutes.

Makes: About 72 biscuits.

Storage time: 6 months.

Six-in-one wafers

METRIC/IMPERIAL	AMERICAN
450 g/1 lb butter	2 cups butter
150 g/6 oz soft brown sugar	¾ cup soft brown sugar
225 g/8 oz granulated sugar	1 cup granulated sugar
1 teaspoon vanilla essence	1 teaspoon vanilla extract
2 medium eggs	2 medium eggs
450 g/1 lb plain flour	4 cups all-purpose flour
1 teaspoon bicarbonate of soda	1 teaspoon baking soda
½ teaspoon salt	½ teaspoon salt

Cream the butter and sugars until light. Beat in the vanilla essence. Beat the eggs until light and stir into the creamed mixture. Sift the flour, bicarbonate of soda and salt into the creamed mixture. Stir until well blended. Divide the dough into 6 portions and leave 1 portion plain. Add one of the following to each of the remaining portions, then shape each portion into a roll 3·5 cm/1½ inches in diameter.

Variations:
Chocolate: Melt 25 g/1 oz plain chocolate and stir into 1 portion.
Coconut: Stir in 50 g/2 oz desiccated coconut.
Fruit: Stir in 50 g/2 oz chopped raisins.
Nut: Stir in 50 g/2 oz chopped walnuts.
Spice: Stir in ½ teaspoon each ground cinnamon and ground nutmeg.
To freeze: Pack the rolls separately in foil. Seal and label.
To serve: Slice the frozen dough 3 mm/⅛ inch thick. Place on lightly greased baking trays and bake in a moderately hot oven (190°C, 375°F, Gas Mark 5) for 10–12 minutes.
Makes: 72 wafers.
Storage time: 6 months.

Freezer cookies

METRIC/IMPERIAL	AMERICAN
200 g/7 oz butter	generous ¾ cup butter
90 g/3½ oz castor sugar	7 tablespoons sugar
275 g/10 oz plain flour	2½ cups all-purpose flour
1 teaspoon coffee essence	1 teaspoon coffee extract
1 tablespoon cocoa powder	1 tablespoon cocoa powder

Cream the butter and sugar together. Add the flour and knead to make a firm dough. Divide the dough into 2 portions. To one add the coffee essence, to the other add the cocoa powder. Knead each until smooth on a lightly floured surface. Roll each portion of dough between two sheets of greaseproof paper to a rectangle, about 18 cm/7 inches by 23 cm/9 inches and about 3 mm/⅛ inch thick. Place the rectangles on top of each other and trim the edges. Roll up the dough like a Swiss roll using the greaseproof paper as a guide. Chill until firm.
To freeze: Wrap closely. Seal and label.
To serve: Defrost in the refrigerator overnight. Cut into 5-mm/¼-inch slices and place on a greased baking tray. Bake in a moderately hot oven (190°C, 375°F, Gas Mark 5) for 10–12 minutes. Cool on a wire tray.
Makes: About 30 cookies.

Storage time: 6 months.
NOTE: The cookies can also be frozen after baking off. Pack in rigid containers for protection.
For the Christmas tree: Brush with beaten egg white and sprinkle with coloured coffee sugar before baking. Pierce with a skewer carefully and hang on the tree with invisible nylon thread.

Three-way cake chain

A simple basic one-stage cake mix with different flavourings and colourings added to each of three portions produces a tempting variety of cakes.

Three-way cake chain

METRIC/IMPERIAL	AMERICAN
450 g/1 lb soft margarine	2 cups soft margarine
450 g/1 lb castor sugar	2 cups sugar
8 eggs	8 eggs
450 g/1 lb self-raising flour	4 cups all-purpose flour sifted with 8
4 teaspoons baking powder	teaspoons baking powder

Preheat the oven to moderate (180°C, 350°F, Gas Mark 4) and grease and line the bottom of 2 1-kg/2-lb loaf tins, 2 20-cm/8-inch sandwich tins and 1 18-cm/7-inch by 28-cm/11-inch Swiss roll tin. Place all the ingredients into a large mixing bowl and beat for 2–3 minutes, until the mixture is smooth and slightly glossy. Divide equally into 3 portions.
Lemon flavour: To 1 portion of the cake mix add the finely grated zest of 1 large lemon. Spread the mixture in the prepared Swiss roll tin and bake in the oven for about 14 minutes, until light golden and firm to the touch. Cool on a wire rack.
Chocolate flavour: To 1 portion of the cake mix add 1 heaped tablespoon cocoa powder mixed to a cream with 2 tablespoons (US 3 tablespoons) hot water and cooled. Divide between 1 prepared sandwich tin and 1 prepared loaf tin. Bake in the oven for about 30 minutes, until firm to the touch. Cool on a wire rack.
Orange flavour: To 1 portion of the cake mix add the finely grated zest of 1 large orange and a few drops of orange food colouring. Divide between the remaining prepared sandwich tin and loaf tin and bake in the same way as the chocolate cakes above.

Tangy lemon bars

METRIC/IMPERIAL	AMERICAN
juice of 1 large lemon	juice of 1 large lemon
75 g/3 oz granulated sugar	6 tablespoons sugar
1 baked lemon cake	1 baked lemon cake

Mix together the juice from the lemon and the sugar. When the cake is baked, brush the top immediately with the lemon juice mixture until it is all used. Leave to cool in the tin. The lemon juice soaks into the sponge and the sugar forms a crisp crunchy topping. Cut into 24 bars.

Chocolate and orange chequerboard cake

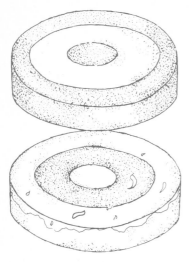

METRIC/IMPERIAL	AMERICAN
100 g/4 oz orange jelly marmalade	⅓ cup orange jelly marmalade
1 baked chocolate sandwich cake	1 baked chocolate layer cake
1 baked orange sandwich cake	1 baked orange layer cake
75 g/3 oz soft margarine	6 tablespoons soft margarine
225 g/8 oz icing sugar, sifted	2 cups sifted confectioners' sugar
1 tablespoon milk	1 tablespoon milk
50 g/2 oz plain chocolate	2 squares semi-sweet chocolate

Sieve the marmalade to remove any shreds of peel. Using a saucer and an egg-cup as a guide, carefully cut each cake into three circles. Spread the cut surface with marmalade and re-shape into two layers alternating the middle rings (see illustration). Place one layer on a serving plate or board and spread with remaining marmalade. Top with the other layer. Cream the margarine, icing sugar and milk until smooth. Melt the chocolate in a bowl over a pan of hot water, cool and beat into the mixture. Use the icing to coat the top and sides of the cake and mark into swirls with the tip of a round-bladed knife.

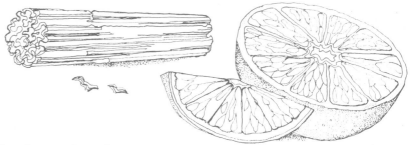

Stripey loaf cake

METRIC/IMPERIAL	AMERICAN
75 g/3 oz soft margarine	6 tablespoons soft margarine
225 g/8 oz icing sugar, sifted	2 cups sifted confectioners' sugar
2–4 tablespoons orange juice	3–4 tablespoons orange juice
1 baked chocolate loaf cake	1 baked chocolate loaf cake
1 baked orange loaf cake	1 baked orange loaf cake
1 small chocolate flake, crumbled, or 25 g/1 oz plain chocolate, grated	1 square semi-sweet chocolate, grated

Cream together the margarine and icing sugar, adding sufficient orange juice to give a soft spreading consistency. Cut each cake into two layers and sandwich all four layers together, alternating the colours and using half the icing. Use the remaining icing to coat the cake completely and sprinkle the top with the crumbled chocolate flake.
To freeze: Pack the lemon bars in layers with dividers. Open freeze the large cakes, then cover with rigid containers or polythene bags. Seal and label.
To serve: Unwrap while still frozen. Defrost lemon bars at room temperature for 1 hour and large cakes for 4 hours.
Makes: 24 Tangy lemon bars, 1 Chocolate and orange chequerboard cake/10 servings, 1 Stripey loaf cake/8 servings.
Storage time: 4–6 months.

Simple bread chain

Bake your own bread in shapes and sizes to suit family needs. Try these nice little Flowerpot loaves, useful Dinner rolls, tasty Supper bread and use the rest of the dough for a large Everyday loaf.

METRIC/IMPERIAL	AMERICAN
700 g/1½ lb plain flour	6 cups all-purpose flour
700 g/1½ lb wholemeal flour	5 cups wholemeal flour
2 tablespoons salt	3 tablespoons salt
40 g/1½ oz lard	3 tablespoons shortening
2 tablespoons sugar	3 tablespoons sugar
900 ml/1½ pints warm water	3¾ cups warm water
2 tablespoons dried yeast	3 tablespoons active dry yeast
¼ teaspoon poppy seeds	¼ teaspoon poppy seeds

Mix together the white and brown flours with the salt and rub in the lard. Stir in half the sugar. Dissolve the remaining sugar in the water and sprinkle the dried yeast on top. Allow to stand for about 10 minutes until frothy, then add to the dry ingredients and mix to a soft dough. Turn out on to a lightly floured surface and knead for at least 2 minutes, until smooth and elastic. Divide as follows:

Dinner rolls: Measure out 8 50-g/2-oz pieces of dough and shape each into a round ball. Arrange them round a greased 20-cm/8-inch sandwich tin with one ball in the centre. Brush tops with salt and water and sprinkle with poppy seeds.

Divide the remaining dough into 4 equal portions and reserve 1 portion for Supper bread.

Flowerpot loaves: Take 2 portions of dough, shape each into a ball and place in a well-greased earthenware flowerpot with a 13-cm/5-inch top. Brush tops with salt and water.

Everyday loaf: Shape 1 portion of dough and place in a greased 20-cm/8-inch cake tin or 1kg/2-lb loaf tin. Dust top of dough with flour.

Cover all the shaped breads with well-greased polythene and allow to rise until double their original size.

Remove the polythene and bake the breads in a hot oven (230°C, 450°F, Gas Mark 8) for 30–40 minutes. Cool.

To freeze: Pack in polythene bags. Seal and label.

To serve: Defrost loaves, still wrapped, at room temperature for 6 hours. To crisp crust, place unwrapped in a moderately hot oven (200°C, 400°F, Gas Mark 6) for 5–10 minutes. If required quickly place frozen loaves, wrapped in foil, in a moderately hot oven as above for 35 minutes. Remove foil and bake for a further 10 minutes to crisp crust.

Makes: 8 Dinner rolls, 2 Flowerpot loaves, 1 Everyday loaf, 1 Supper bread/4 servings.

Storage time: 6 weeks.

Supper bread: Keep the remaining portion of dough in the refrigerator to rise slowly. When the rest of the baking is complete roll it out to fit a 20-cm/8-inch sandwich tin, cover and allow to rise further in a warm place while you prepare the topping. Slice a large onion thinly, cook gently in butter until tender, stir in 4 tablespoons (US ⅓ cup) of grated hard cheese and season to taste. Spread over the risen dough, sprinkle with celery salt or caraway seed and bake in a moderately hot oven (190°C, 375°F, Gas Mark 5) for 30 minutes. Serve warm. Freeze leftovers packed as for other breads.

Rising times:
Quick rise: 30–45 minutes in a warm place
Slower rise: 1–1½ hours at average room temperature
Cold rise: 12–24 hours in a refrigerator

A large packet of brown bread mix and another of white produces four different loaves, a basket of fancy rolls and a batch of sugary buns.

White bread mix chain

METRIC/IMPERIAL	AMERICAN
600 g/1¼ lb white bread mix	1¼ lb white bread mix
400 ml/14 fl oz hand-hot water	1¾ cups hand-hot water
1 teaspoon poppy seeds	1 teaspoon poppy seeds

Place the dry bread mix in a large mixing bowl and add the water. Beat with a wooden spoon or by hand until the water is absorbed. Knead on a floured surface for 5 minutes then divide the dough into 2 equal portions.

Miniature cottage loaves: Take 1 portion of dough and divide into 8 equal pieces. Twist off one-third of each small piece and shape into a ball. Shape the larger piece into a ball and brush the top with water. Place the smaller ball on top of the larger ball and repeat this process with the remaining pieces of dough. Flour the handle of a small wooden spoon and press this down through the centre of each miniature loaf to touch the baking tray.

Poppy seed plait: Take 1 portion of dough and divide into 3 equal pieces. Lay them side by side on a board and, starting in the centre, plait the pieces of dough to one end. Turn the dough and plait to the other end. Place the plait on a greased baking tray and tuck the ends underneath.

Cover the shaped breads with a greased polythene bag and allow to rise in a warm place for 35–55 minutes, until doubled in bulk. Remove the polythene bag, brush the breads with salt and water and sprinkle with poppy seeds. Bake in a hot oven (230°C, 450°F, Gas Mark 8), allowing 10–15 minutes for the miniature loaves and 25–30 minutes for the plait. Cool.

To freeze: Pack in polythene bags. Seal and label.
To serve: See 'Simple bread chain' page 213.

Slashed herby loaf

METRIC/IMPERIAL	AMERICAN
275 g/10 oz white bread mix	10 oz white bread mix
1 teaspoon dried mixed herbs	1 teaspoon dried mixed herbs
200 ml/7 fl oz hand-hot water	¾ cup hand-hot water
¼ teaspoon celery seeds or dried mixed herbs	¼ teaspoon celery seeds or dried mixed herbs

Place the bread mix and herbs in a bowl and add the water. Beat with a wooden spoon or by hand until the water is absorbed. Knead on a floured surface for 5 minutes, then shape the dough into a round and place on a greased baking tray. Slash the top with a cross, brush the loaf with salt and water and sprinkle with celery seeds or dried mixed herbs. Allow to rise and follow all instructions as given above.

Makes: 8 Miniature cottage loaves, 1 Poppy seed plait, 1 Slashed herby loaf.
Storage time: 6 weeks.

Salsicce al vino rosso; Sausage and cheese en croûte; Bangers in blankets; Chicken 'n' chipolata drumsticks (pages 199–201)

Batch baking small cakes: macaroons, almandine tarts, orange tarts, Battenburg fancies, chocolate mint cup cakes, nut and raisin cup cakes (pages 207–208)

Brown bread mix chain

METRIC/IMPERIAL	AMERICAN
600 g/1¼ lb brown bread mix	1¼ lb brown bread mix
400 ml/14 fl oz hand-hot water	1¾ cups hand-hot water
1 egg	1 egg
1 teaspoon sugar	1 teaspoon sugar
1 tablespoon water	1 tablespoon water
1 teaspoon caraway seeds	1 teaspoon caraway seeds

Place the dry bread mix in a large mixing bowl and add the water. Beat with a wooden spoon or by hand until the water is absorbed. Knead on a floured surface for 5 minutes then divide the dough into 2 equal portions.
Flat cottage loaf: Take 1 portion of dough and twist off a quarter of it. Shape the remainder into a ball then flatten it and place on a greased baking tray. Form the remaining piece of dough into a small ball, dampen one side and place in the centre of the larger piece.
Cobblestone loaf: Take 1 portion of dough and divide it in half. Shape one half into an oblong, place in a greased 450-g/1-lb loaf tin and dampen the top. Divide the remaining dough into 6 equal portions and shape each one into a ball. Arrange the balls on the first piece of dough.

Cover the loaves with a greased polythene bag and allow to rise in a warm place for 35–55 minutes until double in size. Remove the bag. Blend the egg, sugar and water and brush the loaves. Sprinkle the flat cottage loaf with caraway. Bake in a hot oven (230°C, 450°F, Gas Mark 8) for 25–30 minutes. Cool.
To freeze: Pack in polythene bags. Seal and label.
To serve: See 'Simple bread chain' page 213.

Rich sugar buns

METRIC/IMPERIAL	AMERICAN
275 g/10 oz brown bread mix	10 oz brown bread mix
75 g/3 oz butter	6 tablespoons butter
175 ml/6 fl oz hand-hot milk	¾ cup hand-hot milk
50 g/2 oz soft brown sugar	¼ cup soft brown sugar
50 g/2 oz demerara sugar	¼ cup granulated sugar

Place the bread mix in a bowl and rub in two-thirds of the butter. Add the hot milk and beat with a wooden spoon or by hand until the liquid is absorbed. Knead on a floured surface for 5 minutes. Roll out the dough to a rectangle 35 cm/14 inches by 23 cm/9 inches. Melt the remaining butter and brush over the dough. Sprinkle with the soft brown sugar and roll up from one long end. Cut the roll into 8 equal portions and arrange these, cut side up, around a 20-cm/8-inch greased sandwich tin, placing one roll in the centre. Cover with a greased polythene bag and allow to rise in a warm place until double in size. Sprinkle with the demerara sugar and bake in a moderately hot oven (200°C, 400°F, Gas Mark 6) for 30 minutes. Cool.
To freeze: Pack the bun ring in a polythene bag or separate and pack individually in cling film and then all together in a container. Seal and label.
To serve: Unwrap and defrost for 3 hours if a ring, 1 hour if separated.
Makes: 1 Flat cottage loaf, 1 Cobblestone loaf, 8 Rich sugar buns.
Storage time: 6 weeks.

Catering for Christmas

Of all family celebrations, Christmas is surely the one most devoted to the pleasures of eating. This places a strain on any hostess because providing home-cooked food of the highest quality, in unlimited quantities, is all part of the great Christmas tradition of hospitality. Every cook prides herself on producing a series of memorable feasts, not only on the great day itself but beforehand, and afterwards as the remaining days of the holiday unwind their relaxing course.

Some of the food and drink is consumed quite informally, with the family grouped round the fireplace or the television. But it all has to be part of the time-honoured festive fare. This does not mean the intermittent re-appearance of mince pies and sausage rolls with monotonous regularity through the holiday, so some of the ideas offered here are rather more original. But we have to admit that Christmas is now at least a four-day event, and menus simply have to be planned ahead. This is where the freezer can be especially helpful as you can earmark space for a number of items you know you will need from the freezer, and cook these ahead. Then you can fit in the last-minute shopping for fresh foods with a flexible attitude towards the final details of the menus. For instance, if you plan to offer a salad, the choice can be decided, whether it is chicory, endive or celery, according to what is best in the market at the time.

The menu plan given here may not exactly suit your own requirements – you may be invited out to parties yourself, or you may not have so many meals to cater for. But it illustrates the kind of plan you should draw up in time to make sure that you have a selection of suitable items ready in the freezer to take out as required. This does ensure that work during the holiday period is reduced to a minimum. Many of the dishes which figure in the menus here are starred to show that the recipes are included in the book and can be cooked ahead of time. The only exceptions are Spiced gammon, where the joint could come from the freezer and the leftovers are used for High rise puffs; and Salamagundy, an elegant salad platter making use of cooked turkey slices. Probably your turkey is a frozen one, so make sure it gets the slow defrosting treatment recommended on the pack. Glancing through the menus, you will notice that the items required on Christmas Eve need only be removed from the freezer that morning along with the frozen gammon joint for Christmas day. The uncooked freezer jam defrosts while breakfast is being prepared, so this need only be removed on Christmas morning at the same time as the Miniature cottage loaves. Other items require little defrosting time, or none. The bread for Boxing Day breakfast and the Cider Christmas cake will be best taken out late on Christmas night.

Cider Christmas cake

(Illustrated on page 198)

METRIC/IMPERIAL	AMERICAN
225 g/8 oz butter	1 cup butter
225 g/8 oz soft brown sugar	1 cup soft brown sugar
3 eggs	3 eggs
225 g/8 oz plain flour	2½ cups all-purpose flour sifted with ½
50 g/2 oz self-raising flour	teaspoon baking powder
pinch salt	pinch salt
2 teaspoons ground mixed spices	2 teaspoons ground mixed spices
225 g/8 oz currants	1⅓ cups seedless white raisins
225 g/8 oz seedless raisins, chopped	1⅓ cups chopped seeded raisins
100 g/4 oz glacé cherries	½ cup candied cherries
1 (35-g/1¼-oz) packet dehydrated apple flakes, or 100 g/4 oz cooking apples, chopped	1¼ oz packaged dehydrated apple flakes, or ¼ lb baking apples, chopped
100 g/4 oz mixed peel, chopped	⅔ cup chopped mixed peel
50 g/2 oz flaked almonds	½ cup flaked almonds
about 3 tablespoons strong still cider	about ¼ cup strong cider
syrup:	*syrup:*
50 g/2 oz sugar	¼ cup sugar
150 ml/¼ pint strong still cider	⅔ cup strong cider

Cream together the fat and sugar until light and fluffy. Whisk the eggs lightly and gradually add to the creamed mixture, beating well after each addition. Sift the flours, salt and spices together, add to the creamed mixture and fold in with a metal spoon. Stir in the fruit, peel, nuts and cider. Place in a 20-cm/8-inch or 23-cm/9-inch round cake tin lined with non-stick parchment or greased greaseproof paper and bake in a cool oven (140°C, 275°F, Gas Mark 1) for 3–3½ hours. When fully cooked, a fine skewer inserted into the cake will come out clean. Allow the cake to stand overnight then pierce holes in the top with a fine skewer. To make the syrup, dissolve the sugar in the cider over low heat. Gradually pour over the cake a little at a time, allowing each amount of syrup to absorb fully before adding more (this may take several hours). Place the cake on a cake board or plate and decorate with moulded icing.

Moulded icing decoration

METRIC/IMPERIAL	AMERICAN
2 tablespoons water	3 tablespoons water
4 teaspoons gelatine	4 teaspoons gelatin
4 teaspoons glycerine	4 teaspoons glycerine
6 tablespoons liquid glucose	½ cup liquid glucose
1 kg/2 lb icing sugar, sifted	7 cups sifted confectioners' sugar
cornflour for sprinkling	cornstarch for sprinkling
when serving:	*when serving:*
candles and candle holders	candles and candle holders
Christmas figures	Christmas figures
few tiny jelly sweets	few tiny jellybeans

To make the icing, stir the water and gelatine in a pan over gentle heat until the gelatine has completely dissolved. Remove from the heat and add the glycerine and liquid glucose. Pour into a bowl. Gradually add the icing sugar and mix to form a stiff paste. Sprinkle a working surface with cornflour and knead the paste until smooth. Reserve one-third of the icing and roll out the remainder to make a circle twice as large as the top of the cake. Put in place and stretch the edge very gently to fit smoothly over the sides to the base all round. Form the rest of the icing into three long narrow ropes and plait together to fit round the top edge of the cake.

To freeze: Open freeze until the decorations are solid. Cover with a rigid polythene container. Seal and label.

To serve: Unpack the cake while frozen and allow to defrost at room temperature for 6 hours. Decorate the top with candles, Christmas figures and tiny jelly sweets.

Makes: 1 cake/20–25 servings.

Storage time: 3–6 weeks.

NOTE: The undecorated cake may be closely wrapped and frozen. Storage time will then be 4–6 months.

No-bake fruit cake

METRIC/IMPERIAL	AMERICAN
16 marshmallows	16 marshmallows
6 tablespoons evaporated milk	½ cup evaporated milk
3 tablespoons orange juice	¼ cup orange juice
1 tablespoon brandy	1 tablespoon brandy
36 digestive biscuits	36 graham crackers
175 g/6 oz seedless raisins	1 cup seeded raisins
100 g/4 oz stoned dates	¼ lb pitted dates
100 g/4 oz walnuts	1 cup walnuts
75 g/3 oz glacé pineapple	3 oz candied pineapple
75 g/3 oz glacé cherries	3 oz candied cherries
25 g/1 oz candied peel	1 oz candied peel
¼ teaspoon ground cinnamon	¼ teaspoon ground cinnamon
¼ teaspoon ground nutmeg	¼ teaspoon ground nutmeg
⅛ teaspoon ground cloves	⅛ teaspoon ground cloves
when serving:	*when serving:*
few glacé fruits	few candied fruits

Cut the marshmallows into quarters, place in a bowl and mix with the evaporated milk, orange juice and brandy. Allow to stand for 10 minutes. Crush the biscuits finely. Chop the raisins, dates, walnuts, glacé pineapple, cherries and peel finely. Stir the biscuit crumbs, chopped fruit, nuts and spices into the marshmallow mixture. Mix until all the crumbs are moistened. Press the mixture firmly into a 1-kg/2-lb loaf tin lined with non-stick parchment, or into two smaller tins. Cover tightly and allow to mature in the refrigerator for 3 days.

To freeze: Remove from tin, leaving paper around cake, and wrap. Seal and label.

To serve: Unwrap and strip off paper. Decorate with glacé fruits. Serve in thin slices.

Makes: 1 1-kg/2¼-lb cake.

Storage time: 3 months.

Basic Viennese pâte brisée

METRIC/IMPERIAL	AMERICAN
350 g/12 oz plain flour	3 cups all-purpose flour
½ teaspoon ground cinnamon	½ teaspoon ground cinnamon
75 g/3 oz castor sugar	6 tablespoons sugar
40 g/1½ oz finely ground coffee	1½ oz finely ground coffee
40 g/1½ oz ground unblanched hazel nuts	⅓ cup ground unblanched hazel nuts
finely grated zest of 1½ lemons	finely grated rind of 1½ lemons
225 g/8 oz butter	1 cup butter
1 egg	1 egg
1 egg yolk	1 egg yolk
Linzertorte:	*Linzertorte:*
450 g/1 lb raspberry jam	1⅓ cups raspberry jam
Citrontorte:	*Citrontorte:*
450 g/1 lb lemon curd	1⅓ cups lemon curd
50 g/2 oz ground almonds	½ cup ground almonds

Sift the flour and cinnamon into a bowl and add the sugar, coffee, nuts and lemon zest. Add the butter and the egg and egg yolk and work the ingredients into a paste, gradually drawing in all the flour. Knead until smooth then chill for 30 minutes. Divide the mixture into 2 portions.
Linzertorte: Roll out 1 portion of the pâte brisée thinly and use to line a 20-cm/8-inch flan ring on a baking tray. Spread the raspberry jam evenly in the pastry case and roll out pastry trimmings to make a lattice over the top.
Citrontorte: Roll out 1 portion of the pâte brisée thinly and use to line a fluted 20-cm/8-inch flan ring on a baking tray. Mix together the lemon curd and ground almonds and spread this in the prepared case.
　Bake the flans in a moderate oven (180°C, 350°F, Gas Mark 4), allowing 25–30 minutes for the Linzertorte and 30–35 minutes for the Citrontorte. Cool.
To freeze: Open freeze the flans then remove flan rings and wrap. Seal and label.
To serve: Unwrap and place still frozen on a serving dish. Allow to defrost at room temperature for 3 hours. If required warm, reheat from frozen in a moderately hot oven (190°C, 375°F, Gas Mark 5) for 15 minutes.
Makes: 2 tortes/12–16 servings.
Storage time: 4–6 months.

Snowballs

METRIC/IMPERIAL	AMERICAN
225 g/8 oz butter	1 cup butter
50 g/2 oz icing sugar	½ cup confectioners' sugar
1 teaspoon vanilla essence	1 teaspoon vanilla extract
250 g/9 oz plain flour	2¼ cups all-purpose flour
¼ teaspoon salt	¼ teaspoon salt
50 g/2 oz chopped walnuts	½ cup chopped walnuts
castor or icing sugar	superfine or confectioners' sugar

Beat the butter until soft. Gradually beat in the icing sugar and vanilla essence. Sift the flour and salt into the creamed mixture, add the chopped nuts and form into a dough. Chill for several hours. Roll the dough into 2·5-cm/1-inch balls and place on ungreased baking trays. Chill for 15 minutes.

To freeze: Open freeze then pack in layers with dividers. Seal and label.
To serve: Place the frozen balls well apart on ungreased baking trays and bake in a moderately hot oven (190°C, 375°F, Gas Mark 5) for about 14 minutes until set, but not browned. While still warm, roll the balls in castor or icing sugar.
Makes: About 48 snowballs.
Storage time: 4–6 months.

Lattice mincemeat tart

(Illustrated on page 197)

METRIC/IMPERIAL	AMERICAN
300 g/11 oz puff pastry, defrosted	11 oz puff paste, defrosted
6–8 tablespoons mincemeat	½–⅔ cup mincemeat
finely grated zest of 1 lemon	finely grated rind of 1 lemon
25 g/1 oz desiccated coconut	1 oz shredded coconut
1 egg, beaten	1 egg, beaten

Roll out pastry on a lightly floured board to 3 mm/⅛ inch thickness. Cut out a circle 20–23 cm/8–9 inches in diameter. Place on a baking tray. Mix the mincemeat with the lemon zest and coconut and place in the centre of the pastry, leaving a border all round the edge. Roll out remaining pastry and cut into long strips. Arrange these in a lattice pattern. Pinch the edges firmly together to seal and brush with beaten egg. Bake in a hot oven (220°C, 425°F, Gas Mark 7) for 10–15 minutes, then reduce the temperature to moderately hot (190°C, 375°F, Gas Mark 5) for a further 10–15 minutes. Cool.
To freeze: Open freeze until solid then pack. Seal and label.
To serve: Heat in a moderately hot oven (190°C, 375°F, Gas Mark 5) for 20 minutes.
Storage time: 4–6 months.

Pavlova mincemeat baskets

(Illustrated on page 197)

METRIC/IMPERIAL	AMERICAN
3 egg whites	3 egg whites
175 g/6 oz castor sugar	¾ cup sugar
2 teaspoons cornflour	2 teaspoons cornstarch
1 teaspoon white vinegar	1 teaspoon white vinegar
450 g/1 lb mincemeat	1 lb mincemeat
finely grated zest of 1 orange	finely grated rind of 1 orange

Whisk the egg whites until stiff. Whisk in half the sugar until the mixture forms stiff peaks. Fold in the remaining sugar, cornflour and vinegar. Place the mixture in a piping bag fitted with a large star nozzle. Pipe baskets on to baking trays lined with non-stick parchment or greased foil and bake in a very cool oven (110°C, 225°F, Gas Mark ¼) for 4–5 hours until dry. Allow to cool. Mix together the mincemeat and orange zest and pile into the meringue baskets.
To freeze: Pack in rigid containers. Seal and label.
To serve: Unpack and defrost at room temperature for 1 hour.
Makes: 6–8 baskets.
Storage time: 3 months.

Pizza party slice

METRIC/IMPERIAL
450 g/1 lb frozen bread dough, defrosted
1 large onion
3 (396-g/14-oz) cans tomatoes
3 tablespoons tomato purée
100 g/4 oz mushrooms, chopped
2 teaspoons dried mixed herbs
salt and pepper to taste
100 g/4 oz strong Cheddar cheese, grated
25 g/1 oz Parmesan cheese, grated
1 (184-g/6½-oz) can red pimientos
1 (56-g/2-oz) can anchovy fillets, cut in
    strips
about 50 g/2 oz stuffed green olives, sliced

AMERICAN
1 lb frozen bread dough, defrosted
1 large onion
3 (14-oz) cans tomatoes
¼ cup tomato paste
1 cup chopped mushrooms
2 teaspoons dried mixed herbs
salt and pepper to taste
1 cup grated strong Cheddar cheese
¼ cup grated Parmesan cheese
6½ oz canned red pimientos
2 oz canned anchovy fillets, cut in strips
about 2 oz stuffed green olives, sliced

Roll out the dough and use to line two trays, 18 cm/7 inches by 28 cm/11 inches. Allow to rise in a warm place until double in bulk. Thinly slice the onion and cook uncovered in a pan with the tomatoes, tomato purée, mushrooms and herbs for about 30 minutes until the liquid is reduced and the mixture thick. Season well with salt and pepper. Spread the mixture over the dough to within 2·5 cm/1 inch of the edges. Sprinkle the cheeses over the top. Bake in a moderately hot oven (200°C, 400°F, Gas Mark 6) for about 20 minutes, until risen and just golden around the edges. Arrange strips of red pepper diagonally across the trays in lines going one way and lattice them with the anchovy fillets going the other way. Put a slice of olive in each space. Cool. Remove from the tins and cut into slices if wished.

To freeze: Open freeze until solid then wrap closely. Pack portions with dividers. Seal and label.

To serve: Unwrap and place on a baking tray. Reheat from frozen in a moderately hot oven (200°C, 400°F, Gas Mark 6) for about 15 minutes.

Serves: 12.

Storage time: 3 months.

Frosted tropical coupe

(Illustrated on page 226)

METRIC/IMPERIAL
175 g/6 oz sugar
100 g/4 oz creamed coconut, grated
300 ml/½ pint hot milk
1 egg white
when serving:
1 (454-g/1-lb) can tropical fruit salad
50 g/2 oz pistachio nuts, chopped

AMERICAN
¾ cup sugar
4 oz creamed coconut, grated
1¼ cups hot milk
1 egg white
when serving:
1 (16-oz) can tropical fruit salad
½ cup chopped pistachio nuts

Dissolve the sugar and melt the coconut in the hot milk. Cool, stirring occasionally. Pour into a shallow container and freeze until mushy. Scoop into a chilled bowl and beat until smooth. Stiffly whisk the egg white and fold into the coconut mixture.

To freeze: Pack in a shallow container. Seal and label.

To serve: Remove from the freezer and allow to soften in the refrigerator for 30 minutes. Place a scoop of sherbet into each of 4 sundae dishes, add 2 tablespoons (US 3 tablespoons) of drained tropical fruit salad and another scoop of sherbet to each one. Chill and serve sprinkled with the pistachio nuts.
Serves: 4.
Storage time: 4–6 months.

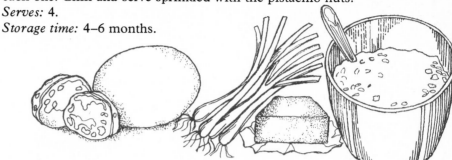

Pastry tricornes and cheese spirals

METRIC/IMPERIAL	AMERICAN
50 g/2 oz spring onions	2 oz scallions
225 g/8 oz pork or lamb fillet, diced	½ lb pork or lamb tenderloin, diced
25 g/1 oz melted butter	2 tablespoons melted butter
½ teaspoon ground cinnamon	½ teaspoon ground cinnamon
1 teaspoon curry powder	1 teaspoon curry powder
1 teaspoon salt	1 teaspoon salt
50 g/2 oz frozen chopped spinach	2 oz frozen chopped spinach
50 g/2 oz walnuts, finely chopped	½ cup finely chopped walnuts
100 g/4 oz cooked rice	⅔ cup cooked rice
450 g/1 lb puff pastry, defrosted	1 lb puff paste, defrosted
1 egg, beaten	1 egg, beaten
2 tablespoons cold water	3 tablespoons cold water
cheese spirals:	*cheese spirals:*
255 g/8 oz goat cheese	½ lb goat cheese

Finely chop the spring onions and toss with the diced fillet in the butter over moderate heat until sealed. Combine the spices and salt, divide and reserve half, stir the remainder into the pan and cook for 1 minute. Add the partially defrosted spinach, walnuts and rice. Stir lightly to combine well, remove from the heat and allow to cool. Roll out the pastry thinly and stamp out 8 rounds the size of small saucers. Reserve the pastry trimmings. Divide the meat mixture between the pastry circles, dampen the edges, pinch in two-thirds of the edge towards the centre, then the final third, to make tricornes. Arrange on a damped baking tray. Brush with the egg and water, reserving part for the spirals. Bake in a hot oven (220°C, 425°F, Gas Mark 7) for 25 minutes.
Cheese spirals: Cut the cheese into matchstick lengths and sprinkle with the reserved seasonings. Bring together the pastry trimmings, re-roll into an oblong and cut into narrow strips. Twist the strips round the cheese fingers. Arrange on a damped baking tray, brush with the remainder of the egg wash and bake in the oven for 15 minutes. Cool on a wire rack.
To freeze: Pack the tricornes in a shallow rigid-based container. Pack the cheese spirals separately in a small container. Seal and label.
To serve: Reheat from frozen in a moderately hot oven (190° C, 375° F, Gas Mark 5) for 20 minutes for the tricornes and 15 minutes for the spirals.
Makes: 8 tricornes, about 80 spirals.
Storage time: 4–6 months.

Cassata bombe (page 240); Peach rice crème (page 240); Toasted nut tortoni (page 241)

226

Frosted tropical coupe (page 223)

Mandarin orange chicken (page 232); Pineappled pork and prawns (page 231)

Mild and hot curry sauces (page 234); Gingered beef curry (page 230); Indonesian chicken curry (page 233)

Dishes from Other Lands

Looking through books of foreign recipes may inspire you to cook a new and unusual dish, maybe one that is a reminder of pleasant holiday experiences in the cuisine of other lands. It will delight your family and may soon become a favourite dish. Enthusiasm is also roused by the idea of producing something exciting and more exotic than usual to offer your guests. So often with foreign recipes one has the impression that the ingredients must be rarities in our own shops and that as foreigners dedicate themselves to cooking, their dishes will take hours of preparation. This is not always the case and here are some exciting ideas to try, all based on ingredients that are reasonable in price and easy to find, to give a world-wide selection of dishes planned to fully exploit your freezer.

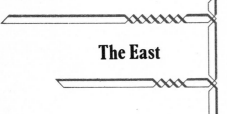

The East

Crispy pancakes with bean sprouts

(*Illustrated on page 117*)

METRIC/IMPERIAL	AMERICAN
100 g/4 oz plain flour	1 cup all-purpose flour
pinch salt	pinch salt
1 egg	1 egg
300 ml/½ pint water	1¼ cups water
oil for frying	oil for frying
filling for each pancake:	*filling for each pancake:*
1 tablespoon bean sprouts	1 tablespoon bean sprouts
pinch salt	pinch salt
few drops soya sauce	few drops soy sauce

To make the pancakes, place the flour and salt in a basin and drop in the egg. Gradually stir in the water to make a batter the consistency of thin cream. Allow to stand for 1 hour. Lightly oil an 18-cm/7-inch frying pan and heat well. Pour a little batter into the pan to coat the base. Cook on one side only until the top surface is dry. Remove from the pan and place pancake cooked side downwards. Continue making pancakes until all but 1 tablespoon of the batter has been used. Turn the pancakes over. Mix all the filling ingredients together and divide among the pancakes, placing in the centre of the *cooked* side. Roll up the pancakes, tuck in the ends and brush with a little of the left-over batter to seal.
To freeze: Open freeze until solid, then pack in convenient quantities. Seal and label.
To serve: Deep-fry the rolls, from the frozen state, in deep hot oil for about 7 minutes until golden brown. Drain well.
Makes: 4–6 pancake rolls.
Storage time: 3 months.

Soup with fenugreek

(Illustrated on page 117)

METRIC/IMPERIAL	AMERICAN
1 medium onion, chopped	1 medium onion, chopped
2 sticks celery, chopped	2 stalks celery, chopped
25 g/1 oz butter, melted	2 tablespoons melted butter
900 ml/1½ pints chicken stock	3¾ cups chicken stock
salt and freshly ground black pepper	salt and freshly ground black pepper
4 heaped tablespoons fenugreek	5 heaped tablespoons fenugreek
2 tablespoons chopped parsley	3 tablespoons chopped parsley

Sauté the onion and celery in the butter until soft but not browned. Stir in the chicken stock and bring to the boil. Simmer gently for 20–30 minutes. Add seasoning, fenugreek and parsley and simmer for a further 5 minutes. Cool.
To freeze: Pack in convenient quantities. Seal and label.
To serve: Defrost at room temperature for 4 hours and reheat to boiling point, stirring well.
Serves: 4.
Storage time: 4–6 months.

Gingered beef curry

(Illustrated on page 228)

METRIC/IMPERIAL	AMERICAN
1 apple	1 apple
50 g/2 oz butter	¼ cup butter
2 tablespoons oil	3 tablespoons oil
600 g/1¼ lb chuck steak, cubed	1¼ lb chuck steak, cubed
3 onions, sliced	3 onions, sliced
1 clove garlic, crushed	1 clove garlic, crushed
2 tablespoons curry powder	3 tablespoons curry powder
2 tablespoons flour	3 tablespoons flour
2 teaspoons paprika	2 teaspoons paprika pepper
600 ml/1 pint beef stock	2½ cups beef stock
2 tablespoons purée	3 tablespoons tomato paste
1 bay leaf	1 bay leaf
3 pieces stem ginger, sliced	3 pieces preserved ginger, sliced
2 tablespoons desiccated coconut	3 tablespoons shredded coconut
2 tablespoons chopped parsley	3 tablespoons chopped parsley
salt to taste	salt to taste

Peel, core and dice the apple. Heat the butter and oil and use to sauté the meat until it changes colour. Remove from the pan. Add the onions, garlic and apple to the fat remaining in the pan and cook for 4–5 minutes. Stir in the curry powder, flour and paprika and cook for 1–2 minutes. Gradually stir all the remaining ingredients and replace the meat. Bring to the boil and simmer very gently for 1½–2 hours, until the meat is tender. Cool.
To freeze: Pack in convenient quantities. Seal and label.
To serve: Defrost and then reheat in a saucepan. Serve with boiled rice.
Serves: 4.
Storage time: 4–6 months.

Pineappled pork and prawns

(*Illustrated on page 227*)

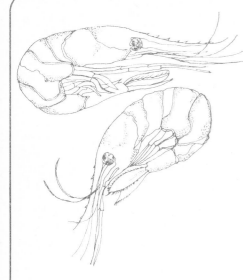

METRIC/IMPERIAL	AMERICAN
1 (227-g/8-oz) can pineapple slices	1 (8-oz) can pineapple slices
1 (91-g/3¼-oz) can prawns	3¼ oz canned prawns
1 chicken stock cube	1 chicken bouillon cube
225 g/8 oz pork fillet	½ lb pork tenderloin
3 tablespoons oil	¼ cup oil
6 spring onions	6 scallions
1 tablespoon mixed pickles in vinegar, chopped	1 tablespoon mixed pickles in vinegar, chopped
2 tablespoons dry sherry	3 tablespoons dry sherry
1 tablespoon liquid from the pickles	1 tablespoon liquid from the pickles
1 tablespoon cornflour	1 tablespoon cornstarch

Drain the juices from the cans of pineapple and prawns. Heat together and use to dissolve the stock cube. Dice the pork and sauté gently in the oil until pale golden. Remove from the pan and keep hot. Finely chop the onions and add to the oil in the pan with the pickles. Cook, stirring constantly, for 1 minute. Add the sherry, liquid from the pickles and the sweet stock. Moisten the cornflour with a little cold water, add to the pan and bring to the boil, stirring all the time until the sauce is slightly thickened and smooth. Chop the pineapple and add to the sauce with the prawns. Cool.
To freeze: Pour into a suitable container. Seal and label.
To serve: Defrost overnight and then reheat gently in a saucepan. Serve with white Chinese vermicelli or boiled rice.
Serves: 4.
Storage time: 3 months.

Hindustani spiced fish

METRIC/IMPERIAL	AMERICAN
1 teaspoon chilli powder	1 teaspoon chili powder
1 teaspoon ground turmeric	1 teaspoon ground turmeric
1 medium onion, grated	1 medium onion, grated
2 tablespoons lemon juice	3 tablespoons lemon juice
600 g/1¼ lb white fish fillet	1¼ lb white fish fillet
flour for coating	flour for coating
oil for frying	oil for frying

Mix together the chilli powder, turmeric, onion and lemon juice. Skin the fish and divide into 4 portions. Coat the fish with the spice mixture and allow to stand for 1 hour. Carefully lift each portion of fish, coat well in flour and fry in hot oil for about 3 minutes on each side, until golden yellow. Drain and cool.
To freeze: Pack with dividers. Seal and label.
To serve: Unwrap and fry the frozen fish portions in hot oil for about 3–4 minutes on each side (depending on thickness), until rich golden brown. Serve with fluffy boiled rice and fried onion rings.
Serves: 4.
Storage time: 3 months.

Mandarin orange chicken

(*Illustrated on page 227*)

METRIC/IMPERIAL	AMERICAN
2 young carrots	2 young carrots
1 piece stem ginger	1 piece preserved ginger
1 (298-g/10½-oz) can mandarin oranges in natural juice	10½ oz canned mandarin oranges in natural juice
1 medium onion	1 medium onion
1 tablespoon vinegar	1 tablespoon vinegar
300 ml/½ pint duck-giblet or chicken stock	1¼ cups duck-giblet or chicken stock
2 frozen chicken breast portions, defrosted	2 frozen duck breast portions, defrosted
1 tablespoon soya sauce	1 tablespoon soy sauce
1 tablespoon ginger syrup from the jar	1 tablespoon ginger syrup from the jar
salt and pepper to taste	salt and pepper to taste

Very finely slice the carrots and onion and the piece of ginger. Drain the mandarins and combine the juice with the vinegar and stock. Use this liquid to poach the chicken portions for about 35 minutes, until tender. Remove from the stock, cool and dice the meat. Add the soya sauce and ginger syrup to the stock. Bring to the boil, season to taste and add the sliced vegetables and ginger. Cook for 3 minutes, or until the vegetables are just tender but still crisp. Return the chicken meat to the sauce and heat through. Cool.
To freeze: Pack in a suitable container. Seal and label.
To serve: Defrost overnight and then reheat gently in a saucepan. Serve with white Chinese vermicelli or boiled rice.
Serves: 4.
Storage time: 4–6 months.

Tandoori chicken

(*Illustrated on page 67*)

METRIC/IMPERIAL	AMERICAN
1·5 kg/3 lb frozen chicken, defrosted	3 lb frozen chicken, defrosted
1 teaspoon ground turmeric	1 teaspoon ground turmeric
good pinch saffron strands	good pinch saffron strands
4 cloves	4 cloves
1 cinnamon stick	1 cinnamon stick
225 g/8 oz long-grain rice	1 cup long-grain rice
pinch salt	pinch salt
1 tiny onion, sliced	1 tiny onion, sliced
1 teaspoon chopped canned red pimiento	1 teaspoon chopped canned red pimiento
2 tablespoons oil	3 tablespoons oil
few watercress leaves, chopped	few watercress leaves, chopped
marinade:	*marinade:*
300 ml/½ pint natural yogurt	1¼ cups unflavored yogurt
1 clove garlic, crushed	1 clove garlic, crushed
½ teaspoon ground ginger	½ teaspoon ground ginger
1 tablespoon paprika	1 tablespoon paprika pepper
few bay leaves and peppercorns	few bay leaves and peppercorns
1 tablespoon tomato purée	1 tablespoon tomato paste
grated zest of 1 lemon	grated rind of 1 lemon

Cut the chicken in half lengthwise and remove the skin. Prick the flesh well with a skewer. Mix together the marinade ingredients and pour over the chicken halves, ensuring that they are well coated. Cover tightly and leave for 24 hours, then remove the bay leaves. Place a wire rack in a roasting tin and carefully lift the chicken halves on to it. Spoon over any remaining marinade. Bake in a moderate oven (160°C, 325°F, Gas Mark 3) for 1½ hours, or until tender, basting frequently. Meanwhile, steep the turmeric, saffron strands, cloves and cinnamon stick in boiling water for 30 minutes then strain the saffron water into a saucepan and use to cook the rice, adding salt to taste. Separate the onion slices into rings and fry with the pimiento in the oil until brown. Drain the saffron rice and fluff up with a fork. Place on a hot serving dish and top with the cooked chicken halves. Garnish the chicken with chopped watercress and scatter the onion rings and pimiento over the rice.

Serves: 4.

Indonesian chicken curry

(Illustrated on page 228)

METRIC/IMPERIAL	AMERICAN
50 g/2 oz butter	¼ cup butter
2 sticks celery, chopped	2 stalks celery, chopped
1 onion, chopped	1 onion, chopped
1 fresh chilli pepper, deseeded and finely chopped	1 fresh chili pepper, deseeded and finely chopped
2 tablespoons flour	3 tablespoons flour
½ teaspoon ground coriander	½ teaspoon ground coriander
pinch chilli powder	pinch chili powder
¾ teaspoon ground cardamom	¾ teaspoon ground cardamom
½ teaspoon ground cumin	½ teaspoon ground cumin
1 teaspoon ground turmeric	1 teaspoon ground turmeric
½ teaspoon ground ginger	½ teaspoon ground ginger
grated zest of ½ lemon	grated rind of ½ lemon
1 tablespoon peanut butter	1 tablespoon peanut butter
600 ml/1 pint chicken stock	2½ cups chicken stock
1 teaspoon anchovy essence	1 teaspoon anchovy extract
4 tablespoons oil	⅓ cup oil
4 chicken portions	4 chicken portions
1 (227-g/8-oz) can pineapple chunks	1 (8-oz) can pineapple chunks
7·5-cm/3-inch piece cucumber, diced	3-inch piece cucumber, diced

Melt the butter and sauté the celery, onion and chilli. Stir in the flour, coriander, chilli powder, cardamom, cumin, turmeric and ginger. Cook for 1–2 minutes stirring all the time. Gradually add lemon zest, peanut butter, chicken stock and anchovy essence. Bring to the boil and simmer for 30 minutes. Heat the oil in a separate pan and use to brown the chicken pieces all over. Remove from the pan, drain and add to the curry sauce. Drain the pineapple chunks and add with the cucumber. Cook for a further 20 minutes. Cool.

To freeze: Pack in convenient quantities in foil containers. Seal and label.

To serve: Defrost and then reheat in a moderately hot oven (190°C, 375°F, Gas Mark 5) for 30 minutes. Sprinkle with salted peanuts and serve with boiled rice.

Serves: 4.

Storage time: 4–6 months.

Mild curry sauce

(*Illustrated on page 228*)

METRIC/IMPERIAL	AMERICAN
50 g/2 oz butter	¼ cup butter
1 large onion, chopped	1 large onion, chopped
2 tablespoons flour	3 tablespoons flour
2 tablespoons curry powder	3 tablespoons curry powder
900 ml/1½ pints chicken stock	3¾ cups chicken stock
1 teaspoon lemon juice	1 teaspoon lemon juice
1 teaspoon ground turmeric	1 teaspoon ground turmeric
2 tablespoons tomato purée	3 tablespoons tomato paste
salt to taste	salt to taste
4 tablespoons chopped parsley	⅓ cup chopped parsley

Melt the butter and use to sauté the onion for 3–4 minutes. Stir in the flour and curry powder and cook, stirring all the time, for 3 minutes. Gradually add the stock, lemon juice, turmeric and tomato purée and bring to the boil, stirring constantly. Simmer gently for 30 minutes and adjust the seasoning. Cool.
To freeze: Pack in convenient quantities. Seal and label.
To serve: Turn frozen sauce into a saucepan and reheat gently, stirring.
Makes: 1 litre/1¾ pints/4¼ cups.
Storage time: 4–6 months.

Hot curry sauce

(*Illustrated on page 228*)

METRIC/IMPERIAL	AMERICAN
2 apples	2 apples
50 g/2 oz butter	¼ cup butter
2 tablespoons oil	3 tablespoons oil
2 large onions, chopped	2 large onions, chopped
2 cloves garlic, crushed	2 cloves garlic, crushed
4 teaspoons turmeric	4 teaspoons turmeric
1 teaspoon ground coriander	1 teaspoon ground coriander
1 teaspoon ground cumin	1 teaspoon ground cumin
1 teaspoon chilli powder	1 teaspoon chili powder
¼ teaspoon dry mustard	¼ teaspoon dry mustard
4 tablespoons flour	⅓ cup flour
generous litre/2 pints beef stock	5 cups beef stock
2 tablespoons black treacle	3 tablespoons molasses
¼ teaspoon chilli sauce	¼ teaspoon chili sauce
salt to taste	salt to taste

Peel, core and dice the apples. Heat the butter with the oil and use to sauté the onions and garlic for 3–5 minutes. Stir in the spices and flour and cook, stirring all the time, for 3 minutes. Gradually add the stock, treacle and chilli sauce and bring to the boil, stirring. Simmer for 30 minutes, season and cool.
To freeze: Pack in convenient quantities. Seal and label.
To serve: Turn frozen sauce into a saucepan and reheat gently, stirring.
Makes: Scant 1·5 litres/2½ pints/6¼ cups.
Storage time: 4–6 months.

Oaty humus flan

(Illustrated on page 237)

METRIC/IMPERIAL	AMERICAN
350 g/12 oz chick peas	¾ lb chick peas
1 large onion, sliced	1 large onion, sliced
2 teaspoons salt	2 teaspoons salt
1 tablespoon tahini (crushed sesame seeds)	1 tablespoon tahini (crushed sesame seeds)
2 cloves garlic, crushed	2 cloves garlic, crushed
1 tablespoon lemon juice	1 tablespoon lemon juice
3 tablespoons vegetable oil	¼ cup vegetable oil
3 tomatoes, peeled and deseeded	3 tomatoes, peeled and deseeded
175 g/6 oz plain flour	1½ cups all-purpose flour
50 g/2 oz rolled oats	scant ½ cup rolled oats
pinch salt	pinch salt
1 teaspoon dried mixed herbs	1 teaspoon dried mixed herbs
100 g/4 oz pure vegetable margarine	½ cup pure vegetable margarine
3 tablespoons water	¼ cup water

First make the filling. Wash the chick peas under running water until the water runs clear. Place in a saucepan, cover with cold water and soak overnight. Drain off the soaking liquid, add the onion and salt to the saucepan and cover with vegetable stock or clean water. Bring to the boil and simmer for 1¼–1½ hours, until the peas are tender and the liquid almost evaporated, skimming as necessary. Place the chick peas, tahini, garlic, lemon juice and oil in a blender and liquidise until smooth. Alternatively, rub the chick peas through a wire sieve then beat in the tahini, garlic, lemon juice and oil. (The mixture should be just thick enough to hold its shape.) Chop the tomatoes and fold into the chick pea mixture. Chill while you make the flan case. Mix together the flour, oats, salt and herbs, then rub in the margarine. Bind with the cold water. Roll out and use to line a 25-cm/10-inch flan tin. Bake blind in a moderately hot oven (200°C, 400°F, Gas Mark 6) for 35 minutes. Allow to cool slightly then remove carefully from the tin and chill. Spread the filling in the pastry case.
To freeze: Open freeze then pack in a rigid-based container. Seal and label.
To serve: Unpack, defrost at room temperature for 3 hours and garnish with a ring of tomato slices topped with olives, and parsley placed in the centre.
Serves: 8.
Storage time: 4–6 months.

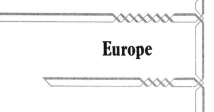

Europe

Granoata

(Illustrated on page 237)

METRIC/IMPERIAL	AMERICAN
450 g/1 lb rolled oats	4½ cups rolled oats
50 g/2 oz chopped nuts	½ cup chopped nuts
100 g/4 oz sesame seeds	¼ lb sesame seeds
50 g/2 oz sunflower seeds	2 oz sunflower seeds
100 g/4 oz wheat germ	¼ lb wheat germ
100 g/4 oz skimmed milk powder	1⅓ cups skim milk powder
150 ml/¼ pint peanut or groundnut oil	⅔ cup peanut oil
150 ml/¼ pint clear honey	⅔ cup clear honey
225 g/8 oz raisins	1⅓ cups raisins

Mix the first six ingredients together in a large bowl. Warm the oil and honey in a small saucepan. Pour over the dry ingredients and mix thoroughly. Spread the mixture on 3 large baking trays and bake in a moderately hot oven (190°C, 375°F, Gas Mark 5) for 10 minutes, stirring occasionally. Cool and add the raisins.

To freeze: Pack in convenient quantities. Seal and label.

To serve: Defrost at room temperature for 1–2 hours or overnight in the refrigerator. Serve as a breakfast cereal or a snack food. If desired, add roasted peanuts and/or chopped dried fruit such as figs, apricots or prunes.

Serves: 15.

Storage time: 4–6 months.

NOTE: This slightly richer version of the Swiss muesli stays crisp and dry if stored in this way in the freezer.

Quick paella

(Illustrated on page 68)

METRIC/IMPERIAL	AMERICAN
750 ml/1¼ pints strong chicken stock	3 cups strong chicken stock
good pinch saffron strands	good pinch saffron strands
2 bay leaves	2 bay leaves
150 ml/¼ pint dry white wine	⅔ cup dry white wine
4 frozen chicken portions, defrosted	4 frozen chicken portions, defrosted
4 tablespoons oil	⅓ cup oil
1 medium onion, chopped	1 medium onion, chopped
1 clove garlic, crushed	1 clove garlic, crushed
350 g/12 oz long-grain rice	1½ cups long-grain rice
12 large prawns or scampi	12 large prawns
generous 1 litre/1 quart fresh or frozen mussels	1 quart fresh or frozen mussels
2 lobster claws	2 lobster claws

Heat the stock, saffron strands, bay leaves and wine together and use to poach the chicken portions until tender. Drain well then strain and reserve the cooking liquid. Heat the oil and fry the chicken joints until golden. Remove the chicken and add the onion and garlic to the pan. Fry gently until softened then stir in the rice and fry over moderate heat until transparent. Add 450 ml/¾ pint/2 cups of the cooking stock and stir well. Cover the pan and simmer gently for about 20 minutes, until the rice is cooked, adding more stock if necessary. Cool. Cook the prawns, mussels and lobster claws (if not already cooked) in the remaining stock. Cool. Remove chicken flesh from the bones.

To freeze: Place the cooked rice in a boilable bag. Place the cooked shellfish and the chicken in a separate boilable bag with 6 tablespoons (US ½ cup) of the stock. Seal and label.

To serve: Place the two bags together in a large pan of boiling water and simmer for about 20 minutes. Open the bags, place a bed of rice on a hot serving dish and arrange the chicken and shellfish on top.

Serves: 4.

Storage time: 1–2 months.

Granoata (page 235); Oaty humus flan (page 235)

Carrot and corned beef hash (page 250)

Chicken Kiev

(Illustrated on page 66)

METRIC/IMPERIAL	AMERICAN
50 g/2 oz butter	¼ cup butter
few drops lemon juice	few drops lemon juice
1 tablespoon chopped parsley	1 tablespoon chopped parsley
1 large clove garlic, crushed	1 large clove garlic, crushed
4 chicken breasts	4 chicken breasts
2 eggs, beaten	2 eggs, beaten
fresh white breadcrumbs for coating	fresh white breadcrumbs for coating

Beat together the butter, lemon juice, parsley and garlic. Form into a short roll, wrap in foil and freeze until hard. Trim the chicken breasts, removing the skin. Place each one between 2 sheets of wetted greaseproof paper and beat out lightly with a rolling pin to flatten. Divide the frozen butter into four. Place a knob in the centre of each piece of chicken and fold up like a parcel. Coat each piece of chicken in beaten egg and breadcrumbs twice, making sure it is well covered.
To freeze: Cover individually in cling film and pack together. Seal and label.
To serve: Fry from the frozen state in deep moderately hot oil for about 20 minutes, or defrost and fry in deep hot oil for 10 minutes.
Serves: 4.
Storage time: 4–6 months.

French oven-steamed chicken

(Illustrated on page 65)

METRIC/IMPERIAL	AMERICAN
8 small onions	8 small onions
1 clove garlic, crushed	1 clove garlic, crushed
2 large carrots, sliced	2 large carrots, sliced
100 g/4 oz mushrooms	¼ lb mushrooms
25 g/1 oz butter	2 tablespoons butter
2 tablespoons oil	3 tablespoons oil
salt and pepper to taste	salt and pepper to taste
1 large lemon	1 large lemon
about 1·5 kg/3–3½ lb frozen roasting chicken, defrosted	3–3½ lb frozen roasting chicken, defrosted
1 tablespoon seasoned flour	1 tablespoon seasoned flour
2 bay leaves	2 bay leaves
sprig thyme	sprig thyme
1 tablespoon chopped parsley	1 tablespoon chopped parsley

Sauté the whole onions, crushed garlic, sliced carrots and mushrooms in the butter and oil for 1 minute. Transfer to a deep casserole and season to taste. Grate the zest coarsely from the lemon and squeeze the juice. Brush the chicken with lemon juice and sprinkle all over with seasoned flour. Put the bay leaves, sprig of thyme and lemon halves inside the chicken and place it on top of the vegetables. Press down well, so that the vegetables are forced partly up the sides of the chicken. Sprinkle the lemon zest and parsley over the chicken, cover and bake in a moderately hot oven (190°C, 375°F, Gas Mark 5) for 1¼ hours.
Serves: 6.

Cassata bombe

(Illustrated on page 225)

METRIC/IMPERIAL

2 (64-g/2¼-oz) packets chocolate ice cream mix
450 ml/¾ pint milk
1 (64-g/2¼-oz) packet vanilla ice cream mix
2 tablespoons dark rum
50 g/2 oz raisins
100 g/4 oz red and green glacé cherries, chopped
25 g/1 oz walnuts, chopped
when serving:
little whipped cream
1 glacé cherry

AMERICAN

4½ oz packaged chocolate ice cream mix
2 cups milk
2¼ oz packaged vanilla ice cream mix
3 tablespoons dark rum
⅓ cup raisins
½ cup chopped red and green candied cherries
¼ cup chopped walnuts
when serving:
little whipped cream
1 candied cherry

Make up the chocolate ice cream mixes with 300 ml/½ pint/1¼ cups of the milk and put into the freezer until firm. Meanwhile, make up the vanilla ice cream mix with the remaining milk and stir in the rum, raisins, cherries and walnuts. Remove the chocolate ice cream from the freezer and spread around the base and sides of a large mould or basin. Pour the vanilla mixture into the centre. Cover the mould and freeze until firm.
To freeze: Check seal and label.
To serve: Dip mould quickly in hot water and turn out on a serving plate. Decorate with piped whipped cream and top with a glacé cherry.
Serves: 6–8.
Storage time: 4–6 months.

Peach rice crème

(Illustrated on page 225)

METRIC/IMPERIAL

50 g/2 oz round-grain rice
50 g/2 oz sugar
600 ml/1 pint milk
300 ml/½ pint double cream, whipped
few drops vanilla essence
few drops almond essence
6 canned peach halves
225 g/8 oz seedless raspberry jam
when serving:
6 blanched almonds

AMERICAN

¼ cup round-grain rice
¼ cup sugar
2½ cups milk
1¼ cups heavy cream, whipped
few drops vanilla extract
few drops almond extract
6 canned peach halves
⅔ cup seedless raspberry jelly
when serving:
6 blanched almonds

In a double boiler mix together the rice, sugar and milk. Cook gently for 1–1½ hours, until the rice is soft. Allow to cool. When cold mix with the whipped cream and flavour with a little vanilla and almond essence. Pour the rice mixture into a glass serving dish and arrange the peach halves on top, making sure that the surface is below the top of the dish. Heat the raspberry jam gently until melted and use to coat the peaches.
To freeze: Cover dish with cling film. Seal and label.

To serve: Uncover and defrost for 4 hours at room temperature. Place a blanched almond on each peach half.
Serves: 6.
Storage time: 4–6 months.

Caramelled oranges

(*Illustrated on page 197*)

METRIC/IMPERIAL	AMERICAN
5 oranges	5 oranges
100 g/4 oz sugar	½ cup sugar
150 ml/¼ pint water	⅔ cup water
225 g/8 oz thick cut marmalade	⅔ cup thick cut marmalade
2 tablespoons cointreau or curaçao	3 tablespoons cointreau or curaçao

Pare the zest from 2 of the oranges in long strips. Peel all the oranges and slice, reserving any juice which runs out during preparation. Place in a suitable container ready for freezing. Dissolve the sugar in the water, add the juice and bring to the boil. Boil rapidly for 3 minutes, or until the syrup is reduced by about one-third. Stir in the marmalade and liqueur. Stir over gentle heat until combined to make a thick sauce. Add the strips of orange and continue cooking for a further 3 minutes. Allow to cool, then spoon over the orange slices. Reserve the strips of zest and use to cover the orange slices and help to keep them moist.
To freeze: Cover the container. Seal and label.
To serve: Defrost the sealed pack at room temperature for about 6 hours.
Serves: 4.
Storage time: 4–6 months.

Toasted nut tortoni

(*Illustrated on page 225*)

METRIC/IMPERIAL	AMERICAN
1 (64-g/2¼-oz) packet vanilla ice cream mix	2¼ oz packaged vanilla ice cream mix
150 ml/¼ pint milk	⅔ cup milk
4 tablespoons sherry, marsala or cognac	⅓ cup sherry, marsala or cognac
100 g/4 oz toasted hazel nuts, chopped	¾ cup chopped toasted hazel nuts
when serving:	*when serving:*
1 tablespoon chopped toasted hazel nuts	1 tablespoon chopped toasted hazel nuts

Make up the ice cream mixture with the milk as directed on the packet and stir in the sherry and nuts.
To freeze: Pack in a shallow container. Seal and label.
To serve: Allow to soften for 20 minutes in the refrigerator then scoop into individual serving dishes and top with a few chopped toasted nuts.
Serves: 4–5.
Storage time: 4–6 months.

Crab bisque with avocado

(Illustrated on page 105)

METRIC/IMPERIAL	AMERICAN
25 g/1 oz butter	2 tablespoons butter
25 g/1 oz flour	¼ cup flour
600 ml/1 pint fish or chicken stock	2½ cups fish or chicken stock
4 (42-g/1½-oz) cans dressed crab	6 oz canned dressed crab
3–4 tablespoons lemon juice	¼–⅓ cup lemon juice
salt and pepper to taste	salt and pepper to taste
when serving:	*when serving:*
1 avocado	1 avocado

Melt the butter, stir in the flour and cook gently for 1 minute. Blend in the stock and bring to the boil slowly, stirring all the time. When thickened, add the crabmeat and lemon juice to taste. Season well and simmer for 2 minutes. Cool.
To freeze: Pack in convenient quantities. Seal and label.
To serve: Defrost and then reheat in a saucepan. Serve garnished with thin slices of avocado.
Serves: 4.
Storage time: 2–3 months.

Frozen Alaska pie

METRIC/IMPERIAL	AMERICAN
600 ml/1 pint chocolate ice cream	20 fl oz chocolate ice cream
600 ml/1 pint strawberry ice cream	20 fl oz strawberry ice cream
1 (30-cm/12-inch) baked pastry case	1 (12-inch) baked pastry case
4 egg whites	4 egg whites
½ teaspoon vanilla essence	½ teaspoon vanilla extract
¼ teaspoon cream of tartar	¼ teaspoon cream of tartar
100 g/4 oz castor sugar	½ cup sugar

Allow the chocolate and strawberry ice cream to soften slightly. Spread the chocolate ice cream over the base of the pastry case. Top with a layer of strawberry ice cream. Place in the freezer. Beat the egg whites with the vanilla essence and cream of tartar until soft peaks form. Then gradually whisk in the castor sugar until the meringue forms stiff peaks. Spread the meringue over the prepared pastry case, carefully sealing to the edge of the pastry.
To freeze: Open freeze until firm then wrap lightly in cling film or foil.
To serve: Unwrap and place the frozen pie in a hot oven (230°C, 450°F, Gas Mark 8) for 5 minutes. Cut into wedges and serve with Hot chocolate sauce.
Serves: 12.
Storage time: 3 months.
NOTE: The surface of the meringue never hardens completely when frozen.

Hot chocolate sauce: Melt 100 g/4 oz plain chocolate in 150 ml/¼ pint/⅔ cup water over low heat. Stir in 50 g/2 oz/¼ cup butter and ½ teaspoon vanilla essence. May be frozen in a boilable bag or polythene container.
Storage time: 4–6 months.

Catering for Special Diets

Most of us have weight problems at some time or another, when we need to prepare dishes with dieting in mind. Cooking for slimming is an art in itself, but with the freezer's help it isn't too trying to make up dishes specially for a slimming diet, or pack portions of the usual family food before the dish is completed – for instance, before thickening the stew. There are other people too for whom dieting would be a problem if there was no freezer to help out; a person on a salt-free or fat-free diet, one who has a particular food allergy, or the diabetic, whose food has to be weighed accurately to the last ounce or gram. Why not weigh it and parcel it up so even the uninitiated person can take out the packs as required? As with all food which is not for ordinary family eating, careful labelling is essential. We cannot disguise that it takes a little time and trouble to do it, but it is important. What peace of mind you get in return, when you know that the doctor's orders can be followed to the letter without difficulty. No shopping mistakes either, when you find yourself suddenly with ordinary jam instead of diabetic, or discover you've forgotten the special packed meal for a dieting daughter who is happily counting on one for lunch.

Fishy foil parcels

METRIC/IMPERIAL
1 clove garlic, cut in half
4 cod steaks
1 small onion, sliced
2 tomatoes
4 teaspoons wine vinegar
pinch ground allspice
pinch ground nutmeg
salt and pepper to taste

AMERICAN
1 clove garlic, cut in half
4 cod steaks
1 small onion, sliced
2 tomatoes
4 teaspoons wine vinegar
pinch ground allspice
pinch ground nutmeg
salt and pepper to taste

Grease 4 sheets of foil, each large enough to enclose a cod steak, and rub them with the cut clove of garlic. Place a cod steak in the centre of each piece of foil and top with onion slices. Peel and slice the tomatoes. Divide the slices among the foil parcels and then spoon a teaspoon of wine vinegar over each. Sprinkle with the spices and salt and pepper.
To freeze: Wrap the foil neatly and seal to make airtight parcels. Label.
To serve: Place the parcels on a baking tray and cook from frozen in a moderately hot oven (200°C, 400°F, Gas Mark 6) for about 55 minutes.
Serves: 4.
Storage time: 3 months.
NOTE: Cooking in foil is ideal for chicken portions or tender cuts of meat.

Slimmers' stock-pot soup

METRIC/IMPERIAL	AMERICAN
100 g/4 oz white cabbage	¼ lb white cabbage
4 sticks celery	4 stalks celery
1 medium cauliflower	1 medium cauliflower
225 g/8 oz courgettes	½ lb zucchini
100 g/4 oz mushrooms	1 cup mushrooms
225 g/8 oz turnips or swede	½ lb turnips or swede
1 large onion	1 large onion
2 tablespoons tomato purée	3 tablespoons tomato paste
1 tablespoon clear honey	1 tablespoon clear honey
1 beef stock cube	1 beef bouillon cube
1 chicken stock cube	1 chicken bouillon cube
generous litre/2 pints boiling water	5 cups boiling water
garlic salt and pepper to taste	garlic salt and pepper to taste

Roughly chop all the vegetables and place in a saucepan with the tomato purée and honey. Dissolve the stock cubes in the water, pour over the vegetables, stir well and bring to the boil. Cover the pan and simmer gently until all the vegetables are tender. Cool slightly, add garlic salt and pepper to taste and liquidise until smooth. Cool.
To freeze: Pack in convenient quantities. Seal and label.
To serve: Turn frozen soup into a saucepan and add 1–2 tablespoons of water. Bring slowly to boiling point, stirring frequently.
Serves: 8–10.
Storage time: 4–6 months.
NOTE: If preferred, the vegetables may be chopped neatly before cooking and the soup frozen without being liquidised.

Smooth kidney soup

METRIC/IMPERIAL	AMERICAN
450 g/1 lb ox kidney	1 lb beef kidney
3 beef stock cubes	3 beef bouillon cubes
1·75 litres/3 pints boiling water	7½ cups boiling water
bouquet garni	bouquet garni
50 g/2 oz butter	¼ cup butter
1 large onion, chopped	1 large onion, chopped
25 g/1 oz flour	¼ cup flour
1 tablespoon tomato purée	1 tablespoon tomato paste
1 teaspoon Worcestershire sauce	1 teaspoon Worcestershire sauce
4 tablespoons dry sherry	⅓ cup dry sherry
salt and pepper to taste	salt and pepper to taste

Remove the skin from the kidney, cut in half and remove the core. Cover with cold water and allow to stand for 30 minutes. Drain, cut into small pieces and place in a saucepan. Dissolve the stock cubes in the water and pour half over the kidney. Bring to the boil, add the bouquet garni and cover the pan. Simmer gently for about 1 hour, until the kidney is soft. Discard the bouquet garni. Meanwhile, melt the butter in a large saucepan and use to fry the onion until well browned. Stir in the flour, tomato purée and Worcestershire sauce and gradually add the remaining stock. Bring to the boil, add the kidney and cooking liquid, the sherry and seasoning to taste. Cook for 10 minutes. Cool slightly then liquidise or sieve. Cool.

To freeze: Pack in convenient quantities. Seal and label.

To serve: Turn frozen soup into a saucepan and reheat gently to boiling point, stirring frequently. Adjust seasoning if necessary.

Serves: 8.

Storage time: 4–6 months.

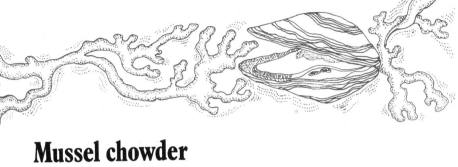

Mussel chowder

METRIC/IMPERIAL	AMERICAN
2 tablespoons oil	3 tablespoons oil
1 large onion, chopped	1 large onion, chopped
1 clove garlic, crushed	1 clove garlic, crushed
1 (396-g/14-oz) can tomatoes	14 oz canned tomatoes
600 ml/1 pint fish or chicken stock	2½ cups fish or chicken stock
½ lemon	½ lemon
about 2 litres/2 quarts fresh mussels	2 quarts fresh mussels
300 ml/½ pint dry white wine	1¼ cups dry white wine
2 sticks celery, chopped	2 stalks celery, chopped
bouquet garni	bouquet garni
50 g/2 oz fine soft white breadcrumbs	½ cup fine soft white breadcrumbs
salt and pepper to taste	salt and pepper to taste
when serving:	*when serving:*
little chopped parsley	little chopped parsley

Heat the oil in a saucepan and use to cook the onion and garlic until limp but not brown. Place the tomatoes and their liquid in a basin and chop roughly with a knife. Add to the pan with half the stock and the juice from the lemon half and bring to the boil. Simmer for about 20 minutes, until reduced by about one-third. Meanwhile, scrub the mussels and place them in a saucepan with the wine, the remaining stock, celery, squeezed lemon half and the bouquet garni. Bring to the boil and cook until the mussels open. Discard any that remain closed. Strain the cooking liquid carefully and add to the tomato mixture with the breadcrumbs. Cook for a further 5 minutes. Shell the mussels. Remove the pan from the heat, stir in the mussels and add salt and pepper to taste. Cool.

To freeze: Pack in convenient quantities. Seal and label.

To serve: Defrost overnight in the refrigerator and then turn into a saucepan and bring to boiling point. Simmer for 3 minutes, adjust seasoning and serve sprinkled with parsley.

Serves: 8.

Storage time: 1–2 months.

NOTE: This recipe could be adapted to make use of frozen mussels. In that case use the wine to make the sauce, then defrost and reheat the mussels in the sauce.

Chicken with baby onions

METRIC/IMPERIAL	AMERICAN
2 teaspoons ground cumin	2 teaspoons ground cumin
1 teaspoon ground allspice	1 teaspoon ground allspice
4 teaspoons plain flour	4 teaspoons all-purpose flour
salt and pepper to taste	salt and pepper to taste
8 small chicken portions	8 small chicken portions
75 g/3 oz butter	6 tablespoons butter
700 g/1½ lb small onions	1½ lb small onions
1 chicken stock cube	1 chicken bouillon cube
1 tablespoon tomato purée	1 tablespoon tomato paste
600 ml/1 pint water	2½ cups water
few drops Tabasco sauce	few drops Tabasco sauce

Mix together the spices, flour and salt and pepper to taste and rub this mixture into the skin of the chicken portions. Melt the butter in a large pan and brown the onions. Remove from the pan. Add the chicken portions, skin side down, and fry gently for about 15 minutes, until golden brown. Turn the chicken, add the stock cube and tomato purée dissolved in the boiling water, and the Tabasco. Return the onions to the pan and bring to the boil. Cover and simmer gently for about 30 minutes, until the chicken is tender. Cool.
To freeze: Pack in convenient quantities. Seal and label.
To serve: Defrost overnight in the refrigerator then turn into a saucepan and reheat gently to boiling point.
Serves: 8.
Storage time: 4–6 months.

Lemony lamb

METRIC/IMPERIAL	AMERICAN
700 g/1½ lb minced lamb	1½ lb ground lamb
finely grated zest of 1 lemon	finely grated rind of 1 lemon
1 tablespoon lemon juice	1 tablespoon lemon juice
1 teaspoon salt	1 teaspoon salt
¼ teaspoon pepper	¼ teaspoon pepper
pinch ground bay leaves	pinch ground bay leaves
pinch dried rosemary	pinch dried rosemary
1 heaped tablespoon chopped parsley	2 tablespoons chopped parsley
when serving:	*when serving:*
2 tablespoons dry white wine for each serving	3 tablespoons dry white wine for each serving

Mix together the lamb, lemon zest and juice, the salt, pepper and herbs. With lightly floured hands, form the mixture into about 40 small balls.
To freeze: Open freeze until solid then pack in layers with dividers. Seal and label.
To serve: Heat the wine in a shallow pan, add the frozen meatballs and cook gently for about 20 minutes, turning frequently.
Serves: 8.
Storage time: 4–6 months.

Rabbit with mustard topping

METRIC/IMPERIAL

2 small rabbits, jointed
1 (225-g/8-oz) piece streaky bacon
4 large onions, quartered
1 tablespoon flour
1½ chicken stock cubes
600 ml/1 pint water
bouquet garni
salt and black pepper to taste
when serving:
1 teaspoon French mustard, 1 tablespoon
    natural yogurt and a little chopped
    parsley for each serving

AMERICAN

2 small rabbits, jointed
1 (½-lb) piece bacon
4 large onions, quartered
1 tablespoon flour
1½ chicken bouillon cubes
2½ cups water
bouquet garni
salt and black pepper to taste
when serving:
1 teaspoon French mustard, 1 tablespoon
    unflavored yogurt and a little chopped
    parsley for each serving

Have the rabbit cut into serving pieces and trim away the rib cages. Remove the rind from the bacon and dice neatly. Heat the bacon dice in a saucepan until the fat begins to run then add some of the rabbit joints and fry lightly. Remove from the pan and repeat until all the joints have been fried. Add the quartered onions to the fat and bacon remaining in the pan and fry until golden brown. Stir in the flour and gradually add the stock cubes dissolved in the boiling water. Bring to the boil, stirring constantly, then add the bouquet garni and seasoning to taste. Return the rabbit joints to the pan, cover and simmer very gently until the rabbit is really tender. Cool.

To freeze: Freeze in convenient quantities in foil containers. Seal and label.

To serve: Defrost overnight in the refrigerator and then reheat in a moderately hot oven (190°C, 375°F, Gas Mark 5) for 30–40 minutes, depending on the size of the pack. Taste and adjust the seasoning. Mix together the mustard and yogurt and spoon over the rabbit. Return to the oven for a further 5 minutes and serve sprinkled with parsley.

Serves: 8.

Storage time: 4–6 months.

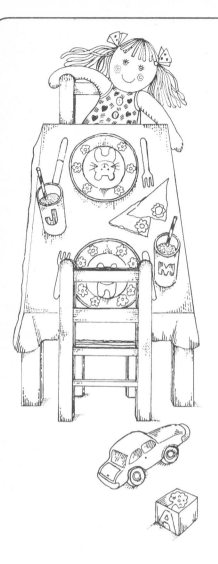

Catering for Children

Simple meals which children enjoy, and which do not strain your housekeeping budget, are a must for the average freezer family. Those who do not enjoy the school meal at lunch-time, especially look forward to a hearty meal at home. The recipes in this section are planned to make an attractive alternative to the favourites you can buy in bulk from the freezer centres, such as fish fingers, peas and ice cream. Many mothers find the school holidays are a great trial to fit into the general catering pattern because their housekeeping plans are not geared to providing children with so many meals. Some of the food suggested here could be packed up and taken out on expeditions – always an advantage. Much of it could be removed from the freezer and prepared ready for eating by older and more responsible members of the family without mother's supervision at all. If directions are clearly given on these packs and if, better still, they are colour identified by a small stick-on label showing that they are not 'out of bounds', this would give young would-be cooks a good start.

Cheesy toad-in-the-hole

METRIC/IMPERIAL	AMERICAN
225 g/8 oz flour	2 cups flour
1 teaspoon salt	1 teaspoon salt
2 eggs	2 eggs
1 teaspoon made mustard	1 teaspoon made mustard
300 ml/½ pint milk	1¼ cups milk
16 chipolata sausages	16 link sausages
50 g/2 oz cheese, grated	½ cup grated cheese
when serving:	*when serving:*
15 g/½ oz grated cheese for each 'toad'	2 tablespoons grated cheese for each 'toad'

Sift the flour and salt into a bowl and make a well in the centre. Drop in the eggs and mustard and gradually mix to a smooth batter with a wooden spoon. Gradually add the milk and beat well. Set aside. Grill or fry the sausages until lightly brown. Meanwhile, grease 8 deep shaped foil containers. Whisk the batter again and stir in the cheese. Divide the batter among the containers to half-fill them. Place two cooked sausages in the centre of each. Cool.
To freeze: Cover containers with lids or foil. Seal and label.
To serve: Uncover and sprinkle with grated cheese. Place still frozen in a hot oven (220°C, 425°F, Gas Mark 7) for 40–50 minutes, until well risen and golden brown. A skewer inserted in the batter will come out clean when it is cooked.
Makes: 8 servings for children.
Storage time: 2–3 months.

Beefburger bonanza

METRIC/IMPERIAL
16 slices white bread
100 g/4 oz butter
225 g/8 oz crumbly cheese (Lancashire or white Cheshire)
1 tablespoon tomato ketchup
8 beefburgers or steaklets

AMERICAN
16 slices white bread
½ cup butter
½ lb crumbly cheese (Lancashire or white Cheshire)
1 tablespoon tomato ketchup
8 beefburgers or steaklets

Trim the bread slices to fit the beefburgers and butter one side of each piece. Grate or crumble the cheese and combine with the tomato ketchup and any remaining butter. Arrange 8 slices of bread buttered side downwards on a baking tray. Put a beefburger on each, spread lightly with the cheese mixture and cover with another slice of bread buttered side uppermost. Bake in a moderately hot oven (200°C, 400°F, Gas Mark 6) for 20 minutes, or until golden brown. Cool.
To freeze: Wrap individually in cling film then pack all together in a large container. Seal and label.
To serve: Unwrap, place on a baking tray and reheat from the frozen state in a hot oven (220°C, 425°F. Gas Mark 7) for about 20 minutes until heated through and crisp.
Makes: 8 servings for children.
Storage time: 2–3 months.

Chicken fritters

METRIC/IMPERIAL
100 g/4 oz butter
750 ml/1¼ pints chicken stock
2 teaspoons salt
¾ teaspoon white pepper
225 g/8 oz flour
6 eggs
700 g/1½ lb cooked chicken, turkey or ham, finely chopped
fat for frying

AMERICAN
½ cup butter
3 cups chicken stock
2 teaspoons salt
¾ teaspoon white pepper
2 cups flour
6 eggs
1½ lb cooked chicken, turkey or ham, finely chopped
fat for frying

Place the butter, stock, salt and pepper in a saucepan and bring to the boil. Add the flour all at once and stir steadily until the mixture leaves the sides of the pan. Cool to blood heat then beat in one egg at a time. Continue beating until the mixture is smooth and shiny after each addition. Stir in the chicken and adjust the seasoning. Using floured hands, shape the mixture into about 30 balls. Heat the fat or oil and use to fry the balls, a few at a time, for 5 minutes. Drain and cool.
To freeze: Pack in convenient quantities. Seal and label.
To serve: Place the required number of fritters on a baking tray and reheat from the frozen state in a moderate oven (180°C, 350°F, Gas Mark 4) for 25 minutes, until browned and heated through. Serve with a fresh tomato salad or a cooked frozen green vegetable.
Makes: About 30 fritters.
Storage time: 4–6 months.

Carrot and corned beef hash

(Illustrated on page 238)

METRIC/IMPERIAL	AMERICAN
50 g/2 oz dripping or lard	¼ cup drippings or shortening
2 medium onions, chopped	2 medium onions, chopped
225 g/8 oz cooked carrots	½ lb cooked carrots
225 g/8 oz cooked potato	½ lb cooked potato
1 (340-g/12-oz) can corned beef	12 oz canned corned beef
salt and pepper to taste	salt and pepper to taste

Melt the dripping and use to fry the onion until soft but not brown. Slice the carrots and dice the potatoes. Add these to the pan and cook gently for a few minutes. Cut the corned beef into neat dice and add to the pan with salt and pepper to taste. Mix well, then press down and cook until browned on the underside. Turn the hash over with the help of a plate and brown the other side. Remove from the heat. Slide the hash out of the pan on to a sheet of foil and allow to cool.

To freeze: Wrap closely in the foil. Seal and label.

To serve: Place the sealed pack on a baking tray and reheat from the frozen state in a moderately hot oven (190°C, 375°F, Gas Mark 5) for about 30 minutes. Open the foil and return the hash to the oven for a further 5–10 minutes to crisp the top. Garnish with chopped parsley and serve with Tasty tomato sauce.

Serves: 4.

Storage time: 4–6 months.

Tasty tomato sauce

METRIC/IMPERIAL	AMERICAN
1 tablespoon oil	1 tablespoon oil
1 teaspoon cornflour	1 teaspoon cornstarch
250 ml/8 fl oz tomato juice	1 cup tomato juice
4 tablespoons tomato ketchup	⅓ cup tomato ketchup
1 tablespoon vinegar	1 tablespoon vinegar
¼ teaspoon dry mustard	¼ teaspoon dry mustard
pinch sugar	pinch sugar
salt and pepper to taste	salt and pepper to taste

Heat the oil in a small saucepan and stir in the cornflour until well blended. Gradually add the tomato juice and when smooth add the ketchup, vinegar and mustard. Bring to the boil, stirring constantly, and season to taste with sugar, salt and pepper. Cool.

To freeze: Pack in a polythene container. Seal and label.

To serve: Place the pack under running water and turn the frozen sauce into an ovenproof sauceboat or dish. Place in the oven with Carrot and corned beef hash to reheat.

Serves: 4.

Storage time: 4–6 months.

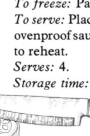

Crumpet pizzas

METRIC/IMPERIAL	AMERICAN
8 crumpets	8 English muffins
25 g/1 oz butter	2 tablespoons butter
2 teaspoons French mustard	2 teaspoons French mustard
2 large tomatoes, sliced	2 large tomatoes, sliced
175 g/6 oz cheese, grated	1½ cups grated cheese
50 g/2 oz streaky bacon	3 bacon slices
50 g/2 oz salted peanuts	⅓ cup salted peanuts

Toast the underside of the crumpets until brown then lightly toast the other side. Spread the lightly toasted side first with butter and then with mustard. Cover the crumpets with tomato slices and sprinkle with grated cheese. Derind the bacon and cut into strips. Decorate the crumpets with crosswise strips of bacon and place salted peanuts in between.
To freeze: Pack with foil dividers in rigid-based containers. Seal and label.
To serve: Unpack and defrost at room temperature for 15 minutes, then grill until heated through and the cheese is bubbly.
Makes: 8 pizzas.
Storage time: 4–6 months.

Sausage and apple pielets

METRIC/IMPERIAL	AMERICAN
450 g/1 lb shortcrust pastry	1 lb basic pie dough
1 medium cooking apple	1 medium baking apple
1 small onion	1 small onion
450 g/1 lb pork sausage meat	1 lb pork sausage meat
1 egg, beaten	1 egg, beaten

Roll out the pastry and use to line 8 deep bun tins. Re-roll the pastry trimmings and cut out 8 7·5-cm/3-inch circles for the lids. Grate the apple and onion and mix with the sausage meat. Divide the filling between the pastry cases, mounding it up well in the centres. Brush the edges of the pastry with a little beaten egg, place on the lids and crimp the edges well together to seal. Add a little water to the remaining egg and brush over the tops of the pielets. Bake in a moderately hot oven (200°C, 400°F, Gas Mark 6) for 30 minutes. Cool.
To freeze: Wrap individually then pack together in a rigid-based container. Seal and label.
To serve: Defrost at room temperature for about 4 hours.
Makes: 8 pielets.
Storage time: 2–3 months.

Sweet and sour relish: Fry 4 rashers streaky bacon until crisp and the fat is rendered out. Remove the bacon, stir 2 tablespoons (US 3 tablespoons) flour into the fat, add 1·50 ml/¼ pint/⅔ cup water, 150 ml/¼ pint/⅔ cup white vinegar, 2 tablespoons (US 3 tablespoons) brown sugar, 1 teaspoon salt and stir over moderate heat until thick and smooth. Core and slice 2 large green-skinned dessert apples and add to the pan with the crumbled bacon. Bring to the boil and simmer for 2 minutes.

Cherry sponge dessert

METRIC/IMPERIAL	AMERICAN
100 g/4 oz butter	½ cup butter
100 g/4 oz castor sugar	½ cup sugar
2 eggs	2 eggs
100 g/4 oz self-raising flour	1 cup all-purpose flour sifted with 1 teaspoon baking powder
when serving:	*when serving:*
1 (396-g/14-oz) can cherry pie filling	14 oz canned cherry pie filling
25 g/1 oz desiccated coconut	⅓ cup shredded coconut

Cream together the butter and sugar until light and fluffy. Gradually beat in the eggs then fold in the flour. Divide the mixture between 2 greased and base-lined 18-cm/7-inch sandwich cake tins and smooth the tops. Bake in a moderately hot oven (190°C, 375F, Gas Mark 5) for 25–30 minutes. Cool on a wire rack.
To freeze: Pack with a divider between the layers. Seal and label.
To serve: Unwrap and place on serving dishes. Allow to defrost at room temperature for 30 minutes. Spread with pie filling and sprinkle with coconut.
Makes: 2 desserts/12–16 servings.
Storage time: 4–6 months.

Marble mocha cake

(*Illustrated on page 37*)

METRIC/IMPERIAL	AMERICAN
65 g/2½ oz butter	5 tablespoons butter
225 g/8 oz castor sugar	1 cup sugar
1 teaspoon vanilla essence	1 teaspoon vanilla extract
225 g/8 oz plain flour	2 cups all-purpose flour
2 teaspoons baking powder	2 teaspoons baking powder
¼ teaspoon salt	¼ teaspoon salt
150 ml/¼ pint milk	⅔ cup milk
2 tablespoons hot, strong coffee	3 tablespoons hot, strong coffee
3 egg whites	3 egg whites
25 g/1 oz plain chocolate	1 square semi-sweet chocolate
2 tablespoons hot water	3 tablespoons hot water
¼ teaspoon bicarbonate of soda	¼ teaspoon baking soda

Cream the butter and sugar until light and fluffy. Add the vanilla essence. Sift the flour, baking powder and salt together and add to the creamed mixture alternately with the milk and coffee. Beat well after each addition. Whisk the egg whites until stiff and fold into the mixture. Melt the chocolate in a basin over a pan of hot water and mix in the hot water and bicarbonate of soda. Divide the cake mixture in half and use the chocolate mixture to flavour and colour one portion. Place alternate spoonfuls of the mixtures in a greased and floured fluted mould or ring mould. Bake in a moderate oven (180°C, 350°F, Gas Mark 4) for 40–45 minutes. Cool on a wire rack.
To freeze: Wrap closely. Seal and label.
To serve: Defrost still wrapped at room temperature for 3 hours.
Makes: 1 cake/8–10 servings.
Storage time: 4–6 months.

Banana chocolate mousse

METRIC/IMPERIAL	AMERICAN
1 (35-g/1¼-oz) packet chocolate blancmange powder	1 (1¼-oz) package chocolate blancmange powder
600 ml/1 pint milk	2½ cups milk
25 g/1 oz sugar	2 tablespoons sugar
2 eggs, separated	2 eggs, separated
2 bananas, sliced	2 bananas, sliced

Mix the blancmange powder with 2 tablespoons (US 3 tablespoons) of cold milk and place the remaining milk in a saucepan with the sugar. Stir until the sugar has dissolved and bring almost to boiling point. Pour the hot milk over the chocolate mixture and return to the pan, stirring constantly. Bring to the boil and cook for 2 minutes, stirring all the time. Remove from the heat and beat in the egg yolks. Allow to cool. Whip the egg whites stiffly and fold into the chocolate mixture with the sliced banana.

To freeze: Divide the mixture between 8 individual containers. Seal and label.
To serve: Allow to defrost at room temperature for 2 hours.
Makes: 8 servings for children.
Storage time: 4–6 months.

Quick lemon cheesecake

METRIC/IMPERIAL	AMERICAN
25 g/1 oz butter	2 tablespoons butter
100 g/4 oz digestive biscuits, crushed	¼ lb graham crackers, crushed
1 (135-g/4¾-oz) packet lemon jelly	1 (4¾-oz) package lemon jello
225 g/8 oz cream cheese	½ lb cream cheese
450 ml/¾ pint canned custard	2 cups canned custard

Melt the butter and mix with the biscuit crumbs. Press into the bottom of a 20-cm/8-inch loose-bottomed cake tin. Bake in the centre of a moderate oven (180°C, 350°F, Gas Mark 4) for 10 minutes. Dissolve the jelly in 150 ml/¼ pint/⅔ cup hot water and leave until beginning to set. Beat the cream cheese, adding the custard gradually until the mixture is smooth. Finally beat in the setting jelly. Pour carefully over the crumb base and leave to set.

To freeze: Open freeze until solid. Dip in hot water, remove from the tin and slide on to a plate. Cover closely. Seal and label.
To serve: Unwrap while frozen and defrost at room temperature for 3 hours.
Storage time: 4–6 months.

Coffee float

(Illustrated on page 35)
Half-fill a glass with milk, add 2 frozen coffee cubes and a generous tablespoon of vanilla ice cream. Stir lightly, allow the cubes to melt and serve with a straw. If liked, sprinkle with a little cinnamon.
NOTE: Coffee made from ground beans, or from instant coffee, can be frozen in an ice cube tray for storage in the freezer. If no cubes are available, dissolve ½ teaspoon instant coffee in 1 tablespoon boiling water and stir into the milk.

Freezing of the Future

As we progress further towards the ultimate ideal of totally trouble-free cooking, new reinforcements appear on the scene. If today you find your freezer essential, tomorrow you will probably feel the same about a microwave oven. It may start off seeming a luxury but once you have learned to use it properly it becomes an essential and economic proposition. Defrosting time is cut from hours to minutes, and cooking times sometimes to seconds. For instance, you can defrost the Sunday joint by the pulse-power method and cook it in 45 minutes from freezer to serving dish. With rising fuel costs, this is a great saving; there is no preheating, and not only is the cooking time reduced – during part of it the oven is not even switched on. The average leg of lamb needs 7 minutes on, 5 off, another 7 on, and 5 off then it's ready to cook. The same technique applies to the cooking – 7 on, 5 off, 7 on, and 5 off. For a larger leg, maybe another 5 minutes cooking time. A meat thermometer shows you just how long if you are doubtful (as it is metal insert it after the meat comes out of the oven). Other methods suggested include roasting continuously for 30 minutes then allowing the joint to stand (covered with foil to retain the heat) during an equivalent equalisation period. This leaves the oven free for cooking the vegetables. You are only using a very small amount of electricity for about 30 minutes to roast the meat. That compares very well with overnight defrosting, or 4 hours roasting time from frozen, in the conventional oven. Fresh and frozen vegetables and fruit can be cooked in loosely sealed roasting or boiling bags. Bread thaws in a flash, small cuts of meat defrost and cook while you lay the table. Every microwave oven is accompanied by a booklet which suggests suitable methods and recipes; just a few foods are not recommended for microwave cooking, and you may find it a problem that the outside of some foods does not brown. Here hints are given for sauces to spoon over the meat to conquer that problem.

Incidentally, meat is expensive. Future freezer owners will be more and more grateful for the saving in using soya meat extenders or soya products which look and taste like meat. For those who truly have an eye to the future, recipes are included using sprouting seeds, such as triticale and mixed salad sprouts, which require no soil to cultivate and increase seven-fold, ready for use on your kitchen shelf, in 3–8 days. The only equipment – empty glass jars and muslin. The only growing medium – water. What could be easier?

Should you still dislike the wearisome washing up, hitherto an inescapable part of food preparation, get in the habit of using freezing bags and wraps in which you can boil, bake or roast. There is never more than the first preparation stage to cause a mess in your kitchen. After that the sink stays clear until the plates are removed from the table. Combine the use of these bags and wraps with the microwave oven and you are really moving into the space-age of cookery.

Integrated microwave meal – before and after
(page 261)

Loaf in a crust (page 266); Lazy lasagne (page 259); Winter cobbler (page 258)

Meatsauce mix

METRIC/IMPERIAL	AMERICAN
500 ml/18 fl oz water	2 cups water
3 (60-g/2⅛-oz) packets soya meat extender	6 oz packaged soy meat extender
1·5 kg/3 lb minced beef	3 lb ground beef
4 large onions, chopped	4 large onions, chopped
4 sticks celery, chopped	4 stalks celery, chopped
3 cloves garlic, crushed	3 cloves garlic, crushed
3 tablespoons oil	¼ cup oil
3 teaspoons salt	3 teaspoons salt
½ teaspoon pepper	½ teaspoon pepper
2 tablespoons Worcestershire sauce	3 tablespoons Worcestershire sauce
450 ml/¾ pint tomato ketchup	2 cups tomato ketchup
150 ml/¼ pint dry red wine	⅔ cup dry red wine
150 ml/¼ pint beef stock	⅔ cup beef stock

Add the water to the soya meat extender as directed on the packet and combine with the minced beef. Sauté the onions, celery and garlic in the oil until limp but not brown. Stir in the minced beef mixture, salt, pepper and Worcestershire sauce. Cook until the meat is nicely browned, stirring occasionally. Add the ketchup, wine and stock and mix well. Cover the pan and simmer for 1 hour. Cool, then skim off excess fat.

To freeze: Pack in convenient quantities. Seal and label.

Makes: 2·25 litres/4 pints/5 pints meatsauce.

Storage time: 3 months.

Use the meatsauce mix for any of the following quick main dishes:

Barbecued meatsauce: Add 50 g/2 oz/¼ cup brown sugar and 3 tablespoons (US ¼ cup) white vinegar to 300 ml/½ pint/1¼ cups meatsauce mix. Bring to the boil, then simmer for 30 minutes. Serve over split and toasted hamburger rolls.

Chilli: Heat equal quantities of meatsauce mix and canned red kidney beans. Add chilli powder to taste.

Spaghetti with meatsauce: Simmer 300 ml/½ pint/1¼ cups meatsauce mix with ½ teaspoon dried basil and 1 teaspoon dried oregano. Spoon over hot cooked spaghetti and sprinkle generously with grated Parmesan cheese.

Stuffed green peppers: Allow the meatsauce mix to thaw in the refrigerator. Mix with an equal quantity of cooked long-grain rice. Spoon into hollowed out green sweet peppers. Place the stuffed peppers in a shallow baking dish and bake in a moderate oven (180°C, 350°F, Gas Mark 4) for 45–50 minutes.

Mock pizza: Allow the meatsauce mix to thaw in the refrigerator. Prepare a basic scone dough and roll out to 3-mm/⅛-inch thickness. Spread a thin layer of meatsauce over the dough. Top with Mozarrella cheese slices. Sprinkle with dried oregano. Bake in a hot oven (220°C, 425°F, Gas Mark 7) for 15 minutes.

Mock Stroganoff: Heat 300 ml/½ pint/1¼ cups meatsauce mix in a large frying pan until completely thawed. Stir in 50 g/2 oz canned sliced mushrooms and 150 ml/¼ pint/⅔ cup condensed cream of mushroom soup. Simmer for 10 minutes. Stir in 150 ml/¼ pint/⅔ cup soured cream and heat through. Serve over hot buttered noodles.

Stuffed French loaf: Hollow out a long French loaf, leaving a 1-cm/½-inch crust. Fill the cavity with equal quantities of meatsauce mix and grated Cheddar cheese. Wrap the loaf in foil and bake in a moderately hot oven (200°C, 400°F, Gas Mark 6) for 30–40 minutes. To serve, slice diagonally.

Barbecue supper savoury

METRIC/IMPERIAL	AMERICAN
2 large onions	2 large onions
2 aubergines	2 eggplants
2 green sweet peppers	2 green sweet peppers
175 ml/6 fl oz water	¾ cup water
1 (60-g/2⅛-oz) packet soya meat extender	2 oz packaged soy meat extender
450 g/1 lb minced beef	1 lb ground beef
4 tablespoons oil	⅓ cup oil
1 (396-g/14-oz) can tomatoes	14 oz canned tomatoes
225 g/8 oz wagon-wheel pasta, cooked	½ lb wagon-wheel pasta, cooked
when serving:	*when serving:*
1 egg for each person	1 egg for each person

Slice the onion, dice the aubergines and deseed and dice the green peppers. Add the water to the soya meat extender as instructed on the packet and combine this mixture with the minced beef. Fry the onion in the oil in a large frying pan for 3–4 minutes. Add the meat mixture and cook gently for 10 minutes, stirring frequently. Add the diced aubergine, green pepper and tomatoes, cover and simmer for 15 minutes. Stir the pasta into the meat mixture. Cool.
To freeze: Pack in convenient quantities. Seal and label.
To serve: Defrost in the refrigerator overnight and turn into a frying pan. Reheat gently, stirring frequently, and when hot make hollows in the mixture with the back of a spoon. Break an egg into each hollow, cover the pan and cook until the eggs have set. Serve with crusty French bread.
Serves: 12.
Storage time: 3–4 months.

Winter cobbler

(Illustrated on page 256)

METRIC/IMPERIAL	AMERICAN
25 g/1 oz dripping or lard	2 tablespoons drippings or shortening
100 g/4 oz carrots, sliced	¼ lb carrots, sliced
100 g/4 oz celery, sliced	¼ lb celery, sliced
100 g/4 oz onions, chopped	¼ lb onions, chopped
100 g/4 oz turnip or swede, diced	¼ lb turnip or swede, diced
salt and pepper to taste	salt and pepper to taste
150 ml/¼ pint beef stock	⅔ cup beef stock
pinch dried mixed herbs	pinch dried mixed herbs
1 bay leaf	1 bay leaf
1 (425-g/15-oz) can soya casserole chunks	1 (15-oz) can soy casserole chunks
cobbler topping:	*cobbler topping:*
175 g/6 oz self-raising flour	1½ cups all-purpose flour sifted with 1½ teaspoons baking powder
50 g/2 oz margarine	¼ cup margarine
1 egg	1 egg
about 2 tablespoons milk	about 3 tablespoons milk

Melt the fat and fry the prepared vegetables until softened. Season to taste and stir in the stock, herbs and bay leaf. Mix well then add the soya casserole chunks and cook in a moderate oven (180°C, 350°F, Gas Mark 4) for about 40 minutes. Meanwhile, place the flour in a bowl and rub in the margarine. Add the egg and sufficient milk to make a soft dough. Pat out on a floured surface and cut into 8 5-cm/2-inch rounds with a pastry cutter. Place the rounds overlapping on a baking tray and brush with milk. Remove the casserole from the oven and cool. Raise the oven heat to hot (220°C, 425°F, Gas Mark 7) and bake the cobbler topping for about 10 minutes, until golden. Cool.

To freeze: Pack the casserole mixture and topping separately. Seal and label.

To serve: Defrost the casserole at room temperature for 6 hours. Place in a moderately hot oven (190°C, 375°F, Gas Mark 5) and reheat for about 45 minutes. Stir well and return to the oven if necessary for a further 5 minutes, until piping hot. Place the frozen cobbler on top of the stew, raise the oven heat to hot, as above, and continue to cook for a further 10 minutes, until the cobbler topping is browned.

Serves: 4.

Storage time: 3–4 months.

Lazy lasagne

(*Illustrated on page 256*)

METRIC/IMPERIAL	AMERICAN
225 g/8 oz lasagne noodles	½ lb lasagne noodles
2 tablespoons oil	3 tablespoons oil
1 large onion, chopped	1 large onion, chopped
1 clove garlic, crushed	1 clove garlic, crushed
100 g/4 oz mushrooms, sliced	1 cup sliced mushrooms
1 (425-g/15-oz) can soya mince	1 (15-oz) can soy mince
1 (396-g/14-oz) can tomatoes	14 oz canned tomatoes
1 tablespoon tomato purée	1 tablespoon tomato paste
½ teaspoon dried mixed herbs	½ teaspoon dried mixed herbs
sauce:	*sauce:*
40 g/1½ oz margarine	3 tablespoons margarine
40 g/1½ oz plain flour	6 tablespoons all-purpose flour
450 ml/¾ pint milk	2 cups milk
salt and pepper to taste	salt and pepper to taste
75 g/3 oz Cheddar cheese, grated	¾ cup grated Cheddar cheese

Cook the lasagne in boiling salted water for about 12 minutes, until just tender. Drain and rinse in cold water. Spread out on a towel. Meanwhile, heat the oil and fry the onion, garlic and mushrooms until the onion is soft. Stir in the soya mince, tomatoes and their liquid, tomato purée and herbs. Melt the margarine in a saucepan, add the flour and cook for 2 minutes, stirring all the time. Gradually add the milk and bring to the boil, stirring constantly, until the sauce is smooth and thick. Season to taste. Layer the noodles, mince mixture and white sauce in an ovenproof casserole, ending with a layer of sauce on the top. Sprinkle with the grated cheese and cool.

To freeze: Cover with lid or foil. Seal and label.

To serve: Uncover and defrost at room temperature for 6 hours. Reheat after defrosting in a moderately hot oven (190°C, 375°F, Gas Mark 5) for about 50 minutes, until heated through and the cheese is golden brown.

Serves: 4.

Storage time: 3–4 months.

Caraway pancakes

METRIC/IMPERIAL	AMERICAN
100 g/4 oz self-raising flour	1 cup all-purpose flour sifted with 1
1 teaspoon salt	teaspoon baking powder
1 teaspoon sugar	1 teaspoon salt
1 teaspoon caraway seeds	1 teaspoon sugar
2 eggs	1 teaspoon caraway seeds
150 ml/¼ pint milk	2 eggs
75 ml/3 fl oz water	⅔ cup milk
50 g/2 oz triticale sprouts	5–6 tablespoons water
40 g/1½ oz butter, melted	2 oz triticale sprouts
fat for frying	3 tablespoons melted butter
100 g/4 oz cream cheese and pineapple	fat for frying
	¼ lb cream cheese and pineapple

Place the flour, salt, sugar and caraway seeds in a large bowl. Put the eggs, milk, water and sprouts in a blender and liquidise until smooth. Pour this into the dry ingredients with the butter and mix well. Use the mixture to fry 8 small pancakes. Cool, then divide the cream cheese mixture between the pancakes and spread evenly. Fold into four.
To freeze: Pack in convenient quantities. Seal and label.
To serve: Defrost at room temperature for 2–3 hours, depending on size of pack.
Makes: 8 pancakes/4 servings.
Storage time: 4–6 months.

Cottage cheese dip

METRIC/IMPERIAL	AMERICAN
225 g/8 oz cottage cheese	½ lb cottage cheese
100 g/4 oz mixed salad sprouts	¼ lb mixed salad sprouts
3–4 tablespoons natural yogurt	4–5 tablespoons unflavored yogurt
1 tablespoon toasted sesame seeds	1 tablespoon toasted sesame seeds
1 tablespoon finely chopped spring onion	1 tablespoon finely chopped scallion
1 teaspoon salt	1 teaspoon salt
¼ teaspoon pepper	¼ teaspoon pepper

Sieve the cottage cheese and beat in all the other ingredients.
To freeze: Pack in small quantities, Seal and label.
To serve: Defrost at room temperature for 2–3 hours depending on size of pack.
Use as a dip or as a sandwich filling with fresh brown bread or crispbreads.
Makes: About 450 ml/¾ pint/2 cups.
Storage time: 4–6 months.

Integrated microwave meal

(Illustrated on page 255)

METRIC/IMPERIAL	AMERICAN
4 frozen sparerib chops	4 frozen spare rib chops
4 medium potatoes	4 medium potatoes
salt and pepper to taste	salt and pepper to taste
50 g/2 oz butter	¼ cup butter
450 g/1 lb frozen peas	1 lb frozen peas
sauce:	*sauce:*
25 g/1 oz butter	2 tablespoons butter
2 tablespoons tomato purée	3 tablespoons tomato paste
1 teaspoon soya sauce	1 teaspoon soy sauce
50 g/2 oz sugar	¼ cup sugar
1 tablespoon vinegar	1 tablespoon vinegar
1 clove garlic	1 clove garlic
1 dessert apple	1 dessert apple
sprigs watercress	sprigs watercress

Microwave Work Plan

1. Separate the chops and place in a shallow ovenproof casserole. Cover and defrost for 2 minutes. Meanwhile, thinly slice the potatoes and place on a large plate. Season, dot with half the butter and cover with another plate.
2. Turn the chops and defrost for a further 2 minutes. Meanwhile, put the ingredients for the sauce into a basin. Remove the chops from the oven.
3. Cook the sauce for 2 minutes then remove from the oven and take out the garlic. Pour the sauce over the chops.
4. Cook the chops for 5 minutes, then remove from the oven. Meanwhile, place the peas in a boilable bag with the remaining butter and seasoning to taste. Loosely seal the top. (Do not use a metal twist tie.)
5. Cook the potatoes for 5 minutes, then remove from the oven. Meanwhile, baste the chops with the sauce, cover the dish and rest while the potatoes cook.
6. Remove the cover and cook the chops for a further 5 minutes, then cover again and remove from the oven.
7. Cook the peas for 3–4 minutes. Meanwhile, core and slice the apple.
8. Serve the chops on a warm serving dish, garnish with apple twists and slices and the watercress. Pour the sauce over. Place the peas in a serving dish.
Serves: 4.

Autumn vegetable medley

METRIC/IMPERIAL	AMERICAN
225 g/8 oz courgettes	½ lb zucchini
1 small aubergine	1 small eggplant
225 g/8 oz tomatoes	½ lb tomatoes
1 medium onion, chopped	1 medium onion, chopped
1 clove garlic, crushed	1 clove garlic, crushed
1 tablespoon vinegar	1 tablespoon vinegar
salt and pepper to taste	salt and pepper to taste
1 tablespoon chopped parsley	1 tablespoon chopped parsley
when serving:	*when serving:*
50 g/2 oz hard cheese, grated	½ cup grated hard cheese

Thinly slice the courgettes and aubergine. Peel and slice the tomatoes. Place these in a boilable bag with the onion, garlic and vinegar. Season to taste with salt and pepper and loosely seal the bag. Cook in the microwave for 12 minutes. Stir in the parsley and cool quickly.

To freeze: Seal tightly. Label.

To serve: Loosen the seal on the bag and defrost in the microwave for 5 minutes. Turn the medley into an ovenproof dish and sprinkle with the cheese. Cook for 5–6 minutes, until the mixture is hot and the cheese has melted.

Serves: 4.

Storage time: 4–6 months.

NOTE: The vegetable medley can be kept warm for a further 4 minutes while thin gammon slices or chipolata sausages are cooked in the microwave. Cook for 2 minutes, turn and cook for a further 2 minutes.

Microcrumble

METRIC/IMPERIAL	AMERICAN
450 g/1 lb blackberries, apples, etc., or a mixture of fruit	1 lb blackberries, apples, etc., or a mixture of fruit
75–100 g/3–4 oz sugar	6–8 tablespoons sugar
2 tablespoons water	3 tablespoons water
175 g/6 oz plain flour	1½ cups all-purpose flour
100 g/4 oz butter	½ cup butter
50 g/2 oz demerara sugar	¼ cup light brown sugar
pinch ground cinnamon	pinch ground cinnamon
finely grated zest of ½ lemon	finely grated rind of ½ lemon

Prepare the fruit and place in an ovenproof dish. Sprinkle over the sugar and add the water. To make the crumble, place the flour in a bowl and rub in the butter. Stir in three-quarters of the demerara sugar, the cinnamon and lemon zest. Sprinkle the crumble mixture over the fruit and scatter the remaining sugar over the top.

To freeze: Cover with lid or foil. Seal and label.

To serve: Uncover and place still frozen in the microwave. Cook for 10 minutes, turn the dish one quarter to the right and cook for a further 10 minutes.

Serves: 4–5.

Storage time: 4–6 months.

Microwave Hints

Defrosting baked goods from the frozen state

Individual pizzas (13 cm/5 inches in diameter): Place on a serving plate, heat for 1½ minutes, give the pizza a quarter turn and heat for 1½–2 minutes. If overheated the edges will be dry and hard.

Small cakes: Place 6 small cakes on a serving plate, making sure they are spread well apart. Heat for 1 minute, rest for 1 minute and heat for a further 30 seconds.

Individual portions of cake: Place on a serving plate and heat for 1 minute.

Large fruit cake: Place on a serving plate and heat for 5 minutes. Rest for 5 minutes and heat for a further 3–5 minutes, depending upon size.

Swiss roll: Place on a serving plate and heat for 2 minutes. This is particularly delicious served hot in slices with ice cream as the hot jam makes the sponge very moist.

Individual pastry fruit pies: Place on a serving plate (removing foil case) and heat for 1½ minutes.

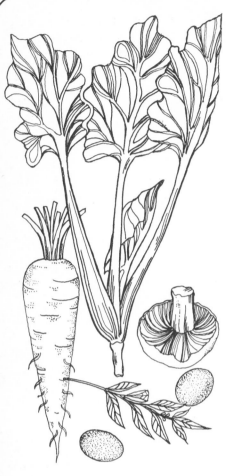

Whole-food and Vegetarian Recipes

Many readers have sincere convictions about the foods to be included in their diet and would not dream, for example, of eating refined white sugar or meat. For them it is essential that the ingredients used in preparing their meals conform with these principles. It can be quite hard to shop for food which is organically grown unless there is a health food store close to where you live or work. Nor is it always possible to 'eat out' at a vegetarian restaurant or even prepare dishes in your own kitchen which conform to strict vegetarian rules. So take advantage of the freezer's capacity to store away nature's bounty for your special enjoyment, even if other members of the family prefer different food.

Vegetarian lasagne

METRIC/IMPERIAL	AMERICAN
75 g/3 oz lasagne noodles	3 oz lasagne noodles
225 g/8 oz spinach	½ lb spinach
100 g/4 oz mushrooms, sliced	1 cup sliced mushrooms
100 g/4 oz carrot, grated	¼ lb carrot, grated
50 g/2 oz onion, chopped	2 oz onion, chopped
1 tablespoon cooking oil	1 tablespoon cooking oil
1 (227-g/8-oz) can tomatoes	1 (8-oz) can tomatoes
3 tablespoons tomato purée	¼ cup tomato paste
50 g/2 oz black olives, sliced	2 oz ripe olives, sliced
1 teaspoon dried oregano	1 teaspoon dried oregano
salt and pepper to taste	salt and pepper to taste
225 g/8 oz cottage cheese	½ lb cottage cheese
225 g/8 oz Mozzarella cheese, sliced	½ lb Mozzarella cheese, sliced
2 tablespoons grated Parmesan cheese	3 tablespoons grated Parmesan cheese

Cook the lasagne in boiling salted water for 8 minutes. Drain thoroughly. Wash the spinach, chop roughly and cook for 3 minutes. Sauté the mushrooms, carrot and onion in the oil until tender. Stir in the tomatoes, tomato purée, olives and oregano. Simmer until thick. Season to taste with salt and pepper. In a deep foil container, layer the lasagne noodles, spinach, tomato mixture, cottage cheese and sliced Mozzarella cheese. Repeat the layers, ending with a layer of cheese. Sprinkle with the grated Parmesan cheese.
To freeze: Put on lid. Seal and label.
To serve: Defrost and then bake in a moderately hot oven (190°C, 375°F, Gas Mark 5) for 30–35 minutes until heated through and bubbling on top.
Serves: 4.
Storage time: 4–6 months.

Asparagus and corn soup

METRIC/IMPERIAL	AMERICAN
1 (283-g/10-oz) can asparagus spears	10 oz canned asparagus spears
1 tablespoon cornflour	1 tablespoon cornstarch
300 ml/½ pint milk	1¼ cups milk
300 ml/½ pint water	1¼ cups water
salt and pepper	salt and pepper
1 (326-g/11½-oz) can sweet corn	11½ oz canned corn kernels
when serving:	*when serving:*
4 tablespoons double cream	⅓ cup heavy cream

Liquidise or sieve the asparagus spears and liquid from the can. Add the cornflour, milk and water, season well with salt and pepper and liquidise again for 30 seconds. You may need to do this in two batches. Pour the asparagus mixture into a saucepan and add the sweet corn. Bring to the boil, stirring all the time, and simmer for 2–3 minutes. Cool.
To freeze: Pack in convenient quantities. Seal and label.
To serve: Turn the frozen soup into a saucepan and reheat gently, stirring occasionally. Swirl 1 tablespoon of cream into each portion of soup in the serving plate.
Serves: 4.
Storage time: 4–6 months.

Vegetable pie with potato pastry

(*Illustrated on page 118*)

METRIC/IMPERIAL	AMERICAN
225 g/8 oz carrots	½ lb carrots
1 small cauliflower	1 small cauliflower
175 g/6 oz French beans	6 oz green beans
100 g/4 oz peas	¼ lb peas
1 teaspoon Worcestershire sauce	1 teaspoon Worcestershire sauce
sauce:	*sauce:*
6 tablespoons skimmed milk powder	½ cup skim milk powder
20 g/¾ oz margarine	1½ tablespoons margarine
20 g/¾ oz plain flour	3 tablespoons all-purpose flour
100 g/4 oz cheese, grated	1 cup grated cheese
salt and pepper to taste	salt and pepper to taste
pastry:	*pastry:*
20 g/¾ oz instant potato granules	¾ oz instant potato granules
150 ml/¼ pint boiling water	⅔ cup boiling water
75 g/3 oz plain flour	¾ oz all-purpose flour
50 g/2 oz hard margarine	¼ cup hard margarine

First, measure the potato granules for the pastry into a bowl and pour over the boiling water. Stir with a fork and allow to cool completely. Meanwhile, chop the carrots, break the cauliflower into florets and slice the beans. Cook the carrots in salted boiling water for 5 minutes, add the cauliflower and beans then the peas, being careful not to over-cook them as the vegetables should be crisp. Drain the vegetables, reserving the cooking water. Divide the vegetables between 2 shaped foil containers and sprinkle with the Worcestershire sauce.

To make the sauce, make up the skimmed milk powder to 600 ml/1 pint/2½ cups with the vegetable water. Melt the margarine, stir in the flour then the milk liquid. Bring to the boil, stirring all the time. Cook for 2 minutes. Add the cheese and season well to taste. Pour over the vegetables in the containers. Cool. To make the pastry, place the flour in a bowl and rub in the margarine. Stir in the cold potato and form into a dough. Roll out on a floured surface and cut lids to cover the vegetables. Use the trimmings to decorate the tops of the pies. Bake in a hot oven (220°C, 425°F, Gas Mark 7) for about 30 minutes, until just golden on top. Cool.

To freeze: Pack in polythene bags or cover with lid or foil. Seal and label.

To serve: Uncover, brush with milk or beaten egg and reheat from frozen in a moderately hot oven (200°C, 400°F, Gas Mark 6) for about 45 minutes, until well browned.

Makes: 2 pies, each 3–4 servings.

Storage time: 4–6 months.

Country pie

(Illustrated on page 118)

METRIC/IMPERIAL	AMERICAN
good pinch chopped mixed herbs	good pinch chopped mixed herbs
1 (127-g/4½-oz) packet instant potato granules	4½ oz instant potato granules
1 medium onion	1 medium onion
25 g/1 oz margarine	2 tablespoons margarine
1 cooking apple	1 baking apple
4 tomatoes	4 tomatoes
350 g/12 oz cabbage	¾ lb cabbage
150 ml/¼ pint vegetable stock	⅔ cup vegetable stock
when serving:	*when serving:*
75 g/3 oz cheese, grated	¾ cup grated cheese
2 tomatoes, sliced	2 tomatoes, sliced
sprig parsley	sprig parsley

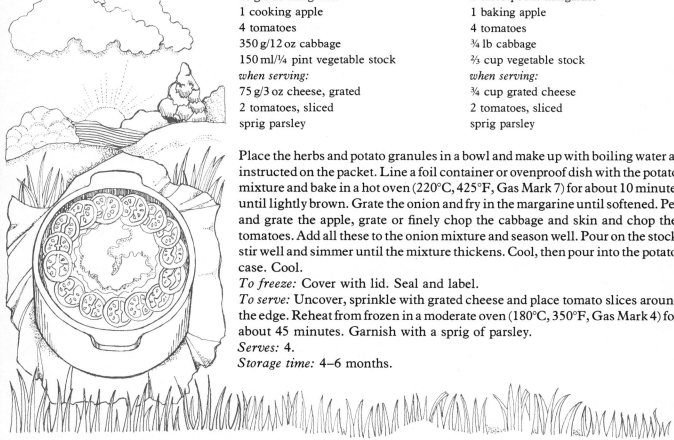

Place the herbs and potato granules in a bowl and make up with boiling water as instructed on the packet. Line a foil container or ovenproof dish with the potato mixture and bake in a hot oven (220°C, 425°F, Gas Mark 7) for about 10 minutes, until lightly brown. Grate the onion and fry in the margarine until softened. Peel and grate the apple, grate or finely chop the cabbage and skin and chop the tomatoes. Add all these to the onion mixture and season well. Pour on the stock, stir well and simmer until the mixture thickens. Cool, then pour into the potato case. Cool.

To freeze: Cover with lid. Seal and label.

To serve: Uncover, sprinkle with grated cheese and place tomato slices around the edge. Reheat from frozen in a moderate oven (180°C, 350°F, Gas Mark 4) for about 45 minutes. Garnish with a sprig of parsley.

Serves: 4.

Storage time: 4–6 months.

Loaf in a crust

(Illustrated on page 256)

METRIC/IMPERIAL	AMERICAN
25 g/1 oz margarine	2 tablespoons margarine
1 medium onion, chopped	1 medium onion, chopped
1 (425-g/15-oz) can soya mince	1 (15-oz) can soy mince
100 g/4 oz fresh breadcrumbs	2 cups fresh breadcrumbs
225 g/8 oz self-raising flour	2 cups all-purpose flour sifted with 2 teaspoons baking powder
pinch salt	pinch salt
1 teaspoon curry powder	1 teaspoon curry powder
3 tablespoons oil	¼ cup oil
about 6 tablespoons water	about ½ cup water
little milk for brushing	little milk for brushing
½ teaspoon sesame seeds	½ teaspoon sesame seeds

Melt the margarine and lightly fry the onion. Add the soya mince and breadcrumbs, then season well. Sift the flour with the salt and curry powder. Add the oil and sufficient water to make a soft dough. Roll out the pastry on a floured surface to a rectangle 30 cm/12 inches by 23 cm/9 inches. Place the filling in a line down the centre, dampen the edges then bring each edge over the filling and seal together. Place the roll, seam side down, on a greased baking tray and make cuts across the top, about 3·5 cm/1½ inches apart. Brush with milk and sprinkle with sesame seeds. Bake in a moderately hot oven (190°C, 375°F, Gas Mark 5) for about 30 minutes. Cool.
To freeze: Pack in polythene. Seal and label.
To serve: Unpack and place on a baking tray. Reheat from frozen in a moderately hot oven as above for about 45 minutes.
Serves: 4.
Storage time: 3–4 months.

Cheese and corn tart

METRIC/IMPERIAL	AMERICAN
65 g/2½ oz margarine	5 tablespoons margarine
1 tablespoon water	1 tablespoon water
100 g/4 oz plain flour	1 cup plain flour
25 g/1 oz butter	2 tablespoons butter
1 medium onion, chopped	1 medium onion, chopped
100 g/4 oz courgettes, sliced	¼ lb zucchini, chopped
300 ml/½ pint savoury white sauce	1¼ cups savory white sauce
75 g/3 oz Cheddar cheese, grated	¾ cup grated Cheddar cheese
1 (198-g/7-oz) can sweet corn	7 oz canned corn kernels
1 teaspoon mustard	1 teaspoon mustard
salt and pepper	salt and pepper

Beat together the margarine, water and one-third of the flour until smooth. Add the remaining flour to form a firm dough. Knead lightly and roll out to line a 20-cm/8-inch foil flan case. Melt the butter and fry the onion and courgettes for 3 minutes. Add to the white sauce with 50 g/2 oz/½ cup of the cheese, the sweet corn, liquid from the can and the mustard. Bring to the boil and remove from the heat. Season to taste, pour into the pastry case and sprinkle the remaining cheese on top. Cool.

To freeze: Open freeze, then wrap in foil. Seal and label.

To serve: Unwrap flan, place on a baking tray and bake in a moderate oven (180°C, 350°F, Gas Mark 4) for 40 minutes until heated through, then raise the temperature to 200°C, 400°F, Gas Mark 6 for a further 10–15 minutes.

Serves: 4.

Storage time: 6 months.

Vegetable wheatgerm scallop

METRIC/IMPERIAL	AMERICAN
1 small cabbage	1 small head cabbage
4 large carrots	4 large carrots
1 medium onion	1 medium onion
25 g/1 oz butter	2 tablespoons butter
2 tablespoons flour	3 tablespoons flour
300 ml/½ pint milk	1¼ cups milk
1 teaspoon prepared mustard	1 teaspoon prepared mustard
pinch salt	pinch salt
150 g/6 oz grated Cheddar cheese	1½ cups grated Cheddar cheese
4 tablespoons wheatgerm	⅓ cup wheatgerm
2 tablespoons soft wholewheat breadcrumbs	3 tablespoons soft whole wheat breadcrumbs
2 tablespoons melted butter	3 tablespoons melted butter

Coarsely shred the cabbage. Slice the carrots thinly. Cook in a little boiling salted water for 10 minutes. Drain well. Chop the onion and fry in the butter until limp, but not brown. Stir in the flour and cook for 1 minute. Gradually add the milk and cook and stir until thickened. Remove from the heat and stir in the mustard, salt, grated cheese and cooked vegetables. Spoon into a foil container and cool. Mix the wheatgerm and breadcrumbs with the melted butter and sprinkle over the vegetable-cheese mixture.

To freeze: Put on lid. Seal and label.

To serve: Remove lid and reheat from frozen in a moderately hot oven (190°C, 375°F, Gas Mark 5) for 35–40 minutes until hot and bubbly.

Serves: 4.

Storage time: 4–6 months.

Honeyed bran loaf

METRIC/IMPERIAL	AMERICAN
1 medium egg	1 medium egg
50 g/2 oz brown sugar	¼ cup brown sugar
4 tablespoons clear honey	⅓ cup clear honey
1 tablespoon melted butter	1 tablespoon melted butter
100 g/4 oz natural bran	¼ lb natural bran
½ teaspoon bicarbonate of soda	½ teaspoon baking soda
2 teaspoons baking powder	2 teaspoons baking powder
1 teaspoon salt	1 teaspoon salt
50 g/2 oz walnuts, chopped	½ cup chopped walnuts
150 g/6 oz dates, chopped	6 oz dates, chopped
275 g/10 oz wholewheat flour	2½ cups whole wheat flour
350 ml/12 fl oz milk	1½ cups milk

Beat the egg with the sugar, honey and melted butter. Stir in the bran. Mix the bicarbonate of soda, baking powder, salt, chopped walnuts and dates and wholewheat flour. Add the dry ingredients alternately with the milk to the bran mixture. Do not over-mix. Spoon the mixture into a lightly greased 1-kg/2-lb loaf tin. Bake in a moderate oven (180°C, 350°F, Gas Mark 4) for 1¼ hours. Allow to cool in the tin.
To freeze: Wrap tightly. Seal and label.
To serve: Defrost, still wrapped, at room temperature for about 4 hours.
Makes: 1 1-kg/2-lb loaf.
Storage time: 4–6 months.

Peanut butter honeys

METRIC/IMPERIAL	AMERICAN
100 g/4 oz margarine	½ cup margarine
6 tablespoons clear honey	½ cup clear honey
100 g/4 oz brown sugar	½ cup brown sugar
1 egg	1 egg
100 g/4 oz peanut butter	⅓ cup peanut butter
¼ teaspoon salt	¼ teaspoon salt
½ teaspoon bicarbonate of soda	½ teaspoon baking soda
150 g/6 oz wholewheat flour	1½ cups whole wheat flour
50 g/2 oz walnuts, chopped	½ cup chopped walnuts

Cream the margarine, honey and sugar together until light and fluffy. Gradually beat in the egg and peanut butter. Mix the salt and bicarbonate of soda with the wholewheat flour. Add the dry ingredients to the creamed mixture, stir in the walnuts and form into a dough. Divide the mixture into 1-cm/½-inch balls. Place the balls on lightly greased baking trays and press the top of each ball with a fork to flatten. Bake in a moderate oven (180°C, 350°F, Gas Mark 4) for 8–10 minutes. Cool on a wire rack.
To freeze: Pack in layers with dividers. Seal and label.
To serve: Unwrap, spread out on a serving dish and defrost for 30 minutes.
Makes: About 48 biscuits.
Storage time: 4–6 months.

Sweet prune pockets

METRIC/IMPERIAL	AMERICAN
1 egg yolk	1 egg yolk
50 g/2 oz light soft brown sugar	½ cup light brown sugar
50 g/2 oz ground almonds	½ cup ground almonds
50 g/2 oz candied peel, chopped	⅓ cup chopped candied peel
50 g/2 oz walnuts, chopped or pecans, chopped	⅓ cup chopped walnuts or pecans
450 g/1 lb large soft dried prunes	1 lb large soft dried prunes

Beat together the egg yolk and brown sugar and add the almonds. Knead in the candied peel and chopped nuts. Stone the prunes and stuff them neatly with the nut mixture.

To freeze: Pack in convenient quantities in layers with dividers. Seal and label.

To serve: Unpack while frozen, spread out on a serving plate and allow to defrost at room temperature for about 30 minutes.

Makes: 48–60 stuffed prunes, depending on size.

Storage time: 4–6 months.

Potted cheese

METRIC/IMPERIAL	AMERICAN
450 g/1 lb Gouda cheese, grated	4 cups grated Gouda cheese
100 g/4 oz butter	½ cup butter
1 tablespoon French mustard	1 tablespoon French mustard
3–4 tablespoons double cream	¼–⅓ cup heavy cream
salt and pepper	salt and pepper

Mix together all the ingredients until smooth and well blended.

To freeze: Pack in convenient quantities. Seal and label.

To serve: Uncover and defrost at room temperature for 3 hours. Serve as a spread with oatcakes.

Makes: 450 ml/¾ pint/2 cups spread.

Storage time: 4–6 months.

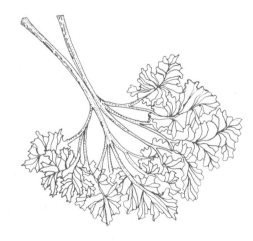

Index